LAW'S MOVING IMAGE

Edited by
Leslie J Moran
Emma Sandon
Elena Loizidou
and
Ian Christie

Birkbeck College, University of London

Cavendish
Publishing
Limited

First published in Great Britain 2004 by
The GlassHouse Press, The Glass House,
Wharton Street, London WC1X 9PX, United Kingdom
Telephone: + 44 (0)20 7278 8000   Facsimile: + 44 (0)20 7278 8080
Email: info@cavendishpublishing.com
Website: www.cavendishpublishing.com

Published in the United States by Cavendish Publishing
c/o International Specialized Book Services,
5824 NE Hassalo Street, Portland,
Oregon 97213-3644, USA

Published in Australia by The GlassHouse Press,
45 Beach Street, Coogee, NSW 2034, Australia
Telephone: + 61 (2)9664 0909   Facsimile: +61 (2)9664 5420
Email: info@cavendishpublishing.com.au
Website: www.cavendishpublishing.com.au

British Library Cataloguing in Publication Data
Moran, Leslie
Law's moving image
1 Law and art   2 Motion pictures – Law and legislation
3 Lawyers in motion pictures
I   Title
340.1'15

Library of Congress Cataloguing in Publication Data
Data available

ISBN 1-90438-501-X

1 3 5 7 9 10 8 6 4 2

Printed and bound in Great Britain

Cover image courtesy of Christina Panagi at the Birkbeck College Photographic Unit

List of contributors

Fred Botting is Professor and Head of the English Department, University of Keele. His monographs include *Tarantinian Ethics* (2001, Sage) with Scott Wilson on the films of Quentin Tarantino. He has published extensively on the Gothic including *Gothic* (1996, Routledge) and *Gothic: Critical Concepts in Literary and Cultural Studies* (2004, Routledge) and with Scott Wilson on the work of George Bataille.

Ian Christie is Professor of Film and Media History at Birkbeck College. He teaches British, Russian and European cinema history, avant-garde film and visual art, media theory and aesthetics. He has published extensively on the cinema of Powell and Pressberger, including *A Matter of Life and Death* (2000, BFI Film Classic), Soviet cinema (*The Film Factory*, 1988; *Inside the Film Factory*, 1991; and *Eisenstein Rediscovered*, 1993: all co-edited with Richard Taylor for Routledge) and on early cinema (*The Last Machine: Cinema and the Birth of the Modern World*, BBC/BFI, 1994).

Lawrence Douglas is Professor of Law, Jurisprudence & Social Thought at Amherst College, USA. He is the author of *The Memory of Judgment: Making Law and History in the Trials of the Holocaust* (2001, Yale University Press), and the co-author of *Sense and Nonsensibility: Lampoons of Literature and Learning* (2004, Simon and Schuster). His work has appeared in *The Yale Law Journal, Representations, The Washington Post, New York Times Book Review* and *The New Yorker*.

Bill Grantham is an Attorney working in Los Angeles, California, USA. He practises entertainment, media and intellectual property law and has represented both European and American clients from the film and television industries. He has acted as a consultant to the European Union's MEDIA programme and to national film development organisations.

Lee Grieveson is a Lecturer in Film Studies at King's College London. He is author of *Policing Cinema: Movies and Censorship in Early Twentieth Century America* (University of California Press) and co-editor, with Peter Kramer, of *The Silent Cinema Reader* (2003, Routledge) and, with Peter Stanfield and Esther Sonnet, *Mob Cultures: Essays on the American Gangster Film* (forthcoming, Rutgers University Press).

Elena Loizidou is Lecturer in Law in the Law School at Birkbeck College. She teaches in the areas of law and film, crime and culture, and gender and the law. She has published in the areas of law and culture, and in gender and the law, and is currently writing a book on cultural formation of the legal subject.

Celia Lury is Professor of Sociology in the Sociology Department, Goldsmiths College, University of London. She has written widely on visual culture, the culture industry and feminist theory. Recent publications include *Global Nature, Global Culture* (Sage, 2000, with Sarah Franklin and Jackie Stacey) and *Transformations: Thinking Through Feminism* (2000, Routledge, edited with S Ahmed, J Kilby, M McNeil and B Skeggs). She is currently completing a book on brands.

Angus MacDonald is a Senior Lecturer in Law at Staffordshire University. His research activity is centred on issues in constitutional law and the application of postmodern theory to that field. He has published work on Dicey and Bagehot and also on critical constitutionalism, on urbanism and on the situationists.

Fiona Macmillan is Professor of Law at Birkbeck, University of London. She is also the convenor of the AHRB Network on New Directions in Copyright Law, which is based in Birkbeck's School of Law. Her published research has focussed on the areas of corporate regulation, intellectual property law and the law of the World Trade Organization. She is the author of *WTO and the Environment* (2001, Sweet and Maxwell) and is currently working on a new monograph entitled *The World Trade Organization and Human Rights*.

William P MacNeil is Co-Director of the Socio-Legal Research Centre and Senior Lecturer in Law in the Faculty of Law at Griffith University Brisbane, Queensland Australia.

Eugene McNamee is currently a Marie Curie Fellow in the Department of Sociology and Politics at University College Cork. He is researching on the relationship between art and constitutional politics in Northern Ireland in the period 1994–2004.

Leslie J Moran is Professor of Law and Head of the Law School at Birkbeck College, University of London. He has written extensively about matters relating to law and culture and teaches postgraduate courses on Law and Film and Crime and Culture in the Law School. In 2000 he organised the UK's first conference on law and film at Tate Britain. His other publications include *The Homosexual(ity) of Law* (1996, Routledge), *Legal Queeries* (1998, Cassells) and *Sexuality and the Politics of Violence and Safety* (2004, Routledge).

M Madhava Prasad is Professor at the Centre for European Studies, School for Critical Humanities, Central Institute of English and Foreign Languages at Hyderabad. He has published a number of articles on film in India as well as a book, *Ideology of the Hindi Film: A Historical Construction* (1998, New Delhi: OUP).

Emma Sandon is Lecturer in Film and Media Studies in the Film and Media Studies Department, Birkbeck College. She teaches history cinema courses, specialising in British cinema, early and silent cinema, documentary film, and issues of gender and ethnicity in film. She has published articles on British silent colonial ethnographic film and has recently completed a historical study of early television in Britain.

David M Seymour teaches in the School of Law, Lancaster University. His current research interests include critical theories of anti-Semitism and cultural expressions of law and ethics.

J David Slocum is Associate Dean in the Graduate School of Arts and Science at New York University, where he teaches in the Cinema Studies Department and the Program in Art and Public Policy. He is the editor of *Violence and American Cinema* (2001).

Scott Wilson is Director of the Institute of Cultural Research and Head of the Department of Culture, Media and Communications at Lancaster University. His monograph on the films of Quentin Tarantino, *Tarantinian Ethics* is written with Fred Botting, published by Sage in 2001. He has also written extensively on the work of George Batailles, including *Batailles* (2001, Palgrave) with Fred Botting.

Alison Young works in the Department of Criminology at the University of Melbourne, Australia. Her research and teaching interests lie primarily within the areas of cultural criminology, criminal law and feminist criminology. Publications include *Imagining Crime* (1996, Sage) and *Judging the Image: Art, Value, Law* (Routledge, 2003). Her current research covers two distinct areas: first, cultural representations of crime (in media such as film, television drama, and newspaper discourse); and secondly, the socio-legal regulation of artworks (with case studies on graffiti, 'disgusting' images, performance art, artwork about HIV/AIDS).

Acknowledgments

Acknowledgments for the illustrations in this book are due to Carlton International (*A Matter of Life and Death*); Charter Films and the British Broadcasting Corporation (*Thunder Rock*); MGM and Hollywood Pictures (*A Guy Named Joe*); Renaissance Films (*Henry V*); Paramount Pictures (*The Castle*); Warner Bros (*Rebel Without a Cause*); Warwick Productions (*The Trials of Oscar Wilde*); 20th Century Fox (*Oscar Wilde*); Spyglass Entertainment and Buena Vista (*The Sixth Sense*); and the British Film Institute Video (*M*). Also to Christina Panagi, Andrew Buchan, Jim Pennington and Beatrice Christie for their help with the cover illustration.

Contents

List of figures

Introduction

Leslie J Moran

Emma Sandon

Elena Loizidou

Ian Christie

The interface between law and film is complex. Law has played and continues to play an important role in the facilitation and regulation of the film business in general and is an inevitable part of the production and exhibition of each and every film. Legal concepts such as property, ownership, obscenity, indecency, immorality, disorder, civil rights, freedom of expression, contractual rights and duties, to name but a few, form and frame film businesses, processes of production and film as a cultural object. At the same time, the institutions and processes that produce and circulate film as a cultural product inform, shape and transform the nature and expression not only of these legal concepts but of the very ideas of law, legality and justice. These encounters and transformations between law and film take place in and through the archaic, discrete and arcane practices and institutions of law, such as the lawyer's office, the text of a binding agreement, the statement of claim, the courtroom encounter or the final judgment. But their location is not limited to those contexts. It also happens in the process of script writing, on the film set, in the close-up and the star's gaze, on the billboards, by way of the toys and other consumer artefacts sold in association with a film, on the screen, be it in the trailers or the main feature itself and in the cinema theatre in general: in short through film as an institution and medium of popular culture. Law and film is the site of an encounter between what might be described as the institutions and practices of high culture (law) and those institutions which might be more closely associated with low or popular culture. It is also an encounter of another kind, between different media, the law, which purports to be exclusively literary (Goodrich, 1995, 1996; Douzinas and Nead, 1999) and another more recent medium, film, that has up until recently been considered to be predominantly visual (Panofsky, 1966; Deleuze, 1986, 1994). The essays collected in this volume take up and engage with these distinctions, differences, encounters and locations, exploring the ways in which law and film are not only produced as separate categories and phenomena, but also how they are deeply implicated in each other, making law and film a problematic if not impossible distinction. Opening up new agendas, offering new insights and setting new parameters of understanding these essays explore that complex intimacy.

As a multidisciplinary collection, *Law's Moving Image* brings together scholars from film studies (Ian Christie, Lee Grieveson, Emma Sandon), literary theory (Fred Botting and Scott Wilson), cultural studies and sociology (Celia Lury, Madhava Prasad and J David Slocum), as well as law scholars, some of whom have practised law in the field of film and cinema. Its many intellectual and scholarly points of departure,[1] engagement and address have been apparent in the challenge of writing with particular disciplinary audiences in mind, and at the same time a desire to engage with other and sometimes new audiences in different but intimately connected disciplines.

---

1   One of its points of origin was a conference at Tate Britain in London in 2001. We are grateful for the financial support of the British Academy whose award made that conference possible.

At the same time the collection has been developed and produced with a view to intervene in particular scholarly debates. One such debate has its origins in the work of US law academics in the late 1980s who, in general, embarked upon an analysis of the role of popular culture in the formation of the legal imagination (Chase, 1986)[2] and, in particular, explored representations of lawyers in that context (Post, 1987; Stark, 1987; Friedman, 1989). From its origins in the analysis of law and lawyers in popular literature, scholars have extended their analysis into the realm of visual culture, first television (Stark, 1987; Gillers, 1989; Rosen, 1989) then Hollywood cinema (Greenfield and Osborn, 1993, 1995; Sheffield, 1993; Shapiro, 1995). As the rate of scholarly publication has grown, collections of essays by Denvir (1996), and Machura and Robson (2001) and books such as Rafter's *Shots in the Mirror* (2000), Greenfield, Osborn and Robson's *Film and the Law* (2001) and Anthony Chase's *Movies on Trial* (2002) have helped to institutionalise law and film as a new scholarly discipline in legal studies and promoted a wider awareness of it.

An orthodoxy, setting the parameters, priorities and methodology of legal scholarship around film, has already emerged. The first, and most dominant feature is a focus on questions of representation. Intimately connected to this is a preoccupation with representations of criminal trials, which are equated with the rather more generous category of 'courtroom drama' and a dominant concern with images of the legal profession, in particular advocates.[3] As others have noted, '... considering law films as only courtroom dramas is a very narrow interpretation of what law is concerned with' (Osborn, 2001, p 173). Another theme is a fixation with classification and taxonomies. Here the organising principle seems to be to invent and police a film genre, be it 'courtroom drama' or 'the trial film' or the more generous category of 'the law film'. For example, the parameters of 'courtroom drama' are a dominant concern in Greenfield, Osborn and Robson's *Film and the Law* (2001) and in essays in the collection *Law and Film* (Machura and Robson, 2001). In that volume, for example, Rafter (2001) devotes her energies to differentiating four sub-groupings (experimental; law noir; the heroic tradition; the decline of the hero) within a subdivision (criminal trial films) of the more general category, 'trial films'; Kuzina (2001) offers 10 subdivisions of 'the courtroom genre' and Drexler (2001) frames his analysis of *Gerichtsmilieu*, German law films, by way of five subdivisions. A fourth common denominator of existing work is the dominance of classical Hollywood cinema and the American way of law. The parochialism of American law and Hollywood as a national cinema (albeit with global impact) is largely unmarked in this work. Methodologically, the predominant approach is a concern with narrative and textual analysis. An analysis of the particular impact of visualisation in general and the audio/visual modes and techniques of cinema in particular have remained beyond the parameters

---

2 The work cited in this introduction does not purport to be an exhaustive list of legal scholarship in the field. The volume as a whole provides a wide ranging bibliography of that scholarship. For a useful historical bibliography see Machura and Robson, 2001, pp 3–8. Several major works now address the interface between law and popular culture: eg, see Leonard, 1995; Redhead, 1995; Sarat and Kearns, 1998; Sherwin, 2000; Ward, 2000; Young, 1996.

3 Bergman and Asimow's edited volume *Reel Justice: The Courtroom Goes to the Movies* (1996) highlights an important influence on the emergence of this scholarship, the use of film as a pedagogic tool within the American Law School. Here the focus has been on the gap between representations of courtroom practice in Hollywood films and the daily practice of American lawyers. Its impact has been to elevate the importance of questions of the accuracy and authenticity of the representations of courtroom practices of lawyers.

of much of this scholarly engagement with representations of law in film. Another methodological characteristic of much of this work is at best a hesitancy, and at worst a complete failure, to engage with related disciplines. For example, there has been a great deal of work by film and cultural studies scholars on censorship and the production code (Carmen, 1967; De Grazia and Newman, 1982; Jacobs, 1992; Kuhn, 1988; McCarthy, 1976; Maltby, 1993; Randall, 1968), regulation (Grieveson, 1997, 1998; Uricchio and Pearson, 1997), notions of law and order in genre study (Cook, 1999; Neale, 1980) and on audience (Clover, 2000). Little attempt has been made to incorporate the specific disciplinary insights that this and other work on film, visual culture, cultural and social theory might contribute to understanding the complex relationship between law and the moving image.

The essays collected in this volume seek to challenge this orthodoxy in various ways, one of them being its multidisciplinarity. Multidisciplinarity is not only reflected in the combination of scholars from different disciplinary backgrounds, but also in the multidisciplinary approach found in the individual essays. In Part 1, *A Fantastic Jurisprudence*, engaging with but not limited to courtroom drama, the essays by Christie, McNamee, MacNeil, Loizidou, and Botting and Wilson draw upon a wide variety of sources through which to explore justice, legality, the Constitution and citizenship. Ian Christie draws inspiration from the critical jurisprudence of Peter Goodrich (1996) to examine the jurisprudence of British wartime cinema. Social and political theory is central to Loizidou's reading of *Rebel Without a Cause* (1955) and Botting and Wilson's encounters with *Toy Story* (1995) and *Toy Story 2* (1999). In Part 2, *Law, Aesthetics and Visual Technologies*, Moran, Douglas, Seymour, MacDonald and Young participate in a common enterprise, engaging with not just the visual, but more specifically the cinematic, audiovisual dimension of representations of, for example, crime and criminality, courtroom representations and justice. Drawing extensively on insights taken from film studies and cultural and social theory more generally, the chapters in this part of the book examine the impact of the medium of the moving image and its aesthetic effects upon perceptions and experiences of law and order, be it in the context of the moving image of lawyers and courtroom encounters or at the more conceptual level of legality or justice. In Part 3, *Regulation: Histories, Cultures, Legalities*, Fiona Macmillan brings an analysis of the political economy of cultural politics in both national and international contexts to bear on the context of her exploration of the interface between Hollywood cinema and national and international codes of law concerned with intellectual property. Celia Lury engages with the idiosyncrasies of trade mark law in her theoretically informed empirical study of the autobiographies of a number of cultural artefacts such as *Toy Story* (1995) and *Trainspotting* (1996). While this does not exhaust the multidisciplinary dimensions of the essays in this volume, it is sufficient to make the point that as a whole this collection exemplifies the importance of multidisciplinarity. It suggests that it is a necessary point of departure.

A second challenge provided by this collection is to be found in the determination evidenced in many essays to situate the complex interface between law and film in its historical, cultural and national context. Examples are to be found in Grieveson's work on early (silent) cinema in the US. Prasad and MacNeil offer an analysis of the colonial context and dynamics of cinema respectively in India in the early 20th century and in late 20th century Australia. Essays by Christie, McNamee and Moran focus on British cinema in relation to war (Christie and McNamee) and a costume drama of sexual politics and human rights in the early 1960s (Moran).

To limit the significance of *Law's Moving Image* to an engagement with work on law and film produced by law scholars is to impose too severe a restraint on the diversity of conversations to be found in the articles collected here. Another important conversation engages with work on deviance, criminality and crime in film and television, be it in the context of criminological (Cohen and Young, 1981; Ericson, 1987 and 1991; Sparks, 1992) and other disciplinary contexts such as cultural history (Munby, 1999; Ruth, 1996) or film studies (see Chibnall and Murphy, 1999; Dyer, 1999; MacCabe, 1998). Like much of the law and film scholarship outlined above, the orthodoxy of much scholarship on the visualisation of deviance, criminality and crime in film and television works with parameters, priorities and methodologies similar to that outlined earlier. Matters of representation, the accuracy or otherwise of the image and a focus on narrative dominate. Perhaps with the exception of some film scholarship (such as Dyer's study (1999) of the film *Se7en* (1995)), it remains the case that little attention is paid to the non-visual dimension of representations of law. Finally, a point of difference from the work of law scholars is that the substantive preoccupation with deviance, crime and criminality gives this body of work a very different edge. Insecurity, danger and disorder, which are explored through the figures of crime and criminality, are considered in the absence of reference to security, safety and order figured in and through law and questions of legality. The focus is driven by the criminological quest that seeks a solution to crime by exploring its causes, which are reduced to the pathological individual. Essays in this collection (Douglas, MacDonald, Moran, Loizidou, Seymour, Slocum, Young) engage with matters of crime and criminality but their approach to such matters differs. Sometimes this is in their engagement with film aesthetics and technology in the generation of the image of crime and criminality (Douglas, Moran, Young). Sometimes it is in the way they situate crime and criminality in the context of problematising ideas of law and legality, citizenship (Loizidou), ethics and justice (Douglas, Young) and in their use of crime and criminality to figure an engagement with social and cultural theory (Loizidou, MacDonald, Seymour, Slocum). Together they challenge the substantive and methodological foundations of work on crime in film.

The three sections of the book gather these diverse essays under the themes of cinema as jurisprudence, the representation of law in cinema and the regulation of film. *A Fantastic Jurisprudence* explores film as a social and cultural practice through which the nature of law and the relationship of law and society can be imagined. Taking familiar themes, courtroom drama, constitutional law, citizenship and family values, the essays provide new approaches to viewing films which engage with law either overtly or implicitly. As such, cinema becomes a screen onto which legal issues can be projected and questioned. Ian Christie takes the courtroom drama as the most familiar point of departure for scholarship on law and film. Yet his examples of films from the US, *A Guy Named Joe* (1944), and Britain, *Thunder Rock* (1942) and Powell and Pressburger's *A Matter of Life and Death* (1946), in the period of World War II, illustrate how in cinema the courtroom is no longer confined to terrestrial jurisdiction but to a celestial one. Extending Peter Goodrich's characterisation of 'minor jurisprudences' to cinema, he posits the films as fantastic concepts of justice, constituting a critique of the limitations of the actual legal process. The concepts of justice in the films offer themselves as 'fictive microjurisprudences', 'courts of conscience' creating alternatives that challenge normal (positive) law and the rationality of thought in a period of wartime, thereby reconnecting law to questions of duty and conscience and to the ethical dimensions of judgements. Eugene McNamee, on the other hand, takes a film made by one of the British film industry's favourite and most successful contemporary actor/directors, Kenneth Branagh, as an example of how British cinema perpetuates the justification of war and notions of the superiority of the British legal system. He reads Branagh's *Henry V* (1989), within the context of Shakespeare on film, as an intervention in the constitutional life of the UK. Focusing on Branagh's declared attempt to create a less propagandistic film than Lawrence Olivier's well-known World War II film version of the play, McNamee traces how the apologetic, yet unrepentant tone that Branagh's characterisation of Henry V embodies undermines any attempt to see the film as carrying an anti-war message. On the contrary, the film, made after the Falklands War, succeeds in reiterating the concept of a 'just war', foregrounding Tony Blair's justification of British involvement in the Iraq War. Whilst his point is that challenges to British territorial claims can be accommodated by British constitutional law, structured as it is by its parliamentary sovereignty, William P MacNeil looks at how land right claims to Aboriginal traditional territories not only challenged constitutional law, but caused a crisis in Australian national identity. He questions to what extent the Australian cult film *The Castle* (1997) explores the constitutional challenge of Aboriginal land claims in Australia. The main theme of *The Castle* is a critique of the compulsory government acquisition of land. He argues that, on the contrary, the film gives expression to the panic generated amongst Australian householders about dispossession, by the legal precedents set by the seminal cases of *Mabo and Others v The State of Queensland* and *Wik Peoples v The State of Queensland*, which led to 'native title'. The film's portrayal of cross-class allegiances amongst white Australians in the face of corporate threats to their property rights, and the conspicuous absence of Aborigines in this narrative of land possession, parallels the existing inequalities in common law with regard to immigrant and native claims to property. Both McNamee and MacNeil explore the role of film in the constitution of legal consciousness as national consciousness.

If ethnic rights to citizenship in the current Australian context are contested through property law in MacNeil's account, notions of political citizenship in America are addressed by Elena Loizidou's analysis of the figure of the rebel in *Rebel Without a Cause* (1955). Her discussion of the film focuses on rebellion as it is articulated through the character of the American teenager, played by James Dean. She suggests that the concept/practice of rebellion, which Hannah Arendt proposed, can usefully be applied to analyse the film. However, rather than limiting rebellion to describing an event which either did or did not achieve political change, Loizidou argues, drawing on Judith Butler, that it should be defined as a practice by which political agency is created through the act of resistance to power. In applying this interpretation to the film *Rebel Without a Cause*, youth rebellion in post-World War II America can be interpreted as a demand for political citizenship. Her reading of *Rebel* accounts for the radical impact of the film, not only on its release, but in the present, which traditional interpretations of it as either a portrayal of individual juvenile delinquency or as a crisis of masculinity which accompanied the breakdown of conservative misogynistic family values, find hard to explain. If the essays in this section so far have either argued for a radical or conservative interpretation of the jurisprudence offered by the moving image, Fred Botting and Scott Wilson look at the dualistic role of film in the imaginary worlds of *Toy Story* (1995) and *Toy Story 2* (1999). Here, family values are challenged by the ambivalent law set down by toys. Through Charles Baudelaire's discourse on toys in modernity, they trace the relationship of toys to cinema, looking at the way in which the aesthetics of the moving image duplicate the structures of modernity which are constituted around routine and excitement. Film, like toys, trains subjects in the routines of everyday life, as well as offering excitement and pleasure. Drawing on Lacan and Derrida, they argue that it is in offering the latter that these toy stories, about animated toys, serve to invert the logics and structures of conventional law, revealing the performative aspects of heterosexual normality in the nuclear family. This allows for the playing out of the fantasy of adult-child love and sexuality and for the formation of new families.

Law, Aesthetics and Visual Technologies turns from the imaginary to the real to address some of the debates raised by the representation of justice through the aesthetics and medium of the moving image. The essays in this section explore various aspects of the impact of the visual, and the aesthetics and medium of the moving image, upon our experience of law, legality and justice, as well as interrogating the way in which the technologies of the moving image have given rise to claims that film can reveal the truth. Leslie Moran's essay raises some of the problems of legal scholarship which assume a direct relationship between film representations of legal issues and cases and the actual events. By contrasting two films, *The Trials of Oscar Wilde* (1960) and *Oscar Wilde* (1960), he raises the different dimensions of realism operating in the films. He argues for a more complex understanding of the nature of realism amongst legal scholars using narrative film. He is not arguing that the moving image does not have a powerful resonance in its representation of the real world, but that the relationship between films' mediation of events and audiences' responses to it operates at multiple levels of cognition and affect. Thus, Moran reflects upon some of the challenges of film as a technology of representation and consumption. Lawrence Douglas takes up this issue in a different form in his essay on documentary representations of the trials of Eichmann. He explores the ways in which four documentary films transform these historical trials into historical events. His close textual analysis of the four films, from the original television documentary shot at the trial to three subsequent interpretations of the Eichmann trials in relation to the Holocaust, illustrates how documentary aesthetics have shifted to engage with the problems of the visualising events. The first film posits the case for the prosecution, the second situates the viewer as witness and judge, the third projects the documentary trial as a history lesson, and the final film proposes documentary as a form of remembrance. He exposes the way in which documentary substitutes itself for the witnesses in its veracity of presenting the Holocaust. David Seymour also points out how video technology is used in M Night Shyalaman's film, *The Sixth Sense* (1999) to expose the ethical dimensions of justice. The film serves to allow him to reflect on some of the problems of interdisciplinary scholarship and to examine the dualism of thought which not only structures the film, but also is to be found in the structure of his examples of critical texts from the fields of film and law. He thus explores one of the difficulties of engagement between the disciplines of law and film: that despite interesting insights, each medium retreats after any encounter. The other difficulty he perceives is that legal scholars use film as an illustrative resource rather than acknowledging the specific properties of film – its visual dimensions. Seymour proposes that a way through the circular engagement and retreat of critical writing on law and film, through the 'jurisprudence of absolutes', might be found in the development of a critical methodology of film and law through the engagement of critical theory from each discipline with each other. Acknowledging the impact of the visual as operating within the symbolic realm of language rather than outside of, and in opposition to it, might yield more productive theories of knowledge. Angus MacDonald's paper on Fritz Lang's *M* (1931), on the other hand, explores the limits of the visual. He finds that the meaning of the film cannot be understood through analysing the plot as a battle between the law and the criminal world. In other words, the narrative is not resolved through recourse to questions of ethics or of superior knowledge based on the point of view of either one or the other. Both the law and the criminal world are after the killer, and neither has superior knowledge of how to apprehend him. Moreover, in the city where the child murder has taken place, and the film itself, it is not what is seen that reveals the murderer, it is what is heard. Using a Deleuzian analysis, he explores the use of sound in *M* to disrupt a series of binary oppositions generated by way of the visual. Only then when understood as a narrative of the competing hermeneutics of sight and sound, in a film made in the early days of sound cinema, can *M* be understood as an allegory in which law is imagined, rather than being an attempt at the realistic representation of law. Alison Young's chapter takes the challenges of the visual image in a different direction. She reflects not so much upon an actual encounter between law, justice and the visual image, but an imagined encounter. She looks at two court cases in Australia in which the gay man as threat is not only imagined, but also recognised legally. The visual fantasy of fear of sexual abuse and HIV infection appears and is embodied as a reality in the image of the gay man within the law. Alternatively, in her examination of Derek Jarman's *Blue* (1993), made while he was living with the increasingly disabling effects of HIV/AIDS, she locates the representation of HIV in cinema through the disappearance of the image of the gay man. *Blue* rejects the moving image in its inability to represent the invisible and instead offers the voice, sound, to the viewer. The essay offers an analysis of the film as one that exposes the impoverished aesthetics of the visual in law, judgment and justice, as imagined and generated in response to HIV/AIDS in Australian litigation.

The third and final section of the book brings together essays around the topic of *Regulation: Histories, Cultures, Legalities*, which trace the way in which law tries to concretise the moving image within its regulatory structures. Under the name of 'regulation' we bring together essays that explore regimes of law that are traditionally kept apart: public law, focusing on relations between subjects, citizens of the state (including corporate citizens) and the state, national and international law, and civil or private law with its focus on the fabrication and enforcement of relations between private persons. They are brought together under this heading in part as a common concern of these essays is an exploration of the different legal contexts in which the very idea of cinema disrupts and confounds cultural expectations outwith but already embedded in the law. In turn, these essays all explore the fashioning and refashioning of ideas of cinema that are produced in and through these legal encounters not only limiting but also forming the very idea of film and cinema at different times and in different national, social and cultural contexts. The section opens with two essays that explore the impact of the new technology of cinema in two very different contexts and settings, the US and India, in the early 20th century. Both draw attention to the disruptive effects of the new medium of film and the struggles to make sense of film, which both shaped and confined not only the meaning of cinema, its consumption and its consuming subjects, but formed (and was informed by) the fabrication of social relations more generally. Grieveson's study of the early cinema in the US examines the ways in which instances and expectations of social disorder surrounding the showing of *The Birth of a Nation* (1915) and other contemporary films generated demands for regulation. Rather than working with a model of regulation as being concerned with prohibition, Grieveson draws out the role of censorship in the production of the very idea of cinema. He explores the way in which censorship becomes a context in which the cultural functions and relative weighting of different ideas of cinema, (is it 'entertainment' or 'education', fiction or non-fiction, indexical or realist?) is fabricated and institutionalised. The cultural and wider political dimensions of regulation are also of concern in Prasad's essay, which examines the colonial struggles generated in and through the importation of film images of and from Britain and America which are recorded in the papers of the Indian Cinematograph Committee (1928). Provoked by a perception that these images were corrupting Indian audiences, causing them to lose respect for the ruling race, the Committee embarked upon an inquiry into the truth of this allegation and had the objective of recommending interventions. Prasad's essay offers a fascinating account of the disruptive effects that the cinematic image introduced into colonial relations and the efforts made, under conditions of colonial rule, to come to terms with the novelty of the film image. He explores the way the colonial relation, based on fairly well-established ideas (the coloniser as agency of reform, the native as the object of reformist projects) is both challenged by a new cultural institution unanticipated by colonialism and managed in and through the shadow of that perceived threat. The cultural and wider social factors at play in regulation are also the focus of Slocum's analysis of a more contemporary event, the release of the film *Bonnie and Clyde* (1967). Drawing upon the insights generated by a broad engagement with an interdisciplinary sociology of popular media, Slocum offers an analysis that situates the more conventional legal, institutional and statutory instruments governing film violence within the wider parameters of cultural regulation concerned with the social control of deviance, the disciplining of individual bodies, and the production of knowledge through criminalisation, pacification and the civilising process.

Examining the interface between the state, cultural policy and the film industry, Grantham's essay turns our attention to a very different context of government intervention in response to different dangers, the development of policies, strategies and institutions dedicated to fighting the incursion of Hollywood cinema into Europe, leading to the perceived erosion of cultural identity as national identity. Continuing the debate found in the first three essays in this section, to re-imagine regulation, Grantham explores the challenges of nationalism, regionalism and globalisation to the assumptions of those who seek to define culture and cultural regulation in terms of the nation state. Thereafter, the focus shifts to bring regulation by way of private law into the frame. Fiona Macmillan refashions Hollywood cinema in the image of corporate power and examines the impact of that institutional power upon cultural production through the lens of national and international codes of law that seek to produce a common global regime of intellectual property. Framing culture in general and visual culture in particular as a matter of property and ownership, her essay explores the problems this generates when read through the real politik of institutionalised economic power. Finally, Celia Lury's essay returns us to the significance of the social and cultural context in which the private law of copyright has emerged as a key means of regulation. Based upon an empirical study and using the methodological device of biography, the essay explores the social life of a number of cultural products, including the film *Trainspotting* (1996), the animated features starring Wallace and Gromit and the computer animated film *Toy Story* (1995). The device of the biography is adopted to facilitate not only a mapping of the movements of these cultural objects across space and time, but also to map transformations in time and space. Two general principles of product transformation are explored: translation and transposition. The chapter documents and examines the way copyright and trademark support these complex processes in many different ways.

PART I
A FANTASTIC JURISPRUDENCE

Chapter 1
Heavenly justice
Ian Christie

> Why should not Conscience have vacation
> As well as other courts o' the nation?
> (Samuel Butler, *Hudibras* ii 2)

Cinema has long had a guilty conscience about the supernatural. Although its photographic resources soon made possible the realistic portrayal of ghosts, visions and all forms of the paranormal, much of cinema's history seems to have been governed by a form of collective self-denial which has confined the supernatural to such codified genres as the gothic or juvenile fantasy. After the extraordinary popularity of the essentially supernatural trick film between 1898 and 1906, realist narrative became the dominant industrial form, with décor and spectacle substituting for what came to be regarded as the primitive, often fanciful pantomime of early cinema (Hammond, 1981). Although there would continue to be supernatural-allegorical interpolations, such as the rocking cradle of *Intolerance* (1916), the Dürer-inspired figures of *Four Horsemen of the Apocalypse* (1921) and the vision of Moloch in *Metropolis* (1926), these were generally subordinated to realist narrative, until the emergence of a new naturalistic supernatural in the 1930s. The harbingers of this were the passengers in *Outward Bound* (1930),[1] the Christ-like stranger in *The Passing of the Third Floor Back* (1935), the eponymous protagonist of *Death Takes a Holiday* (1934) and the weary angel of *It's a Wonderful Life* (1946). It was also paralleled by a strong current of new supernaturalism in the theatre, notably in JB Priestley's 'time plays', from *Dangerous Corner* (1932) to *An Inspector Calls* (1946), and in Thornton Wilder's *Our Town* (1938).

A parallel trajectory might be traced, which would begin by noting that the key technique of stop-action was often used to confer 'magical', but illegal, benefits in early films, allowing assorted mischief-makers to steal, cheat and insult, and escape with impunity (Shale, 1996a, p 4). Soon filmmakers began to make extensive use of mistaken inference, where visual evidence is misconstrued, as the basis for many kinds of realist narratives. And from an early date, the trial and the detection process, either separately or combined, would account for a large proportion of all screen drama. Carol Clover has recently drawn attention to the long-standing relationship in, especially, American cinema between the trial movie as a specific genre and a more general equation in cinema between audience and jury (Clover, 2000). The term 'diegesis', commonly used in film analysis to denote narrative content, was originally the recital of facts in a Greek law court before its adoption by Aristotle in the *Rhetoric* (p 247).

The courtroom drama may indeed only be an explicit instance of cinema's more pervasive interpellation of its viewing subjects as jurors, granted special privileges of access and insight.[2] My concern here, however, is with a limited area of convergence between the naturalistic supernatural and the court drama: films from World War II

---

1 Based on a 1924 play by Sutton Vane, remade during World War II as *Between Two Worlds* (1944).
2 Louis Althusser observed that bourgeois ideology's concept of the 'subject' was itself borrowed from the legal category of the 'subject in law' (Althusser, 1971, p 160).

in which there is an appeal to a 'higher jurisdiction', where matters that lie beyond the scope of immediate human responsibility may at least be debated, if not resolved. *Thunder Rock* (1942) is set in a remote lighthouse, where an intellectual has taken refuge from the imminent war against Nazism, but is haunted by the ghostly victims of a 19th century shipwreck, who enjoy a supernatural afterlife only thanks to the power of his imagination.[3] When he accuses them of cowardice in their own time, running away from persecution, they challenge him to stand up for his beliefs in the present. In *A Guy Named Joe* (1944), a pilot killed in action 'discovers' that he now has a celestial Commanding Officer and a new mission, which is to mentor living pilots, one of whom becomes the new boyfriend of his former fiancée.[4] The hero of *A Matter of Life and Death* (1946) is a bomber pilot who 'should' have died after bailing out without a parachute, but finds himself alive, while awaiting a trial in heaven to decide his case for staying on earth.[5] Only the last of these literally portrays a celestial court and centres on a trial, but all appeal to fantastic concepts of justice, which also constitute a critique of the limitations of actual legal process.

Figure 1: *Thunder Rock*, **Boulting, 1942.**

---

3 *Thunder Rock* (1942), directed by Roy Boulting, from a script by Jeffrey Dell and Bernard Miles, based on the play by Robert Ardrey. With Michael Redgrave, Lilli Palmer, Barbara Mullen and James Mason.

4 *A Guy Named Joe* (1944), directed by Victor Fleming, from a script by Dalton Trumbo. With Spencer Tracy, Irene Dunne and Van Johnson.

5 *A Matter of Life and Death* (1946), directed and written by Michael Powell and Emeric Pressburger. With David Niven, Roger Livesey and Kim Hunter.

It might be argued that all films with a counterfactual or fantastic legal theme constitute in some sense a critique of the existing legal process; that they represent a fictive 'return of the repressed' of natural law as against positive law. But I want to suggest that these particular fictions might usefully be considered 'minor jurisprudences', in the sense proposed by Peter Goodrich (Goodrich, 1996, p 2). The historical examples he gives include 'ecclesiastical courts, civilian courts, courts of conscience, of equity, of inquisition; and also such locally defined jurisdictions as forests, circuses, fairs, manors'. In Britain, all of these gradually came within the emerging common law from the 16th century onwards, in some cases shaping its forms. Canon law survived longest as a separate jurisdiction, with responsibility for a range of issues considered to have religious underpinning, before it too gave way to secular law. Goodrich suggests that these minor jurisprudences, having been repressed by common and statute law, have nonetheless left 'phantoms' of discarded tradition. They define 'a space within which radical legal studies can explore alternative legal forms', using them to help construct 'a history of the legal unconscious'. My proposal here is to consider the fictive micro-jurisprudence of such films as *A Guy Named Joe*, *Thunder Rock* and *A Matter of Life and Death* as fantastic alternatives to positive law, which function in ways analogous to the medieval and Renaissance practices Goodrich cites. Like these, they may serve to reconnect law to questions of conscience, and to the ethical dimensions and indeterminacies of judgment (Goodrich, 1996, p 4). These films precisely seem to raise issues which 'rational' thought about personal and national values in wartime cannot progress, and cannot finally arbitrate.[6]

A fantastic jurisprudence

Thunder Rock began its life as a play by an American dramatist Robert Ardrey, written in mid-1939 and premiered that November at the New York Group Theatre in a production supervised by Elia Kazan.[7] The message of the play was anti-isolationist. Inspired by Ardrey's own sojourn on the island of Nantucket, his hero is a widely travelled reporter and political commentator, David Charleston, who has become a lighthouse-keeper as a gesture of withdrawal from a world seemingly hell-bent on war. His solitude is broken by the arrival of an inspector and a pilot about to volunteer for foreign service against Japanese aggression in China. The three debate activism versus cynicism in face of rising international tension; after the visitors leave, the debate is continued in Charleston's mind, as he imagines a group of historical characters, based on a shipping disaster of the previous century which took place near the lighthouse. Blending symbolist and modernist aesthetics,[8]

---

6 The wartime context is significant, since it led to a specific revival of long-forgotten forms of representation and rhetoric. David Mellor has referred to a 'new symbolic order' in British war-related art, in which Renaissance and older forms were remobilised 'under the ideological aegis of the Churchillian renaissance' (Mellor, 1982, p 70).

7 This account of *Thunder Rock* owes much to the invaluable account by Anthony Aldgate (Aldgate and Richards, 1986, pp 168–86).

8 Ghostly characters who are explicitly products of the imagination were a feature of the symbolist theatre of Maurice Maeterlinck, Emile Verhaeren and August Strindberg between roughly 1890 and 1910. Breaking the theatrical illusion was an important feature of Luigi Pirandello's *Six Characters in Search of an Author* (1921) and Bertolt Brecht's early plays, both influences on the Group Theatre, which nurtured Ardrey.

Ardrey has Charleston summon a representative group of victims of past injustice and intolerance whom he can accuse of defeatism, before they voice the same accusation towards him. Having convinced himself that action is preferable to inaction, he announces at the end of the play that he will leave the lighthouse to 'fight ... not for fighting's sake, but to make a new world of the old' (quoted in Aldgate and Richards, 1986, p 175).

Although unsuccessful in America, then sharply divided over the European war that had just broken out, *Thunder Rock* became a focus of attention in London during the summer of 1940, when it opened shortly after the debacle of Dunkirk and Churchill taking over from Chamberlain as Prime Minister. Negotiations were soon underway for a screen adaptation, which was undertaken by the producer-director team of John and Roy Boulting, from a script adapted by Bernard Miles and Jeffrey Dell, and starring the actor who had played Charleston on stage, Michael Redgrave. Aldgate has pointed up the two major changes made in the adaptation from stage to screen, apart from various devices of narrative 'opening up' and Charleston becoming an Englishman. The first of these is to give the ghostly passengers, drowned in 1849, more detailed histories of oppression in England and Austria: a labourer who has developed lung disease working in the Potteries aims to take his family to California; a spinster, disowned by her wealthy father after she has been imprisoned repeatedly for agitation on behalf of women's rights, who now hopes to find a husband in the United States; and a doctor, drummed out of Vienna by his colleagues, after pioneering the use of anaesthetics. These 'back stories', realised with considerable scenographic invention, become a substantial part of the film's body, giving it a pervasive atmosphere of social exposé and of struggle against both legal and moral repression.

They are counterbalanced by the film's other main departure from the play. After Charleston has accused his 'ghosts' of cowardice, the captain of the ship in which they perished challenges him on their behalf to justify his own retreat to this refuge. In reply, as it were, the film offers a rapid montage summarising Charleston's career as a crusading political correspondent. It does this by reference to the chapters of his book, *Darkening World*, each devoted to one of the major political crises of the 1930s, from the Japanese in Manchuria, to Abyssinia, Spain, the Anschluss between Germany and Austria, and German rearmament. The interweaving of newsreel and dramatised 'eye-witnessing', together with a commentary on British newspapers' desire to censor reports such as Charleston's, reaches its climax in a cinema when, after a dispiriting campaign of anti-fascist public meetings, he is surrounded by patrons, oblivious to the newsreel report of Hitler entering the Sudetenland, who only want cartoon entertainment. This is what has led to his retreat from active struggle, which we might conclude, in psychoanalytic terms, has prompted the return of the repressed in the form of the phantasms of earlier struggles. There are many possible determinations at work here: from the trans-historical viewpoint of Wilder's *Our Town*[9] and Priestley's 'time plays'[10] to the dazzling kaleidoscopic

9 Aldgate notes (Aldgate and Richards, 1986, p 170) that Ardrey studied with Wilder at the University of Chicago, although this would have been before *Our Town* was written.

10 The cycle of 'time plays' by JB Priestley that includes *Time and the Conways* (1937), *I Have Been Here Before* (1937) and *An Inspector Calls* (1946) makes use of mystical ideas of precognition and recurrence, influenced by PD Ouspensky and Carl Jung.

flashback structure of Orson Welles' recent *Citizen Kane* (1941), and from agitprop to psychoanalysis. But given that the film's completion in late 1942 precluded any of the play's predictive urgency, what might strike us are its elaborate dramaturgy of conscience and its self-conscious modernisation of the apparatus of consciousness and memory. Recalling elements of both the pictorial 'memory theatre' tradition studied by Frances Yates and Griffith's interweaving of temporally distinct narratives exemplifying 'intolerance', *Thunder Rock* creates a modern phantasmagoria, in which the past permeates the present, and the personal is imbricated with the political.[11]

The film's Charleston is less a modern Everyman than a *case*; one who has seen and understood too much, and who has attempted to become a modern hermit, retreating from the clamorous evils of the present to the ivory tower of a lighthouse. But his unconscious cannot accept this repression, and although he believes he has conjured the historical figures, Prospero-like, as creatures under his control, they revolt and reveal themselves as analogues of himself, symptomatic projections of his guilty conscience. Now, rather than pursue the vulgar Freudianism of this reading, I will suggest it is equally, if not more, appropriate to conceive the apparatus of *Thunder Rock* as a modern 'court of conscience' which focuses upon that which is 'subjugated' (Goodrich, 1995, p 234), in the positivising tendency of common law. The 'court of conscience' offers a mystical jurisprudence. This mysticism Goodrich traces back to the theological conception of an 'outward' and an 'inward' eye, the latter, according to St German, 'the eye of reason, whereby [man] knows things invisible and divine' (p 236). In this perspective, matters of ethics and conscience are hierarchically and ontologically prior, relating to 'the substance of subjectivity, to an unconscious discipline or juristic soul' (p 236). Common law's adjudication of external conflicts is 'a living metaphor or allegory for the courts of conscience and of the spirit' (p 236).

Like the mock-legal court of history before which Byron is arraigned in *The Bad Lord Byron* (1949), Charleston stands accused in, literally, a court of conscience, where his transgression is that of the ethic that he professes and applies to others. What the film's elaborate dramaturgy works to achieve is our belief in this 'case of conscience', in the relevance of its phantom evidence, its trans-historical principles, and its 'spiritual' verdict, to which are attached special powers of enforcement, which must dictate the subject's future conduct. But why should this model reappear at such a juncture? An important aspect of World War II was the sense it brought to many of spiritual renewal or exaltation. The eschatological tenor of TS Eliot's *Little Gidding*, published in the same year as *Thunder Rock*, claims that 'Every phrase and every sentence is an end and a beginning' as it moves towards the ecstatic 'History is now and England' (Eliot, 1969, p 197). In appropriating Ardrey's Charleston to the wartime England of 1942, the Boultings needed to create a court of conscience that, however spectral and speculative, would be seen to reassert the forgotten pre-eminence of spiritual justice in a momentary, emblematic return of law's repressed.

---

11 On the classical and Renaissance mnemonic tradition, see Frances Yates, 1966.

Both *A Guy Named Joe* and *A Matter of Life and Death* participated in the last phase of an early 20th century preoccupation with the flyer as modern hero and also as mythic figure. This is hardly surprising, in view of the speed with which powered flight had developed in less than 30 years after centuries of myth and speculation. During the 1920s and 1930s, flyers such as Lindbergh and Johnston undertook remarkable solo journeys which gave them an aura of distinctively modern heroism, celebrated by artists as diverse as WB Yeats, Filippo Marinetti, Bertolt Brecht, Fernand Léger, WH Auden and Paul Nash (Wollen, 1999, p 10; Christie, 2000, pp 13–14). The main characteristics of this modern myth would seem to have been the risk of absolute dependence on a machine; the extreme isolation of the long-distance flyer; and, more difficult to define, the sense of transgression attaching to flight, reflected in the myth of Icarus, combined with the idea of a vantage point on human affairs that evokes, perhaps blasphemously, the angelic or divine. One imaginative work of the 1930s, above all, encapsulates the image of the aviator as a superior being, and as the arbiter of a new world order: HG Wells' novel *The Shape of Things to Come* (1933), filmed by Alexander Korda three years later.[12] In this, the collapse of modern civilisation in the aftermath of a devastating world war is followed by regeneration under the benevolent dictatorship of an order of aviators known as 'Wings Over the World', who impose rationality and progress, like the guardians of Plato's *Republic*. The Wells-Korda fantasy image of the aviator as all-powerful arbiter might be considered to mark the climax of the myth of the flyer, since, as Wollen observes (1999, p 10), after the bombing of Guernica, air power began to seem more threatening. However, the chivalric image of the pilot as a 'knight of the air' revived during World War II, and it is through this specific mythology that both *A Guy Named Joe* and *A Matter of Life and Death* create their fantasies of otherworldly duty and justice.

The hero of *A Guy Named Joe* is presented as an irreverent, supremely confident and somewhat cynical pilot who decides in the heat of battle to take his damaged bomber suicidally close to an enemy aircraft carrier rather than bail out after the rest of the crew. He next finds himself walking across a dazzling plain, where he meets a fellow pilot, who he realises is already dead. Recognising the commanding officer as 'one of the greatest fliers of all time', he soon discovers that 'here' he must learn a new humility and a new discipline. He is rebuked by 'The General in Heaven' for presuming that he learned to fly by his own ability, rather than as the beneficiary of all who preceded him. His new work turns out to be as the invisible mentor of young flyers, one of whom will eventually become the partner of his own former fiancée. The immediate wartime messages are clear enough: duty must come before sentiment; we are all dependent on each other; and life will go on beyond individual tragedy and loss. But are these enough to merit any more than historical curiosity? Supernatural fantasy was far from unusual in Hollywood cinema of the 1930s and 1940s, from the ghostly detective of the *Topper* series[13] to *Here Comes Mr*

---

12 *Things to Come* (1936), directed by William Cameron Menzies, from a script by Wells. With Raymond Massey, Ralph Richardson and Margaretta Scott.

13 *Topper* (1937), based on a comic novel by Thorne Smith about a banker helped to solve crimes by the ghosts of his dead friends; followed by two sequels, *Topper Takes a Trip* (1939) and *Topper Returns* (1941).

Jordan (1941) and *It's a Wonderful Life*, usually played for whimsical comedy or easy pathos. For some contemporary critics, the film's emotional excess was already risible or distasteful. One wrote of 'fake philosophy, swimming eyes and all',[14] while another noted how 'it neatly obtunds death's sting as ordinary people suffer it by ... assuming ... a good busy, hearty hereafter'.[15] Such responses convey the unease that has affected much 'discriminating' response to cinema's treatment of emotionally charged issues, but they also miss the point of modernised melodrama and its play with the supernatural. Although the film carefully avoids explicit religious trappings, Pete Sandige has become, in effect, a guardian angel, and it is from this unusual viewpoint that we witness the further unfolding of the narrative.

The circumstances of the film's creation are unclear, with four writers credited and its director, Victor Fleming, usually considered more workmanlike than a creative force. The concept of a wartime pilots' heaven may owe something to a 1943 training film, *Learn and Live*, produced by the Army Air Corps' First Motion Picture Unit.[16] In this, 'Joe Instructor' climbs through the clouds to visit 'Pilots' Heaven', where he is greeted in traditional fashion by a benign St Peter who is

Figure 2: *A Guy Named Joe*, **Fleming, 1944.**

---

14 Richard Mallet review, *Punch*, 1944.
15 A contemporary review by James Agee.
16 *Learn and Live* appears to have been the first of 12 training films produced between 1943 and 1945 by the Army Air Corps' First Motion Picture Unit, under the supervision of Paul Mantz.

concerned about overcrowding due to the many elementary errors made by trainee pilots, seen lounging unhappily in their celestial mess. *Learn and Live* reviews a series of case histories in flashback to drive home its training message. Another precursor is the comic fantasy *The Remarkable Andrew*, scripted from his own novel in 1942 by the scenarist for *A Guy Named Joe*, Dalton Trumbo.[17] In this, a timid accountant who has been falsely accused of embezzlement is advised on his defence by a succession of ghosts from American history, including Andrew Jackson, George Washington, Benjamin Franklin and Thomas Jefferson. Neither of these films, however, aspires to the full-blown melodramatic intensity of *A Guy Named Joe*, and neither posits a realm of transcendence in other than essentially comic terms. The significance of the wartime context in creating a framework of acceptance for the emotions of *A Guy Named Joe* was underlined when Steven Spielberg undertook a remake in 1989, entitled *Always*.[18] Here, by common critical consent, the central issue of Pete's duty to accept his guardian angel role is weakened by a modern peacetime setting, with the pilots involved in forest firefighting. As a result, Pete now 'returns' as much because of a romantic attachment as out of any sense of duty, even though the duty of the original film is necessarily partisan.

The emotional conflict of *A Guy Named Joe* could certainly be aligned with the familiar themes of wartime romantic pathos, in which couples are routinely parted, wives and fiancées bereaved, and the miraculous occasionally intervenes to engineer a form of qualified happy ending, as in Borzage's *Seventh Heaven* (1927), or epiphany. But it is also possible to read the film allegorically, as we would perhaps normally read tales involving supernatural agency, and for this approach we have the encouragement of Sergei Eisenstein's interpretation (1980, p 224).[19] What Eisenstein found particularly admirable was the simplicity and directness of the philosophy spelled out by the General, with its emphasis on the common task to which all contribute.[20] This embodied the idea that there is 'an unbreakable chain of human experience ... a creative inheritance which is transmitted down the generations, so that even victims are not without value, since their sacrifices make possible the achievements of others'. From this perspective, he suggests, every flight becomes a creative performance by all flyers, adding that, if he were 20, he'd probably be inspired to become a pilot. In a broader sense, Eisenstein was reading the celestial mission as a parable, which fitted well with the Russian Symbolist tradition of collective creative inheritance, as proposed by Vyachslav Ivanov.[21]

---

17 *The Remarkable Andrew* (1942), directed by Stuart Heisler, from a script by Trumbo. With Brian Donlevy and William Holden.

18 *Always* (1989), directed by Spielberg, from a script by Jerry Belson, based on the original script by Trumbo and Chandler Sprague. With Richard Dreyfuss and Holly Hunter.

19 This text appears in a collection of late writings speculatively regarded as part of Eisenstein's memoir, composed between 1946 and 1947, during his convalescence after the heart attack brought on by the banning of *Ivan the Terrible Part 2* in 1946. The wartime alliance had made possible an unusual degree of access to American films in the Soviet Union during 1944–45, before post-war relations soured, and Eisenstein, like other Russian artists with an international reputation, was obliged to adopt a hostile stance towards all things American.

20 This also recalls the influential Russian religious thinker Nikolai Fedorov, with his 'philosophy of the common task' (Fedorov, 1990).

21 Ivanov developed the ideas of the 19th century philosopher and poet Vladimir Solovyov and the 'new dawn' current in Russian Symbolism around 1900, proposing a form of 'racial memory' and emphasising the idea of salvation through death and resurrection.

Such an interpretation, helped by its impressive pedigree, is valuable in countering the prevailing tone of much Anglo-American criticism, focused narrowly on questions of credibility and sympathy: do we 'believe' in this story and in these characters and actors? The theme of the film, underpinning its romantic, sentimental story, is in fact propaedeutic: it teaches the idea of a collective, trans-individual morality, in which the misfortune of the individual may still contribute to the common good. And through our identification with the star, Spencer Tracy, we are encouraged to un-learn the hubris of mastery, and begin instead to understand a new ethic of humility and submission to the contingency of war. Like Charleston in *Thunder Rock*, Sandige is being 'sent back' into the world, although this is not the result of a celestial judgment, as, for instance, in *Liliom* (1934), where a brutal fairground barker is required to expiate his wrongdoing before he can enter heaven.[22] In *A Guy Named Joe*, the avuncular Heavenly General is only identified as a 'great flyer' who is apparently the commander of a ghostly legion of instructors whose intervention remains invisible, like the guardian angels of Handke's and Wenders' *Wings of Desire* (1987). These instructor-angels seem to be following a mystical, yet secular, code of obligation.

This might be seen as defusing unwanted theological complexity, by giving the General an authority based on professional status and charisma rather than through being an 'official' archangel, as in the heavenly hierarchy of *A Matter of Life and Death*. Similarly, the bare office in which he interviews Sandige avoids any direct equation with heaven (or purgatory or limbo) through its functional informality: it appears to be, quite simply, a briefing room, where flyers receive their orders for posterity. Yet Sandige has to overcome his pride and egocentricity, and be 'tested', like a novice entering a religious or chivalric order. Unlike the eschatological justice of Yahweh, this is therapeutic or propaedeutic, offering its subjects the chance to play their part in the 'creative chain' by aiding the living. Theologically, this is no doubt heretical, since it ignores the whole apparatus of repentance, salvation and final judgment. But it evokes a modern form of the code of chivalry, which was one of the important minor jurisprudences, and is significant not only for 'reconnecting law to ... the ethical dimensions ... of judgment', but also in spiritual terms (Goodrich, 1996).

A Matter of Life and Death, unusually, and perhaps uniquely in cinema, takes up the challenge of figuring both heaven and a full-scale trial therein. Yet this is a resolutely modern, bureaucratic heaven, in the tradition of Kipling's World War I story, *On the Gate*, and the trial is framed exclusively in political and poetic terms, devoid of any conventional religious trappings. Mischievously, it is a trial, not about seeking admission to eternity, but about the 'right' to remain mortal. The film originated in an invitation in 1944 to Michael Powell and Emeric Pressburger from Britain's Ministry of Information to consider ways of improving post-war Anglo-American relations, which seemed likely to deteriorate even further after the end of hostilities (Christie, 2000, p 12). By the time it was completed in 1946, there was

---

22 Ferenc Molnar's 1909 play *Liliom* was filmed by Fritz Lang in France in 1934, and later served as the basis for Rogers' and Hammerstein's musical *Carousel*. In it, a fairground barker killed during a robbery has to return to earth for one day to redeem his brutal behaviour while alive. His sentence is handed down in a celestial police-court.

something amounting to paranoia on both sides of the Atlantic, with Britain deeply in debt to America and fearing it would be demoted to second class status in the post-war political settlement, and American popular sentiment increasingly suspicious of British colonialism, of long-term involvement in Europe, and of a successor to the League of Nations.

In this climate, the task of *A Matter of Life and Death* was to create a fiction capable of dealing with such large and seemingly abstract issues. Its chosen method, in a nutshell, was to attempt a bold fusion of the Shavian problem play with the newly revived tradition of the early 17th century allegorical masque.[23] As in *Thunder Rock*, the protagonist is an anguished intellectual, poised between past and future, a 'man who knows too much'. The solution in both cases is for the hero to become, at least temporarily, mad, to fantasise or hallucinate a world beyond the confines of space and time where his 'case' can be heard. For Peter Carter, the bomber pilot and poet of *A Matter of Life and Death*, the immediate dilemma is both personal and political. Having bailed out of a damaged bomber without a parachute, he should be dead, but due to an error in the celestial system, he has not been brought to heaven and has fallen in love with the last person he reached by radio from the plane, an American radio operator. Suspended in an earthly limbo, he is diagnosed as needing cranial surgery to alleviate the hallucinations, which tell him of an impending trial in heaven to decide his fate. Technically, in this fantastic jurisprudence, the case is about whether Peter's *de facto* escape from death constitutes grounds for an extended reprieve. At issue also is the question of what constitutes 'sanity', in a fascinating exploration of the conjuncture between medical and legal categories: Peter is simultaneously, and paradoxically, a subject of these different discourses and jurisdictions. But in the ideologically charged rhetoric of the trial, which parallels his operation, it is Britain itself that is on trial. For Peter to deserve an extended life with June, the prosecuting counsel argues, Britain must be deemed able to offer a worthy home for an American, and to do so, it must overcome the legacy of its colonial tradition.

In a fuller exploration of the film's many and varied sources, I have suggested that it can be seen as a reinvention and combination of two traditional forms: the allegory and the masque (Christie, 2000, pp 14–19). These were indeed originally linked, since the court masque which flourished in England during the early 17th century was intrinsically allegorical in its use of mythological figures, 'personified' by courtiers and even royalty, to celebrate contemporary political events such as a marriage or an investiture. Their elaborate and costly spectacle was justified by their political significance in court life and in international diplomacy, with ambassadors often actively involved (Lindley, 1998, p ix). It has also been noted that the masque was frequently self-referential:

---

23 Vaughan Williams' 1930 ballet *Job*, subtitled 'a masque for dancing', and Benjamin Britten's coronation opera *Gloriana* (1953) are the best known examples of a renewed interest among musicians in the masque. Pageants, albeit treated obliquely or ironically, became popular among writers seeking alternatives to conventional realism and ways of dealing with the legacy of English history. Examples would include EM Forster's *England's Pleasant Land* (1938) and Virginia Woolf's last novel, *Between the Acts* (1941).

In *Pleasure Reconciled to Virtue*, for example, the masquers are returned to the hill of virtue, and reminded of the struggle they must continually make to live up to the roles they have enacted (Lindley, 1998, p xii)

In *A Matter of Life and Death*, not only does a rehearsal of Shakespeare's *A Midsummer Night's Dream* recall the presence of the masque in more familiar Renaissance drama and imply that these latterday lovers are subject to higher powers, but the film also makes frequent allusion to the mechanics of illusion, from the doctor's *camera obscura* to the heavenly conductor remarking, 'One is starved for Technicolor up there', as he appears on earth amid luridly coloured rhododendrons.

Figure 3: *A Matter of Life and Death*, Powell and Pressburger, 1946.

The terms in which Peter represents England, and June stands for America, conform closely to the diplomatic traditions of the court masque, underlined by the film's origins as a propaganda intervention. But another tradition is also invoked by references to the most famous allegory in English literature, John Bunyan's *The Pilgrim's Progress* (1678). Peter's defending counsel, who has also been his physician, is escorted into heaven after a fatal road accident by a figure identified as Bunyan. Dr Reeves effectively 'goes ahead', like an amalgam of several of Bunyan's characters, such as Mr Valiant-for-Truth and Mr Standfast; however, in this case his role is not to 'conduct' Peter into heaven, but instead to argue that he should be returned to earth and a life with June. If we try to decipher the course of the heavenly tribunal, it can perhaps be divided into three stages. First, there is the question of contingency. Because of a dense fog over the English Channel, Peter has not been brought to heaven by his appointed Conductor, a cynical victim of the French Revolution, so the Records department is at fault. He has fallen in love with June, and so acquired an 'obligation', as his counsel argues, deploying the terms of a court of love. This obligation would lead to June living in England, but the prosecuting counsel, who died in the American War of Independence and is no friend of Britain, questions whether this is desirable, opening up the main ideological-political debate over Britain's post-war values and identity.

During the two-year interval between the film's conception and completion, the war had ended, leaving Britain bankrupted and heavily dependent on American goodwill. American public opinion, however, was suspicious, believing that Britain would seek to keep its colonies and to 'drag Americans into things which were not in their interest' (Ryan, 1987, p 28). While there is no evidence that Powell and Pressburger received specific briefing during late 1945, their film directly engages with the issues that British diplomats considered crucial in Anglo-American relations, particularly colonialism and the need for a continuing post-war alliance. The case is heard in a vast arena, which evokes both the ancient theatrical and communal origins of law, and the elemental ethos of modern drama from Wagner to Max Reinhardt. A striking feature of its fantastic jurisprudence is the interplay between the multitude of spectators, representing the diversity of both past and present 'humanity', and the six-person jury. In its first incarnation, the jury represents historically different phases of Britain's impact on the world, from Napoleonic France, India and South Africa to the modern Irish struggle for independence. The original script proposed an elaborate structure of 'empty' point-of-view shots from jury members, which would isolate them from the spectators, apart from the 'Sinn Fein rebel', who would address a full amphitheatre.[24] This was discarded, but what remains is the dramatic device, proposed by Dr Reeves in response to the challenge by an American prosecutor from the War of Independence era, of the jury members all being 'magically' changed into modern Americans, although of the same ethnic background as before. In this masque-like moment of transformation, a complex idea is conveyed by visual metaphor: that modern American society is less a challenge to the British Empire than a continuation of its diversity by other means. In the context of 1946–47, when the film was released, its massed representation of different nationalities could also hardly fail to suggest an historicised fantasy of the emergent United Nations Organisation.[25]

The new jury's first request, reflecting American pragmatism and fairness, is that the trial should move from heaven to earth, so that the defendant can be cross-examined; and so legal and medical jurisdiction converge as the heavenly court enters the operating theatre when Peter is undergoing cranial surgery. His case, however, will now be determined according to the steadfastness of the couple's love, and it is this that the opposing counsels seek to determine. First, Peter affirms

---

24 See references to shooting script annotated by Powell in Christie, 2000, p 70.

25 The United Nations Organisation was formally proposed at a conference in San Francisco in April to June 1945 and the first General Assembly took place in London in October of that year.

that he would be prepared to die on behalf of June, who is frozen in the stasis that represents the mortal world from heaven's perspective. Next, June is admitted into the limbo world of the trial and put to the test, first by the prosecutor, Farlan, asking if she would take Peter's place in heaven to prove her love, then by Reeves urging her to do this and so prove by deed her love. This substitution evokes the classical myth of Alcestis entering the underworld in order that her husband Admetus can enjoy the eternal life promised him by Apollo. As June mounts the escalator, Farlan warns, 'Take care, Dr Reeves! In the whole universe, nothing is stronger than the law'. Then, in a dramatic metaphor, the celestial machinery shudders to a halt, as if unable to resolve the contradiction posed by Reeves' and June's challenge to an implacable fate in the name of individual love. Reeves responds: 'Yes, Mr Farlan, nothing is stronger than the law in the universe, but on earth nothing is stronger than love.' When the jury agrees that Peter should remain alive to live out his life with June, the heavenly judge quotes Walter Scott on love in times of peace and war, ending with the lines:

> Love rules the court, the camp, the grove,
> And men below and saints above;
> For love is heaven and heaven is love.

Functioning like a latter-day version of the medieval court of love, this celestial tribunal accepts that Peter has acquired 'superior rights and duties' through falling in love with June; hence his life span will be 'generously' increased. The tone of this conclusion may indeed recall the typical ceremonial ending of a masque, in which conflict or opposition is happily resolved. But the final exchange between Farlan and Reeves gives it a pointed significance in the immediate post-war context. 'The rights of the common man' is amended by common consent to 'the rights of the uncommon man must always be respected'. I have suggested elsewhere that this cannot be read, as it sometimes has, merely as a defence of elitism or an anti-socialist barb; but that it coincides with a major post-war insistence on the rights of the individual. In his 1945 lecture 'Existentialism is a humanism', Jean-Paul Sartre argued that to choose one's own freedom was unavoidably to choose freedom for others, by treating them as ends in themselves (Sartre, 1973), while the United Nations' 1948 Declaration of Human Rights insisted that 'everyone has the right of life, liberty and security of person' (Harris, 1998, p 631). Powell's and Pressburger's existential couple celebrate in the final scene having 'won', and while their victory may seem merely romantic, it clearly also has an allegorical dimension as much as the endings of *Thunder Rock* and *A Guy Named Joe*.

Goodrich proposes the study of minor jurisprudences as 'a history of law's residues, of imaginary and fictive laws', which challenges the 'phantasm of an all-powerful law'. The three wartime fictions discussed here extend this domain into the fantastic, with their supernatural jurisprudences of duty and conscience extending beyond mortality. Their common reliance on evoking the supernatural may recall the historic growth of interest in both conventional religion and spiritualism during wartime.[26] In so far as they enact symbolic forms of trial by

---

26 The scale of death in World War I prompted mass interest in spiritualism, and also such quasi-religious fictions as HG Wells' *Mr Britling Sees It Through* (1916) and Kipling's story, *On the Gate*, which although written in 1916 was not published until 1926 in *Debits and Credits*.

ordeal, they remind us that, as Shale has observed, 'rational narrative adjudication seems by and large appropriate to us, but it is important to recognise that it is a specific form of legal adjudication rather than the only one' (Shale, 1996b, p 101). More generally, these instances of the legal paranormal might be considered forms of return to the religious metaphors that produced the concepts of the Western legal tradition. Harold Berman has characterised modern law as a 'secular theology', whose origins lie in the metaphors arising from beliefs and institutions of the medieval Christian church and from social relations of the feudal era (Berman, 1983, p 165). Central to these were the overarching concept of the Last Judgment, sited in a heavenly court and served by a hierarchy of angels, and the feudal relations of honour and duty. The heavenly tribunals of the films discussed, and of others belonging to this spectral genre, could therefore be seen as evidence of the return of both law's ancestry and its repressed, and as such might take their place in the ambitious 'genealogy of jurisprudence' proposed by Douzinas and Warrington (1994). Rather than be dismissed as 'light eschatological whimsies', they may be regarded as fulfilling an aspect of the general function of the uncanny that Freud identified as a symbolic 'preservation against extinction' (Freud, 1990, p 356) as well as admitting the return of cinema's own repressed magic. They assert a persistent belief in a redemptive rather than a damning justice: a protest against the 'law of the law – destiny' (Douzinas and Warrington, p 222), and offer a range of speculative answers to Antigone's question: 'Who knows what the rules are among the dead?'

Chapter 2
Once more unto the breach: Branagh's Henry V, Blair's war and the UK Constitution

Eugene McNamee

Introduction: approaching the Constitution filmically

A peculiarity of the UK legal system is that the Constitution rests completely on the principle of parliamentary sovereignty, rather than on a document of constitution. Neither entry into the European Union nor legislative initiatives such as the Human Rights Act 1998, which might be thought to represent profound constitutional events, either necessarily or inevitably change this state of affairs. It remains the case that no law has any greater formal weight than another and none has a superior formal quality that can protect it against being superseded.[1] In effect the Constitution is continually remade as more law is passed. At the same time there is no notion that the Constitution is incomplete; rather the basic idea is that the Constitution is always complete but always open to change by way of just another law. This cleavage is mirrored in the metaphysics of the state, which Kantorowicz (1997) explored in his study, *The King's Two Bodies*. The state is manifest in the simultaneous double body of the sovereign, one physical/natural and the other abstract/metaphysical: both human and divine; both perfect and lacking in perfection; both frail and eternal. In the UK, the body of law that is the Constitution shares these characteristics, but the turnover of that particular body is much more rapid; each day the body of constitutional law dies and another takes its place, while all the while the Constitution remains extant and in perpetuity. To put it another way, there is a condition of permanent plenitude which pre-supposes continuous breach.

The fact that constitutional questions are debated and constitutional law enacted in the same register as all other law (indeed there is no necessary distinction in substance or in form) renders the British Constitution extremely permeable to ongoing change in the developing social and cultural climate. Such flexibility and responsiveness is a proud boast of many Anglophile constitutionalists when comparing this system to the relative inflexibility of the 'written constitution' system. Furthermore, the flexibility of the Constitution is really the embodiment of the idea that the Constitution is nothing more than the implicit accord of the people as to the basics of good government, that finds expression through parliamentary enactment. The Constitution is the ongoing state of how the nation is constituted, which laws attempt to reflect and which law will inevitably shape. The most basic

---

1 There is a long tradition of legal scholarship that explores this state of the Constitution. The classic exposition is to be found in Dicey, 1965; Heuston, 1964; Marshall, 1971; and Wade, 1955.

element, however, is not law, but the ongoing lives of the people and some spirit of the nation is postulated as underpinning this (Ward, 2000).

This point may be more deeply illustrated by considering the nature of the 'common law'. 'Common law', as a term used in reference to the UK legal system, may mean two things. It refers to the entirety of the legal system (deriving from the systematisation of the laws of England that are taken to be common to all that domain and timeless).[2] It is also a phrase that is used to name a sub-species of law based on decided cases rather than on legislation (primarily law concerned with relations between persons, contract and torts, rather than between the subject and the sovereign/state). In the process of decision making, the transition from one case to the next is aided by the generative myth that the 'common law' exists as complete in some alternative realm. The bending and shaping of new decisions, where there is an obvious and necessary gap between the facts of a previous case and those in the case to be decided and therefore a gap in how the law may be applied, is based on the calling of a portion of this mythical complete legal system into the realm of the actual. It is imagined then not as creating law, but rather calling already-existing law out from the shadows and into the light. If the legitimisation of legislation is based on parliamentary sovereignty as the proper means for the voice of the people to find expression, then the legitimation of such legal development in the common law is the idea of a spirit of the people which resides within the ongoing development of their laws, and which judges, through their long exposure and expert training, are uniquely qualified to access. The judges form a kind of priesthood who serve before the altar of the legal system, with privileged access to its spiritual heart. The common law as judge-made law is, like the legislative part of the legal system, always suspended in a state of supposed plenitude yet with an ongoing process of filling up the holes which appear. It too is in a condition of permanent plenitude, which is also a condition of permanent breach. There is an ongoing tension both in legislative and in 'common law' terms as to how directly the law should embody the general will; here we might think of the supposed majority in favour of hanging. The tension can only be sustained by a semi-mystical idea that there is a difference between the general will and the 'spirit' of the nation. Access to the latter, it seems, demands some degree of initiation to the judicial or political class.

The calling up of the spirit of the nation is a process not confined, of course, to legislators but an enterprise shared by cultural commentators of all kinds. When judges call up the spirit of the law, they do so in order to make law, and thus a kind of permanence is guaranteed to their pronouncements. When others make a call to the spirit of the nation, the permanence must be achieved voluntarily on the part of the people themselves. It is on this basis that it is often said that poets are the unacknowledged legislators of a community, in that they write their text directly into the mind of the people rather than have it imposed on their bodies through external command (Ward, 2000). In the British context, the chief poet legislator is

---

2 Sometimes the temporal origin is imagined by reference to a fixed point, such as the reign of William the Conqueror; at other times its temporality has a more abstract quality, 'time immemorial'. See Goodrich, 1990 and 1992.

surely William Shakespeare (Ward, 1999). The permeability of the UK Constitution invites breaches in the legal fabric to be filled by just such kind of poetic legislation that makes a direct appeal to the spirit of the nation.

The major premise upon which this chapter rests is that film, as an aspect of culture, is an intervention into the ongoing constitutional life of the UK which needs to be taken seriously.[3] Film is often a particularly vibrant intervention, given its mass-market nature. As film scholars have noted, indigenous cinema in general (Higson, 1993, 1995, 1996; Monk and Sargeant, 2002) and historical and costume drama in particular (Cook, 1996; Sargeant, 2002)[4] plays an important role in the production of an idea of nationhood in general and Britishness in particular. My interest in Shakespeare and *Henry V* in particular is a reflection of the way in which that play is not only the most blatant of Shakespeare's comments on the nature of Englishness/Britishness,[5] but as Ward notes, it provides a context in which the political nature of an elision of sovereign and nation might be imagined in a very particular context: in relation to war (Ward, 2000, pp 52–53). *Henry V* most basically deals with the story of Henry's battle to assert his claim of right over the throne of France and his conquest of France in the pursuit of that claim, culminating in the decisive battle of Agincourt. The more general question of the play is the legitimacy and nature of war. These themes inform the instances in which the stage play has been transposed into the different medium of film. When Laurence Olivier, with the support of the British Ministry of Information, made the first film version of *Henry V* (1946) during World War II, it was made as a straightforward propaganda exercise to rally the troops and the people of Britain in the face of Nazi aggression. The second film version of the play, Kenneth Branagh's *Henry V* (1989), came after the Falklands War, a conflict which more directly echoes the narrative of the play in that it sought to establish a claim to non-national territory by force. Branagh stated that he thought the time was ripe for a 'darker and less jingoistic' version of the play (Branagh, 1989). Branagh's film version was a self-conscious approach to these themes in the wake of the Falklands War, with a nod to the earlier canonical version by Olivier, which stands as a great cultural edifice (Quinn and Kingsley-Smith, 2002).

To engage in a critical evaluation of Branagh's version of *Henry V* is also to ask what kind of running repair it attempts to make to the spiritual breaches in the constitutional wall. What kind of Britain and what idea of sovereignty and nationhood does it attempt to conjure up and pass on? More specifically, what attempt does it make to address the warrior soul of the British nation, and is this address forceful and persuasive enough to leave a lingering trace in the memory? In this chapter, in placing Branagh's film into a contemporary context of

---

3 Within a UK context little attention has been paid to film as a medium of the constitutional imagination. Ward's work on the English Constitution in the popular imagination (2000) has its origins in the law and literature movement and makes no reference to film.

4 On Kenneth Branagh's *Henry V* in relation to costume drama, see Quinn and Kingsley-Smith, 2002.

5 This conflation of national identity occurs within the text itself, where at times an issue is made of the separate nationalities of English, Scottish, Welsh and Irish, while at times the difference is occluded beneath Henry's calls to his 'English' followers.

constitutionalism in relation to the UK's engagement in the Iraq War, it is not my intention to suggest that this film can be causally or even directly connected to the constitutionalism that informs the government's rationalisation of that engagement, or in the context of a whole series of wars in which the UK has become involved since Branagh's film was released. Any connection must be seen rather as a matter of resonance with existing or nascent cultural currents.

Figures 4a–g: *Henry V*, Branagh, 1989.

Mud! Glorious mud! Anatomy of a film

Branagh's desire to make a 'darker' interpretation of *Henry V* is immediately made manifest in the filmic presentation, in that the action begins in darkness. The first pulse of light in darkness is the striking of a match to reveal the face of the speaking chorus, who then pulls down a main switch lever to illuminate the strewn detritus of an abandoned film set. This action is accompanied by the chorus' plea for the audience to allow its imagination to run beyond the limits of what the players and their props can accomplish in bringing before them 'the vasty fields of France', and to bear with their conversion of 'the accomplishment of many years into an hour-glass'.

The schematic of darkness continues throughout the film in terms of lighting, costume and, perhaps most notably, in the presentation of the entire French campaign as having been conducted in torrential rain and amidst a sea of unending mud. This is a very dirty Harry, and the exterior dirt brings out Branagh's sub-textual theme of Henry's interior turmoil over the conduct of war and the terrible responsibilities of kingship. However, while the prologue to the film introduces the idea of artifice and deliberate production, of light being withheld and then forcefully cast on chosen objects, the second scene of the film, a scene which introduces Henry and illustrates his decision to go to war (a scene which maintains the representational quality of darkness) moves completely away from the deliberate display of artifice and into the realms of realism, both physical and psychological. The rest of the film remains in this realm of realism. We are presented with a young man, costumed as a medieval king, in the throes of a dreadful dilemma as to whether to go to war, acutely aware of the terrible consequences his decision may bring in terms of human suffering. To be weighed against these consequences are the issues of basic right, whether his claim to the throne of France is just. The arbiters of this justice are the Archbishops, the representatives of divine law, reading the charters of succession which dictate who rightly has claim to a throne. Henry agonises and finally accepts the religious counsel that he must pursue his just claim and make war on France to retrieve a crown which is properly his. From this opening scene to the end of the film, the only breaks in the almost unremitting gloom are the playful and brightly lit scenes of the French Princess Catherine being taught English by her maid, and the eventual courtship scene between Henry and Catherine. This Harry does not enjoy war; he is good at it, and he is resolute in pursuit of righteousness, but only love can take away the darkness in his soul which war brings.

Henry's interior darkness is underlined by Branagh's adoption of Orson Welles' trick, from *Chimes at Midnight* (1966), of placing in the film flashbacks to scenes from other Shakespeare 'history' plays to highlight the close relationship between Henry and his drinking companion Falstaff (as well as the minor 'common' characters of Pistol, Bardolph and Nym). It is these immature friendships which Henry eventually casts off as he assumes the responsibilities of kingship. Branagh has Henry (tearfully) assent to the hanging of his old companion Bardolph for stealing from a church in France. The discipline of the army is reluctantly placed before his personal friendship, and the twisting of Henry's soul is illustrated on Branagh's muddy, tear-stained, chubby, boyish face. Henry, then, is presented as a deeply religious and deeply responsible man, coming into the fullness of what he sees as divinely ordained authority. Nevertheless he is also a fully human figure, a muscular Christian who likes to drink, to joke and to have good friends. We are privy to the development of his character whereby this side of his nature is gradually brought under control and within the service of the former. His pleasure and his human sympathies must take second place to his sense of mission, and his mission is to conquer for God and his right. Henry, as written in the Shakespeare text, never doubts the righteousness of his cause and, once decided for war, never relents an inch on his purpose to win. He includes them, this 'band of brothers', in the general mission appointed by God, and ridicules the idea that the king who leads his men to slaughter should have a hard reckoning on the day of judgment, since every man is the master of his own soul and this is what is important at the last judgment. The king is pre-absolved for responsibility for the death of his men and for others; the king must do what the king must do. What Branagh adds to this is that his Henry is a kind of Christ-like figure, who feels so deeply for the suffering of his men, who asks nothing of them that he is not prepared to do himself and who measures his own suffering with theirs.

The cultural resonances of Branagh's dark and dirty adaptation are examined by Kenneth Hendrick (1997). He concludes that the principal resonance of Branagh's Harry is precisely with Eastwood's character in the title role of Don Siegel's film, *Dirty Harry* (1971); a good man hauling himself up through sheer personal charisma to do a dirty but necessary job. This neglects the very strong religious slant that Branagh gives to his Henry. Where Branagh might have made Henry's pleas to God and thanks to God simple formal gestures (much in the manner of how these were treated in the Olivier version), Branagh produces a Henry who speaks from the bottom of his heart when he talks to God. Indeed, when Henry, on the eve of the battle of Agincourt, calls on the 'God of battles' to 'steal my soldiers' hearts', and begs pardon for his father's sin of taking a crown rightfully his cousin's, Branagh's portrayal of Henry's utter anguish can only recall the plight of Jesus in the garden of Gethsemane awaiting his death the following day. When the French herald arrives after the battle to inform Henry that he has won the day, he declares from his knees 'Praised be God, and not our strength, for it'. What we have then is a portrayal of the internal anguish of an extraordinary and yet fully human man, fighting for a cause that he not only believes in, but believes in with religious fervour, a fervour so intense that it negates all qualms of the means by which the causal end is achieved.

The emphasis on the tension between ends and means in the film is further underlined by the prominence given to the 'ordinary' (non-noble) people in the film; that is the characters of Pistol, Bardolph, Nym, Mistress Quickly and the foot soldiers. These characters are given a rich internal life, a pathos and plenty of time and space within the arrangement of the film to display that their lives have dignity and value. To achieve this, Branagh had to work fairly hard to cut and paste the received text into a pattern of some kind of grandeur for his ordinary characters. The most moving scenes in the film are not those played by Branagh, either exhorting the troops to battle or grieving the loss of life, but the scenes when Pistol pleads for Bardolph's life and when he mourns the death of his wife, Mistress Quickly; or when the soldier Williams (played by the actor Michael Williams) ponders on the guilt of the king if he is taking his army into an unjust conflict, leaving all the hacked off arms and legs to come together on the day of judgment to cry out for justice against the king that led them to the slaughter. The text for these 'ordinary' characters is written in non-metrical form, and so the attribution of psychological realism is already there to some extent within the Shakespearean form. What Branagh does is to foreground the scenes of the ordinary people as a filmic gesture towards the ideas that 'war is hell' and 'it's the little people who suffer most'. Branagh's Henry can feel for the ordinary people, but must put their pain into the larger context of what is right and what is necessary for the war to be won.

The playing of Henry himself in a purely realistic way is more of a problem. In purely formal textual terms, Henry's lines are mostly in metrical form (per the Shakespearean convention that noble characters speak in metre and ignoble characters in blank verse), and trying to play poetry as a form of realist speech is a kind of violence to the text. Heightened speech in this film is played down into the register of an ordinary man's language (and then often times reinflated by a clumsy musical score welling up underneath). Apart from this, there is the problem that Shakespeare's original play, written in 1600 at the zenith of Elizabethan power, was a work of propaganda in itself, written within an atmosphere of censorship such that it was required to praise resolutely the actions of the monarchy. It was blatantly unrealistic in its portrayal of war, even to the extent of having the English slay 10,000 French at Agincourt, while the French could only manage to kill 29 English. Furthermore, the complications of the Henry character written into the play's text were something more than Branagh could bear to give even his realistic Henry. The 'realistic' filmic Henry was shorn of his two moments of bad conduct which are clearly laid out in the play; first when he orders the slaying of the French prisoners to free up his own soldiers, who guard them, for the battle, and secondly when he jokes lewdly about the sexual conquest of Catherine that he will soon make.

To create this realistic Henry then, a large amount of selection and work is involved, and this work tends towards the promotion of a character so elevated that even his doubts are noble ones, his every action honest and true, his hatred of war outweighed only by his commitment to justice, his sympathy for the little people profound but tempered by his knowledge of the need for sacrifice. This is a nub of where the film backs away from its seeming intent to throw into relief the question of war's legitimacy and falls down into an outright support for just war. There is a definite sense that Branagh, while having a stated commitment to produce a less jingoistic 'post-Falklands' Henry, fell so much in love with the idea of playing an utterly noble character that he compromised the overall film as any kind of critical comment on war and emerged with his own hymn to the glory of just war.

The core of the filmic message is that war is a dirty job and that just war must be waged, whatever the human cost. Branagh emphasises the anachronisms at play here by foregrounding the religious basis of Henry's conviction as to his own right to territorial expansion, and the religious basis of his own right to send men to their death. Where we are invited to identify with Henry, however, is in his humanity and in his dignity in response to the hard questions that life thrusts upon him. It is here that the dice are loaded by Branagh, by his excision of any negative side to Henry's character in favour of a kind of liberal egomania that sees all the gravity and dignity of its own dilemmas in the world, but is blind to any possible tawdriness, ignobility, venality or even stupidity in its own actions.

From Agincourt to Downing Street: good intentions

In the *London Review of Books* of 8 May 2003, David Runciman, using a Weberian typology, analyses the politics of Tony Blair under the title 'The politics of good intentions'. Weber, in his essay 'Politics as a vocation' (1978), suggested that the responsible politician calculated on the basis of consequences. Where unintended consequences were negative, the responsible politician might express a personal regret, but would take the political responsibility to do something about the negative consequences. The only worthwhile course of action in the face of negative and unintended consequences was to exhibit 'manliness' and to get on with things. The irresponsible politician proceeded by way of good intentions and attempted to use these good intentions to justify the (predictably disastrous) consequences of their political actions. For Weber, the whole business of politics was inevitably a dirty one, and to rely on good intentions as a motive or justification in any political context was a dangerous naivete bordering on madness. Runciman notes that Blair has managed to pull off a successful political trick of conflating the Weberian typology and being both a responsible and an irresponsible politician. His responsibility lies in his willingness to acknowledge the limitations of good intentions. His irresponsibility is to proceed on the basis of good intentions despite the acknowledgment of their limitation. This circle is usually squared by taking what for Weber was a mark of personal virtue in a responsible politician, regret for negative, unintended (yet predictable) consequences, and turning it into a public political tool. The depth of his regret and the detail of his awareness of the limitations of his extremely good intentions all somehow work together to convince himself and, it seems, the majority of his party and the public that whatever is proposed or whatever has already been endured is or was the best that could be or could have been achieved. Runciman notes that this kind of manoeuvre inhabits many phases of the Blairite political project, for example, when finally acknowledging the disastrous financial adventure of the Millennium Dome as a failure of government, he 'took full responsibility that the Dome did not achieve what it set out to achieve but he would not apologise for trying'; a typical, according to Runciman, Blairite non-apology apology.

It is, however, in times of war that the full weight of unintended consequences and necessary regret for them comes to bear. Here Runciman notices a progression in the war-like behaviour of regret that Blair exhibits, to the point where, in the run up to the war on Iraq, he seemed to be actively inviting public occasions where he would be prevailed upon to display regret for the inevitable losses that war would bring. Blair, for example, took part in an ITV televised debate on 10 March 2003 where he was confronted with a hostile audience, several of whom had been recently bereaved by terrorism and who were implacably opposed to the war in Iraq. Rather than avoid such a no-win situation, the opportunity was used by Blair to show just how deeply he could appreciate the pain of these people, and just how deep was his own pain about the suffering that war would inevitably bring to others. Yet still it must happen, and they surely could see in his drawn and exhausted face, feel in his racked presence, the depth of his suffering and his conviction that this was the only way. While such a political manoeuvre seems to be something that Blair can carry off successfully, the effect of it is to deflect attention from a politics of consequences onto the need for personal suffering in order that justice be done in a larger sphere. The measuring of personal suffering during the course of a televised debate against that of those bereaved by war is not something which convinces Runciman. His acid final comment is, 'Knowing that good intentions aren't enough isn't enough'.

The telling point of Runciman's article in the context of this essay is the remarkable resonance between Blair's vision of just war – and the responsible way to take responsibility for the unintended consequences of war – with the representation of these same themes in Branagh's version of *Henry V*. Branagh's Henry, like Blair, is convinced that in law and in justice (and both figures bear a strong religious conviction as to their justice) he is right to press on with the war and, like Blair, his very suffering over the consequences of this conviction is used as a prop to the necessity of pressing ever more resolutely forward. The argument develops a circularity: 'the more I suffer at the terrible consequences of my actions, the more right I must be; why else would I bring this upon myself?' The why else can surely only be explained as a form of madness, yet neither Blair nor Henry seem mad. Indeed, Blair is generally successful at establishing that precisely what distinguishes the just from the unjust is that they are sane, while Saddam, Milosevic *et al* are indeed mad.

What both Shakespeare's *Henry V* (as directed and performed by Branagh) and Tony Blair seem to share is the form of logic which dictates that, when it comes right down to it, war is what the English/British can do very well, and war is the way that they will go about sorting things out. When an issue is turning into an intractable problem, the solution of fighting it out becomes an attractive one. The resonance with the conduct of Mrs Thatcher in relation to the Falklands/Malvinas conflict should be obvious. The issue of right is coupled, or subsidiary to, an attitude of confidence that military action on a grand scale can reap long-term rewards. This issue is complex, since the lack of military intervention is often as controversial as intervention. The point is not the righteousness of any particular war, simply the ongoing attitude that Britain is a warrior nation that, residing in the spirit of the place, is an impulse to settle conflict by force.

It should not be overlooked that in the context of war there is no requirement for the Prime Minister to seek the approval of Parliament that military action should be commenced; this lies within the Crown prerogative as exercised by the government. In the British system of Cabinet government, it is often suggested that we have evolved a system which locates power in a single individual even more thoroughly than in Presidential systems, since the dominance of a charismatic leader with the power to replace Cabinet colleagues at will ensures the possibility to drive through a particular project or style of government. Furthermore, the fact that the government is necessarily composed of leaders of the majority party in Parliament normally ensures that government policy will prevail. This structure of governmental organisation exists by virtue of constitutional convention, that is, it has developed as 'the way things are done'. Once again there is a filling of what might be regarded as a gap with an entry into a complex of institutional practice coupled to an idea of underpinning spirit.

This conventional location of power in a single individual surrounded by a council of advisors re-emphasises the link between a contemporary Prime Minister and a historical figure such as Henry V, each with the effective power to decide that war will be waged. This power, despite the undoubted supremacy of Parliament and the numerous wars that Britain has waged, has never been challenged by Parliament, despite the fact that Parliament could easily change this. The figure of the single strong leader who leads us into battle is an extremely live one in British culture.

The further resonance of Blair's conduct and Branagh's particular take on the Henry themes of the legitimacy of war and the balance of ends and means, is that both, one in the aesthetic and one in the political realm, utilise their own nobility of intention and, secondarily, their own suffering at their awareness of how others must suffer as a prop to the legitimacy of their mission. They both know that good intentions are not enough, but their awareness of bad consequences does not deflect them one whit; the consequences are absorbed on a level of identification into their own bodies. Like Christ in the garden, or like so many leaders with a sense of mission, they feel the pain and do it anyway. The persistent nagging question remains of how much of this pain is really theirs.

Conclusion

In political-aesthetic terms then, Branagh's *Henry V* and Blair's contemporary conduct in relation to war form a couplet of mutual commentary, which rests, in the first place, on an established axis of the acceptability of war. In Constitution terms, the various breaches in the fabric of our constitutional system need to be continually filled, by legal measures supplemented by conventions. Equally importantly, there must be a sense that national culture has a fullness to it, that there is a reality of

British spirit which will always provide a reserve which can be drawn upon for law and convention to be made, particularly in times of crisis. This spirit, on occasion, will find embodiment in the single heroic figure exercising (as convention demands) strong leadership to take us into conflict. Branagh's film provided a foreshadowing of how the major constitutional question of the propriety of force being used as a means to assert national self-interest would develop within our political culture. The Branagh film and the Blair political project, particularly in relation to war, are both aspects of preserving a memory and a sense that part of being British is about uniting around a leader and fighting the good fight. The danger in this is twofold: first, in the persistent readiness to see fighting as a ready option rather than as a last resort; secondly, in that the persistent reinforcement of this message leads to a form of circularity wherein it becomes acceptable that 'it must be a good fight, since we are fighting it'.

Chapter 3
'It's the vibe!':
the common law imaginary Down Under[1]

William P MacNeil

'It's the Constitution, it's *Mabo* ... it's the vibe!' So goes one of the most memorable lines of dialogue from Rob Sitch's cult Australian film, *The Castle* (1997). Now a hook of Australian popular culture as well as that nation's legal consciousness, this phrase makes reference to the Constitution and the landmark judgment of the High Court, *Mabo and Others v The State of Queensland (No 2)* (1992),[2] hereafter referred to as *Mabo*.[3] It is a phrase that has been repeated, just as feebly, by scores of flummoxed law students from Toowoomba to Tasmania grasping at constitutional straws in public law exams or essays, as it was in the film by the character of fly-by-night solicitor, Dennis DeNuto. DeNuto (played here to 'wog-boy' perfection by Tiriel Mora) utters these immortal words before the Federal Court,[4] after losing his administrative appeal challenging the federal government's 'compulsory acquisition' of the modest (to say the least) Melbourne home of his truckie client, Aussie Everyman, Daryl Kerrigan (a role brilliantly taken by character actor, Michael Caton). DeNuto's *mot (in)juste*, however, is memorable not only for its catchphrase quality, but also as an outstanding example of what semiotics would call 'empty discourse', worthy to chime in along with Daryl's meaningless mantras like 'He's an ideas man', 'Tell 'em they're dreamin' or, my personal favourite,

1 Versions of this article were given at: Griffith University's Faculty of Law Seminar Series, Brisbane (December 2000); the Law and the Moving Image Conference, Tate Gallery and Birkbeck College, University of London (January 2001); The Nation is My Thing Conference, University of Sydney and the University of New South Wales (August 2001) and the Faculty of Law, Australian National University (June 2003). Thanks also to the students in the Legal Fictions seminar (2001) for their valuable feedback, and as well from the following friends, colleagues and conference confrères: Robert Burrell and Lindsey Duncan (ANU); Peter Fitzpatrick, Leslie Moran and Emma Sandon (Birkbeck); Pam Adams, John Dewar, Shaunnaugh Dorset, Rosemary Hunter and Shaun McVeigh (Griffith); Aileen Moreton-Robinson (Queensland); Slavoj Žižek (Ljubljana); Anne Barron (LSE); Peter Rush (Melbourne) and Jennifer Rutherford (Sydney). This article is dedicated to my friend and colleague, Bridget Cullen-Mandikos: a screening of *The Castle* at her very salubrious home on Laurel Avenue, Brisbane, Queensland, Australia was the very first time I saw this film and the inspiration for this article. As Daryl himself would say: 'Good on ya' Bridget!'

2 The case has a long and involved procedural and substantive history, the proceedings having been initiated in 1982. The original challenge concerned legislation enacted by the State of Queensland extinguishing Aboriginal land claims as contravening the Racial Discrimination Act (1975). For a resolution of that specific issue, see *Mabo v Queensland (No 1)* (1988).

3 At the time of this article's writing, the scholarly output on *Mabo* had reached fever pitch in Australia and around the common law world. For a selection of some of the most interesting analyses, see Perrin, 1998; Povinelli, 1998; Motha, 1998; Ivison, 1997; Edgeworth, 1994; Webber, 1995.

4 The presiding judge is played by the extremely *distingué* Robyn Nevins.

'How's the serenity?'. But, however much this filmic reference to the *Mabo* case parodies, even trivialises, that High Court decision, declaring the indigenous Meriam people to be the owner-occupiers of Queensland's Murray Islands, DeNuto's declamation points to the very real re-vision which that case was and is for Australia. A landmark judgment in the most literal sense of that word, *Mabo* instituted, for at least some of the Aboriginal peoples of the Commonwealth, a new property regime, *native title*,[5] thereby bringing indigenity into the field of vision of that *salon des glaces* of what I call the Anglo-Australian common law imaginary (Althusser, 1971; Lacan, 1977, pp 292–325). Now focalised around the new imago of the native title holder (the land claims of Eddie Mabo, David Passi and James Rice constituting the *objet petit a* (Lacan, 1977, pp 83, 268–74) of not just the Meriam but all Aboriginal peoples), *Mabo* shattered the anamorphic 'glass darkly' of *terra nullius*, the legal fiction rendering Australia a 'no man's land' at the time of its European colonisation, thereafter blinding the courts to the very presence, let alone priority of any claims to land or compensation of the indigenous population.

Figure 5: *The Castle*, **Sitch, 1997.**

---

5 For the standard British Commonwealth text on native title, see McNeil, 1989. For a more recent comparative treatment of two major British Commonwealth jurisdictions, see Dorsett, 1995.

Not that the Aborigines and/or the Torres Strait Islanders figure very much in *The Castle*, other than by way of citation, like Daryl's *en passant* references to Cathy Freeman and Yvonne Goolagong. In fact, indigenes are conspicuous by their absence here, a strange cinematic reinscription of *terra nullius*, particularly in a film that goes out of its way to represent post-colonial Australia's much vaunted ethnic diversity (self-consciously showcasing Italian, Greek and Arab 'New Australians' as well as the native-born Kerrigans). But if the actual people referenced and represented by the *Mabo* decision are nowhere to be found in the film, then it is my contention that the case's core principles are to be felt everywhere throughout the film. They power its plot, in its valorisation of the courts over the legislature, the common law over policy. They inflect its language, not just in its footnoting of *Mabo*, but in its historical allusions to White Australia's land grabs and in the metaphor of 'the castle' itself, with all of its resonance of conquest and settlement. They inform its theme, with its focus on property and the legality of ownership, dispossession and reclamation. But the film does more than just reflect *Mabo's ratio decidendi*. The film reads the decision critically, ambiguating, problematising, even subverting it to the extent that I will claim *The Castle* puts *Mabo* on trial. In so doing, *The Castle* exposes not only *Mabo's*, and native title's, internal contradictions, but also its own conflicting politics: activist or reactionary? Pearsonite or Howardist? Additionally, it gestures to the profound cultural, social and particularly legal ambivalences, which the decision has aroused in Australia. The effect is to transform this self-described 'feel-good' film into one of the bitterest of 'black comedies', or more accurately a '(tragi-)comedy of jurisprudence' (Frye, 1957).

Central to the film, and functioning something like a Lacanian *point de capiton* by 'quilting' (Lacan, 1993) together the narrative's issues of land, community, identity, politics and, especially, the law, is the eponymous 'castle' of the title: 3 Highview Crescent. A 'home', not just a house (a sentiment that the script insists upon several times, having been coined by Daryl at the tribunal, commended by Farouk afterwards and, finally, repeated by Laurie at the High Court) to that most 'unhomely' or, to give the term its full Freudian spin, that most *unheimlich* (Freud, 1924–50, pp 368–407) of families, the Kerrigans of Cooloroo, Victoria. The Kerrigans are a kind of 'Royle family Down Under', a sort of Simpsons of the South Pacific, though neither of these analogies does justice to the way in which Australian cinema and television of late has outpaced the Northern Hemisphere in its celluloid and video representations of domestic dysfunction.[6]

Even gauged, though, by these productions' exceedingly broad standards of farce, *The Castle* presents in the Kerrigan clan a picture of working class, suburban Australian life which borders on the satirically sour, glibly patronising, at the very same moment it purports to gently rib this very 'ocker' world of mullet haircuts and daggy trainers, of dodgy DIY home 'improvements' and stodgy 'Women's Weekly'

---

6 Think of PJ Hogan's disturbing depiction of the maladjusted Hislop brood of Porpoise Spit in *Muriel's Wedding* (1994), or Baz Luhrmann's discomforting portrayal of the almost as equally bizarre Hastings mob of Sydney in *Strictly Ballroom* (1992), not to mention the small screen household grotesqueries of the Shanes and Charlenes, Pippas and Toms of, respectively, TV's *Neighbours* (1985–) (eg, the Robinsons of Ramsey Street) and *Home and Away* (1987–) (eg, the Fletchers of Summer Bay), to name just two.

cookery, of daft cosmetology and naff pool rooms full of kitsch memorabilia and tourist tat. What with Dad Daryl's greyhounds (not only 'Coco', but 'Son of Coco'), Mum Sal's handicrafts (the bedazzled jean jacket, the stencilled serving tray, etc, all rapturously greeted by her husband with 'You could sell that!'), daughter Tracey's beauty salon quiff ('Now that is a head of hair!' enthuses her father), and their sons' respective foibles (Wayne's incarceration for armed robbery of the local petrol station, Steve's incessant 'Trading Post' call and response, and narrator Dale's questioning overkill), the Kerrigans are designed to send a collective shudder of self-recognition (as much as a frisson of relief, owing to one's ironic distance from them) down the spines of all antipodean viewers. Particularly targeted are those urban, university-educated, media-savvy 'chattering class' trendies of Melbourne's Glebe-St Kilda axis, in fact just like the quartet of writer-director-producers of the production company Working Dog[7] whose sentimental fantasy and worst nightmare this tribe of *bogans extraordinaire* are.

What prevents this cinematic essay in Aussie *grand guignol*, by turns witty and sneering about the heavily overdetermined 'worker's paradise' it posits, from degenerating into the kind of prole bashing rife in American sitcoms like *Roseanne* is the timely arrival of Airlink's letter 'compulsorily acquiring' the Kerrigan house. This narrative turn shifts the rather hamfisted irony away from the taste-challenged dystopia (at least, from a yuppie perspective) to a more acceptable object of critique, namely, 'Big Government'. Though privately funded, Airlink is a state sanctioned and fronted consortium intent on levelling all of Highview Crescent[8] so as to make way for the expansion of the freight facilities of Melbourne's airport, soon to be 'the largest in the Southern Hemisphere'. Now there is nothing illegal about what Airlink wants to do here. In fact, the consortium is acting well within its statutory authority, as a simpering city official, full of *faux* sympathy, is at pains to point out to Daryl. Airlink's power to expropriate is conferred by, and exercised lawfully under, the Airport Commission, itself warranted by 'iron-clad' agreements between federal, state and municipal governments. Moreover, it's an argument endorsed and upheld by two tiers of adjudication: at the Administrative Appeals Tribunal and the Federal Court. So Airlink appears to be holding all the legal cards here, and may even occupy, as its lawyers argue at court, the high moral ground because it is acting in the public interest as measured by the utilitarian yardstick of the 'greatest good for the greatest number'.

But, of course, the referencing of the utility principle by Airlink's counsel here works in precisely the same cynical way Marx (2000) said all Benthamism did. Its calculations of felicity, maximising pleasure and minimising pain across the broadest possible spectrum really amount to nothing more than an ideological smokescreen, masking the private interest (the desire of the ruling few) under the guise of public welfare (and the needs of the labouring many). Certainly it is the intensely private motive of profit that drives Airlink's intention to bulldoze

---

7 Tom Gleisner, Santo Cilauri, Jane Kennedy, as well as Rob Sitch. Working Dog is an extremely successful Melbourne production house behind such popular Australian television shows as *The Panel, Frontline, Funky Squad, A River Somewhere*, etc, as well as the recently released feature film, *The Dish*. See their website: www.workingdog.com.

8 Jack's, Farouk's and Evonne's 'castles', as well as Daryl's.

Highview Crescent. The alternative, landfilling the neighbouring quarry, might prove too expensive, upping costs, thereby cutting into returns. So Airlink is acting on behalf of the public only incidentally, if at all. Just consider who they really are. They are government fronted, but funded and principally controlled by the Barlow Group. These mysterious financiers, as Dennis warns Daryl, not only 'write the rules' through their travelling claque of legal counsel, but enforce these semi-sovereign commands through their gang of 'hired thugs' (remember the leather jacketed hood 'just passing on a message' at the Kerrigan's doorstep one night, to 'take the offer'). Sequestered behind their security systems, and never more than a disembodied voice over the tannoy, the Barlow Group represent a new stage of Capital for the 'lucky country' which exceeds, in its unseen malignancy, even the corrupt cronyism of the 1980s (at least Alan Bond and his ilk were identifiable) because it is so decontextualised, invading but also evading the state, here today and gone tomorrow. So what *The Castle* dramatises here are the massive inroads this globalising form of anarcho-capitalism, acting both within and outside the law, is making into the hitherto tightly protectionist and highly unionised economy of Australia under the guise of 'privatisation'. Airlink embodies the monstrous hybridity that policy creates, which like all the other unholy alliances of state and market are intent on demolishing, as much at Jabiluka[9] as at Highview Crescent, all that the nation holds dear (ecosystems, beauty spots, even sacred sites) to carry out their 'development' projects.

It is at this point in the narrative that the film comes closest to articulating a critical legal, even Marxist analysis, aligning the Kerrigans' plight with the class struggles that beset contemporary Australia's 'politics of the law' (Kairys, 1982). But class is not the only basis for critique here. Race, in particular indigenity, is alluded to and cited directly by the film's script and scenery, analogising and equating the situation of the whiter than white, Irish Catholic Kerrigans with the fortunes of Australia's enraced 'Other', its Aboriginal peoples. Consider, for example, the actual physical site of 3 Highview Crescent: wedged between power lines, lead dumping and one of the airport's busiest runways. This 'no man's land' at once lampoons estate agent-ese ('location, location, location' as Dale says at the opening of his narration), all the while literalising the doctrine of *terra nullius*, thereby evoking the pre-*Mabo* juristic fantasy, or more properly delusion,[10] of Australia as uninhabited at the time of colonial contact, and ripe for the imperialist picking. No wonder then that Airlink has opted to 'kick out', as Steve phrases it, the occupants of Highview Crescent. To the powers-that-be they, like the Aboriginal people, were never really there in the first place, a presence which is really an absence, the erasure of which merits only the most minimal recompense as a form of largesse.

Daryl responds to the offer with true bevan bluffness: 'get stuffed!' because his 'castle' is not something reducible to Airlink's exchange values. It's a point which the Aborigines, as the traditional custodians of Australia, have been arguing for

---

9 Other examples in Australia include the extractive industries.
10 Disarticulated, most notably, in *Milirrpum v Nabalco Pty Ltd* (1970). See also *Coe v Commonwealth* (1979).

years: that their land is not a commodity, mere real estate (Pearson, 1997, p 223). It is their community's context, saturated with, and the source of, spiritual, psychic and aesthetic meaning which, in turn, defines their collective and individual identity. Consider the 'strong relationship',[11] as Moynihan J put it in *Mabo* at the Queensland Supreme Court, between the Meriam people and their 'garden lands', significant not only 'from the point of view of subsistence', but also for 'the various rituals associated with different aspects of community life' (marriage, adoption, *rite de passage*, etc), as well as 'prestige' and 'cohesion'.[12] For the Meriam people (as for the Kerrigans), the land ('the castle') is a space that is imbued with the very 'ethical substance' of their sociality.[13] In the film, Laurie Hammill gestures towards this at the High Court when he talks, in his closing argument, of the 'love', 'care' and 'memories' which Highview Crescent holds for its owner-occupants. No surprise then when Daryl exclaims to Sal while packing up the pool room after losing at the Federal Court, 'I'm beginning to understand how the Aborigines feel', because their home is 'like their land', adding like an Outback black fella 'talking up', the white man: 'This country has to stop stealing other peoples' land' (Moreton-Robinson, 2000).

But indigene *manque-à-être* is precisely what Daryl Kerrigan is not. The threatened dispossession of his home was, and never will be, as far-reaching and final as what in fact happened to Aboriginal Australia. His owner-occupancy was always recognised as such at law, giving rise to a right of compensation which, however unsatisfactory, was never, ever offered to the indigenous peoples (even by the majority in *Mabo*).[14] Nor is Daryl the class warrior he may appear, *prima facie*, to be, because the neighbourhood committee he convenes remains just that: not a Leninist cell raising revolutionary consciousness, but a special interest group of property holders which he heads up by virtue of his race and gender power. As the white male patriarch, who better to lead a group consisting of a pensioner, a single woman and a 'New Australian'.[15]

All this situates Daryl and his struggle against the corporate 'Goliath', as the Channel Nine newscast puts it, within a particular political tradition. The Hollywood version pits a motley group of outsiders (whose ethnic, class, gender and age group variety reflects America's ideological *amour propre* as the great 'melting pot'), lead by a small 'l' liberal, rugged individualist, revelling in his autonomy and doing battle against some pernicious system of political economy. But, in Frank Capra's films,[16] whose stock-in-trade this kind of narrative is, the point is never actually to change the system (substituting, say, socialism for capitalism). Rather, the point is to restore it, by delivering the system from the corrupt aberration distorting its original imperatives (for example, defeating the

---

11 Moynihan J at pp 155–56 quoted by Toohey J in *Mabo v The State of Queensland (No 2)* (1992) 107 ALR 1 in Bartlett, 1993.

12 Determination of Moynihan J quoted in Brennan J in *Mabo* (1992), p 9.

13 Hegel describes it as *Sittlichkeit*; see Hegel, 1945.

14 Though Toohey J raises the possibility of compensation for native title land 'wrongfully' extinguished by the Crown; see *Mabo*, p 169.

15 Despite 20 years of official multiculturalism, Kerrigan (the Anglo-Celtic) represents the continuing hegemonic (monoculturalist) position of Australia.

16 See, especially, *Mr Smith Goes to Washington* (1939) and *It's a Wonderful Life* (1946).

monopoly and allowing the 'free market' to be truly free). By invoking this genre, *The Castle* reveals Daryl to be anything but a threat to the established order. Indeed, he is its staunchest supporter, seeking not so much a departure, as a return to the Australia of the 1950s, where 'every man's home is his castle', flash financial types are unheard of, and 'sheilas' and 'wogs' know their place. In light of this politics and aesthetics of nostalgia, one could even go so far as to suggest that *The Castle* might be retitled *Mr Kerrigan Goes to Canberra* or *It's a Wonderful Barbie*.

This longing to return to a past, which may only have existed on celluloid, extends as much to the law as the politics and aesthetics of *The Castle*. Consider, for example, the narrative and juristic climax of the film; the hearing before the High Court of Australia. There, a kind of jurisprudential nostalgia suffuses the proceedings, harking back to a very traditional kind of legal argument, even a particular type of 'Establishment' practitioner. Gone are the references to *Mabo*, a silence suggestive of its dubious status within the common law canon, as a *cause célèbre* rather than a sound authority, to be trotted out only as an eleventh hour, 'Hail Mary' defence by no-hopers like solicitor Dennis DeNuto.[17] Even when the Kerrigan's barrister, Lawrence Hammill QC departs from the rules and turns, as Ronald Dworkin (1977, 1985, 1986) might say, to the realm of principle, he positivises it in terms of the Constitutional framers' original intentions, arguing that the 'just terms' qualifying the federal power of expropriation could never have been intended to justify dispossessing a family of their 'home'. Why? Presumably because the framers themselves were common lawyers for whom the time honoured, traditional maxims of the common law, like 'An Englishman's home is his castle' of the *Semayne's Case* (1605), were bred in the bone.

So *The Castle* looks back to what Isaiah Berlin (1969) would call the classic common law tradition of 'negative liberty', and its most hallowed right to be left alone, free from interference, especially by the state. At the very moment it raises, in its references (express and implied) to *Mabo*, it skirts the prospects afforded by a new, post-*Mabo* era of judicial activism; of a more 'positive' conception of liberty (Berlin, 1969) authorising state intervention for resource redistribution. But what is truly striking about the double movement enacted by the film, of one step forward (in the citations of *Mabo's* positive liberty) and two steps backwards, applying the negative liberty of *Semayne's Case* (1605), is that it repeats the very 'skeletal fracture' exemplified by *Mabo*. It throws into bold relief the jurisprudential and political cross-purposes at work in the decision, at once regressive and progressive, proactive and conservative. Consider the most 'Whiggish' of the judgments, and the source of the striking skull 'n' bones similitude, that of Mr Justice Brennan, who repeats the 18th century's characteristic platitude of 'progress', ironic in an era, postmodernity, which has proclaimed the end of all such metanarratives. By repudiating *terra nullius* on the grounds that it is 'imperative in today's world that the common law should

---

17 The character DeNuto is relegated to the judicial sidelines as a waterboy (filling glasses or passing notes like 'Fucking brilliant'), as the magisterial Lawrence Hammill QC (played with patrician ease by Charles 'Bud' Tingwell) takes to the curial centre field, kicking off his case, and indeed carrying the day, by adducing solid, 'black letter' law, be it legislative (s 51 of the Constitution) or judicial (*Commonwealth v Tasmania* (1983)).

neither be, nor be seen to be frozen in an age of racial discrimination' (*Mabo* (1992), p 29), one which treats the 'indigenous inhabitants ... as [so] "low in the scale of social organisation", [that] they and their occupancy ... were ignored' (*Mabo* (1992), p 28), Brennan J implies that the common law is a dynamic force, evolving in response to the nation's economic, political and social changes. Given this, one would expect 'public policy', hitherto a largely American judicial heresy, to loom large in a decision which, in its anti-racism, rights consciousness and social justice concerns is redolent of the 'grand style of adjudication' (Llewellyn, 1960), being concerned more with the law's results rather than rules, its 'spirit' instead of 'letter', even when this means, as Brennan acknowledges, 'overruling ... cases which have held the contrary' (*Mabo* (1992), p 29).

But the bench's nascent proactivity is contested and complicated by the very rhetoric of the decision itself, which invokes the ghost of Blackstone and his declaratory theory when Brennan J holds:

> In discharging its duty to declare the common law of Australia, this court is not free to adopt rules that accord with contemporary notions of justice and human rights if their adoption would fracture the skeleton of principle which gives the body of our law its shape and consistency. (*Mabo* (1992), p 18)

Now the interesting thing about this tropological appeal to tradition's 'bare bones', that judges declare rather than find the law, is that it enables Brennan J to do exactly the reverse: to manipulate precedent's frame, like some sort of juridical chiropractor, realigning the lumbar of a long line of disjointed authorities, cracking the spine of domestic (*Administration of Papua and New Guinea v Daera Guba* (1973)), imperial (*Amodu Tijani v Secretary, Southern Nigeria* (1921)), British Commonwealth (*Calder v Attorney General of British Columbia* (1973)) and international (*Advisory Opinion on Western Sahara* (1975)) sources, so they uphold, at common law, the co-existence and compatibility of native title with the Crown's 'radical title'.[18] This is about as radical as this judgment gets. Its standard interpretive move is one of infinite regress, going as far back as the early 17th century cases of *The Case of Tanistry* (1608) (concerning the survival at common law of 'tanistry', a form of property inherited from Irish Brehon law) and *Witrong and Blany* (1674) (affirming the continuity of Welsh proprietorial interests predating the introduction of the common law). Given this sort of legal historical anachronism, one might suspect that what the first British colonists to the Murray Islands, the police, the London Missionary Society and others would have found there are nothing less than the dry bones of the common law itself, marking since time immemorial the cadastres of native title. All of this suggests another inflection of Brennan's skeletal analogy: that of the common law as a *corpus delicti* whose dead hands, the touch of which is mortified and mortifying, as Maitland once said of the forms of action, 'rule us from the grave' (Maitland, 1909), controlling policy, containing activism and ensuring that every political progression is a regression to common law origins.

---

18 Here interpreted as a postulate necessary to legitimise the tenurial system, put in place in a territory recently acquired by a colonial sovereign, but not to be equated with 'absolute beneficial ownership' which would extinguish all other prior – read indigenous – claims. See *Mabo* (1992), p 34.

The 'mythos of return' staged here is precisely why Noel Pearson, amongst others, dismissed *Mabo* as a profoundly 'conservative' decision (Pearson, 1997, p 214), regardless of all the triumphalist self-congratulation with which liberals greeted the ruling when it was handed down. Despite its 'reformist' agenda, or perhaps precisely because of it, the judgment largely ignored activist claims that native title's recognition went to the heart of the 'human rights' debate in Australia, 'presenting an opportunity to radically reassess the relationship between Indigenous and non-Indigenous Australians' (Pearson, 1997, p 219). That opportunity, however, was lost because the court elected to 'take rights less seriously', reading native title restrictively. Though recognised as a proprietorial interest of the 'indigenous inhabitants in land, whether communal, group or individual, possessed under the traditional laws acknowledged by ... traditional customs' (*Mabo* (1992), p 41), that interest was reduced by the judgment to something less than a 'common law tenure', like that of an 'estate in fee simple' or an 'estate in freehold' (*Mabo* (1992), p 55). Even when deemed 'good against the state' (*Mabo* (1992), p 55), so to approximate ownership, native title was undercut by a rather pejorative characterisation, as a 'burden' (*Mabo* (1992), p 35) on sovereignty.

The problem with this sort of description is that 'burdens' can be and often are laid down. So *Mabo* goes on to elaborate in great detail how sovereignty can relieve itself of native title's weary load, a final about-face in a judgment marked by a peripatetic doubling back. But not much interpretive to-ing and fro-ing is required here on the part of Mr Justice Brennan and the rest of the judges. Native title is so internally conflicted that it might well be said to carry the seeds of its own destruction. It sets up the conditions for the disavowal of indigenous land claims at the very moment it purports to acknowledge them, repealing but also reviving a kind of *terra nullius* at one and the same time. How does native title pull off this legal *legerdemain* (now you see the property interest, now you don't)? No other way than by means of the concept of 'extinguishment' (Dorsett, 1995), and its corollary 'inconsistency', as qualifying all land claims made pursuant to native title. For native title was never intended to secure in perpetuity indigenous land claims, but rather to accommodate them, temporarily, with those of the coloniser's white settlers. This envisages their eventual obliteration by 'extinguishment', as the American Native Peoples (and later the Canadian 'First Nations' peoples) discovered to their detriment in the germinal judgment, *Johnson v McIntosh* (1823). There, Chief Justice Marshall articulated the extinguishing doctrine, which Brennan J succinctly summarises in his judgment in *Mabo*. Native title is 'extinguished' if land claimed under it is subject to any 'valid exercise of sovereign power inconsistent with the continued right to enjoy', whether that inconsistency takes, for example, the form of 'alienation' to private interests or 'appropriation' for the public benefit (*Mabo* (1992), p 51).

It is precisely this doctrinal delimitation that has become the source and site of curial controversy post-*Mabo*, particularly following on from the 1993 enactment of the Native Title Act 1993 which codified, *inter alia*, the 'past acts' (s 228) requisite for extinguishment. *Wik Peoples v The State of Queensland* (1996) (hereinafter referred to as *Wik*) is the most prominent of native title 'test cases'.[19] In *Wik*[20] a determination

---

19 Others include *Fejo v Northern Territory* (1998) and *Western Australia v The Commonwealth (the Native Title Act Case)* (1995).

20 *Wik* has generated almost as much academic commentary in Australia as *Mabo*. For two of the best commentaries on the case, see Rush, 1997; Godden, 1997.

was sought regarding the status of pastoral leases, and whether they, like freehold tenure, evinced to use the common law formula developed in *Mabo*, a 'clear and plain intention' (*Mabo* (1992), p 46) to extinguish native title. Even though the High Court upheld the legality of the pastoral leases, the judgment set off another wave of '*Mabo* madness' (Pearson, 1997, p 273) because it overturned the Queensland Supreme Court's ruling extinguishing native title, finding instead that native title survived, but was subordinated to the pastoral leases. The ruling, of course, stopped far short of recognising the co-existence of native title and the pastoral leases, let alone the priority of native title. Nevertheless, even as cautious a decision as this was enough to rattle the national psyche, raising anxieties, bordering on hysteria, about dispossession in and among a land of householders already insecure, both financially and psychically, because of the economic and social dislocations wrought by globalisation's relentlessly *laissez-faire* initiatives.

Following upon the High Court's judgment in *Wik* late in 1996, *The Castle*, with a national cinema release in 1997, taps into, and gives expression to, the panic, moral or otherwise, generated by the case. In its story of a family threatened with the loss of their home, the film's narrative reiterates, visually, the curially-sanctioned, Capital-driven 'plague of fantasies' (Zizek, 1997) haunting suburban Australia for the last decade, shattering its 'dreamtime' of quarter acre lots, by driving home the point that there are no tenurial fixities in the new Australia, and that any usufruct they enjoyed yesterday could disappear tomorrow. By suggesting through its plot line this sort of (not so) quiet desperation, *The Castle* shifts the identification of the Kerrigans, and the rest of Highview Crescent, away from indigenity, never a strong connection given that even Jack, positioned by Daryl as the *ur*-resident of the district, has only lived there for 'three years'. No wonder, then, that there are no Aboriginal characters in *The Castle*. Not only aren't they there, as suggested earlier, but, more to the point, there is no such thing as indigenity in Australia, everyone being an 'import' from somewhere else, 'squatting' on land, unencumbered by prior proprietorial interests, though now threatened by malign, even alien forces. All this suggests another identification for the Kerrigans, one more consonant with their claims as much as their colour. Far from being stand-ins for Aboriginality, which the film seems to want them to be, Daryl, Sal and their kids come to resemble no group more than those representative figures of the post-*Mabo* 'white backlash', the squattocratic pastoralists of and mobilised by *Wik*.

Nothing, however, would appear to be, at first blush, further apart, in class terms, than the (sub)urban lumpen proletariat of Highview Crescent and *Wik's* rural squattocrats – Australia's historic answer, for all its self-proclaimed egalitarianism, to the landed gentry of the Mother Country, though here the 'broad acres' of Gloucestershire have been transmuted into the even vaster stations of the Outback. Now more than ever commercially viable because of rich mineral deposits, these huge tracts of leased land often lure corporate interest, thereby rendering the pastoralists anything but 'pastoral', especially when intent on strip-mining their bucolic idylls. But whether landed or commercial, the pastoralists, so-called, duplicate the strategies of self-presentation of their natural class antagonists, the Kerrigans, by portraying themselves, just like the residents of Highview Crescent do in the film, as underdogs battling an inequitable system. For example, throughout the controversies triggered by *Wik* and, before the Native Title Act 1993,

Mabo, the pastoralists struck a deep populist chord by repeatedly sentimentalising themselves in the media as modest stakeholders on the verge of being driven out of their homes and off their land, callously, even viciously, like the Joads of Steinbeck's *The Grapes of Wrath* or, for that matter, the Kerrigans of *The Castle*.

Now this sort of mimicry might be dismissed as just that, a sham, with the ruling class wolf slumming in the sheep's clothes of the working man. However, both the pastoralists and the Kerrigans support their respective claims on eerily analogous grounds: by insisting upon a proprietorial interest, pre-eminent over, and dispositive of, any prior less 'posited' arrangement. Consider the pastoralists, who maintained successfully at the Federal Court that their statutory leases extinguished any previous native title claims to land that the Aboriginal people argued they enjoyed, as the Land Sales Act 1842 put it, by 'Contract, Promise or Engagement preceding the statute' (*Wik* (1996), p 649). Daryl himself counters the legalism of the city official's defence of their power of expropriation, with the sharp comeback about his own lack of privity of contract: 'Where's the agreement with Daryl John Kerrigan?' The question arises: why this shared rhetoric of counter-, even anti-contractualism? I would like to suggest that it is because both the pastoralists and the Kerrigans are positioned against the rewriting of the nation's social contract. This kind of novation, whether Airlink driven or *Mabo* inspired, puts on notice if not ousts White Australia from its 'castle', be it grand (like the pastoralists of *Wik*) or grunge (the Kerrigans of Highview Crescent).

It is here that *The Castle's* many frustrating, even maddening inconsistencies, its wavering attitudes towards native title (satirical or serious? critical or celebratory?), its shifting characterisations (indigenes or pastoralists? heroes or villains?), its uncertain narrative tone (contemptuous or sentimental? feel-good or ironic?) begin to exhibit a particular logic, ushering the viewer into the film's ideological core, the traumatic kernel of which is *la patrie en danger*. Threatened from outside (by the incursions of global Capital, instantiated in Airlink) and, now, from the inside (by the redistributions of native title, allegorised in the expropriation of Highview Crescent), the film portrays Australia as a land divided against itself. It is split into 'two nations' of 'haves' and 'have-nots', owners and dispossessed. What then, or more precisely who, will suture this split and heal the divisions of the country, restoring Australia as 'One Nation'? That is the question the film seems to pose and answer. It raises in its representation of working class *ressentiment*, the spectre of Pauline Hanson's reactionary One Nation Party, the loose cannon of federal politics, which in its *Auslander, raus!* and, especially, anti-reconciliation stances, threatens a return of the fascist repressed and the worst of the 'White Australia' policy.[21] But a 'working class hero', or its demonic parody, as Pauline Hanson, the Queensland (Ipswich) fish 'n' chip shop owner certainly is, is not the salvific figure *The Castle* vouchsafes. Instead, deliverance comes from top-down, in the very aristocratic shape of Lawrence Hammill QC, retired Victorian barrister and constitutional law authority who lends his considerable expertise, as well as stately courtroom presence, to the case, willingly dispensing with payment in order to see justice

---

21 For an interesting psychoanalytic take on Australia's race politics, and the 'return of the fascist repressed' which 'One Nation' promises, see Rutherford, 2000.

done. Now there's a real case of filmic wish fulfilment that would make even Capra arch a brow: a lawyer prepared to forgo a fee, *pro bono publico*!

All of this plays into a politics of 'One Nation' which is more Disraelian Tory than dizzy Queensland. It turns on the fantasy of a benevolent ruling class, acting on behalf of the lower orders, though ultimately this *noblesse oblige* is intended to restore the status quo, keeping us all in our 'proper stations'. Now this scenario, which *The Castle* fully realises in the *deus ex machina* of Hammill's improbably timely intervention, would be laughable but for the fact that it stages the kind of fantasy which features so prominently in the 'politics of nostalgia' of Prime Minister John Howard, the leader of Australia's Conservatives (the misnomered Liberal Party) whose intolerant illiberalism is made all the more transparent by his rhetoric of 'mateship'. In the run-up to the 2000 referendum on the republic, the crypto-monarchist Howard promoted 'mateship' as an addition to the proposed constitutional preamble. Presumably it was offered as an 'inclusive' move, but one which, given mateship's blokey, cobber-ish overtones, looks more like a code for the new alliance the Prime Minister was forging in Australian politics, between the traditional Liberal constituency of the professional-managerial classes and the erstwhile Labour voting, (now disaffected) white working class. Realigned here, and acting in tandem, it is an alliance which threatened to roll back the inroads made by cultural diversity in the new Australia, of which native title was the most prominent symbol and most reviled target.

Surely there is no better imaging of the strange bedfellows made by Liberal Party politics than the 'mateship' which develops, across class lines, between Daryl and Lawrie (Hammill), who, by the film's finish, are photographed cray fishing together in that ironic island of 'serenity', Bonnie Doone, the Kerrigans' holiday home. Moreover, this friendship proves strategic as well as satisfying. It is Lawrie who represents Wayne at his parole board hearing, securing his release from prison, thereby enabling a partnership with his father (Kerrigan and Son Towing). This will not only rehabilitate him ('Dad's prouder of him now than he was when he was in prison', says Dale) but embourgeoisify the family, now with eight tow trucks and prospects of further expansion. So the film ends with a vision of consensus politics, or, at least, the Liberal Party's version of it. Farouk, Evonne, Jack and the Petropoulouses are no more than walk-ons at that showcase of what Stanley Fish would call 'boutique multiculturalism' (Fish, 1997), namely, the party scene. Here the real foci are the Hammills, *père et fils*, modelling their very middle class values which the now fiscally and physically fecund Kerrigans all too easily mimic. The closing 'snapshot' epilogue is of Sal and her mugs, Daryl on his new patio contemplating the power lines, and the kids with their kids, not just Trace and Con, but Steve and his girlfriend, all with babies. *The Castle* concludes with the Kerrigans firmly, even dynastically *in situ*, barricaded behind their 'castle's' wrought iron gates.

However, the last image, of the portcullis, nicked by Daryl and Steve, bespeaks a mentality more of siege rather than security and raises all the ambiguities with which the trope of the 'castle' resonates. For the symbol of the castle connotes, no matter how cosy the film wants this figure of speech to be, conquest, like a Norman redoubt rising above and ruling over Britain's first colonial subjects: the Anglo-Saxons. Only that, under common law, a conquered people, like the Anglo-Saxons, and latterly the Welsh, the Irish, the Québécois, retained rather than forfeited their prior rights to, and claims over, land. Given that legal history, what the analogy of the 'castle' conveys, when recontextualised as a metaphor for Australia, (which is, indeed, what 3 Highview Crescent, Cooloroo really is) is that its settlement was, in fact, what many activists have long claimed, an invasion. So *The Castle's* overarching and controlling emblem might suggest a new era for Australia, one of 'co-existence', where everyone is secure in their castellated retreats, be they Anglo-Celt or Aboriginal. The problem though with this optimistic (naive) reading is that it falsifies the way in which the common law actually operates, treating some properties as less equal than others, subordinating, even extinguishing, particular interests. That these sidelined and suppressed interests always turn out to be those of native title should come as no surprise because they never quite fit in the first place into the feudal tenurial categories of the common law's conception of property. This might serve as a warning to those who would put their faith in the common law, with its private, individualising and, ultimately, retrograde imperatives, as a vehicle for the very public and political issues of social change, and the construction of a better, fairer world. The imaginary of the common law is, as Leslie Moran (2001) would put it, fundamentally 'Gothic', organised around and informed to this day, as much as in Blackstone's day (Hutchings, 2001) and earlier,

Figure 6: *The Castle*, **Sitch, 1997.**

by the castle of the overlord in all his guises, coloniser, patriarch, capitalist. In the image of the castle is a form of property which will trump all other antecedent and future interests, however valid, however equitable, however just, because *all* property, as Proudhon and the French socialists said 150 years ago, as much as Noel Pearson and the Aboriginal peoples know today, is theft (Proudhon, 1969).

Chapter 4

Rebel without a cause?
Elena Loizidou

> What is a rebel? A man who says no: but whose
> refusal does not imply a renunciation.
> (Camus, 2000, p 19)

The figure of the rebel and the practice/idea of rebellion feature in a variety of intellectual writings. Albert Camus' famous book *The Rebel* (2000) and Hannah Arendt's socio-philosophical reading of revolutions in her equally famous book *On Revolution* (1990) are works that discuss and analyse the concept/practice of rebellion as well as the figure of the rebel. They both elaborate on these terms by drawing on the socio-historical conditions from which they emerge. Arendt's book, as the title suggests, is concerned with establishing the 'meaning' of the practice/concept of revolution, by drawing upon the American and the French Revolution, and upon post-medieval rebellions. Her thesis on revolution, as I explain later in the chapter, emerges through the differentiation of events/concepts/practices that appear to be similar to it. Rebellions and the figure of the rebel are theorised by Arendt in this context. Camus' book is more concerned with the figure of the rebel. He primarily focuses upon the French Revolution of 1789 and the Russian Revolution of 1917 and utilises philosophy to paint a widely humanist account of the figure of the rebel. However, rebellion and the rebel have not only been read through, and in relation to, the concept and practice of revolution.[1]

Rebellion or the figure of the rebel has also been the focus of work by cultural analysts and thinkers. In these instances the rebel or rebellion is not read as a historical phenomenon (though they might be historically located), but rather as a private mode of expressing individuality and responding to an existing state of affairs or the status quo. Dick Pountain and David Robins, in their book *Cool Rules: An Anatomy of an Attitude* (2000), trace the rebel or rebellion through the phenomenon of 'Cool' (that can be located in artistic movements, youth culture, celebrated figures and generally popular culture) and point out that 'Cool' '... can be seen as a permanent state of private rebellion' (p 19). Pountain and Robins' book begins its investigation of 'Cool' in the 1950s. While they are aware of cross-cultural and cross-historical figures of cool and rebellion (p 12), they decide not to develop a genealogy of the concept. The phenomenon of 'Cool' they say can best be defined as an attitude, and more precisely as an:

---

1 There is an interesting footnote in relation to Camus' book, Arendt and Ray's film that is worth mentioning. Arendt had read Camus' book and had sent him warm congratulations. Camus had deep respect for Arendt's work. He never, though, read *On Revolution* (1990), since it was originally published three years after his death in 1963. Ray, on the other hand, had read Camus' *The Rebel* in 1954, when the book was first published in English, and was deeply influenced by it. It is well documented that Camus' work has made the director keep the word 'rebel' in the title of the film; for more on this, see Eisenschitz, 1993.

... oppositional attitude adopted by individuals or small groups to express defiance to authority – whether that of the parent, the teacher, the police, the boss or the prison warden. Put more succinctly, we see Cool as a permanent state of private rebellion. Permanent because cool is not just some 'phase that you go through', something that you 'grow out of', but rather something that if once attained remains for life; private because Cool is not a collective political response but a stance of individual defiance, which does not announce itself in strident slogans but conceals its rebellion behind a mask of ironic impassivity. (p 19)

The marking of 'Cool' as an attitude makes their analytical schema both trans-historical and trans-cultural. Their conception of 'Cool' as an oppositional attitude of permanent and private rebellion is useful for my argument here. It introduces (albeit not for the first time ever, but in a concentrated way that makes it unique) an idea of rebellion that is not inextricably linked to a big historical event but to a rather private and individual situation. It is this particular position that I want to bring to Arendt's reading of the figure of the rebel and an analysis of citizenship.

Whilst so far the figure of the rebel, along with the concept of rebellion, has been discussed either in relation to historical contingency or in relation to cultural location, this chapter makes an attempt to think of the figure of the rebel, along with the concept/practice of rebellion, through and beyond historical contingency (history in this particular context makes reference to grand history, history of grand event). By this I do not mean that I will attempt to talk about the rebel as a private figure that through the act of rebellion reflects one's individuality as Pountain and Robins might want us to believe. I will rather attempt to read the figure of the rebel and his/her act of rebellion as a figure that through the very public act of rebellion tells a story about citizenship. The rebel and rebellion, in other words, could be read as indexes of 'alternative' and possible citizenship. By 'alternative' of course I do not mean ultimate. The argument will be made by firstly scrutinising the way in which Arendt gives meaning to these terms and the meaning she ascribes to them. Thereafter I develop a new reading of the figure of the rebel as articulated and depicted in Nicholas Ray's film *Rebel Without a Cause* (1955). There I will focus on two scenes of the film. The first depicts an encounter in the police station between Jim Stark (played by James Dean) and a sympathetic police officer. The second scene is located in the planetarium and depicts an exodus from that place.

At this point one might wonder to what extent this chapter is about Nicholas Ray's film *Rebel Without a Cause* or whether it is rather a study in the concept/practice of rebellion and the figure of the rebel. One analytical approach to *Rebel Without a Cause* might be within the 'Law and Film' tradition. 'Law and Film' as a category of critical law scholarship is relatively new. If one is to locate its emergence (I don't think one can precisely locate its time of emergence) one can say that it has roots in *Law and Literature* (White, 1973) and critical legal studies scholarship. 'Law and Film' scholars have been primarily preoccupied with 'the use of film in the service of a legal goal' (Black, 1999, p 133). Films have been used in explaining constitutional issues (Soifer, 1981) and legal interpretation (Lawrence, 1989), films have been used to analyse how lawyers (Sheffield, 1993) are represented and more generally how law is represented (Black, 1999). Films have also been used as an offering of an alternative legal imagination (Sarat, 2000) or jurisprudence (Young, 1997; Loizidou, 1998; Moran, 1998a). In many respects, I am using *Rebel*

Without a Cause to talk about something else, therefore falling outside the 'traditional' scholarship in 'Law and Film', but at the same time I am using the film to talk about a subject that is of particular interest to lawyers or legal scholarship. I am using *Rebel Without a Cause* to talk about the rebel as a figure that can tell an alternative story about citizenship.

The question of citizenship has been prominent in contemporary academic inquiries within the disciplines of political theory, cultural studies and geography, amongst others. Such discussions have challenged traditional conceptions of citizenship, which relied heavily on discourses of rights, obligations and entitlement (Marshall, 1950). Instead they have focused on discourses of 'hegemony' (Mouffe, 1992), 'practices of citizenship' and 'wounded attachments' (Berlant, 1997, 2000; Brown, 1995; Loizidou, 2001)[2] to deconstruct concepts of citizenship that are constituted upon rights, obligations and entitlement. It is with these critical concepts that I will concern myself here. *Rebel Without a Cause* does not become an excuse for me to talk about the concept/practice of rebellion, or the figure of the rebel of law for that matter, but rather it is a film that is paradigmatic of a series of films in the 1950s that question and represent the American teenager and its demands.[3] An esteemed feminist academic had suggested to me, amongst other things, that I should have used another film to make the point. She suggested that *Rebel Without a Cause* is a very conservative and misogynous film, a popular and ordinary film. In response, and in defence of the importance of using *Rebel Without a Cause*, I would like to address the issue of ordinariness. As Berlant explains, 'Its very popularity or its effects on everyday life or its expression of emblematic knowledge makes it important. Its very ordinariness requires reflecting on what is merely undramatically explicit' (Berlant, 1998, p 119).[4] Here, Berlant suggests that ordinary images ought to be investigated and questioned. In analysing Nicholas Ray's *Rebel Without a Cause* I will be doing precisely this. I will firstly offer a historical and cultural analysis of the 1950s, the context in which the film and the figure of rebellious youth emerge. Then I will offer a critical analysis of the way Arendt reads the term 'rebellion' or 'rebel'. Finally I will be using my critical perspective on Arendt to read the film. My main aim here is to read *Rebel Without a Cause* not as the film has been ordinarily read, namely as a film that primarily tells the story of juvenile delinquency or youth rebellion in suburban America during the 1950s, but rather as a story of youths' demand for recognition, not only of their individuality, but also their demand for political citizenship.

---

2   These contemporary critiques of citizenship have supplemented more traditional readings by offering writings on citizenship. Lauren Berlant, in her essay 'The subject of true feelings: pain privacy and politics' (2000), explains how the juridical discourse can't capture the demands of contemporary American citizens. One of the allegories that she uses to explain how citizens demand their rights to be recognised is the allegory of wound. Citizens feel wounded if their citizen rights are not respected and thus make claims to that effect.

3   Films that fall within the same genre are *On the Waterfront* (1954) and *The Wild One* (1953).

4   While James Dean occupied and still occupies to some extent an iconic position within American culture, I argue that he does so because his cinematic persona is inextricably linked to ordinary figures. Put differently it is the very ordinariness of his cinematic persona that makes him a Hollywood icon.

An American context: individuality and citizenship

Rebel Without a Cause takes place in mid-fifties USA in a Los Angeles suburb. The director, Nicholas Ray, and the scriptwriter, Steward Stern, set out to portray the life of the American teenager at the time. The story is organised around Jim Stark, played by James Dean, who is new to the suburb where the film takes place. His parents moved him there after he was involved in a violent incident with another boy, in the hope that he will conform and lose his rebellious streak, to make 'a right step in the right direction'. Jim soon manages to get into trouble again. After being challenged by Buzz, the popular kid in town, to a 'chickie run', where two drivers of a stolen vehicle drive towards a cliff – the one that jumps out first is considered to be a chicken, that is, a coward or not a man – Jim survives the run whereas Buzz drives over the cliff and dies. Against his parents' advice, Jim goes to the police station to report the event, but on arriving he does not confess because he does not find the sympathetic police officer, Ray (who had taken care of him when he was first arrested for being drunk), at the police station, and he leaves. Buzz's friends, fearing that Jim had indeed reported the event to the police, pursue him. Jim, by now in the company of Judy (Natalie Wood), Buzz's girlfriend, and Plato (Sal Mineo), a young boy who also becomes his friend, hides in a deserted mansion. The mansion is not a safe haven for long and events turn nasty when Buzz's friends and the police discover the three characters. Plato shoots and injures one of Buzz's friends, and then runs and hides, fearing that the police will shoot him. Jim and Judy run after him whilst the police surround the planetarium where he is hiding. Jim convinces Plato to walk out having also negotiated a peaceful 'arrest' for his friend Plato. However, Plato panics and, holding his bullet-less gun, runs out and is shot dead by the police. At the end of the film, in the face of this tragedy, Jim and his parents reconcile their differences.[5]

The film offers a startling counter-perspective to the political rhetoric of the post-World War II period, which depicted the US as a prosperous, homogeneous nation bereft of any social conflict. During the post-World War II years, the US had undergone a transformation in the social, economic, political and military domain. The effects (long-term health effects and destruction of civilians) of the use of atomic bombs by the US in Hiroshima and Nagasaki made President Truman and his administration realise that the existence and future of nations and their populations was at risk; at risk that they could be destroyed or might vanish in a single stroke (Brogan, 1988, p 604). Coupled with the fear of the USSR and the realisation that the US could not be protected from a Soviet invasion by merely relying on the Navy or missile weapons, the US resumed an aggressive production of weapons, more often described as the 'arms race' (Brogan, 1988, p 605).

The economic effects of the arms race were remarkable. Brogan (1988) suggests that the arms race rejuvenated the American economy and moved the country into an economic growth period (pp 605–06). For the first time, Americans found

---

5 Throughout the film there are images of confrontations between Jim and Judy and their respective parents.

themselves in secure employment and earning steady salaries (Hurley, 2001, p 2). This outcome, Hurley points out, was '... celebrated by going into a consumer binge' (p 2). Hurley's statistical information is telling:

> In just the four years following the end of the war, Americans purchased 21.4 million cars, 20 million refrigerators, 5.5 million stoves, and 11.6 million television sets. During the late 1940s and 1950s, annual expenditures on jewelry, toys, and kitchen appliances were twice what they had been in the immediate pre-war era. (p 5)

In the post-World War II period, the purchase of goods, such as cars and televisions, became for Americans a way of expressing their aspirations and celebrating the fact that their fear of a recession after the war was not vindicated (p 6). This economic growth permeated the whole of society. Blue-collar workers were earning as much as white-collar workers. For the first time blue-collar workers found themselves able to afford the goods that the middle classes had been able to enjoy in previous decades. On the basis of purchasing power it is suggested that during this period the rift between the working and middle classes became smaller (pp 6–12). One important effect was the emergence of a larger middle class. This new middle class was characterised by domesticated family life and its purchasing power targeting domestic family goods. Its primary location was the suburbs.

The American 'way of life', a popular cliché of the time perpetrated by consumer culture, became the symbol of what it was to be an American. This notion of Americanism was supported by the political and financial institutions of the time.[6] Hurley suggests that:

> Indeed, the premise became a kind of party line among nationalistic pundits who sought to distinguish the United States from its communist rivals. A consumer culture that denied class distinctions evinced proof of the nation's enduring democratic culture. Its ability to absorb people from working class backgrounds and foreign ancestries testified to the superiority of the American way, namely free market economy. (p 274)

The 'class-less' American society that was emerging in the 1950s also forced manufacturers and advertisers to search for new markets and target new consumer groups, as class could no longer be their guide for either production of goods or advertising. Suburban family life and domestication became instead the focus of production and advertising (p 278). Manufacturers and advertisers found a way to exploit and capitalise upon not only the institution of family and the moral values that it was depicting, but also upon members of the family who previously could not be considered as consumers or as individuals with dispensable incomes or consumer desires. Women and teenagers became the focus of advertising and product campaigns. Advertisers and manufacturers '... positioned themselves as surrogate families ...' and '... encouraged men, women, and children to find fulfilment and pleasure beyond the family circle' (p 291).[7] A good example of this commercial encouragement was the production of cars for women and teenagers.

---

6 Hurley is alluding to an America in a period after the McCarthy 'witch hunts' (which ends in 1954). One could perhaps argue that the McCarthy 'witch hunts' against 'unpatriotic communists' strengthened the concept of an American 'way of life'.

7 For an alternative feminist reading of the suburban housewife, see Friedan, 1965.

Housewives were encouraged by advertisers to develop out-of-home activities. In return they had to have their own car to carry out these activities. Teenagers were also encouraged to invent their own individual personalities. Manufacturers and advertisers rewarded them with low-frame fast cars (pp 290–99). Yet the commercial industry was not wholeheartedly promoting the development of individuality outside of the institution of the family: whilst encouraging housewives and teenagers to become more independent in relation to their mobility, they simultaneously supported the homogeneous and respectable idea of the family, with the father being the head and controller of this institution.

While in the aftermath of World War II and the atomic bomb, a lot of its citizens were better off and the US was growing economically and financially, the country was still not without its social problems. At the heart of this economic growth is a growth of social problems and in particular juvenile delinquency. Criminologists sought to explain this rise of juvenile delinquency.[8] Sociologists of crime such as Shaw and McKay (1942) suggested that crime was related to population movements. They suggested that, while economic prosperity stabilised city areas, increased the value of property and the cost of living, people were forced to move into new areas in order to maintain a better standard of living. These new areas, suburbs, were characterised by Shaw and McKay as disorganised spaces that gave rise to very little community cohesion, a sense of instability and the erosion of family ties. This translated into individual dissatisfaction and loss of any moral direction. This in turn led to conflicting moral and social values that encouraged lawbreaking and delinquency.

Other criminological studies, belonging to the category of strain theory, suggested that the lawbreaking acts of juvenile youths reflected a normal response to abnormal societal or personal circumstances. Here, juvenile crime is understood to be caused by societal failure. Merton (1938, p 672) states that juvenile crime represents the failure of the social system to provide and enable ways in which young people could access material success. Others, such as Cohen (1955), moving away from strain theory, explain delinquency as being a reaction to status formation: youths invert middle class values and through them oppose the middle class status quo. In other words, the inversion of middle class values and taking up and creating violent and hedonistic youth gangs is a way of resolving their opposition to the middle class values through a collective reaction to them.

In some respects, Nicholas Ray's *Rebel Without a Cause* could be seen to be a mid-1950s representation of youth discontent and a critique of family cohesion and suburban affluence. At some level, the story that Nicholas Ray and Steward Stern narrate is a story of discontented teenagers, youth that is rebelling against '... the suffocating web of family ties, school, suburban respectability and labour discipline that the new "mass society" imposed' (Pountain and Robins, 2000, p 70). One can read the character of Jim and his actions either through Shaw and McKay's scheme of analysis: as a reaction to a system that could not provide him with material recognition, or through Cohen's scheme of analysis: as reacting against status formation by the formation of a youth gang. Nevertheless, in my opinion, neither of

---

8 For a general discussion of crime and causes of crime, see Henry and Milovanovic, 1996.

these analyses really provides us with a full description of Jim Stark's character and the effects of his actions.

Jim's material desires are fully provided by his parents. We see his father at the beginning of the film being perplexed by his rebelliousness, for it could not be explained by factors such as material deprivation. At the very beginning of the film his father asks him why he is breaking the law. Cohen's theory if applied to the film can't provide an adequate analysis of Jim's character or effects of his actions. As we see, Jim rebels against his family and the status quo, but nevertheless his rebellion is an insular rebellion rather than one that is associated with the formation of a gang that perpetrates mindless violence. Additionally, an effective reading (one that is read through the effects of his actions) of his rebellion shows that his rebellion, while without a strategic motivation, is not necessarily without a cause. An effective reading will allow us to read his 'cause' as one that desires to transform his private, intimate and familial environment. This differs from Cohen's theory, which suggests that the formation of gangs and the use of mindless violence become the end of juvenile delinquency. Additionally, one of the problems of criminological understanding of youth discontent is that, no matter how radical the theoretical framework used, the behaviour of discontented youth groups or discontented young individuals is interpreted in negative terms, even if their actions are a reaction to an abnormal society as Merton suggests: as law and norm-breaking actions. These readings are limited in their analysis by focusing on the behaviour and the social conditioning of the groups that they analyse. Such readings, I argue, can be both challenged and supplemented by an affective reading of the practices of discontented groups and more specifically in our case, youth. An affective reading of their practices reads their practices not so much as lawbreaking actions but as demands for change, reconstruction and youth citizenship.

I am not interested here in what particularly brings about Jim's 'rebellious' streak. Hurley suggests that by the 1960s, young men and women were growing critical of the emptiness of the consumer culture and conformism. Jim's 'rebelliousness' might be read as an early critique of consumer culture. Other explanations might come from a combination of the suggestions that the criminologists discussed above have offered: lack of cohesive community, competing moral values and general dissatisfaction with the social mores.

As I said, I am not interested in the aetiology of rebellions. I am interested in reading how either rebellion or the figure of the rebel, affect the social and political arena. A critical analysis of Arendt's work on revolutions demonstrates why it is important to adopt an affective reading of events or characters. I want to draw upon it in analysing the film *Rebel Without a Cause*. As suggested above, an affective reading of practices refrains from offering an ontological understanding of action (of what they are) and offers a practice-based analysis which explains what they do or demand.

What is a rebellion? Who is a rebel?

Hannah Arendt's *On Revolution* (1990) offers both a sociological and philosophical analysis of the modern phenomenon of revolution. Arendt looks into the principles that underlie the concept/practice of revolutions and how they developed both in practice and theory since the landmark revolutions that she analyses, namely the American Revolution (1775–83) and the French Revolution of 1789. The book, as the title suggests, is mostly preoccupied with how we are to understand the idea/practice of revolution. In doing so, Arendt engages in a practice of writing that allows her to differentiate and 'purify' the concept/practice of revolution from concepts/practices that appear to be similar to that of the revolution. The meaning of revolution, in other words, comes out from the 'destruction' of dissimilar concepts/practices of struggle that are not necessarily opposite to the concept/practice of revolution. Through this process of 'purification', Arendt's quest is to establish both that the concept/practice of revolution is a unique modern phenomenon (located in the latter part of the 18th century) and that it is different from rebellion, war, the birth of Christianity, and the concept of revolution that was developed in the natural sciences.

While it is significant to look at how Arendt purifies the concept/practice of revolution from all the terms identified above, of particular interest here is the way she differentiates revolution from rebellion. Arendt, in defining revolution, seeks to differentiate it from other similar concepts and attribute to it specific characteristics. For Arendt, the modern concept of revolution is inextricably linked with two ideas: the idea of novelty and the idea of freedom. For a revolution to have taken place, she suggests that these two ideas must coincide. In relation to the idea of novelty, Arendt characteristically writes:

> The modern concept of revolution, inextricably bound up with the notion that the course of history suddenly begins anew, that an entirely new story, a story never known, or told before is about to unfold, was unknown prior to the two great revolutions at the end of the 18th century. (Arendt, 1990, p 28)

The idea/practice of revolutions (as a modern phenomenon) as presented by Arendt appears to be doing something, bringing something into effect. Arendt suggests that revolutions uproot the foundations of the old or ancient regime and write their own history in its place. Revolutions transform the socio-symbolic system to such an extent that it becomes unfamiliar, anew, a new story. It is in this sense that modern revolutions are seen to be effecting something new. It is in this sense that Arendt understands the idea of novelty as being connected to the idea of revolution. Arendt also states that: 'Crucial ... to any understanding of revolutions in the modern age is that the idea of freedom and the experience of a new beginning should coincide' (Arendt, 1990, p 29). She is suggesting that for a revolution to be successful the idea of freedom should also appear to be doing something novel or something anew. She clarifies how the concept/practice of freedom ought to be understood by contrasting it to that of liberty.

Freedom, she says, should not be understood as being synonymous with liberty or liberation. Liberation, she states, '... may be the condition of freedom but by no means leads automatically to it ...' (Arendt, 1990, p 29). In proving the difference between the terms, Arendt resorts to an explanation that focuses on what these two ideas effectively do, as opposed to a traditional approach to political theory that focuses on what the concepts are. The idea of liberation or liberty, she argues, leads to the formation of civil liberties, civil rights and constitutional governments. But neither the institution of civil rights nor the institution of constitutional governments can 'capture' the 'desire for freedom' (Arendt, 1990, p 29). This precise 'desire for freedom', leads to the doing of something new. The institutionalisation of civil liberties in the aftermath of the French Revolution and the American War of Independence, Arendt argues, 'meant no more than freedom from unjustified restraint ...' (Arendt, 1990, p 32). What liberty and liberation effectively achieved was to bring into being something that was already there, rights that were not new but rather pre-existed the revolutions. In exemplifying her argument Arendt points out that the core idea that supports civil rights is that of 'freedom from unjustified restraint'. The origin of this idea, as she points out, can be traced back to Blackstone's idea of 'power of locomotion ... without imprisonment or restraint, unless by due course of law' (Arendt, 1990, p 32). If revolutions would have only aimed at guaranteeing civil liberties, she argues, they would have had as their aim the control of governments that violated 'well established rights' (Arendt, 1990, p 32). The idea/practice of freedom that is paramount to the idea/practice of revolution, she suggests, does something else. The idea of freedom desires to make freedom a way of political life, and for freedom to be a way of political life, means that freedom is to give people access to the public arena and participation in the making of public affairs (Arendt, 1990, p 32). This understanding of freedom, which Arendt suggests is not a complete novelty to the modern era,[9] is new in the sense that the revolutionaries, for the first time after centuries, put themselves in a position of using their faculties to make something new. Arendt points out that what they felt through the practices of speech making, decision making, thinking and persuasion was an experience of freedom. These practices are represented by Arendt as an index of freedom as a way of life.

As for the idea of 'violence' that is so often used, at least in lay terms, to describe events that are seen to be revolutionary, Arendt suggests that 'violence' is not a term that conveys the meaning of revolution. She points out that, while violence becomes an ingredient of a revolution, we can't say that a revolution took place because there was violence (Arendt, 1990, p 35). Violence can contribute to the establishment of a new order of things that in turn opens a space for access to public political participation, to freedom as Arendt understands it, but violence is not an index that can on its own describe revolutions. For Arendt then, our modern understanding of revolution is embellished with the idea of a new story that comes into being through the demolition and uprooting of the old and holds with it the promise (desire) that freedom, as a political way of living, will come into being.

Arendt suggests though, that the concept/practice of modern revolutions, exemplified by the French Revolution and the American War of Independence, is not synonymous with that of rebellion. In showing the difference between the two, Arendt resorts to looking at the history of rebellions and their achievements. She focuses particularly on rebellions that took place between the medieval and post-medieval period.

---

9   Arendt points out that this it is very similar to the concept of isonomy, 'that can be understood as a form of political organisation in which the citizens lived together under conditions of no-rule, without division between rulers and rules' (Arendt, 1990, p 32).

Unlike revolutions, which aim to transform the whole socio-symbolic realm, Arendt claims that rebellions merely manage to remove one ruler and lead to the appointment of a new leader, in the same position, who appears to be less tyrannical (Arendt, 1990, p 40). Rebellions for Arendt fail to be 'transformative', to uproot the old, the ancient and invent in its place a new political system. The difference between rebellions and revolutions for Arendt does not though remain at the level of the kind of changes that takes place. She is quick to point out that the role the rebels played in rebellions was very different:

> ... the people might be admitted to have the right to decide who should not rule them, they certainly were not supposed to determine who should, and even less do we ever hear of a right of people to be their own rulers or to appoint persons from their own rank for the business of government ... In order to rule, one had to be a born ruler, a free-born man in antiquity, a member of the nobility in feudal Europe, and although there were enough words in pre-modern political language to describe the uprising of subjects against a ruler, there was none which would describe a change so radical that the subjects became rulers themselves. (Arendt, 1990, pp 40–41)

Rebellion, as a concept/practice, becomes in Arendt's writing an event that does not re-write history. Rebellion does not re-write history not only because it does not alter the political structure, but rather more importantly Arendt suggests because it does not alter the political position of the rebels. The rebel becomes just a figure that contributes to the removal of the ruler, but never becomes a ruler because he is not born a ruler. Rebellions, one could say, construct the rebel as a non-agentic political subject. This is primarily what allows Arendt to differentiate the concept/practice of revolution from that of rebellion.

However, Arendt's idea of the rebel as a figure without political agency limits an understanding of revolutions and rebellions. Arendt focuses constantly on events that are historical in character to explain the meaning of concepts and practices; to explain what these concepts 'do'. I contend that her focus on historical events to explain meanings is of a teleological nature. By this I mean that Arendt can only understand what a rebellion or a revolution 'does' and therefore 'is' by looking at their ends; by which I understand their effects. She reads rebellions and revolutions as complete, closed events. This reading I think is problematic for three reasons. First, it relies heavily on the achievements or what events do. Secondly, the doing of events is not read beyond linearity and conclusion (achievement). Thirdly, it fails to understand the contribution of the subject, that is, the contribution of the rebel to the event – the event is somehow disembodied, alienated from the subject.

The third point of critique in particular is highly problematic in Arendt's writing and, I would suggest, is very much linked to reading the concept/practice of revolution and rebellion in a historical and teleological way. It fails to evaluate significantly the contribution that rebels have made in removing a ruler from power. Arendt, rather, evaluates their contribution in terms of what they have not achieved, namely not gaining power in themselves. In doing so she disenfranchises the practice that the rebels are engaging in from the arena of political transformation. This disenfranchises the rebel twice: she is not only insignificant politically because she never gets public political power, but also because her political agency is only understood in terms of an end, and hence without a cause. In Butler's words, what Arendt fails to understand is that:

Agency exceeds the power by which it is enabled. One might say that the purposes of power are not always the purposes of agency. To the extent that the latter diverge from the former, agency is the assumption of a purpose unintended by power, one that could not have been derived logically or historically, that operates in a relation of contingency and reversal to the power that makes it possible, to which it nevertheless belongs. This is, as it were, the ambivalent sense of agency, constrained by no teleological necessity. (Butler, 1997, p 15)

Butler's formulation of power and agency is enabling in understanding how power and the subject might be politically franchised. Unlike traditional Marxist Feminist models of power promoted by the likes of MacKinnon (1991) and Dworkin (1981), Butler uses a Foucauldian framework to explain how subjects come into being. Her explanation formulates an effective discourse of power, where power is not external to the subject and can be attained through restructuration, but rather constituent to it and therefore both open to resistance and reconfiguration. Butler, in this respect, understands the agency of the subject as being derivative from subject resistance to the power figuration that brings it into being. Finally, Butler argues it is impossible to talk of a pre-existing already configured agentic subject, but rather one that comes into being through the affective practice of resistance. In contrast, Arendt's understanding of the rebel as a powerless figure constructs power as an external entity that can be possessed. Once power is set up as something external that can be possessed, the rebel (in Arendt's historical sense) is seen as one that does not possess political power and henceforth agency, political agency. But what this construction fails to understand is that agency operates in a non-teleological way and resists the very power that brings the rebel into being. Butler's analysis of agency shows that despite the fact that a subject might be subordinated, feel the pain of subordination, and might in everyday terms be understood as powerless, she still possesses political agency. This political agency enables the subject to resist subordination, to resist being identified as a victim of power. Instead the resistance to subordination communicates that the subject desires to be dis-identified from the position of victim and be identified with a subject that talks through his/her actions about a different world than the one that already exists. It is in this sense that I would like to talk of political agency as that which 'resists the power that brings it into being by projecting a desired political world' (Berlant, 2000, pp 42–43), one that dis-identifies with the identification.

Can I read a rebel? Can I read a rebel with a cause?

Arendt's reading of rebellions and the rebel fails to read the rebel as a subject that possesses a political agency that comes through his/her resistance to power. I have also pointed out that Arendt's reading fails to understand how political agency operates and what it demands, because she focuses primarily on reading both the terms rebellion and revolution in historical terms and through their ends. In being critical of Arendt's reading of rebellion and the figure of the rebel, I have suggested that we can understand the figure of the rebel and his/her acts as demands for recognition of political agency and, ultimately, political citizenship. It is this definition of rebellion and the rebel that I will use to read Nicholas Ray's film, *Rebel*

Without a Cause. In doing so, I want to examine the figure of Jim Stark,[10] the protagonist in the film, focusing on two scenes of the film.

The first scene takes place in the Juvenile Division of the police station. It is the encounter between a sympathetic police officer, Ray, and Jim Stark. It is a scene in which Ray, the sympathetic officer, distances Jim from his parents and his grandmother who have arrived to pick him up after he has been arrested for being drunk and disorderly. Prior to the encounter between Ray and Jim, Jim's father tries to apologise to the police officer for his son's behaviour. Jim's father also attempts to understand why his son behaves in this way. He states that he can't understand Jim's behaviour. Jim's actions are not justified since they give him everything. Jim breaks down. The sympathetic officer, Ray, removes him from the room where his parents are. Ray tries to get to the cause of Jim's discontent.

Figure 7: *Rebel Without a Cause*, Ray, 1955.

---

10 See Dyer, 2001, pp 52–54, on Hollywood's use of charismatic actors such as James Dean in playing rebellious characters. Dyer offers a sociological and semiotic analysis of stardom. In relation to the type of the rebel, he argues that one should question the rebelliousness of such types in Hollywood films. James Dean in Nicholas Ray's *Rebel Without a Cause*, Dyer argues, is not a rebel, for his character recuperates the institutional family values. He suggests that the life and death of stars such as James Dean is used by Hollywood to lure the audience into perceiving the character of the film as rebellious. He also warns us of the ways in which the type of character is used to situate other types of characters, such as women, homosexuals and blacks, within a hierarchy. In the case of *Rebel Without a Cause*, one might suggest that the type of the masculine young rebel that James Dean depicts through the character of Jim Stark positions the female character Judy, played by Natalie Wood, as subordinate.

Jim looks back at his family through the spy hole. He sees his family (mum, dad and grandmother) arguing. He wishes that his dad had:

> ... the guts to knock his Mom cold once, then maybe she'd be happy and then she'd stop pickin' on him, because they make mush out of him ... I tell you one thing, I don't ever want to be like him. How can a guy grow up in a circus like that? ... Boy, if I had one day when I didn't have to be all confused, and didn't have to feel that I was ashamed of everything ... If I felt that I belonged someplace, you know, then ...

Jim expresses here, in the eyes of (to the eyes of) his surrogate father, the officer of law and order, that he does not belong. Jim does not belong in 'a circus like that': his family. 'Circus' is used by Jim metaphorically. It transmits both his distaste and disapproval of his family. As a metaphor, 'circus' connotes a confused state of affairs. In this particular instance, Jim's reference to his family's state of affairs as being 'a circus' exposes his understanding of the failure of his family to successfully carry the family and gender values of post-World War II middle class. His family fails in being united and warm. Any form of family respectability that he could have disappears amid their everyday fights. Family respectability is translated into the act of keeping up appearances for the sake of the public. His family gender relations are also a sham. His mother is portrayed as being in control of his father. Jim's desire for his dad to have the 'guts to knock Mom cold once' registers further his anger with his family's gender relations. If we were to apply Arendt's historical analysis of rebellions to this private rebellion, as expressed by Jim's actions and words, we would construct it as one relating to his familial affairs. Jim can be read as being disempowered by the failed institution of the family. In a criminological sense he would be read as acting delinquently, either because he is not satisfied with his material provisions, or because he is refusing the status quo or authority. All these explanations though are inadequate, because they fail to transmit how Jim's individual agency is produced through this scene. Jim's critical reflections of his family talk volumes about his relation to his condition of subordination and his 'delinquent' status. Jim's actions and words could be read as practices of resisting the 'circus' and registering his demand to be recognised, not as a victim of his familial or social environment, but as an individual that is searching to find somewhere else to belong. His wish that he was able to feel that he belonged somewhere else is paradigmatic of this. Through his actions he is transmitting a desire to be recognised as an individual that demands to belong in a space that does not accept the values of middle class respectability, gender relations and the American way of life that are typified by his family. He is also demanding an inversion of his own family gender relations. From his father he is demanding a transformation into a strong masculine figure that can resist his mother's demands and control. His rebellion thus transmits his request for a change in the family figurehead and also the recognition of his own individuality and opinion within his family. It is perhaps to some extent true to say that the film recuperates the institution of the family and does not transgress it, but it is also true to say that Jim Stark's yearning to belong somewhere else outside the 'circus' of the family, somehow transgresses the idea of the mid-1950s suburban middle class family.

I want to turn now to the second scene. After Plato is shot by the police, we see Jim feeling both guilt and confusion, being unable to understand Plato's senseless death. He did attempt to negotiate with the police and resolve this issue peacefully.

This attempt to negotiate with the police brings Jim closer to his father; he identifies, or more precisely comes close to identifying, with his father. The scene that I am about to analyse shows a father that comes close to his son for the first time by telling him that they will face things together. Jim hugs him after asking his father to help him. This could be considered as a reconciliation of father and son.

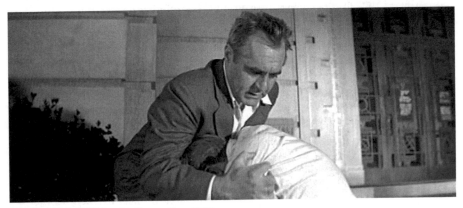

Figure 8: *Rebel Without a Cause,* **Ray, 1955.**

Jim now finds himself at the location of reconciliation. He does not demand answers anymore from his father. Somehow, having confronted the law and having failed to reconcile with it (having failed to stop the shooting that caused Plato's senseless death), no answer could alleviate the pain. The open wound,[11] brings him down to his knees, asking for help from the very figure that he has throughout the film been demanding answers from and demanding changes from, his father. Has this wound transformed into a wound that suddenly made him recognise what she[12] is? Has he given up the dream, his political dream, has he been brought down to his knees, has he forgotten the dream? Jim's father explains:

> Look Jim. You can depend on me. Trust me. Whatever comes, we'll, we'll fix it together. I swear it. Now Jim, stand up. I'll stand up with you. I'll try to be strong as you want me to be. Come on.

You never choose a ruler, rebel. You contribute only in replacing him. You gain no power. You fall to your knees and cry (you fail), you ask for help. But I wonder. How can I remove a ruler (the father) without making a replacement? How come the new ruler, the 'new' father, talks to him? Have my cries of resistance effected this transformation?

---

11 Here I am using the allegory of the wound to ironically suggest the impossibility of the wound being 'healed' by a juridical discourse.

12 Here I am using the feminine pronoun 'she', for I want to suggest that Jim's disempowerment and demands for citizenship are not dissimilar to those of women. In addition, the 'she' introduces a poetic nexus between the character of the film and the writer of this article, one whereby the figure of analysis and the writer can't be differentiated. The significance to this is an attempt to point out that every analysis of a text, albeit a cinematic one, carries with it an autobiographical reference.

Jim's father speaks to him. He tells him that he'll be as strong as he wants him to be. He answers partially to his wound. He answers partially to what he wants and dreams of being a political citizen. He puts down the façade of respectability, of middle class values, of not standing up to his mother and for once dreams with him. 'Come on', perhaps this also means let's go on, 'we'll fix it together', perhaps this means we'll pull apart the void of our difference that differentiates us, perhaps it means we'll put an end to the story that reads through the end, that resistance, that rebellion and the rebel have no cause.

Conclusion: citizenship and private rebellion

Political citizenship has traditionally been read as a possession of public institutions. Marshall's book *Citizenship and Social Class* (1950) argued that citizenship is a possession of the state, which in return cares for the welfare and rights of its citizens. State citizenship, Marshall also argues, binds and brings together socially members of a state. More recently, cultural theorists such as Lauren Berlant (1997) have transformed the terrain of discourses surrounding citizenship. Berlant's critique of US citizenship during the Reaganite era demonstrates that the idea of public political arena has been transformed into 'intimate public' sphere. Our contemporary idea of citizenship, she argues, is measured against our private acts. In analysing Nicholas Ray's *Rebel Without a Cause* through a critical reflection of Arendt's understanding of rebellion, I have demonstrated that youth rebellions that can be traditionally understood as being delinquent acts or as being politically insignificant hide within them a political message. Private and individual acts of rebellion might not be revolutionary, might not in other words transform the socio-symbolic order that is being challenged, but they carry within them a demand that an individual's critical opinion and demands be recognised. This demand for individual recognition, I have argued, resists the power relations that bring an individual into being and give rise to an articulation of political citizenship that is different from the one that one is experiencing. Jim Stark's words and actions articulate his demand for a familial environment that does not hide behind the façade of middle class values, a rejection of consumer values, and recognition that he is also an individual, along with being a family member. The end of the film does not necessarily address all his demands. He does not find that other space where he could feel that he belongs. Instead his family 'circus' transforms in such a way as to come closer to his ideal place. Private rebellions, no matter how apolitical they might appear to be, I have argued, still offer an affective reading of practices whereby they might not only 'transform' the status quo, but more importantly, also inform us of individual demands of citizenship and a critique of existing conceptions of citizenship. At the time that one is rebelling against particular values a complete transformation might not take place. A future socio-political arena could, though, bear the fruits of individual and private rebellions.

Chapter 5
Toy law, toy joy, *Toy Story 2*
Fred Botting and Scott Wilson

'Life's only worth living if you are being loved by a kid'
(Toy Story 2, 1999)

A philosophy of toys

Toys, operating uncomfortably within and in excess of homogeneous systems, situate their subjects in a double relation: on the one hand as subjects of rules, moves, exchanges, circulating within a closed structure; on the other, as insubordinate and playful entities refusing any subjection to dictates of reason, use or morality. Goods and the good encounter diabolical and irregular elements in play, heterogeneous forces refusing to respect the dictates of order. Bataille's (1973) distinction between law and value is crucial: 'the law (the rule) is a good one, it is Good itself (Good, the means by which the being ensures its existence), but a value, Evil, depends on the possibility of breaking the rule' (p 186). Toys, in their ambivalent movements of subjection and subversion, institute both law and the heterogeneity on which it depends and which it cannot contain.

Toys lay down an ambivalent law. Forming part of a process of acculturation and socialisation, toys serve as instruments of training and discipline, objects involved in the making of the subjects who manipulate them. Barbie dolls, for example, are supposed to be instruments of heteronormative hegemony. As an object encouraging play, however, a Barbie might also become a prototype 'queer accessory' (Rand, 1995; Botting and Wilson, 2002a). Toys introduce an excess that threatens and defines modes of organisation and homogenisation: play wastes time and energy as much as it enables the development of rational, moral and useful skills. While 'the *fun* of playing resists all analysis, all logical interpretation', 'pure play is one of the main bases of civilisation' (emphasis added, Huizinga, 1949, pp 3, 5). Originating in ritual and festival, play shapes bodies and identities within cultural formations. Since the late 18th century, play has been integrated into the temporality and workaday rhythms of modernity, like the playtime that forms an integral part of the disciplinary regime of schools. But the usefulness of play is also contested: Roger Caillois (1962) argues its significance lies in the fact that 'it creates no wealth or goods' and thus belongs neither to the category of work nor to that of art. Aneconomic, games are repetitive, ending only to begin again without delivering an aesthetic or material product. Nor do they allow capital to be accrued. Hence, 'play is an occasion of pure waste: waste of time, energy, ingenuity, skill and often of money' (pp 5–6). Toys, then, as objects fashioned or purchased for purposes of play, are things on which time and money has been expended in order that further, often useless, expenditures of energy can occur.

Charles Baudelaire's essay 'A philosophy of toys' (1964), first published in 1855, discloses the other side of bourgeois modernity, revelling in the aesthetics, desires and commodities which exceed rationality, use and morality. Recounting one of his earliest memories, Baudelaire describes a visit to a party hosted by Mme

Panckoucke, a celebrated *salonniere* of the time. There he encounters toys in the context of art and extravagance in the form of a young Alexandre Dumas and his consort, Elsa Mercoeur, who appears 'dressed as his page'. But it is not Dumas' playful pederasty that arrests the boy's attention so much as the hostess who, clad as she is 'in velvet and fur', resonates with the literature of 19th century sexual fetishism. The hostess leads the boy away and opens a door to her 'children's treasury' – a room filled to bursting with every type of toy. For Baudelaire the sight of this room, with its 'efflorescence of toys', is a 'fairylike spectacle', and one which stays with him for the rest of his life. Since he is a 'nice little boy', his hostess invites him to choose one toy as a 'souvenir' of her. With an impulsive yet unerring movement in which 'desire, deliberation and action make up, so to speak, a single faculty' (p 197), the young Baudelaire chooses the single most beautiful and expensive toy in the shop, much to his mother's embarrassment. This embarrassment is a symptom of the rational and moral 'degeneracy' that Baudelaire, in a proto-Nietzschean gesture, believes condemns 'man' to the absurdity of an infinite 'deliberation' that 'absorbs almost the whole of his time' (pp 197–98). Such deliberation is of course precisely the thing that 20th century consumer capitalism will break down.[1] Consumer capitalism will seek to invoke and lay down the toy law that seizes thought and action in the unity of one childlike movement of desire and consumption.

The gift of the toy, furthermore, and the whole scenario of its giving, proves to be a determining experience for Baudelaire. Even as an adult, he notes how he is unable to pass a toyshop without thinking of the 'velvet-and-fur-clad lady' who remains forever his 'Toy Fairy'. Better than any fine bourgeois apartment, the toyshop has become the most aesthetic of places, a realm in which all life is found 'in miniature' and 'far more highly coloured, sparkling and polished than real life'. Unsurprisingly, the aesthetic dimensions of toys figure most prominently in Baudelaire's account. Though commenting on the differences between rich and poor at play, and noting the practical and educational benefits of toys, it is their role in imaginative life that most appeals to him. Indeed, the focus on aesthetic qualities and effects answers his own question as to whether children dominate or are dominated by their toys: Baudelaire, aesthetically at least, has fallen fully under their thrall. As a child's 'earliest initiation into art', toys (and theatres) have powers of 'predestination', giving shape to the artistic or literary imagination.

Mechanisms and mechanical metaphors are never far away from the imagination in Baudelaire's discussion. His account of the way that toys represent life in miniature, and at its most dramatic, for the children who play with them, notes how these toys or 'actors' are 'reduced in size by the *camera obscura* of their little brains' (p 198). The analogy between a child's brain and an early form of visual technology blurs the distinction between subjects and objects of play, rendering the mind as already the toy or theatre that it is predestined to become. The association is later underlined by the type of toys Baudelaire discusses towards the end of his essay.

---

1   An embarrassment that will give way to the embarrassing spectacle of Christmas shopping mothers fighting over the last Buzz Lightyear in the shop, something referred to in Pixar's sequel *Toy Story 2*.

The 'Stereoscope' (which presents a flat image in the round) and the 'Phenakistoscope' (a circular card covered in images of dancers which, when rotated, appear to dance as one) are both optical toys that delight with their illusions of depth or movement. Neither of these 'scientific' toys are cited by Baudelaire as examples of educational play, however. In developing 'a taste for marvellous and unexpected effects', their value lies in their aesthetic predispositions and in their stimulation of imaginative play.

That optical mechanisms, used increasingly since the end of the 18th century to entertain audiences, should inform the development of the artistic imagination is at odds with the idea that 'mechanical reproduction' effaces the Romantic aura of the work of the art. This, of course, is the transformation that Walter Benjamin identifies in modernity, in essays that draw heavily on Baudelaire's writings and his poetic persona. For Benjamin (1973), an organic and humanistic imagination seems to give way to an imagining bound up with industrial mechanism. A different aesthetic moves imagination away from nature and into the rapid movements of the urban scene where the fast flow of crowds and the glittering surfaces of arcades intoxicate the viewer who passes by. It is a visual and kinetic environment in which Baudelaire comes into his own. The child captivated by the room full of toys and, still impressed by the wonders of toyshops, has his predispositions shaped early on. The *camera obscura* of little brains, however, is transposed onto the urban exterior, the shopfront-as-screen duplicating the toys of visual illusion and inculcating 'a taste for marvellous and unexpected effects'. This exteriorisation, of course, informs the aesthetics of early cinema, where the mechanisms of optical observation and experimentation are deployed as devices of perceptual excitement and stimulation. The 'cinema of attractions' produces moving images to cause sensation in spectators, thrilling them with the strange and unexpected, shocking them with visual marvels (Gunning, 1996).

The aesthetics of early cinema duplicate the dominant structures of the modernity in which they emerge. Imagining is not performed over and against the mechanisms of urban mass (as it had been in previous eras) but is defined and evoked in the very terms of modern mechanism. Cinematic effects, for Benjamin (1973), participate in an aesthetic that shatters tradition with the shock of modern life: sensations and shocks mark the transformation of (human) experience, and the aura of creation. They intensify the shocks that constituted the basis of everyday experience in the crowd or at the factory, where repetitive labour is calibrated to the hard rhythms of the machine. 'There came a day', writes Benjamin, 'when a new and urgent need for stimuli was met by the film. In a film, perception in the form of shocks was established as a formal principle. That which determines the rhythm of production on a conveyor belt is the basis of the rhythm of reception in the film' (p 177). Modern aesthetics, which film comes to embody, has to exceed the shocks of everyday life through the provision of yet more shocks. Benjamin uses Freud's notion of the 'protective shield' which defends the organism from the intensities of external and unconscious stimulation. Industrial labour and urban living dulls sensation through repeated shocks, engendering habituation. To break through the protective screen and succeed in stimulating an audience, the shocks have to be more intense. The rhythm becomes one of repetition and excess, habituation and excitement, boredom and intoxication. The process, however, offers Benjamin a glimpse of how 'technology has subjected the human sensorium to a new kind of training' (p 176).

Film aesthetics thus operate in a doubled fashion, training subjects in the rhythms of industrial production and overstimulating them at the same time. With the *flâneur*, existence is similarly divided by intoxication and ennui, an immersion in the flow of crowds and wonderment at the phantasmagoria of the arcades. Like film, which replaces a human-centred aesthetic with a new mode of industrial-cinematic production, the *flâneur* inhabits a system of values determined by commodities and exchange rather than useful production: 'empathy with the commodity is fundamentally empathy with exchange-value itself. The *flâneur* is the virtuoso of this empathy' (Benjamin, 1999, p 448). With Freud, on whom Benjamin also draws extensively in his account of modernity, both the mechanism of training and the imperatives of two economies – of pleasure and death – hinge on repetition and come to the fore in the observation of a child playing with a toy.

'O-o-o-o!' In *Beyond the Pleasure Principle*, Freud (1984) notes how this exclamation accompanies his grandchild's game of throwing a cotton reel on a piece of string over the side of his cot. He translates the sounds into 'fort!' (gone) and 'da!' (here), attached as they are to acts of making the toy disappear and subsequently return. Initially, it seems that the greater pleasure is attached to pulling the reel back, and Freud posits the dominance of the pleasure principle at work. Pleasure results from a 'diminution' in unpleasurable neural excitation and a decrease in tension (p 276). Here it appears that the child compensates for the absence of his mother, and for Freud this act of 'instinctual renunciation' is presented as a 'great cultural achievement' (p 285). But things are not so clear, as further observation makes evident. Often the act of throwing the reel away 'repeated untiringly as a game in itself' (p 284). Since the return of the reel yields greater pleasure for the child, Freud proposes that the repeated act of throwing away manifests an 'instinct for mastery' in which absence is dealt with by moving from a passive position, 'overpowered by the experience', to one in which the child assumes an active role (p 285). The spectacle of repetition announces the possibility of a principle at odds with that of pleasure, a compulsion in excess of pleasure's economy and governed by the death drive.

Identity begins with a toy and situates the subject between economies of pleasure and death, subordinated, through repetition, to a bifurcated system in which self can never fully be assumed and objects never fully mastered. Indeed, the game is played with a mirror as well as a reel, the child making his inverted image disappear and return. For Lacan (1977), the disappearance of the mother is 'of secondary importance'. That the game involves 'one of the first oppositions to appear' is of greater significance: 'it is in this object to which the opposition is applied in act, the reel, that we must designate the subject' (p 62). A fundamental alienation, a splitting of biological being and cultural identity, is at stake, the loss and recovery of subjectivity at the level of signification: 'in his phonematic opposition, the child transcends, brings onto the symbolic plane, the phenomenon of presence and absence. He renders himself master of the thing, precisely insofar as he destroys it' (Lacan, 1988, p 173). The child, in this loss of the mother, accedes to the law of the signifier, defines himself through his utterance in terms of the symbolic oppositions of which 'fort' and 'da' (which have no meaning except in their difference from the other term) constitute early examples.

Identity, and the law of the signifier on which it dangles, remains at stake, however, in the fort-da game; self-constitution by way of the toy is always threatened by a daemonic and mechanical power beyond its grasp. Derrida's account of Freud is attentive to the automatism that the compulsion to repeat discloses, and he finds in the movement of disappearance and return, an iteration which does not necessarily mean that the subject returns to himself on a symbolic plane. A new technical metaphor appears in the utterances of the child:

> He speaks to himself telephonically, he calls himself, recalls himself, 'spontaneously' affects himself with his presence-absence in the presence-absence of his mother. He makes himself *re-*. Always according to the law of the PP [pleasure/paternal principle]. In the grand speculation of a PP which (who) never seems to absent itself – (himself) from itself – (himself). Or from anyone else. The telephonic or telescripted recall provides the 'movement' by contracting itself, by signing a contract with itself. (Derrida, 1987, p 319)

The movement is automatic. And demonic, too:

> The demon is that very thing which *comes back* [*revient*] without having been called by the PP. The demon is the *revenance* which repeats its entrance, coming back [*revenant*] from one knows not where ('early infantile influences' says Freud), inherited from one knows not whom, but already persecutory, by means of the simple form of its return, indefatigably repetitive, independent of every apparent desire, *automatic*. (Emphasis added, Derrida, 1987, p 341)

The autoaffectivity of the game opens onto another automatism:

> ... this automaton comes back [*revient*] without coming back to [*revenir à*] anyone, it produces effects of ventriloquism without origin, without emission, and without addressee. ... Tele without telos. Finality without end, the beauty of the devil. (p 341)

Another direction is announced, one resolutely automatic, one in which the autos is no longer self in human form, but technology itself, having absorbed the human figure in its screens.

Thrown forwards, jerked back, modernity has played itself out on its own technological string. Baudelaire, who glimpsed marvels in the toys of modernity and attributed an artistic and imaginative predestination to them, also hinted at another aesthetic, an aesthetic in which mechanical reproduction succeeds imaginative power and simultaneously transforms, as Benjamin comments, the human sensorium. The cinema screen duplicates and replaces the 'protective shield' of perception-consciousness, calling up and sending away the subject of modernity down another (ateleological) teletechnological line.

The living toy

Alongside toys in Baudelaire's philosophy are related supplementary figures of modernity: the artist that the boy will become, the women that are the condition of that artistic gift, and the poor that evoke feeling amid the urban mass. These figures are crucial in constituting the utopian possibility of modernity, and for Comtean sociology offer the possibility of resistance to the economists and jurists carving up the world. Women, artists and proletarians represent the treasury of 'social feeling' and, imaginarily at least, sustain an idea of humanity against the agglomeration of marketised individuals (Goux, 1998, p 43). On these figures, for Comte, 'all the utopias of the reappropriation of the social bond' rest (Goux, 1998, p 46). But, according to Jean-Joseph Goux (1998), sociology and its visions of human social reconstruction have been surpassed by political economy. Aristotle's three forms of justice – the corrective, the distributive and the commutative – have been replaced by just one, the latter, in the form of 'equivalent exchange'. With the market becoming the 'sole regulator of social life' all bonds dissolve in the face of exchange (pp 37–38). For Goux, 'a new, extremely powerful form of legitimation' (p 41) comes into existence: an 'objectivised and autonomised medium of exchange has created its own order' (p 48). The proletarians, women and artists, that represented for Comte the hope of the human social realm against the incursions of economic modernity, are absorbed: 'we are all, structurally and ontologically, proletarians, women, and artists', it declares (p 49). A 'generalised ontological aesthetisation', rendering each unlocatable and the latter 'the paradigm of all activity', consumes the entirety of experience (pp 49–50), to the point that 'only aesthetic machinations allow the production of lived experience' (p 52).

There is possibly one figure to which these 'aesthetic machinations' still refer. Hollywood and the American culture industries in particular continue to organise their representations in relation to one centre of feeling above all, though this figure around which the economy of autonomised exchange pulsates no longer has anything to do with humanity, women, workers or artists. Utopian potential collapses on a single, ambiguous figure: the child. As Lauren Berlant (1997) argues, in the context of US political economy, 'the nation's value is figured not on behalf of an actually existing and labouring adult, but of a future American, both incipient and prehistorical: especially invested with this hope are the American foetus and the American child' (p 6).

A philosophy of toys might go hand in hand with a concept of childhood, and indeed a certain powerful conception of childhood emerges, as an effect of Romanticism, at the political, philosophical and poetic vanguard of modernity. Most notably, for radicals like Jean-Jacques Rousseau and William Blake, the Romantic child provided a point of natural authority, virtuous innocence and quasi-divinity that was used to denounce and combat the social utilitarianism and secular rationalism that sought to render every aspect of life productive. In such a system, working class children were simply part of the labour force, particularly useful in narrow mine shafts and chimney stacks, so childhood was over by the age of five or six, when the child was ready to earn its living.

In his essay, Baudelaire (1964) also ruminates on the playthings of the poor, and introduces a concept of the toy that exceeds even the most beautiful and expensive toy that captures his own imagination in Mme Panckoucke's toyshop. Baudelaire constructs an almost Dickensian tableau in which two children confront each other either side of a wrought-iron grille, the signifier of the profound divisions of luxury, freedom and class that separate the children. On one side is a pretty, coquettish child who has discarded 'a splendid doll, as neat and clean as its master, rich and glittering, wearing a fine dress and covered with feathers and glass beads' (p 200). Indifferent to this splendid doll, however, the rich child's gaze is intent on the object held by the snot-streaked urchin who stands, among nettles and thistles, in the road on the other side of the grille:

Through those symbolic iron bars the poor child was showing his toy to the rich child, who was greedily examining it, as a rare, unknown object. Now this toy which the little brat was teasing, rattling and shaking in a box with bars, was a live rat! To save money his parents had taken the toy from life itself. (Baudelaire, 1964, p 200)

The joy and fascination offered by an animated rodent, a 'living toy' teased in a box, exceeds the charms of the most beautiful and expensive doll. Moreover, it becomes the model – both in Baudelaire's essay and in the history of the 20th century – for the 'scientific' toys that produce the moving images and animated tricks that become the stock-in-trade of the Hollywood vision machine, to such an extent that the image of a little animated rodent now stands at the masthead of a massive multinational corporation. Mickey Mouse presides over the 'generalised ontological aesthetisation' that consumes the entirety of experience: Disney's machinic productions of animate experience saturate the memory and overwrite the life of contemporary childhood worldwide.

As Goux (1998) argues, postmodernity works like a game which casts modernity away only to return to it, evacuated of human ('adult') illusions, bonds and signifying supplements. But it takes up the 'telos of modernity' in the form of the child and thereby actualises an aesthetic entirely confiscated by economic ideology, in which deliberation is totally absorbed in childlike desire and consumption. Without future or past, it is an aesthetic whose repetitions and escalations are thoroughly ateleological. The social bond is cast away and returned to as a 'commercial and aesthetic production of that bond', no more than a 'spectacle' (p 53), but a spectacle governed by the imagined sensitivities of a child that represents the 'treasury of feeling' in the late 20th and 21st centuries. All mainstream media productions in the US must be suitable for 'family viewing', the benchmark for which is determined by a notional six-year-old child. There is no law governing the social bond, then, but that of the screen and its banal projections, locus of all 'interactivity', all work and all play, aesthetic and economic at the same time, but evacuated of all content.

The Romantic child 'was largely figured as an inversion of Enlightenment virtues and was thus strangely hollow right from the start: *un*corrupted, *un*sophisticated, *un*enlightened ... oddly dispossessed and eviscerated, without much substance' (Kincaid, 1998, p 53). This child, moreover, is sustained in postmodern capitalism as the vacuole around which its commodities, its toys, its luxuries, its candy and its pornography circulate and expand. Everything is sold as if it were a 'toy', an object of play or pleasure, even as desire in its repetition ('fort', 'da') brushes up against the limit of the pleasure principle. At this point, the vacuole is disclosed as precisely an absolute *moral* void, an abyss, at the edge of which structures of parental authority and control tremble. At the edge of this precipice provided by the extimate (interior-exterior) threshold of the child and the child within, social and economic life becomes a highly ambivalent toy law, supplemented by an obscene toy joy that the transgression of that law promises. The joyful supplement of toy law is already implicit in Baudelaire's short essay, not just in the form of the cross-dressed page boy, but primarily in the narrator's auto-affective enjoyment of his own image, as a boy overexcited and stimulated by the velvet and the furs, an excitement that is appropriately sublimated in an image of the child's spontaneous, joyful consumption.

Although toy law, and its terrors, animate all of Hollywood's products, two movies conjure up the spectacular life of living toys more effectively than most. The first fully computer animated movies, *Toy Story* (1995) and *Toy Story 2* (1999), are exemplary in the way that they invert or re-fold the conventional structure of law so that toy adult figures become objects of childhood play. A different order of law and desire is thus introduced in which toy-adults are bound to the arbitrary tyranny of children who are in turn the focus of the economic law of the commodified media images driven by constant technological innovation and obsolescence. This law does not, of course, appeal to the needs and interests of rational subjects ('adults'), but unfolds, as a principle of difference and repetition, in the sovereign world of childhood. An infinity of images and objects stretch into the beyond, the oscillation of childlike desire for novelty providing its only point of limit and regulation. As these movies show, this is the only law that matters: it provides the locus of recognition, utility, morality and love. To be abandoned by the child, who provides the nodal point of desire, use and identity, is to find oneself forgotten, discarded as junk or cryogenised in a heritage museum awaiting rediscovery and re-animation in a retro future. In these movies, made for Disney by Pixar, nostalgia opens onto a vision of human toydom, in which the world is subject to the arbitrary tyranny of a new techno-economic order that takes childhood as its point of sovereign authority, moral value and commercial utility.

Toy Story stages the ambivalence of toy law through juxtaposing the play and the toys of two children, Andy and Sid. Andy appears to be a highly conventional child who plays with his toys in a way prescribed by the manufacturers, supplementing them with the appropriate merchandising – wallpaper, bedspread, lunch box. Meanwhile, his neighbour Sid destroys and dismantles his toys, frequently reassembling them in bizarre and disturbing ways – a baby's head on a mechanical spider's body and so on. These two modes of play provide the basis of two readings of the first movie by Thomas Dumm (1997) who situates the lives of the toys governed by Andy in the context of corporate America and white masculinity. Dumm argues that 'the thematic heart of the film and the major plot device is an allegory about white collar unemployment. The toys live in constant fear that they will be thrown away or put into storage, no longer loved by Andy' (p 90). Significantly, Dumm also notes that *Business Week* reported, shortly before the film's release, that on *Toy Story* 'Only 27 animators were used, as opposed to the 70 or so who worked on *Pocahontas*. Animators make $100,000 or more per year, so Disney saved $10 million on the film' (quoted in Dumm, 1997, p 94). The Disney Corporation therefore participated 'in the very event it reports on and celebrates' (p 94).

But while Dumm's 'majority reading' explores the movie as 'a parable in learning to accept one's diminished circumstances in a post-productive corporate order', he also offers a 'minority reading' that focuses on Sid and his mutant toys. For Dumm, Sid is in 'full-scale subversive rebellion against the consumer order', and his toys are examples of 'genetic subversion', cyborg alternatives to, and transgressive reworkings of, fetishised, white heteronormative commodities. Dumm associates Sid with a kind of 'guerrilla warfare' that is imagined smuggling 'black sperm into white sperm banks', and sees him living out Donna Haraway's Cyborg Manifesto (p 94). This is an optimistic reading of the film. However, *Toy Story 2*, which excludes anyone like Sid, suggests that the biotechnical science that makes possible the 'genetic subversion' and re-engineering of identities, is simply another aspect of the toy law that takes childhood and childhood play out of the purview of the family. Indeed the problems and anxieties concerning identity facing the toy adult figures precisely recall those associated with subjection to a law of playful genetic manipulation, cloning, quasi-corporate parentage (sperm banks), and the latest fantasies concerning biotechnological constructions of identity. Dumm imagines Sid, 'if he succeeds in being employed in future years, as either a computer hacker, or a drug dealer, or perhaps a combination of the two' (p 93), but *Toy Story 2* seems to suggest that Sid would be more likely to become the new creative consultant of Disney Biotech Corp. Sid's childhood play in the first movie has prepared him to fully exploit and exacerbate the anxieties caused by the disruption of heteronormative identity in the playful space of corporate econopoetic experimentation.[2] *Toy Story*'s sequel fully opens out both the movie and its fragile familial referent to this space, disclosing narrative, identity and the family as ateleological aesthetic simulacra whose survival depends upon their success as performances sustaining economic desire. Buzz and Woody are both confronted with their multiplication, redundancy and death, and are given the challenge of finding new uses and joys in a world of playfulness generalised beyond the restricted world of the traditional family and the childhood it defines. In *Toy Story 2*, the remnant of paternal law, cut off from any heritage other than that of the toy museum, is rendered totally subject to the obscene joy of toy law.

Toy joy before death

In November 1999, the *Landover Baptist* reported the following story:

> Children At Risk!
> *Toy Story 2* isn't polluting theatres yet, but *Landover Baptist* has already seen an early script for this disgusting little movie. ... The movie company Walt Disney, run from top to bottom by sodomites, has once again thumbed its rodent nose at traditional family values. ... *Toy Story 2*, a stealthily packaged 'children's' movie, doesn't even pay lip service to the original *Toy Story*. No, instead, it picks up where Caligula left off! This stomach-turning tale is so sexually offensive that even that ungodly crippled pervert Larry Flynt would throw his fat little body from his wheelchair and drag his carcass to the lobby to avoid seeing such putrid computer-generated mess as *Toy Story 2*. The cute boy from the first movie has turned so queer and wears so much eye make-up he looks like he should be in the cast of 'Rent'. And his innocent, sweet toys of youth have now been turned into a minefield of deviant adolescent sexual experimentation. Buzz Lightyear is no longer a battery powered spaceman, but is a turbo-activated hand-held rectal-stimulator with two rotating heads worthy of Black & Decker. ... Woody, living up to his smutty namesake, spends the entire movie spiking the other toys' batteries with powdered Viagra, as all of the toys compete with each other to see who can be the first to mount the sweet little springer spaniel puppies that live in the basement. (Harper and Americhrist, 1999)

---

2 For a discussion of 'econopoesis', the aneconomic principle of creative play integral to postmodern capitalism, see Botting and Wilson, 2000 and 2002b.

It was an internet spoof, of course, its target the illiberal, anti-Semitic, anti-gay, anti-Hollywood American Right. But the power of the joke works precisely at the level of the momentary double take. Woody and Buzz? A Viagra evangelist and a rectal stimulator? Is some Sid-like mischief maker at Pixar having a laugh at the expense of children?

On the shiny, reflective surface of the *Toy Story* movies, some kind of unconscious desire begins to twitch. Looked at from a different perspective, turning on the figure of the child as the point of anamorphosis, another picture emerges from the blurred moral void (see Lacan, 1977). Emptied of all substance, blankly innocent, the child suddenly becomes filled with the banishing summons of a sexual negation. 'Few stories in our culture right now are as popular', notes James Kincaid, 'as those of child molesting' (Kincaid, 1998, p 3). Suddenly, retrospectively, *Toy Story* depicts recognisably adult figures whose all-consuming desire is to be played with by children. Indeed, in the first movie, the main plotline involves the intense rivalry between two men over the affections of a little boy. The last straw, for Woody, comes when Buzz replaces him in Andy's bed, Woody being relegated to the toy box. In the second movie, Buzz is able to restore Woody to his desire for Andy by reminding him of his own advice to Buzz: 'life's only worth living if you are being loved by a kid.' Since child molestation is currently the most powerful taboo in American culture, the joys of playing with children are no doubt highly problematic. In a context where it is no longer possible for adults to 'toy' or 'dally' with children, the *Toy Story* movies play out a fantasy of adult-child love in the utopian space of computer animatronics.

As the *Landover Baptist* suggests, *Toy Story 2* subjects 'traditional family values' to a thorough examination, though not simply through hinting at an unconscious eroticism evident in the games children play with their toys – or in the games toy manufacturers play with the desires of children. *Toy Story 2* is partly about the fate of the family in a corporate culture driven by market imperatives that render it virtually obsolescent, destined for the museum: inefficient, they impede the development of the really flexible labour market that economic competitiveness and growth requires.

Further in this register (rather than that of sexual transgression), *Toy Story 2* is ordered according to a logic of obscenity, designed primarily as a marketing tool rather than as a stand-alone, autonomous film. Like so many Hollywood movies, *Toy Story 2* shamelessly foregrounds its promotional function and is dominated by normally off screen 'extra-textual' elements that formally draw attention to it. The 'obscene' is brought on screen from the opening scenes of the movie. It begins with a parody of *Star Wars: The Phantom Menace*, Buzz battling with the evil Emperor Zurg. This sequence is quickly revealed to be not from a movie as such, but to constitute the climax to one of the levels of the *Toy Story 2* video game.[3] The moment that 'Buzz' dies at the hands of Zurg, the words 'GAME OVER' appear and

---

3   The video version of the first movie, *Toy Story* opens with a trailer for Disney Interactive's CD Rom Storybook and video game available in both Sega Mega Drive and Nintendo formats.

the camera 'pulls back' to reveal Rex the dinosaur gripping the handset of a SNES games console, watched admiringly by a Buzz who comments that, despite Rex's recent failure, he is better at being Buzz than the toy space ranger himself. Later, Buzz, whose 'education' in the first movie required him to renounce his delusions of authenticity and accept his status as a simulacrum, will be confronted with the dizzying spectacle of hundreds of Buzz clones in Al's Toy Barn superstore, as a Barbie 'tour guide' comments on the failure of retailers to anticipate demand for the Buzz Lightyear doll following the success of the first movie in 1995. Elsewhere, Rex is described as 'the toy that comes with the meal', and Woody discovers his 'real' identity as the missing piece of a large collection of merchandise from a 1950s TV cowboy puppet show called *Woody's Round Up*. The obscenity reaches a bizarre climax when, after the closing credits, a series of 'out-takes' are shown depicting the toys fluffing their lines, playing practical jokes on one another, letting fly involuntary, improbable farts and, in the case of Stinky Pete, trying to get into a threesome with twin Barbies. 'Are you two really identical', purrs the stinky old prospector as he promises them a larger role in the movie. This 'postmodern' playfulness apparently transgresses the traditional limits of the movie world and its frame, as if blurring the boundaries between the film and its context, the work and its process of production, between the real and the artificial, the original and the copy. But it can do this in such a seamless way because everything has been rendered equivalent according to a techno-economic logic of infinite exchangeability, something that is precisely made possible by the digital reformatting of all phenomena. That is the hypermodern, 'post-human' promise of the movie.

It is in this way that the movie's ambivalent toy law continues to operate, in which a certain heteronormativity is disclosed to be the purely performative, secondary effect of a general digital iterability opening on to an infinite exchange of possibilities. In a process that marries Judith Butler's queer theory with postmodern capitalism, the movie's self-reflexivity reminds us that these toys are 'realised' through a process of speculative 'performativity'. Woody and Buzz bring themselves into being as real toys through the 'speech act' of movie marketing and the successful merchandising. Further, the second movie makes it clear that there is no contradiction between Tom Dumm's 'majority' and 'minority' readings. Sid's 'genetic subversion' is the general condition of reproduction, as reproduction takes place according to biotechnical corporate lines of economic performativity, rather than through the metaphor of the traditional family. Buzzes multiply or Buzzes disappear according to their performance.

This transformation is of course what underlies anxieties in the plots of both pictures, supposedly set, as they are, in the context of a normative family. A curiosity of the first picture, however, was that Andy was apparently part of a one parent family; he has no father, and his toys seem to express their anxieties in, as Dumm (1997) says, 'corporate submissive terms' (p 89). This continues in *Toy Story 2*, where Woody gives a seminar to the other toys on what to do while he's away at cowboy camp with Andy. Woody's torn arm, and his placement on the broken toy shelf, precipitate Woody's nightmare of redundancy, becoming waste and disappearing into a trashcan. From the toys' point of view, this 'family' operates according to the most ruthless economic principles in which desirability and performance totally determine survival. Ironically, it is while he is trying to rescue Wheezy (the plastic penguin who has lost his squeak) from a yard sale that Woody's value as rare merchandise is recognised by a toy collector who steals him in order to sell him on to a toy museum in Japan. It is this discovery that causes a crisis in Woody, and in the movie.

Woody discovers his 'true' toy family, the 'Round Up Gang'. Though he has presumably never met them before, this is where he symbolically 'belongs' and they greet him as if he were a long lost family member. Unlike Andy's family, there is no mother, but Woody has a cowgirl sister-figure called Jessie, a pet mule that behaves like a puppy, and an obscene father-figure called Stinky Pete, an old prospector. Significantly, Stinky Pete remains mummified in his box, having never been desired, bought and played with by a child. The Round Up Gang have been left in a state of suspended animation, awaiting the discovery of a Woody in some yard sale somewhere, so that they can be reunited in the museum. At first, Woody is appalled by the prospect, but a combination of his narcissistic affection for the authenticity of his image in the pantheon of merchandised TV toys, and the horror of the inevitable abandonment by the child that Jessie's song relates – the sentimental tour de force of the movie – succeeds in reconciling Woody to his fate. This fate, a curious combination of archivisation and cryogenics in which an imaginary identity might be held in suspension in a symbolic order, is perhaps the destiny of everyone in so far as everyone has become film, ready to be re-animated as a ghost in a film, video album or photo archive of popular memory.[4] Or as a TV re-run. Certainly, it is the destiny of the traditional, heteronormative, nuclear family as it has been relayed on proliferating TV screens since the 1950s. As *Toy Story 2* demonstrates, the traditional family still retains a nostalgic charge, but largely as a repressive structure against which to project more exciting variations. Significantly, successful representations of family life are only possible through re-routing the family through a logic of deviancy and dysfunction, as shown in *The Simpsons* or *The Osbournes*.

Accordingly, Woody's heterogeneous assortment of chums from Andy's toy box rescue him from his newly discovered family and he resolves to go back to Andy's bedroom, taking his new family with him. The final sequence of the film follows the adventures of the toys as they take their homeward journey, Woody heroically rescuing Jessie from the aeroplane scheduled for Japan. Significantly, however, Stinky Pete is lost along the way. With the obscene 'father-figure' gone, the film ends with a series of affirmations of romantic and familial heteronormativity. 'Oh Bullseye', says Jessie to the mule, 'We're part of a family again'. However, though Jessie is rescued by Woody in the manner of a screwball romantic adventure, his relationship with her is apparently too fraternal to end in a fully acknowledged romance or 'marriage'. Back at Andy's, Woody returns to the insipid Bo Peep, and the hitherto exclusively homosocial Buzz notices, after a particularly impressive bit of athletic business, the energetic cowgirl as if for the first time. It's love. Even Mr Potatohead returns to adopt, with Mrs Potatohead, all the little arcade aliens with

---

4   It is also a little reminiscent of Walt Disney himself, whose interest and faith in biotechnology was such that he apparently had his head cryogenised, thus leaving his fate at the hands of the biotechnoscience of the future.

the cargo-cult culture. As a series of climactic reunions, it is positively Shakespearean.

However, as so often with Shakespeare, there is something about these pairings that does not quite ring true. The instant attraction of Buzz and Jessie is particularly unsatisfactory. Totally unprepared in the narrative, it only makes sense in movie-psychoanalytic terms as a displacement, and sublimation, of Buzz's buddy-romance with Woody. And it is her tomboy athleticism that particularly impresses him, after all. But Buzz's buddy romance with Woody is reaffirmed by the latter in the final statement of the movie. 'It'll be fun while it lasts', says Woody, referring to his uncertain future in Andy's affections, 'and when it ends I'll have old Buzz Lightyear to keep me company – to infinity and beyond!' It is Buzz and Woody, not Buzz and Jessie, who are imagined living together (happily or not), in the unknown future beyond their existence as Andy's playthings. Similarly, Jessie's future is re-routed elsewhere, in the direction of Andy's little sister. All the toys are returned to the 'reality' of an existence at the whim of a child's playful desire and the toy law that articulates it. This law of repetition, that is sustained by the introduction of minor differences, has already suggested an infinite number of different and endlessly repeated possibilities for the toys.

Buzz himself has already glimpsed a different future for himself earlier in the mall. The new Buzz-upgrade (with whom 'old Buzz' wrestles in the mall) discovers, in a parody of the *Star Wars* movies, that Buzz's arch enemy, the evil Emperor Zurg, is in fact his long lost father. Just before his cliffhanging death in the elevator shaft, Buzz says to Zurg: 'You killed my father', to which Zurg replies, 'No, I *am* your father'. Buzz's rapid acknowledgment, horror and grief, 'father', he cries as Zurg plummets down the elevator shaft, is just as rapidly resolved a few scenes later when Buzz and Zurg are rediscovered playing frisbee together in a moment of paternal bonding, again centred on play: 'You're a great Dad', says Buzz. An instant oedipalism is resolved into a utopia of game playing in a rapid oscillation of thrills, spills and comforting returns. Just like the video game with which the film began, in which Buzz and Zurg endlessly fight it out on different levels of difficulty, each conflict and death heralding a comforting return of a new Buzz and a new Zurg in the form of another game. Oedipal romance has here become re-routed and hard wired into the structure of computer software, the economic mechanism of a child's game.

PART 2
AESTHETICS AND VISUAL
TECHNOLOGIES

Chapter 6
On realism and the law film: the case of Oscar Wilde

Leslie J Moran

Introduction

Writing in the 1940s, Hesketh Pearson (1946) noted a common characteristic of biographical accounts of the life of Oscar Wilde; they were dominated by Wilde's encounters with the criminal law in a series of three trials.[1] Wilde's prosecution of the Marquis of Queensbury for criminal libel was the first. The two subsequent trials were prosecutions by the state against Wilde on the basis of charges of gross indecency with various men. In the final trial, Wilde was found guilty and sentenced to two years' imprisonment with hard labour which he served in Reading Gaol.[2] The first two films of Wilde's life[3] (both were made in Britain), *Oscar Wilde*, directed by Gregory Ratoff (1960), starring Robert Morley as Wilde and *The Trials of*

---

1   Pearson's own biographical project was to challenge this tradition, to recreate Wilde, to emphasise his wit and humour rather than his martyrdom by way of the law. Pearson explained that this required that the criminal trials be put in perspective and not allowed to 'overshadow the rest' (Pearson, 1946, pp 2–3). More recently, Neil Bartlett's seminal work on Wilde (1988) raises a similar issue about the framing of Wilde's life (p 29).

2   The charge of criminal libel, initiated by Wilde against the Marquis of Queensbury, related to Queensbury's allegation that Wilde was posing as a 'somdomite' (*sic*). In the charge of criminal libel, Wilde claimed that this libel threatened the peace. Queensbury's defence was that the statement was true. The first trial collapsed when it appeared that Queensbury had evidence in support of his claim. The second and third legal actions, initiated by the state against Wilde for the offence of gross indecency, arose out of Queensbury's allegations and evidence. Gross indecency was and continues to be an offence in English law. At the time of Wilde's prosecution, it was to be found in s 11 of the Criminal Law Amendment Act 1885 which reads as follows:

> Any male person who, in public or private commits or is party to the commission of, or procures or attempts to procure the commission by any male person of, any act of gross indecency with another male person shall be guilty of a misdemeanour, and being convicted thereof shall be liable at the discretion of the court to be imprisoned for any term not exceeding two years, with or without hard labour.

The offence is now to be found in s 13 of the Sexual Offences Act 1956. Reform proposals published in 2002 propose the abolition of gross indecency.

3   This was not the first time Wilde had appeared on the big screen. The earliest film versions of Wilde's work dates from 1915. There is a lost Russian version of *The Picture of Dorian Gray*, directed by and starring Meyerhold, and a British *Lady Windermere's Fan*, also of 1915. The first talking film version of a Wilde play, *Lady Windermere's Fan*, directed by Ernst Lubitsch, appeared in 1925. Productions of Wilde's book, *The Picture of Dorian Gray* (1945), and the plays, *An Ideal Husband* (1947) and *The Importance of Being Earnest* (1952), followed. Clearly these are films of Wilde's literary works. However, this does not necessarily mean that they were unconnected with the Wilde of the criminal trials. Arthur Ransome, one of Wilde's early literary champions, commented that such was the pervasiveness of stories about Wilde's encounters with the criminal law that commentators on Wilde's writings found '... a law court ... and heard the clink of handcuffs ...' (Ransome, 1912, pp 9–10) in all of Wilde's work. Thus, while these films are in one sense remote from the criminal trials, it would be wrong to conclude that their production, distribution or consumption are necessarily unconnected with those trials in particular, or stories of law and (in)justice more generally. As I've suggested elsewhere, Wilde is something of an iconic figure in the context of matters of law and homosexuality: see Moran, 1998a.

Oscar Wilde,[4] directed by Ken Hughes (1960), starring Peter Finch in the title role, follow this pattern.[5] The triangular relationship of Wilde, Bosie (Lord Alfred Douglas) and Bosie's father, the Marquis of Queensbury, dominates both films. In both, law frames this relationship and has a pivotal organisational role in the narrative. The criminal law in general, and courtroom scenes in particular, provides the dramatic core of the two films (Baker, 1960; Elley, 1994, p 946). More specifically, much of each film is dedicated to a representation of courtroom processes associated with the first two trials: the reading of the criminal charges; the examination-in-chief of various witnesses and their cross-examination; various interactions between senior counsel and between counsel and the judge. In each film, much of the rest of the story is devoted to setting the scene for the trials. In addition to this focus on the courtroom, the two films deal with a range of other legal issues, such as blackmail, human rights (Anon, 1968) and wider matters of social justice and injustice (NH, 1960).[6]

The dominance of the courtroom and of legal themes within these two films readily brings them within the general category of a law film (Black, 1999; Chase, 2002; Denvir, 1996; Greenfield, Osborn and Robson, 2001; Machura and Robson, 2001). In addition, as biographical and historical works these films situate the law theme in a particular context: both films have a concern with the representation of actual events. Greenfield, Osborn and Robson note (2001, Chapter 3) law films based on real events provide a particular instance in which there is a strong demand for, and expectation of, the truth of the image, its accuracy and its authenticity. Other factors add further weight to the importance of these characteristics in relation to the two Wilde films. As costume and historical dramas, the demand for and expectation of the accuracy and authenticity of the cinematic image is of great importance (Cook, 1996).[7] Accuracy and authenticity are also traits associated with 'quality British cinema' (Cook, 1996, p 53), a category which may be applied to both films. Together these demands work to situate the two films about Wilde's encounters with law within the cinematic context of realism. My objective in this chapter is to use these two films of Wilde's encounters with the law to explore the

---

4   In the US the film had a different title, *The Man with the Green Carnation*.

5   The third biographical film, *Wilde*, again made in Britain, starring British comedian Stephen Fry playing Wilde, directed by Brian Gilbert, premiered in 1997. Gilbert's film offers something of a departure from the earlier representations of Wilde's life. Much more time is devoted to Wilde's relations with his wife and children as well as with his various male lovers. While the law, in the form of trial scenes, still plays a significant role within the biographical film, there is a shift to emphasise Wilde's experience of punishment, focusing on the brutality of it (cf Ryans, 1997).

6   Many of these issues echo debates arising out of a contemporary review of the laws which criminalised consensual sexual relations between men ('homosexual offences'), and proposals for reform which arose out of a government sponsored review of the current law undertaken by the Wolfenden committee (1957).

7   Richard Dyer (2002, Chapter 14) makes no reference to *Oscar Wilde* or *The Trials* in his filmography of gay and lesbian heritage cinema. He does include *Wilde* under that category. In part this reflects the way the category is associated with the late 1970s and 1980s. In part it reflects a difference that Dyer draws between historical drama and heritage. The former, he argues, is concerned with enquiry into the past which seeks to understand the past in contrast to heritage which is, 'an attitude towards the legacy of the past [that] values [things past] for their own sake ...' (p 206). On *Wilde* as heritage cinema, see Davis, forthcoming.

nature of realism in the context of the law film. In doing so, my objective is to engage with and problematise the dominant realist assumptions and demands that have not only informed so much law and film scholarship (cf Bergman and Asimow, 1996; Greenfield, Osborn and Robson, 2001; Rafter, 2000), but are also central to the creation, production and wider reception of law films.

The contested and contentious terrain of realism within film and television production and scholarship[8] has produced a series of different approaches to realism which are concerned with both forms of content and forms of expression and their interrelationship. Realism is in general a mode of description/depiction that refers to a particular relation between two objects: the thing described/depicted (that which is outside and before the text) and the result of the process of description/depiction (that which is 'in' the text). Quoting Roman Jakobson, Paul Willemen explains realism in the following terms, as 'an artistic trend which aims to reproduce reality as faithfully as possible and which aspires to achieve the maximum of verisimilitude' (Jakobson quoted in Willemen, 1972–73, p 36). The term verisimilitude, Willemen explains, suggests that the truth of the representation is influenced by social convention which may be understood as 'rules of a genre' or artistic conventions which are understood as a 'set of restrictions within a particular culture' (p 38). Jakobson highlights the way in which realism may be used in various contexts: as a tendency or aspiration that informs the process of production; a subjective value judgment made by the reader/viewer and as a movement (originally a literary movement with its origins in the 19th century) that now operates as a more general yardstick by which representation is understood (cf Williams, 1977). The importance of realism in relation to cinema (and television), Corner (1992) suggests, is associated with the apparent ability of cinema to record visual likeness and to move a viewpoint through space (p 98). I want to refer to three forms of realism (cf Williams, 1994, p 277). The first is described as 'empiricist realism'. This category of realism emphasises the ability to close the gap between the thing represented and the representation, be it in relation to the likeness of setting, social action or theme (Corner, 1992, p 101). Here an assumption is that the world can be both fully known and fully reconstructed in front of the camera, in the pro-filmic event (Willemen, 1972–73, p 38), and recorded by way of the film (or television) camera. As an ideal type, this provides one model of realism which may be realised with varying degrees of success. A second form of realism has been described by some as 'bourgeois realism' (Gaines, 1999, p 2) and more commonly as 'classical realism', being a realism commonly associated with 'Classical Hollywood Cinema' (Williams, 1994, p 277). Central to this model is a realism produced by way of the suppression of the marks of cultural production which, explains Ang (writing in the context of television), works to produce and sustain the seamlessness that is 'the realistic illusion' (Ang, 1982, p 38). The third form of realism I want to refer to has been called 'emotional realism' (Williams, 1994, p 277). Emotional realism operates by connotation. Ang (1982) explains it in the following terms:

---

8 My use of scholarship concerned with television in the context of this chapter on cinema is not to suggest that cinema and television are the same media. As Corner (1992, pp 97–98) suggests, the text/reality relations in the context of television are significantly different from those in relation to cinema. I have attempted to draw on insights from television scholarship which are equally significant in relation to cinema.

... the same things, people, relations, and situations, which are regarded at the denotative level as unrealistic, and unreal, are at [the] connotative level apparently not seen at all as unreal, but in fact as 'recognisable'. (p 42)

I want to use these three models of realism to examine the operation of realism in the context of the two law films about Wilde's life mentioned above. I begin my exploration of realism in relation to the scripts of the two films, albeit in perhaps an unexpected context, litigation before the English High Court, *Warwick v Eisenger and Others* (1969). While the script, and narrative more generally, may occupy an important position in the fabrication of realism in cinema, I do not want to limit my consideration of realism to the narration of events. To do so would be to ignore a wide range of other dimensions of cinema that are at work in the generation of realism (Williams, 1994). I then turn my attention to material produced by the film companies to promote the consumption of the films. A study of these materials provides an opportunity to bring other dimensions of the apparatus of realism in cinema into view. My third source of data is a small selection of contemporary reviews of the film. These offer a different context in which to consider the nature and operation of assumptions of realism (the reader/viewer perspective), albeit a rather specialist reader/viewer: the film critic. The two films provoked very different reactions from contemporary film critics.[9] *The Trials* was critically acclaimed, winning prizes at various film festivals in Moscow and Venice. In sharp contrast, *Oscar Wilde* was described in withering terms as 'a bad bad film' (Baker, 1960).[10] Together, the judgment of the litigation, the publicity materials and the contemporary reviews of the films offer various insights into different aspects of realism in relation to law films.

The truth of The Trials in court

Judicial consideration of the truthfulness and authenticity of the depiction of Oscar Wilde's criminalisation in the scripts of the two films is to be found in a law report relating to litigation arising out of the simultaneous production and release of the two films. In April 1960, Warwick Film Productions Ltd, the production company of *The Trials of Oscar Wilde*, petitioned the High Court in London on the basis of breach of copyright, to obtain an interlocutory injunction against the scriptwriter (Jo Eisenger), director (Gregory Ratoff), production company (Vantage Films Ltd) and distributor (20th Century Fox) of *Oscar Wilde*. Warwick's immediate objective, to obtain an injunction to stop the premier of *Oscar Wilde*, was unsuccessful. That film premiered first, just five days before *The Trials*.[11]

---

9 Similar contrasting reactions to the film are to be found outside Britain. Eg, see Bosley Crowther's reviews of the two films in *The New York Times* (1970a; 1970b).

10 The fate of the films is also significantly different: *The Trials* has been shown on British TV on a regular basis, while *Oscar Wilde* has largely disappeared from view. There is perhaps a need for some caution here as there may be other factors limiting the availability of the latter, such as ownership of the rights of distribution and reproduction.

11 In the wake of this failed application the plaintiffs, the subsequent trial judge, Mr Justice Plowman, explained, 'lost any enthusiasm they ever had for bringing their action to trial' (*Warwick v Eisenger* (1969), p 512). The litigation relating to the substance of the copyright claim lingered on for a further seven years.

Central to Warwick's legal action were two books that purported to be verbatim accounts[12] of the trials based on the notes of contemporary shorthand writers: H Montgomery Hyde's *The Trials of Oscar Wilde* (Montgomery Hyde, 1948) and an earlier text of the trials (first published anonymously) by Christopher Millard,[13] *Oscar Wilde: Three Times Tried* (1912). It was these 'verbatim accounts' which made up the dramatic core of the two films. Resort by the respective scriptwriters in both films to these supposedly verbatim accounts of the trials is an aspect of the realist tendency or aspirations of both films. Warwick claimed that the script of the defendants, in its account of the trials, violated its rights of copyright in the texts of Montgomery Hyde and Millard.

Jo Eisenger is a key figure connecting the verbatim accounts of the trials in these books to both film projects. Eisenger developed his interest in making a film about Oscar Wilde after seeing a stage play *Oscar Wilde*, written by Leslie and Sewell Stokes and starring Robert Morley in the title role, in New York in 1938. A distinctive feature of the play was its use of extracts from accounts of the three criminal trials involving Wilde. The play drew upon Christopher Millard's book of the verbatim records of the trials. Drawing inspiration from the stage play, Eisenger planned to develop a film that would not only make extensive use of the trial scenes in the play and Millard's verbatim accounts, but also use Montgomery Hyde's more recent (and purportedly more accurate) account as a key source of information.[14] Early discussions about the making of such a film, with 20th Century Fox in the USA came to a halt on the basis that the censorship code, the American Motion Picture Producers Code, would make the film difficult to produce and distribute. Eisenger then pursued his project in Britain with a number of individuals, including the director Ken Hughes. When these discussions broke down, in good part due to Eisenger's failure to write the script, Eisenger went on to develop and realise his project, *Oscar Wilde*, with Gregory Ratoff, Vantage Films and 20th Century Fox. Working with Warwick Film Productions, which obtained rights in Montgomery Hyde's text, Ken Hughes wrote the script and subsequently directed *The Trials of Oscar Wilde*.

Warwick's copyright claim had two connected dimensions: exclusive rights in Montgomery Hyde's text and rights in Millard's text. In part this reflected the fact

---

12 These verbatim accounts have their origins in a well-established literary tradition of Wildean scholarship, part biography and part true crime story, which purported to reproduce the authentic transcripts of the criminal trials. The Wildean trials literature is probably older, and certainly as durable, as biographical and literary writings about Wilde's life and work. The first example is an anonymous pamphlet published in April 1895, *Just Out. Complete. The Life of Oscar Wilde as Prosecutor and Prisoner* (Anon, 1895), being closely followed by a pamphlet entitled *Gentle Criticisms on British Justice*, 'authored' by I Playfair (1895). Charles Grolleau's *The Trial of Oscar Wilde from the Shorthand Report* (1906), printed privately (500 copies) and published for Charles Carrington, was one of the first books to be published on Wilde after his death in 1900. A new volume within this tradition was published by Merlin Holland (2003), Oscar Wilde's grandson. It purports to be the full transcript of the criminal libel trial in which Wilde prosecuted the Marquis of Queensbury.

13 Christopher Millard also wrote under the pseudonym of Stuart Mason.

14 Montgomery Hyde's text was reprinted in 1962 and 1973. The 1973 edition was also an amended version of the account. Montgomery Hyde explained that the changes were made as he was no longer shackled by the threat of prosecution under the obscenity laws. He explained that 'paraphrase' could now be replaced by 'verbatim' account.

that Montgomery Hyde's text drew extensively on the 'verbatim accounts' found in Millard's text. The court accepted Warwick's rights in Montgomery Hyde's text, but rejected their interests in Millard's text on the basis that the plaintiffs could not prove their interest in Millard's text.[15] First, I want to briefly address the conundrum raised by the court's conclusion that Montgomery Hyde's 'verbatim accounts' of the trials gave rise to interests in copyright.

In order to unravel this, we need to consider the relationship between the two texts. Having concluded that the Millard book was 'a literary work' in which copyright subsisted (*Warwick* (1969), p 516), the court's rejection of Warwick's copyright interest in that text threatened to undermine the possibility of Montgomery Hyde's copyright in the trial accounts; Montgomery Hyde had made extensive use of Millard's text (pirated material) and no copyright can exist in a pirated (unoriginal) text (*Warwick* (1969), p 530). However, ultimately this did not prevent a conclusion that copyright did exist in Montgomery Hyde's text. His book, the court concluded, amounted to something more than the mere copying of the Millard text; it contained material gathered from various other sources. In addition, while some parts of Millard's text had been edited and some parts merely copied, they were also conjoined[16] with new additions made by Montgomery Hyde. Their combination, the court concluded, made Montgomery Hyde's text a literary work. However, despite this conclusion, Warwick's action for breach of copyright both at the interlocutory and final hearing failed. Eisenger's script, the court concluded, combined edited and unedited trial accounts, being a selection of materials from Montgomery Hyde's work, many of which were sections copied from Millard. His use of these extracts did not amount to a breach of Warwick's interests in the copyright of Montgomery Hyde's book (*Warwick* (1969), p 533). In giving judgment on these matters, Mr Justice Plowman explored the history and nature of both the 'verbatim accounts' of the trials found in the books of the trials. He also examined Eisenger's assumptions about these accounts and the way they informed his use of them in the development of the script of *Oscar Wilde*. It is to these matters that I now want to turn.

An important finding by the court is in the judge's descriptions of 'the verbatim accounts' produced in the book by Millard, which the judge described as a 'source-book for subsequent studies in the same field' (*Warwick* (1969), p 516) and specifically for Montgomery Hyde's book. Mr Justice Plowman found that Millard had engaged in an extensive project of selecting, editing and changing material. Millard's 'verbatim accounts', Plowman J concluded, were far from a report of every word of the trials, being more the result of 'a drastic process of selection'. Furthermore, that selection, and the process of production in general, reflected the fact that the text was produced by someone who 'was sympathetic to Oscar Wilde'

---

15 Millard's book had originally been published anonymously. In such an instance, s 20(4) of the Copyright Act 1956 brought into play a presumption that the copyright was in the publisher. The court concluded that Warwick had made no attempt to trace their title in the work through the publishers and had failed to provide sufficient evidence to set aside the presumption, and as such could not rely on an argument which located their interests in the author, Millard. See *Warwick* (1969), pp 516–24.

16 The judge uses the term 'collocation', which is a process of joining together, to explain how copyright relating to the book as a whole may include the use of unoriginal material. The right has its origins in the labour through which the text is produced.

(*Warwick* (1969), p 516). Likewise, Montgomery Hyde's book is described as an assemblage of many different sources of material (*Warwick* (1969), p 524), including substantial amounts of the Millard text. In general, Plowman concluded that, in producing his version of the 'verbatim accounts', Montgomery Hyde had:

> ... added material, omitted material, made verbal alterations, rearranged material, transposed material and abbreviated material ... [and] frequently put into *oratorio recta* speeches which were reported in [Millard's text] in *oratorio obliqua*. (*Warwick* (1969), p 525)

The 'real life' of the trials, connoted by way of the phrase 'verbatim accounts' in relation to these two books of the trials, is shown here to be a fabrication deeply informed, at least, by the creative process of writing according to particular conventions of storytelling associated with writing famous trials for popular consumption, and informed by a particular perspective on the proceedings.

It is these already mediated accounts of 'real life' that were the point of departure for the films. The judicial revelation and determination that these texts were already mediated representations of the trials should not distract from Eisenger's apparently different point of departure. From the judgment it would appear that he took the work of Montgomery Hyde to be little more than a transcript, an unmediated record of the event. This was illustrated by way of his use of the texts. He explained to the trial court that he only copied those parts of Montgomery Hyde's text that purported to be true reports of the trial record, leaving out material in brackets which was said to be Montgomery Hyde's commentary on the trial texts. Not only was this material (speeches of counsel, words of the judge and questions to and answers by Oscar Wilde) set out as a verbatim exchange in Montgomery Hyde's book, but, Eisenger explained, their repetition in other works, in particular in Millard's book, led him to conclude that they were nothing other than verbatim accounts. This approach to the text was central to his successful defence that in copying the courtroom exchanges he had not violated copyright. As actual records of the proceedings, he argued, neither Millard nor Montgomery Hyde, as mere copiers of prior shorthand accounts, could have rights in those records. Eisenger added a final flourish. He explained he had never 'heard anybody screaming that, "This belongs to me"' (*Warwick* (1969), p 527). These assumptions of the truth of the texts and their relation to the courtroom interactions evidence the realist tendencies and aspirations at work in the production of the script.

However, there is a need for caution here, as this is not to suggest that Eisenger's script is merely a compilation of these 'verbatim accounts'. Eisenger explained that his approach was more creative than this might suggest. He also made additions and joined extracts up with other extracts from other texts. During the course of the cross-examination, he explained the techniques used to weave these various texts together in the following terms:

> When I sat down to work with the Hyde book and with the Stokes play, I also had other material-sources. I had the Hesketh Pearson book and various others. I marked the Hyde book, comparing it with the testimony which I found in the Stokes play; and then I looked to see if there was other testimony which would be useful in the cinema which Stokes had not used out of the trial record ... I did not follow the continuity of the actual trial record. Some scenes were taken. I say 'scenes', I mean some actual portions of the actual trial I took out of context, either ahead or behind their actual point of development. (*Warwick* (1969), p 526)

Eisenger went on to explain that once he had compiled his notebook from the various texts, a further reshaping took place:

> I then created many passages in the trials, which actually never took place in the trials - passages between Sir Edward Carson and Oscar Wilde. I did not falsify, but I dramatised the prevailing attitudes between Carson and Wilde by creating passages. (*Warwick* (1969), p 527)

Subsequently, as a result of conversations with Robert Morley who had played Wilde in the Stokes' stage play *Oscar Wilde*, Eisenger made further changes to the script (including changes to the trial scenes) to enhance its dramatic value.

This judgment offers an insight into the significance and operation of realist tendencies and aspirations associated with the resort to particular sources of information about real life events, the 'verbatim accounts', and the interface between these 'real life' sources and the script. The evidence of the scriptwriting process found in the judgment draws attention to the way in which the 'real event' of Wilde's encounters with the institutions and processes of criminal justice is both a key point of reference and something of a receding point of origin that is not so much captured by the process of recording and writing, but something that always escapes the various attempts to faithfully represent the real event. The persistent absence of the 'real event' is not peculiar to the script that is to be transformed into the visual medium of cinema, but a characteristic of all the texts that purport to offer authentic accounts of real events. Eisenger's explanation of scriptwriting as a process of writing real life into the script highlights the artifice through which the 'reality' of the courtroom encounters[17] is mediated in the service of the production of drama for the cinema.

How are we to make sense of this in terms of realism in the cinema? The three models of realism outlined above offer some assistance here. Realism seems to operate in various ways in this context. Perhaps the strongest realist aspirations are those associated with 'empiricist realism'. The importance given to the 'verbatim accounts' in the fabrication of the scripts suggests an aspiration towards the production of a representation that seeks to achieve a likeness of social interaction and social setting. Yet, at the same time, Eisenger's description of the process of scriptwriting makes it difficult to sustain this particular approach to realism. However, it would be premature to reject the realist aspirations on this basis alone. Eisenger's reference to the importance of dramatic effect and his fabrication of courtroom interactions to articulate and depict 'prevailing attitudes' might suggest that the process also engages with another realism, emotional realism. Finally, the demands of dramatisation might also relate to 'bourgeois' or 'classical' realism, which works to ensure that the narrative sustains an illusion of cinematic 'real life', which may have particular importance in the context of costume, historical and indigenous cinema. It is perhaps in the combination of these different realisms that we need to understand the realist tendencies and aspirations of the resort to, and

---

17 Richard Sherwin (2000) argues that law cases always engage in a battle over the construction of reality. As such, there is never an unmediated reality either in law or prior to law's representation in other cultural forms.

the significance of, the verbatim accounts of the trials in the generation of the script and narrative of the two films about Wilde's encounters with the criminal law. But an analysis of realism in this cinema of law that focuses only on the script of the films or more generally on the narrative of the films is problematic. Christopher Williams (1994) has argued realism in the cinema is not produced by way of the script/narrative alone. While it may play a significant role, the narrative needs to be placed within the context of a wider and more complex ensemble of techniques of representation. It is to these other dimensions of cinema that I now want to turn.

The institutions and aesthetics of authenticity

I want to begin my consideration of the wider apparatus of realism as it is found in these two films about law by turning to the Press Book of *Oscar Wilde*[18] and the Campaign Book of *The Trials*. Both contain a wide variety of 'exploitation strategies' which highlight the 'real life' basis of the two films. In this context, the realist tendencies and aspirations appear in the context of the promotion and commodification of the film. The Campaign Book contains a wider variety of 'exploitation strategies' designed to promote the sale of the film. I want to focus here upon that text. It includes model press stories serialising and summarising the film's story and telling of the making of the film, star biographies, 'catchlines' (model headlines) offered as devices 'to sell the picture', ideas for various games and competitions such as a crossword puzzle and a 'coach and cab stunt', a wide catalogue of pictures and posters for widow displays, free gifts ('star postcard size throwaways') and information about book tie-ups, to name but a few. Under the headline, 'Authentic and Beautiful – "The Trials of Oscar Wilde"', a model press story reads:

> In exciting Technicolor and Super Technirama it brings all the colour of Wilde's day to the screen. The interior and exterior of the old St James's Theatre in all its glittering glory ... the interior of the Café Royal ... exteriors of London recapturing the gaslight and hansom cab atmosphere of Victoriana ...

Later in the same article we are informed that the production designer, Ken Adam:

> ... spared nothing in reproducing the atmosphere of the period ... He roamed the antique shops to ... dress his gigantic sets ... authentic to the very last detail. (*The Trials of Oscar Wilde* Campaign Book, 1960)

These extracts from the Campaign Book draw attention to two further dimensions of realism in these law films. The first and perhaps the more familiar realism, that associated with 'empiricist realism', takes the form of a range of techniques that seek to reconstruct Wildean London as a pro-filmic event according to requirements of authenticity associated with meticulous attention to the detail of the sets. The use of the term 'atmosphere' is of interest here as it suggests not so much a realism that is a literal reproduction (denotation) of Victorian London, but a realism that is produced in the context of something less tangible than specific selected objects. At

---

18 The only remaining archive copy of the Press Book is described in the British Film Institute Library as a 'Small Press Book'. It is much less extensive than the Campaign Book of *The Trials*.

the same time, the atmosphere is generated through these specific objects, by connotation. As such, the reference to atmosphere points towards the significance of emotional realism in the fabrication of the pro-filmic event. The second dimension of realism in these extracts is perhaps less familiar. It is to be found in the references to the technology of cinema: 'Technicolor and Super Technirama'. One of the model headlines (the 'catchlines') suggested for use in writing stories to sell the film is, 'So big it could only be told in Technirama and Technicolor'. In sharp contrast to the other suggested headlines that might locate the realism of the film by way of familiar aspects of the narrative of Wilde's encounter with the law, such as 'The Story of a Love That Dare Not Speak Its Name', 'The Shocking Scandal That Shook a Nation', 'He Was Condemned as Being at the Centre of a Circle of Corruption', 'So big ...' focuses attention upon the technology of the cinema. More specifically, 'So big ...' frames the depiction by reference to the novelty and specific features of the medium through which the story is told, the visual image, the cinematic apparatus, and more specifically, with particular reference to the size and shape of the film stock and a new technology of wide screen cinema (Technirama). As Willemen (1972–73) notes, many technological developments in cinema have been informed by realist assumptions and aspirations about the nature and role of the movie technology, and of the need to improve that technology with a view to improving its ability to reproduce reality accurately (p 38).[19] In this instance, Technirama was a technological development designed to correct distortions of the image found in other wide screen technologies (Neil, 1996), and Technicolor, a particular colour cinematography that could improve the quality of the coloured image. In the catchphrase 'So big ...', the largeness of the screen and the clarity of the image connote the authenticity of the image projected onto that screen, its concordance with reality and its truthfulness, which is further amplified by the vivid and brilliant colour of the screen image associated with Technicolor.

I now want to turn to my final source of information about realism, a selection of contemporary reviews by film critics. The simultaneous release of the two films fostered many comparisons. Film critic Peter Baker (1960) described Ratoff's *Oscar Wilde* as 'a bad bad film' in contrast with *The Trials*, which he concluded was 'a magnificent achievement'. He was not alone in drawing such conclusions. The categories of 'bad film' and 'good film' are a useful distinction through which to examine the nature of cinema.[20] As Christian Metz (1976) explains, the two terms are not equally positioned. Good film (the film as good object) is the aim of the cinematic institution, which includes film critics. It is, he suggests, a goal of the institution to constantly attempt to maintain or re-establish good film (p 18). Bad film is a failure of the cinematic institution.[21] In addition, good film is intimately

---

19 See Kipnis, 1998. Kipnis notes the impact of digital technology on the relation between the visual technology of cinema and reality.

20 I am not suggesting here that there is a necessary connection between realism and the good/bad distinction used by Metz.

21 Perhaps this is too simplistic as a 'bad film' may become a cult classic. *Myra Breckinridge* (1970) directed by Mike Sarne is an example of this. Made by 20th Century Fox, the film was a box office disaster and described as one of the worst films ever made. It has now become something of a cult hit.

associated with filmic pleasure. The cinema industry depends upon good films (in order to make profits), although it may produce bad films (p 20). When used in the context of realism in cinema, the good/bad distinction may be a useful heuristic device to explore the meaning of realism as it informs the assumptions, expectations and judgments of the film critics, who play an important role in the wider cinematic institution, as reader/viewers.

Contemporary reviewers rehearse their realist assumptions and aspirations of the two films in their acknowledgment of the importance of the verbatim accounts of the trials. For example, PJD (1960), writing of *Oscar Wilde*, gives particular importance to those moments in the film which appear to be most faithful to the records of the trials, being nothing more than the reproduction of the cross-examination of Wilde. These are reported as the most successful moments in the whole film. More specifically, this reviewer suggests that it is these moments that most faithfully capture the proposed director's 'primary object', which is described as the desire to produce a 'living portrait' of Wilde. The phrase 'living portrait' highlights the importance of veracity to the film project as a whole and the courtroom exchange is nominated as the exemplar of that objective; 'the records' the critic explained, 'speak for themselves'. Here, realism (taking the form of empiricist realism) is presented both as an aspiration of those involved in making the film as well as an important aspect of this viewer's evaluation of the success, or failure, of the film.

Yet this is not enough in itself, there being other elements of realism that the film has to comply with. The review of fellow critic Peter Baker offers insights into the nature of realism that go beyond the focus on narrative. Under a subtitle, the 'Crux of Drama', Baker explores some of the aspects of *Oscar Wilde* that lead him to the conclusion that it is a 'bad bad film'. 'It is not enough' he explained:

> ... to take a record of the trials (anyone can read a detailed account of them anyway, by taking a trip to the nearest public library) and to pick a team of actors to recreate the sensational bits. This is what happened in Gregory Ratoff's *Oscar Wilde* ... After an appallingly acted introduction, the film settles down to just such a series of extracts from the trials. (Baker, 1960)

Here, the verbatim accounts are only part of a more complex approach to realism. While *The Trials* shares the same preoccupation with extracts from the courtroom encounters, Baker concludes, the end product is very different. By way of contrast, *The Trials*, he explains, is 'always a pleasure to the eye'.

In these comments, the assumptions and expectations of realism that inform the characterisation of *Oscar Wilde* as a bad film begin with the contrast between the Wilde trials as a printed text and, as a record of a performance, a film. In the first instance, the contrast between the two seems to relate to the institutional location of the particular texts, but the location also emphasises the differences between texts; between the library and a literary text and the cinema/film which combines the spoken word and the visual (moving) image. The contrast is also one between the trials as a literary work and the trials as a filmed record of a performance of the text by actors. It is in this context that Baker begins to offer an insight into the wider ensemble of realist techniques in the cinema.

Of particular importance are the actors and more specifically their performance. Bad cinema, Baker suggests, is little more than a visual record of a performance, whereas 'magnificent' cinema suggests something more. A review of *Oscar Wilde* in *Monthly Film Bulletin* (PJD, 1960) complains of the 'stiff and stagy look' of the film and its 'funereal' pace. Various performances were described as 'cautious', 'petrified', 'inhibited' and 'lifeless'. In Baker's review, Robert Morley's portrayal of Wilde in *Oscar Wilde* (a role he had performed on stage in the Sewell play in the 1930s) is contrasted with that of Peter Finch in *The Trials*. The former, he suggests, made Wilde, 'look like a mad scientist from a horror movie'.[22]

Figure 9: *Oscar Wilde*, **Ratoff, 1960.**

This is in contrast to Finch's portrait of Wilde as a 'man at peace with himself', a heroic martyr, a man of strength.[23]

Baker pursues his evaluation of the performances of the stars playing other key roles, Lord Alfred (Bosie) Douglas, the Marquis of Queensbury, Constance Wilde and Sir Edward Carson. With the exception of the last, in which Ralph Richardson's

---

22 A more recent evaluation of Morley's performance by Andy Medhurst (1997) described it in the following terms: '... a cross between Denis Healey [a retired Labour politician] giving a lugubriousness masterclass and an owl with piles.' (p 32)

23 Evaluation of the roles of the stars in Brian Gilbert's *Wilde* has also been a key figure in reviews of that film.

Figure 10: *The Trials of Oscar Wilde,* **Hughes, 1960.**

performance in *Oscar Wilde* is praised, in contrast to a more critical response to James Mason's portrayal in *The Trials,* the respective performances in *Oscar Wilde* are criticised for being 'too theatrical' and 'not fully rounded'.

These distinctions focus particular attention upon the significance not just of the performance of the actors in the fabrication of realism in the cinema, but upon the actors as stars (Metz, 1976, p 67). Stars are part of the wider institution of cinema, fabricated not only by the media industries and other connected agencies, but also made by the stars themselves. Richard Dyer offers an insight into the role of stars in relation to realism in the cinema. He explains that stars work to 'articulate what it is to be a human being in contemporary society' (1987, p 4). A key component of this, he suggests is 'a rhetoric of sincerity or authenticity' deployed in the fabrication of the star image, which 'guarantee, respectively that the star really means what he or she says and that the star really is what she or he appears to be' (p 11).[24] Through this rhetoric, not only is the truth of the image produced, but it is produced in a particular form and context: it is personified and individualised through the star's

---

24 In Brian Gilbert's *Wilde,* the sexuality of the actor who played Wilde, Stephen Fry (as well as the supposedly similar physical resemblance), highlights the role of the star in constituting the authenticity of the representation of Wilde's life. See Andrews, 1997.

image. Dyer also notes that the camera and editing techniques play a role here (cf Sibley, 2001). The close up, he explains, separates out the star, and in its focus on the face ('the window to the soul') provides a potential experience of unmediated intimacy with the star and the character portrayed (p 11). Furthermore, as a recorded image, the truth produced through the star image has a certain fixity and durability (Metz, 1976, p 67).

The significance of the rhetoric of sincerity and authenticity produced in relation to stars and their performance is one context in which realism in law films may be produced. The critical comments made by the reviewers suggest that it plays an important role in the distinction between good and bad films. For example, the characterisations of *Oscar Wilde* as a bad film share a common concern, which is the inauthenticity and insincerity of the performances, not only in the context of the character, but also through the character/star as a metonym for the film as a whole. The 'stiff' and 'stagy' characteristics of the star's performance seem to emphasise the constructed nature of the film, violating some of the assumptions which are associated with bourgeois/classical realism; of narrative continuity. Here the performance exposes the distance between the motion picture camera in particular, cinema in general, and reality. In contrast to this is the more successful realism of *The Trials*, associated with Finch's more 'authentic' performance; the film appears to confirm a reality. The sincerity and authenticity of the star performances generates and sustains the realist expectations that inform the critic's comments. The disappearance (forgetfulness) of signs of the film's fabrication is celebrated.

It is not my intention to suggest that this exhausts the many different ways and contexts in which the realism of law films is fabricated. Much more could be said about the topics already touched upon, such as acting (McDonald, 1998) and, especially in relation to costume and historical drama, costumes (Cook, 1996; Dyer, 2002; Gibson, 1998), as well as extending the parameters of analysis, for example, to include music (Gorbman, 1998) and sound more generally.

Realism as 'an air of truth'

As film scholars have noted, a great virtue of much critical work on realism in cinema is that it has played a key role in fostering critiques of cinematic representations. The same observation can also be made in relation to the emerging body of work on law and film. However, much of this critical commentary, be it in relation to film in general or law films in particular, in the final instance, emphasises the illusory effect of realist representations and highlights spectatorial naivety (Gaines, 1999, p 2). My concern here is that the reduction of a critical analysis of the realism in law films to one that promotes such conclusions is problematic. It is a matter I want to address in the final section of this chapter.

If we return to the two films, the 'bad film', *Oscar Wilde*, highlights the illusory effect of cinema, emphasising that film's *failure* to sustain the make-believe; it fails to sustain a deception that gives film the appearance of truth. In contrast, the *success* of 'good film', *The Trials*, suggests that the artifice is always effectively denied, that the spectator might be readily duped. I want to suggest that this either/or approach to realism is perhaps too extreme. Christian Metz (1976) offers one response in the following terms:

... the screen presents no more than a fiction. And yet, it is of vital importance for the correct unfolding of the spectacle that this make-believe be scrupulously respected (or else the fiction film is declared 'poorly made') and that everything is set to work to make the deception effective and to give it an air of truth ... (Metz, 1976, p 66)

I want to suggest that in the phrase 'air of truth', Metz intimates that realism is more diffuse, partial and relative. Stephen Neale (1980) argues that to be successful, 'realistic' genres do not involve total belief in the accuracy or the reality of the modes of characterisation. Metz and Neale point to the need to avoid a situation of either/or: either totally effective realism or empty (in terms of reality) illusion; either total spectatorial belief in the truth of the image or total naivety and cynical/critical distance. Successful cinema within a realist canon, following Metz, involves an 'air of truth', a degree of (self) deception. Christopher Williams offers a more complex and nuanced approach to realism and the techniques of realism, '[t]he directions, the modes and the force of these references vary, exercising them in different ways and in relation to different aspects of film ...' (1994, p 282). Both realist and non-realist tendencies and aspiration may simultaneously work together in the realisation of the 'air of truth' in realist cinema in general, and in the law film in particular.

Celia Lury (1991) offers another useful insight. Each media and representation, she suggests, is produced and read within the codes that have historically been developed to ensure credibility and truth for the particular discipline/practice/technology of representation: an 'aesthetics of authenticity'. Neale's work has pointed to the importance of genre in the generation of sustainable representational credibility (Neale, 1980, p 37, see also Gledhill, 2000; Ryall, 1998). Genres, he suggests, '... are determining factors not simply determined ones' (Neale, 1980, p 16). The genre has its '... own laws of verisimilitude' (Neale, 1980, p 39). These laws provide the guide by which the credibility or the 'truth' of the representation associated with a particular genre is guaranteed. Verisimilitude refers not to what may or may not actually be the case, but rather to what the dominant culture believes to be the case, to what is generally accepted as credible, suitable and proper. Krutnick (1991) adds another important dimension, that genre is a 'mental machinery' of the cinematic institution which ought to be understood as systems of orientations, expectations and conventions that circulate between industry, text and subject. Generic verisimilitude provides for a considerable play with fantasy inside the bounds of generic credibility. Neale argues that it is when generic verisimilitude, which refers to the rules of a particular genre (genre conventions), and cultural verisimilitude, the norms, mores, and common sense of the social world outside the fiction, come together that representation is taken as an experience of the real. Within this scheme of things, the 'real life' of the verbatim accounts might be understood in terms of, at best, particular requirements of cultural verisimilitude. At the same time, its ability to be experienced as an instance of the real in the context of cinema is also dependent upon the particular figures of generic codes of verisimilitude. The various reviews of the two trial films do seem to add some support to the suggestion that genre has a role to play in the distinction between the cinema of the trials as an accurate and authentic portrayal of the event (the good film), or a bad film which fails to capture the truth of the event. The good film, *The Trials*, is a costume drama, a melodrama and sometimes described as 'an epic', an 'honest tragedy', in contrast to the bad film, *Oscar Wilde*, which is categorised as 'gothic' and 'horror' (Baker, 1960, p 23).[25] An attempt to understand the 'air of truth' in relation to both law films suggests that these generic distinctions need to be understood as being implicated in the production of realist law cinema, rather than being at best remote from it or at worst contrary to it.

A return to some of the critical commentary about the performance of the stars in the Wilde films provides further insight into the success of *The Trials* in this respect. As has already been noted, Peter Finch's performance as Wilde attracted widespread praise. Some critics described it as the best of Finch's career, as 'a wholly thought-out performance'. One reviewer described Finch's performance as embodying 'a definably solid understanding of any public figure who is privately sick, vulnerable and tormented' (NH, 1960). Another, Baker, concluded Finch portrayed Wilde as a man 'of dignity' and a man 'at peace with himself', making Wilde 'a martyr'. These comments arise within a particular context in Baker's review. They are made in relation to André Gide's plea, found in his essay *Corydon*, for a public figure 'charged with homosexuality' to be a martyr, 'a man of strength' who refuses to deny his 'philosophy' and way of living. Gide's comments suggest an absence of such a figure at the time of his writing. Baker (following Gide) finds the demand for a martyr satisfied in Finch's performance. The praise given to Finch's performance of Wilde as a martyr (as a sign of good cinema), in contrast to the derision heaped on Morley's performance of Wilde 'as a mad scientist' (bad cinema), might suggest a shift in the terms of cultural verisimilitude. It might also suggest a new (and different) arrangement between particular generic codes of verisimilitude, epic tragedy, historical costume drama and a courtroom drama, and that changed cultural verisimilitude. This is also brought out in the dissonance associated with a more gothic aesthetic of authenticity, which was dismissed as dated, giving rise to the charge of bad film. Attention also needs to be drawn to the changes in the codes of verisimilitude, both generic and cultural, taking place at the time the Wilde films were in production, the mid to late 1950s, around sexuality in general and sexual criminality in particular, produced in and through the process of law review and debates surrounding reform and in cinema (Gledhill, 1997, p 360). Such changes are important in another way, as it suggests that the demands of what can be expected from representations of reality shift the debate from one about the relationship between representation and reality to one about interests, stakes and investments in various codes of verisimilitude (both cultural and generic).

25 Another instance of the impact of genre on the 'reality' represented in the two films of the trials of Oscar Wilde is to be found in the context of contrasts between those films and another contemporary film that dealt with the topic of law and homosexuality, Basil Dearden's *Victim* (1961). Both Russo (1981) and Dyer (1993) suggest *Victim* is a more radical film with greater political impact and significance than the two Wilde films. In part, they make this conclusion based on the fact that the 'h' word, 'homosexual', is spoken in *Victim* but not in the two Wilde films. In part, this radicalism also seems to be associated with the fact that *Victim* takes the form of a contemporary police procedure thriller rather than a historical costume courtroom drama. Bourne (1996) suggests that the two Wilde films did have a political impact, paving the way to challenge formal censorship prohibitions on explicit references to homosexuality in films. On law and film in relation to *Victim*, see Moran, 1998b.

This enables a link to be made between the apparatus of representation and the contemporary political moment. As a form of convention, genre takes on an inherently conservative connotation, its main function being to reproduce and reinforce normative meanings and values that are generated elsewhere. For example, the Press Book of *Oscar Wilde* suggests that, 'without the Wolfenden Report on vice in Britain, such a film production as OSCAR WILDE would never have dared been made' (*sic*). Furthermore, as a means of standardisation in the production process, genre tends towards the generation of a product which has an already established look and feel to it. However, this does not exclude the possibility that through repetition, 'the pleasure of recognition' may also be conjoined with 'the frisson of the new' (Gledhill, 1997, p 355). The combination of sameness and difference produced through genre may facilitate (and reflect) change. One dimension of change by way of courtroom costume drama is illustrated by way of a reviewer's comments on Peter Finch's performance and responses to it, '... it was a feminine patron who, weeping buckets, confided as we emerged from the press show, "I never thought I would cry over Oscar Wilde"' (BC, 1960). Here the reviewer points to the possibility of a different reaction, which in this example might be described as a new emotional experience, a new emotional realism.

Conclusion

A reviewer, BC, writing in *The Daily Cinema*, explained the superiority of *The Trials* in the following terms:

> ... excelling in colour and spectacle, finely cast, acted and directed with a script that is just that much larger than fiction to give it maximum popular impact. This Oscar Wilde is a credible tortured individual ... (BC, 1960)

This captures several of the dimensions of realism in relation to law films discussed in this chapter: the script/narrative, the visual spectacle made by way of props, settings and costumes, cinema technology, and the performance by the stars of the film. In offering an analysis of various dimensions of realism, my objective has been to make our understanding of the nature and techniques of realism in the context of the law film more complex. My challenge to the focus on 'empiricist realism' and narrative in law films by law and film scholars is not to suggest that this model of realism or narrative has no place in developing our understanding of the nature and effects of realism. It is to demand a more nuanced understanding of their particular contribution and their limited significance in the representations of law in film and to widen the agenda relating to the nature and techniques of realism in that context. In general, my analysis argues for a more complex understanding and approach to realism in relation to law and film. It seeks to draw attention to the need to consider the encounter between law and film as an encounter with a particular medium and apparatus of representation, to take seriously cinematic technology and cinema as cultural institution. The visualisation of the trials of Wilde in the two films, *The Trials of Oscar Wilde* and *Oscar Wilde*, particularly in their juxtaposition, offers the potential to both expose the artifice of the image of the trials and to take seriously the power and persistence of the air of truth that informs law's moving image in general, and in particular the capacity of that image to represent the real world.

Chapter 7
Trial as documentary: images of Eichmann
Lawrence Douglas

In examining documentaries made about the trial of Adolf Eichmann in Jerusalem in 1961, my interest is in exploring the role that film plays in transforming historic trials into historical events. In so doing, I want to consider how trials, staged to define the terms of responsible remembrance, have themselves become digested into collective memory. The Eichmann trial provides an exemplary subject for such a study inasmuch as the trial marked an unprecedented intrusion of television-video technology into a legal setting. As is well known, Capital Cities, an American film and television company, agreed to film the Eichmann trial in its entirety. The three-judge panel that presided over the case, concerned that the presence of movie cameras might diminish the dignity of a proceeding already troubled by the spectre of the carnivalesque – the zoo-like glass booth designed to protect the defendant, the reconverted theatre in which the trial was staged – granted permission to Capital, but only after the production company convinced the tribunal that its four hidden cameras and newly developed sound-dampened equipment would not disturb the proceeding. In the pre-trial hearing to consider the feasibility of filming, Capital surprised the judges by revealing that the hearing itself had been filmed using the very stealth technology that would be used at trial (Pearlman, 1963). Capital also decided to use another new technology, video tape, which could be quickly copied and distributed to broadcasting outlets around the globe. Capital did this all as a public service, offering copies to broadcasters at no profit and supplying the court with a complete set at no cost. And so the Eichmann proceeding became the first televised trial. Long before Court TV, long before OJ, there was Eichmann.[1]

Unprecedented as it was, the filming and televising of the trial was no mere ancillary or idiosyncratic feature of the proceeding. The trial, as many have noted, was staged not simply to submit the crimes of the Holocaust to legal judgment, but also for didactic reasons. In the words of Israeli Attorney General and chief prosecutor Gideon Hausner (1966), the trial intended to provide a younger generation of Israelis with 'real knowledge ... of the way in which their own flesh and blood had perished' (p 291). As a second matter, the trial aimed to educate the world at large, 'which had so lightly and happily forgotten the horrors that occurred before its eyes, to such a degree that it even begrudged us the trial of a perpetrator' (p 291). Broadcasting the event was thus instrumentally of a piece with the very pedagogic ends the trial meant to serve.

Whether the ends of justice and didactic history are compatible is, of course, a matter of controversy. Hannah Arendt, in her famous critique of the Eichmann proceeding, argued that the 'purpose of a trial is to render justice, and nothing else'

---

1 In Israel, however, the fledgling communications infrastructure didn't include television and so the trial was broadcast live on radio – also, for the time, an unprecedented event (Segev, 1993, p 350).

(1963, p 254). We must be wary, Arendt insisted, of subjecting the trial to pressures that may distort the solemn dictates of justice. The danger of turning a trial into a pedagogic spectacle is that it becomes a legal farce, a show trial lacking the element of 'irreducible risk' that Otto Kirchheimer identified as the *sine qua non* of a just legal proceeding (quoted in Arendt, 1963, p 244). Other scholars, however, such as Michael Marrus (2000), have offered a critique that is the obverse of Arendt's.[2] Here the argument is not that law's tutelary role will distort its solemn responsibility to do justice to the accused. Rather, it is that when called upon to clarify the past, trials fail to do justice to the historical record. However we might feel about these matters,[3] they underscore the point that the filming of the trial was a critical extension and manifestation of the logic of the trial itself: to create a record of the Holocaust for the present and posterity.

It is hardly a surprise, then, that a trial that accepted, if not invited, cameras into the courtroom has been the subject of a number of film documentaries. My interest is in considering four: *Verdict for Tomorrow* (1961), created and broadcast at the time of the trial itself; *Witnesses to the Holocaust* (1987), produced roughly a quarter of a century later; *The Trial of Adolf Eichmann* (1997), a PBS-ABC collaboration of a decade later; and finally, *The Specialist* (1999), an independent film released by an Israeli-French film team in 1999. While each film relies on a particular documentary idiom for the purposes of capturing the trial, together they dramatise evolving understandings of the meaning and nature of the proceeding and, in so doing, highlight and underscore both the attractions and dangers of turning courtrooms into filmic events.

Verdict for Tomorrow, with a running time of 30 minutes, was the first documentary made about the Eichmann trial. Produced by the Anti-defamation League and Capital Broadcasting, it was directed by Leo Hurwitz who, with producer Milton Fruchtman, had arranged and overseen the filming of the trial by Capital. An early member of the leftist Film and Photo League, Hurwitz had made his name during the 1930s with a number of edgy documentaries exploring hunger, oppression and racial intolerance in depression America. These included his famous examination of civil rights, *Native Land* (1942), made with Paul Strand and narrated by Paul Robeson. His contempt of Hollywood and his interest in using film as a tool of social justice earned him a blacklisting in the 1950s, though he continued to find work with certain outlets such as Capital.

Verdict for Tomorrow, which received Emmy and Peabody awards, was completed and screened between the conclusion of the trial phase of the Eichmann proceeding in August 1961 and the delivery of the court's judgment several months later in December. Narrated by Lowell Thomas, a pioneering broadcaster best known for his work in radio, the documentary explicitly understands both the trial and its filming as instruments of legal justice. Beginning with archival images from *Kristalnacht*, and concluding with pictures of corpses discovered in the 'liberated' camps, the film uses the camera both to track the course of the trial and to link it to

---

evidence of criminality captured filmically at both the onset and conclusion of the Nazi campaign against the Jews. The camera in *Verdict for Tomorrow* serves then as the tool of justice in a double sense: it both displays the drama of legality as it unfolded in Jerusalem and indexically supplies, through archival cross-cutting, evidence of the very crimes for which Eichmann was being tried. The documentary supplements this material by providing extended excerpts from the testimony of two survivor witnesses who, within the documentary, remain nameless. These two witnesses, familiar to students of the trial, provided the proceeding with two of its most spectacular testimonial moments: in the first, we witness Yehiel Dinur, better known by his pen name Katzetnik – a novelist and writer who wrote chilling accounts of life on 'planet Auschwitz' – collapse in the stand; in the second, we watch Rivka Yoselewska, who suffered a mild heart attack on the eve of the day she was originally scheduled to testify, describe how she climbed out of a mass grave after being left naked and for dead during a mass killing. Within the context of the documentary, both testimonial gestures are offered as evidence of the accused's crimes, though conceived strictly as a juridical matter, Dinur's and Yoselewska's appearances can be understood to complicate rather than simplify the legal task that faced the prosecution.[4] Dinur's collapse, so understood, stands as a powerful reminder of the difficulty of translating Holocaust trauma into legally digestible narrative, while Yoselewska's hellish tale widens, rather than bridges, the gulf between personal tragedy and legally probative evidence. These problems, which loomed large at trial and would play a critical role in Arendt's famous critique, are resolved within the documentary by a bold switch. The narration gradually assumes the burden of presenting the state's case, as Lowell Thomas seizes the mantle of prosecutor from Gideon Hausner. The film shows clips from Gideon Hausner's opening address, and his famous words, 'Here we shall also encounter a new kind of killer, the kind that exercises his bloody craft behind a desk' (*Trial of Adolf Eichmann*, 1992–95, Volume 1, p 62). It then cuts to Lowell Thomas, who essentially completes the prosecutor's statement. Thomas stands directly before the camera; he addresses us in the same incredulous and sardonic tones that Attorney General Hausner reserved for Eichmann. 'And what explanation did Eichmann have?' Thomas asks, contemptuously, 'I was the little man'. Later, commenting on Eichmann's cross-examination by the Attorney General, Thomas observes, 'A pattern emerges: when Eichmann couldn't deny the facts, he denied responsibility'. The film relies, then, on a technique described by Bill Nichols as 'evidentiary editing': 'two pieces of space' – here the shots of the courtroom and those taken from wartime archives – 'are joined together to give the impression of one continuous argument' (Nichols, 1991, p 20).

In turning the narrator into a proxy for the prosecution, the documentary turns its viewers into surrogate judges, a point made explicitly in Thomas' concluding remarks, a court summation of sorts: 'What will the verdict be? What purpose has the trial served? ... We hope this has made you stop and think, so as to render your own final verdict.' The judgment requested of the viewer contains two distinct aspects: we are asked both to return a verdict on the accused and on the trial itself,

---

4   For a more in-depth discussion of this point, see Douglas, 2001.

which, the film has reminded us, was staged against the backdrop of myriad jurisdictional and procedural challenges. Thus, in the same gesture that we are urged to return a guilty verdict against the accused, we are asked to acquit the trial. The film ends by defending the integrity of the proceeding, reminding us that it has been fairly and scrupulously conducted – in short, that it was no 'show trial', a fact complicated, if not belied, by the very existence of the documentary. Yet the appeal to the viewer to serve as judges complexly serves to justify the trial by reminding us that, weight of the evidence notwithstanding, the verdict has not been fixed or predetermined; each of us is free to reach our own principled judgment. In this final remarkable way, the film serves not simply to document a landmark juridical proceeding, but to legitimate it. The film is no mere witness to a trial; it is an instrument of the prosecution.

If *Verdict for Tomorrow* turns the documentary into a prosecutorial weapon, *Witnesses to the Holocaust* presents the trial in its didactic role, as a teacher of history. Produced in 1987 by the Jewish Museum of New York in co-operation with Yad Vashem, the Israeli state-supported Holocaust research institute, *Witnesses to the Holocaust* relies on an idiom of documentary representation significantly different from *Verdict for Tomorrow*. Instead of immediately confronting us with images of violent crimes, *Witnesses to the Holocaust* begins with a scrolled text that summarises the understanding of the trial that will be presented in the remaining 90 minutes of the film: 'The Trial of Adolf Eichmann was more than just the trial of a single man. The eyewitness testimony gathered for the trial and video taped for posterity examines the entire apparatus of persecution during the Holocaust.'

The documentary's focus on the trial as history lesson structures the film. The narrator, in this case the actor Joel Grey, never appears before the camera as did Lowell Thomas. Instead, his presence is limited to a conventional voiceover: his is a disembodied, roving omniscience, occupying a position of neutral detachment, a formal analogue to the hovering but invisible presence of the professional historian in his or her text. Having described the trial as an exercise in recording history through survivor testimony, the film, recapitulating the gesture of *Verdict for Tomorrow*, immediately identifies itself with the ambitions of the trial itself; in this case, however, the end is pedagogic, not prosecutorial. The documentary, Grey's narration reminds us, seeks to 'educate a new generation' to the history of the Holocaust so that 'once more the world should not forget'. Such invocations are of course familiar, particularly at the present moment, as the generation of survivors gradually passes and the last expressions of exigent memory are gradually absorbed into history. Yet these concerns sounded with particular force at the time of the documentary's production in 1987. In 1985, on the 40th anniversary of the end of World War II, President Reagan visited a German military cemetery at Bitburg. For many, the President's words and actions 'reflected an erosion of historical memory and a desire to have the past press less demandingly on contemporary consciousness' (Rosenfeld, 1986). During the 1987 trial of Ivan Demjanjuk in Jerusalem, prosecutors likewise bemoaned, 'the Holocaust seems to have been forgotten from the collective memory' (quoted in Teicholz, 1990).

Witnesses to the Holocaust gives voice to this sense of urgent remembrance, however, in a strangely self-referential fashion, for it is not the vanishing of the witnesses that troubles the film, but the vanishing of *film itself*. After presenting a clip of Hausner's opening statement, the documentary tells us, via Grey's narration, that of the 500 hours of film originally prepared by Hurwitz for Capital Broadcasting, less than a third, only some 170 hours, remain. As we shall see, this statement was later proved incorrect. The temporal vulnerability of video to decay and destruction thus stands as a trope for the passing of the witnesses themselves. Saving the film of the trial from further erosion, and the complementary gesture of preserving memory from forgetfulness, describe the documentary's urgent logic.

By using the trial as a vehicle for teaching the history of the Holocaust, the film remains faithful to one of the principal goals of the trial itself. The trial presented the history of the Holocaust in astonishing detail, with careful attention paid to each stage in the killing process – from persecution, to ghettoisation, to extermination – and thus by following the chronology of the trial, *Witnesses to the Holocaust* succeeds in presenting a condensed chronology of the Holocaust itself. This structure permits the witnesses to serve as mouthpieces of the larger general history related in Grey's impersonal narration. The relationship between history and testimony is made explicit by the film's heavy use of cross-cutting, from footage of survivors telling their stories on the stand to archival material. Thus, for example, Abraham Aviel's shocking description of surviving an Aktion is interspersed with photographs of Einsatzgruppen killings.[5] Later Yitzhak Zuckerman's description of resistance in the Warsaw ghetto is punctuated with images of the ghetto uprising.[6]

This use of archival footage serves, however, not simply to supplement or illustrate survivor stories. Instead, by supplying a visual corollary of the spoken word, this technique importantly serves to translate testimony into a historical document, establishing an irrefutable indexical referent for narratives shaped by memory. The conclusion of the film both underscores and enlarges this point. The judges rise, Eichmann exits the glass booth, and the narrator explains the tribunal's judgment and the method of the accused's execution. But the documentary does not end with the end of the trial. Rather, it circles back to Abraham Aviel, the survivor of the Einsatzgruppen Aktion. Now, however, Aviel describes not how he escaped, but how he was sustained by the idea of sharing his story: 'It was always my thought: one must survive, one must remain behind ... so he can tell what happened.' If the survivor is the living embodiment of traumatic history, then first the trial and now the film serve as the means of history's transmission to a new generation. The trial, which created the original public opportunity to teach Holocaust history through survivor testimony, is now passed on again through the vehicle of the documentary. Here, then, the indexical quality of documentary comes to embrace the survivors themselves: they are the authentic artifacts and bearers of history. The documentary thus offers itself as an instrument of the selfsame pedagogic mission of the trial.

And so we come to appreciate the interesting ambiguity of the film's title. At first glance, the title, *Witnesses to the Holocaust*, seemingly refers to the survivors who testified in Jerusalem. By the film's end, however, we realise that the title also names the film's viewers, who, like the original spectators of the proceeding, have learned history from being made into witnesses of the witnesses.

---

5   For a transcript of Aviel's testimony, see *Trial of Adolf Eichmann*, 1992–95, Volume I, pp 495–99.
6   For a transcript of Zuckerman's testimony, see *Trial of Adolf Eichmann*, 1992–95, Volume I, pp 409–20.

A decade later, in 1997, the third important documentary appears, *The Trial of Adolf Eichmann*, a two hour co-production of PBS and ABC, broadcast on PBS. Like its 1987 precursor, the PBS documentary relies heavily on a technique of cross-cutting from trial to archival footage. And like *Witnesses to the Holocaust*, *The Trial of Adolf Eichmann* uses a narratorial voiceover, in this case supplied by David Brinkley. *The Trial of Adolf Eichmann* begins, however, not with Brinkley's sonorous voice, but with melodious, dimly melancholy chords of piano music. The use of a musical soundtrack is striking, if only because it is so deeply conventional. Like a standard Hollywood feature or a televised Olympic moment, the PBS documentary deploys sound to prepare, stimulate and organise the viewer's emotional response to the film's words and images. When the defendant delivers a crisp 'Ja wohl' to the court's, 'Are you Adolf Eichmann?', the accused's words are underscored by an ominous drum roll meant to remind us, if somehow this weren't already clear, that the moment when the defendant first faced his judges was one of high drama.

The use of sound is novel in a second regard. In *Verdict for Tomorrow* and *Witnesses to the Holocaust*, the voices we hear issuing from the court are those of the simultaneous interpreters rendering the polyglot of tongues spoken at trial into imperfect English. In *The Trial of Adolf Eichmann*, by contrast, professional actors have replaced the court interpreter. Ed Asner provides the English of Robert Servatius, Eichmann's lead counsel; Eli Wallach supplies the voice of David Ben-Gurion; and the likes of Eric Bogosian and Tony Roberts speak for the various witnesses. Here, then, we find a splintering of the indexical and the representational, as the documentary threatens to transform itself into a recreation, a re-staging of the original trial.

And yet the film's use of cross-cutting serves to verify the authenticity of the proceeding from such stagy effects. The cuts in *Witnesses to the Holocaust*, we recall, were always to antecedent archival material; this technique, I have argued, offers an indexical referent, a visual corroboration, of the history told at trial in testimonial form. In *The Trial of Adolf Eichmann*, however, the cross-cutting is both *retrospective*, to archival images of the Holocaust, and *prospective*, to post-trial interviews with various participants in the proceedings. On one level, these juxtapositions, between the black and white footage from the courtroom and the full colour interviews, serve to transform the trial itself into an article of history, placing it in the context of its staging. For example, Yaakov Baror, the assistant state attorney at the trial, confesses in an interview that, at the beginning of the case, the prosecutors themselves knew little about the Holocaust; they, too, had to 'learn to never forget'. Gabriel Bach, at the time also an assistant prosecutor and later a justice on the Israeli Supreme Court, offers a poignant story of his struggle to maintain composure during the testimony of Auschwitz survivor Martin Földi (Douglas, 2001, pp 162–65). As he tells the story, the camera cuts from the present day interview with the elderly Bach, back to the courtroom, where we see the young assistant prosecutor briefly faltering. Eliahu Rosenberg, a trial witness, describes in another present day interview how, prior to the proceeding, Israelis used to call Holocaust survivors 'cowards, pieces of soap'. The commentary is often fascinating, enriching an understanding of the trial as a historic undertaking.

But as opposed to *Witnesses to the Holocaust*, *The Trial of Adolf Eichmann* does not use the proceeding to teach afresh the underlying history of the Holocaust; nor is the goal simply to offer a history of the trial itself. Instead, the complex cross-cutting from trial to archival footage to recent interviews serves another distinct end: it turns the film into a continuation of the drama of remembrance staged at the trial. The subsequent interviews, particularly those with survivors, serve less to historicise the trial than to keep it fresh in the collective memory. When trial witness Israel Guttman, in an interview, describes how many of the witnesses were reluctant to testify, it's as if he were once again on the stand, extending and supplementing the testimony he offered decades before.

The film's end, a concluding interview with Michael Goldman, most dramatically accomplishes this purpose. Goldman, an officer in the special 06 division of the Israeli police responsible for investigating Nazi crimes and himself a famous figure of survival at Auschwitz by virtue of Haim Gouri's 1974 documentary, *The Eighty-first Blow* (1974), was responsible for throwing Eichmann's ashes into the Mediterranean. In relating this story, the concluding gesture of the case, Goldman reveals that the act of handling Eichmann's ashes suddenly reminded him of a moment at Auschwitz, when he came upon a veritable mountain of cremated human remains. 'When I saw the remains of Adolf Eichmann', Goldman says, that small pile, 'I knew how many hundreds of thousands had been in the Auschwitz mound'. Watching Goldman tell his story, we forget we are listening to an agent of the state describing the aftermath of the condemned's execution. Instead, we cannot help but feel that we are watching a clip from the trial, listening to the difficult testimony of yet another survivor witness. Although Goldman's story seemingly details the concluding chapter to the Eichmann affair – the scattering of the perpetrator's ashes at sea – it also bears witness to the continuing legacy of the executed man's crimes, how they remain troublingly alive in the memory of survivors. The act of bearing witness, of keeping memory active, is thus vital and ongoing: a project stimulated by the trial and continued by the documentary about it.

In this final regard, the documentary's most objectionable features, its use of a carefully orchestrated soundtrack and actors to supply the voices of historical figures, can be grasped as not a trivialisation of the juridical project, but very much in its spirit. For just as the prosecution strove to turn bleak tales of Holocaust survival into displays of heroic memory, the documentary likewise labours to confer poignancy and meaning to the memories captured in its frame.

Altogether different are the representational strategies of *The Specialist*. Directed by Eyal Sivan, an Israeli-French filmmaker, and written by Rony Braman, likewise an Israeli-born, French resident, *The Specialist* is in many ways the most interesting, complex, intriguing and problematic of the documentaries about the Eichmann trial.

In contrast to its documentary predecessors, *The Specialist* entirely eschews the use of a narratorial voiceover responsible for organising and explaining the film's images. Moreover, the film presents no archival footage of the Holocaust; nor does it include any material compiled in the decades after the trial. The absence of a voiceover and of archival material invites immediate comparisons with Claude Lanzmann's *Shoah* (1986), arguably the greatest documentary ever made about the Holocaust. In the case of Lanzmann's masterpiece, however, the eschewal of archival material supports the central problematic of the film, the 'historical crisis of witnessing', explored by critics such as Shoshana Felman (1992) and Dominick LaCapra (1998). While *The Specialist* relies on a similar representational strategy, one seemingly influenced by Lanzmann, the logic behind such documentary austerity is far from clear. The entire 150 minutes of film remains within the confines of the proceeding; the camera never exits the courtroom. The effect is a bit claustrophobic, though the footage is frequently striking, at least in part because it includes much material not seen in the earlier documentaries. Sivan and Braman, after a Sisyphean struggle with the Israel state archives, discovered nearly twice as much film as had previously been thought to have survived. Unfortunately, much of this material was in terrible condition, the result of decades of neglectful storage. As Stuart Liebman (2002) has noted, the footage had to be reformatted and digitally enhanced, and the soundtrack had to be overdubbed in places with the radio transmissions from the trial.

These elaborate techniques, however, do as much to problematise and reconfigure the original as they do to restore it. Though *The Specialist* never leaves the theatre-turned-courtroom, a logic of theatricality controls its images, as the film relies on techniques far more stylised than those deployed in its documentary predecessors. In the earlier films, 'evidentiary editing' is used to create the semblance of a coherent argument; here the cross-cutting serves to disrupt the trial's chronology. Indeed, the very technology that made possible the restoration of the damaged footage is deployed to transform its content. Through digital manipulation, reflections of the courtroom are projected onto the accused's glass booth. Voices are overdubbed, creating a menacing cacophony. The musical soundtrack is arresting. In contrast to the innocuous dulcet chords of the PBS film, *The Specialist*'s soundtrack is like a composition of high modernism: strident bow work, plucked strings, random notes: sounds of discord, disruption and disharmony.

The use of these elaborate techniques, along with the curious absence of any narrative or supplementary images, makes *The Specialist* a difficult film to read, and even the knowledge, supplied in the credits, that it was inspired by Arendt's *Eichmann in Jerusalem* hardly simplifies the matter. Certainly Arendt's influence is apparent in certain of the film's more heavy-handed sequences. Arendt has very little good to say about lead prosecutor, Gideon Hausner, and the film likewise portrays him as a histrionic figure, given to bloated rhetoric and goofy, melodramatic poses. (The film amplifies and overdubs his voice, creating an incoherent acoustical wave of accusation.) The concluding shot also finds its inspiration in Arendt. Digital technology is used to make the surrounding courtroom, the golem-like guards and the glass booth, slowly vanish so that finally Eichmann sits alone before a desk – an image which is then colourised, presumably to remind us that a similarly bland bureaucrat can be found virtually anywhere, a point, I should add, that does not really find support in Arendt's controversial text.

Still, the film cannot be seen simply as a documentary illustration of Arendt's banality thesis. In particular, the absence of a voiceover finds little analogue in Arendt's book, which is very much about *voice*. The book condemns both the prosecution and, to a lesser extent, the court, for failing to frame Eichmann's offences in an adequate legal idiom. The book ends with a remarkable inversion, in which Arendt substitutes her voice for the court's, supplying the very terms of judgment she found wanting in the court's opinion (Arendt, 1963, pp 245–46). The film's silences, if they deconstruct the prosecution's and the court's controlling narratives, provide no substitute framework, no clearly articulated rival interpretation of the trial. On the contrary, the film's highly stylised documentary idiom is significant not because it offers a fresh or pointed reading of the trial, but because it rejects the framing logic of both the trial *and* Arendt.

In this regard, *The Specialist* represents a powerful reorientation of film's relationship to the proceeding. In the first three Eichmann documentaries, trial footage is worked with to invite judgment, or to teach history, or to sacralise memory; now the footage is worked *upon*. In *The Specialist*, the trial has passed from occasion to object, and the accused appears not as index or juridical trope, but as a cultural icon. Here again, the film is notable for many of its omissions and exclusions. In contrast to the other documentaries, the survivor witnesses play a marginal role in *The Specialist*. If one of the aims of the trial was to puncture the numbing anonymity of genocide by providing witnesses an opportunity to present narratives of their victimisation, resistance and survival, the film rejects this gesture, rendering the voice of memory disembodied and incoherent.[7] In a notably disturbing sequence, the testimony of numerous witnesses is run together through a series of quick cuts, their elaborate stories reduced to disjointed, fragmented and isolated utterances:

> ... Eichmann ...
> ... a head, a foot ...
> ... keep beating us ...
> ... dead!
> ... I don't sleep ...

Likewise, the spectators at the trial, who, in the earlier documentaries, are often captured reacting either to the words of a witness or of the accused, barely appear. The banishment of the witnesses and the spectators to the margins of the film places the defendant all the more in the centre: in *The Specialist*, Eichmann is very much the star of his trial and the documentary. His gestures are exaggerated: as the camera focuses on him cleaning his glasses, the squeak of cloth on lens is digitally enhanced. Close-ups likewise track his copious note taking, the scratch of pen on pad building ominously in volume, slowly drowning out the speech in the courtroom.

Not all the effects are born of digital manipulation. In a remarkable sequence, footage captures Eichmann's exiting the glass booth to better explain the logistics of the deportations he oversaw. He stands before a large map of Europe, pointer in hand, and close beside him stands Attorney General Hausner. With their backs to the camera, the men, balding, bespectacled, of identical height, look virtually like twins. It is an astonishing moment, but little more or less than that. Beyond noting the odd instant of forced kinship, we are not moved to make any grander or more profound observations, beyond the relatively banal one (though not in the sense

---

7   For a detailed discussion of the complex and contested role that survivor testimony played at the trial, see Douglas, 2001, pp 150–82.

intended by Arendt) that all human beings look more or less alike. Any deeper reading of the image would be tendentious, if not perverse.

More interesting is the footage of Eichmann responding directly to questions from the bench. In contrast to the exchanges between prosecutor Hausner and Eichmann – Hausner's blustery challenges, sarcastic asides and impatient interruptions; Eichmann's defensive evasions and bureaucratic hair splitting – the exchanges between the accused and the judges are characterised by a peculiar delicacy. The judges, dispensing with the artifice of simultaneous interpretation, address Eichmann in the language that is both the defendant's mother tongue and theirs as well. They do not seek out eye contact, but they also do not refuse it, and they speak in calm, even tones. Eichmann, visibly relieved to be free, at least for the moment, from Hausner's verbal pummelling, answers courteously, respectfully even. Still, these exchanges provide no deeper insight into the character of the accused. There is no moment of epiphany when the man suddenly reveals himself; nor can the absence of revelation be construed as essentially revealing. At most, the exchanges direct attention to an aspect of the trial not typically associated with a spectacular criminal proceeding: its capacity to create moments of intimate exchange.

Yet the refusal of the film to sponsor any deeper reading of the trial, is, I believe, not its failure but its most interesting signature, the surest indication of the documentary's transformation of the proceeding into pure representation. The absence of archival or supplementary footage, then, is hardly accidental, for it has the effect of releasing the proceeding from the pressures of time and place. By remaining in the courtroom, *The Specialist* turns the trial into an object of art, a thing not to be understood, contextualised or assessed, but to be manipulated, appropriated, acted upon. Here we can appreciate the irony implicit in the filmmakers' avowal of their indebtedness to Arendt. For far from revealing the banality and extreme limitations of the accused, the film, by micro-examining his skewed grimace, nervous blinking, compulsive note taking and attentive responses, confers upon Eichmann iconic status. This is not to say the film endows Eichmann with complexity; on the contrary, it turns him into a cultural trope of his own indecipherability. Like Marcus Harvey's oversized painting of convicted murderess Myra Hindley,[8] Eichmann finds celebration as a cipher, a pure trope of our cultural over-investment in images of unreadable evil.

Trials are not about the production of rival meanings. Though numerous commentators have noted that trials provide a site of contestation, an arena in which narratives compete and clash, the very intensity of this competition is born of the fact that each story strives for dominance, aims to be inscribed as authoritative in the court's judgment (Brooks and Gewirtz, 1996). As I have noted, Arendt faults the court not for silencing rival narratives, but for championing the wrong one. *The Specialist*, by contrast, does not condemn the trial. Condemnation implies argument. The film's ultimate gesture of antagonism toward the trial is its refusal to indulge simple critique. Ultimately, then, the film challenges the trial in a far more radical fashion: by aestheticising it. In *The Specialist*, the trial is no longer in control of its meaning.

---

8 On Myra Hindley, see Julius, 2003 and Kemp, 1998.

This point is underscored in the film's concluding shots, in which footage of Eichmann is interspersed with the credits. For the first time we see the defendant smiling, smirking perhaps, and the soundtrack, departing from its signature discordant chords, now plays Tom Waits' jaunty *Russian March*. Accustomed as we are to the defendant's dour bank teller appearance, we are unprepared for his smile, and are discomfited by it, not because it suddenly humanises him, but because it testifies to the strange power of film to manipulate our responses by marrying image with sound. The jaunty tunes and the sly smile suggest Eichmann has outfoxed the court. And in a sense he has, through the instrument of the film itself. By turning the accused into pure representation, the film frees Eichmann, both literally and figuratively, from the juridical box in which the trial tried to contain him. It is an ironic acquittal.

The documentary forerunners of *The Specialist* all recapitulate the essential gesture of the trial: they are structured as arguments. In *Verdict for Tomorrow*, we encountered the documentary as the ally of the trial, a tool of the prosecution. *Witnesses to the Holocaust* similarly turned itself into a tool of the trial by dedicating itself to the proceeding's ulterior project of teaching traumatic history. *Eichmann on Trial* conjured the proceeding as a means of preserving memory, a goal to which the film also pledged its assistance. Each film, through different effects, captured a single aspect of the competing purposes that were provocatively pursued and balanced in the Jerusalem court; and in so doing underscored the affinities between the didactic aims of law and documentary film.

With *The Specialist*, however, we move beyond law, history and memory. Here, documentary no longer serves as a tool of paraphrase or even critique. Its hostility to the trial is the hostility of image to word, of art to law: not a simple binary antagonism, but a complex collision over the control of meaning. The film liberates Eichmann from the debilitations of history, law, and memory; he is now free to circulate in our culture as sheer image.

Chapter 8
Film and law:
in search of a critical method[1]
David M Seymour

Introduction

On reviewing the burgeoning literature of film and law, two general but important characteristics emerge. There is the tendency of scholars to reduce film to a resource for specific legal issues, points or questions (Greenfield, Osborn and Robson, 2001). As a consequence, the specificities of film, its particular properties as *film* disappear from view (Black, 1999). Secondly, despite the often interesting engagement between law and film, after its engagement, each medium retreats to its own corner relatively unscathed and looking pretty much as it had before the encounter. Later rather than sooner, it occurred to me that these two limiting factors of the study of film and law – erasure and the durability of the status quo – are the issues most recently and radically confronted by both critical legal and critical film theory.

In the light of this realisation the best place to begin a critique of the current condition of the study of film and law is with these critical texts. Rather than posit a critical methodology at the outset that could then be 'applied' to the relevant materials, I allow the methodology to emerge from a critique of the materials themselves. The materials used are Douzinas and Warrington's *Justice Miscarried* (1994), Barbara Creed's *Horror and the Monstrous Feminine – An Imaginary Abjection* (1986) and M Night Shyamalan's film, *The Sixth Sense* (1999).

The reason for the choice of these works is that, despite the fact that none of them addresses the question of the interdisciplinary study of law and film directly, each is able to throw some light onto the issue. Each work expresses both a dichotomy and an engagement between two seemingly discrete fields. Creed expresses the duality through the concepts of the symbolic and the abject, Douzinas and Warrington through the legal and the ethical, whilst the facets of *The Sixth Sense* that I focus upon conflate each of the poles of these dualisms into that of the legal symbolic and abject ethical respectively. Because of the central role of visual reproduction, this film is of especial benefit in bringing to light these replications of durability and erasure and their implications for the study of film and law.

One of the issues to emerge, however, is the way in which these respective critical engagements reproduce the very problem each sought to solve; each work culminates by erasing one element of a duality in the name of the other, and ends with a return to the pre-existing status quo. Given this similarity of result, I began to think about a relationship between critical work of this kind that deals with the broad question of law and ethics and the current condition of the study of law and film. It is the exploration of this question that forms the substance of the following

---

1 Thanks go to Alison Diduck, Robert Fine, Leslie Moran, Elena Loizidou and Max 'is it a grown-ups' film?' Seymour.

essay, in which I attempt to point a way forward in the search for a critical method of the study of law and film.

In the light of these reflections, the essay is structured in the following way. The first two sections address the questions of the durability of the status quo and erasure respectively. Having identified and discussed these tendencies in the relationship *between* disciplines, the third section uncovers their presence within the individual concepts that comprise that relationship. The essay concludes with some reflections on the way in which the critiques offered here may be of potential benefit in developing a critical methodology of film and law.

The durability of the status quo

Drawing on the work of Julia Kristeva (1982), Barbara Creed outlines the structure of the horror film as follows:

> The central ideological project of the popular horror film [is the] purification of the abject through a 'descent into the foundations of the symbolic construct'. In this way, the horror film brings about the confrontation with the abject (the corpse, bodily wastes, the monstrous feminine) in order, finally to eject the abject and re-draw the boundaries between the human and the non-human. (Creed, 1986, p 53)

Having laid out the formal structure of this genre, Creed then attempts to subvert its meaning through a trans-valuing of its terms. The threatening abject becomes transformed from the force of evil, to Irigaray's 'sexual difference', the excluded feminine upon which the symbolic or the social is constructed. To Creed, therefore, the horror film serves an ideological function: it represents the potential terror and destruction brought about by the intrusion of the feminine into the seemingly sealed masculine symbolic. In then also representing the necessary destruction of the intruder, the status quo is re-established.

Douzinas and Warrington's work, *Justice Miscarried* (1994), can also be opened to constructive critique. Whilst their account of the symbolic and the abject shares similarities with Creed's discussion of the horror film, in other ways they differ from the archetype. This difference is less in terms of formal structure, though, than through a further subversion of its meaning. As does Creed, Douzinas and Warrington remould the value of the abject into a positive symbol. Unlike Creed, however, they seek a way through which the abject can be absorbed within the symbolic or the law without the risk or realisation of the law's destruction. Whilst the success in avoiding the erasure that comes with the ultimate defeat of the abject is in question (see later), they nonetheless cannot escape the realisation of the re-drawing of the boundaries, of the restoration of the status quo.

Re-interpreting Sophocles' ancient Greek tragedy, *Antigone*, Douzinas and Warrington offer an account of the dichotomy between the symbolic and the abject, through their subsumption into law and ethics respectively (Douzinas and Warrington, 1994, pp 25–93). They argue that the motive for Antigone's disobedience of Creon's edict not to bury Polynices stems not from appeals to 'eternal unwritten laws' (recast as a precursor of natural law) (Douzinas and Warrington, 1994, pp 27 and 70), but from the ethical obligation brought about by the 'call of the Other' (Douzinas and Warrington, 1994, p 57). Although they do not refer to the abject directly, Polynices, the issuer of the 'call', shares many of its characteristics. The first is the nature of Polynices' death; he was killed in battle by his brother (who also perished). Secondly, and more importantly, he remains trapped between the realm of the living and the realm of the dead, which places him in the nether region of the abject. The very content of the ethical obligation, therefore, is to ensure that the correct order of things is restored; it is right and proper that Polynices reaches Hades. The abject nature of this call comes through Douzinas and Warrington's emphasis on the abject presence of Polynices' disembodied head:

> It is Polynices' head, in its beloved physicality, suspended between the earth from which he has departed and Hades where he cannot arrive without the love of Antigone, that gave her the 'law whereby I held you first in honour' ... The ethical demand arises not out of a form or an idea but out of a desire, in a somatic encounter and through the *epiphany* of a head in need. (Emphasis provided, Douzinas and Warrington, 1994, p 57)

Drawing on the moral philosophy of Emmanuel Levinas (1995),[2] the origin of the obligation is said to originate from the responsibility one owes to the Other *prior* to the self's constitution in and through legal relations. Existing outside the law as a symbol of its transgression, it follows that the nature and content of the obligation, from the point of view of both the issuer and the receiver, is correspondingly beyond law. This point is described succinctly:

> The other comes first. (S)he is the condition of existence of language, of self and the law. The other always surprises me, opens a breach in my wall, befalls the ego. The other precedes me and calls upon me: where do you stand? Where are you now and not who are you. All 'who' questions have ended in the foundational moves of (de)ontology. Being or the I of the Cartesian *cogito* and the Kantian transcendental subject, starts with the self and creates other as an *imitatio* ego. In the philosophy of alterity, the other can never be reduced to the self or the different to the same. Nor is the other an instance of otherness or of some general category, an object to a subject that can become a move in dialectics. (Douzinas and Warrington, 1994, p 164)

The example of *Antigone*, in which the entire edifice of the city and its political constitution is put into crisis, illustrates the potential of this ethical imperative to, at best, undermine and, at worst, unravel, the entire network of legal and social relations. It is for this reason, then, that Douzinas and Warrington claim that one of the most important functions of law is to bind itself against any potentially devastating incursion of the ethical (Douzinas and Warrington, 1994, pp 1–24, 80–92). This attempt at boundary marking operates through the juridical sense of 'justice'. In this sense, justice arises from the formal equality of abstract right by which all difference and contingency is expelled from the legal purview. If it does reappear, it is thereby recast as a non-legal, often a 'medical' or 'psychological', problem:

> Within the framework of [Creon's] political rationalism, Antigone can only act for gain or as part of a conspiracy to overthrow him. The only alternative is that she is mad ... To use psychoanalytic terminology, justice is a 'fantasy', a frame we construct to explain

---

2 See also Vasseleu, 1998.

away the unknown desire of the other but which at the same time constitutes our own lack and desire for the other ... Justice is the fantastical screen that philosophers, poets and lawyers have erected to shield themselves from the question of the desire of the other. (Douzinas and Warrington, 1994, pp 79–80)

Despite their attempt to secure complete closure, Douzinas and Warrington point to a possible breach in the law's defences through which the Other may present itself within the legal without the danger of the destruction of either. This small aperture, and one that they acknowledge is constantly narrowing, is the *audi* rule:

[T]he legitimacy of adjudication is largely based on the oral character of that procedure. But ... the *audi* rule shows the law concerned to hear the concrete person who comes before it, rather than to calculate and adjudicate the general qualities and characteristics of the abstracted legal person. Not to give the other a hearing is to deny her humanity, to treat her as someone without the basic qualities of moral worth and capacity. Even more, the demand to hear the concrete other undermines the persistent claim of the law that persons must be judged exclusively according to their classification in broad categories and be treated equally as instances of the application of general rules. The *audi* rule turns the ethical obligation to treat the other as a full and unique person into a logical prerequisite of all judgment. (Douzinas and Warrington, 1994, p 176)

This reliance upon the *audi* rule as the potential space through which to allow the voice of the concrete or 'authentic' person is fraught with problems. Most notable is its implied claim of an unmediated presentation of difference within a judicial setting. Participation within the legal process, whether at court level or not, is, by definition, imbricated with law. It is not the extra-legal or 'pre-legal' person who appears, but the person as client, complainant, accused, lawyer, judge, jury member, etc. Indeed, this inheres within the concept of 'person' itself,[3] which, strictly speaking, means one who is recognised by law.

Accepting for a moment the claim Douzinas and Warrington make for the *audi* rule, it is nonetheless the case that once this 'safe space' has been utilised, all previously existing lines of demarcation have been redrawn. On the one hand, the excluded Other has been given the opportunity to narrate its own difference; on the other hand, in retaining its power of judgment and, by definition, its own discretion in judgment, the law reassembles itself immediately, continuing as it did before. Nowhere is this more the case than in *Antigone* itself. By the end of the tragedy, indeed a tragedy the motivation of which is premised upon transgression, order has been restored; the dead and the living returned to their rightful environments. If this was not the consequence, then the attempt to provide access to and from 'beyond the law' would be subject both to ultimate and total destruction.

M Night Shyamalan's *The Sixth Sense* dovetails with many of Creed's and Douzinas and Warrington's arguments outlined above. *The Sixth Sense* focuses on the character of Cole Seer (Haley Joel Osment) a nine-year-old child with the ability to see and hear the dead. The essence of the film is his journey from denial and fear

---

3 *Audi alteram partem* (hear the other side) is an element of the procedural rules of 'natural justice'. It states that a decision cannot stand unless the person directly affected by it was given a fair opportunity both to state (their) case and to know and answer the other side's case.

of his 'gift' to that of acceptance by himself, his mother (Toni Collette) and his psychiatrist, Malcolm Crow (Bruce Willis). The first relevant scene, which represents law as excluding the abject appearance of the ethical, takes place in an interchange at Cole's school between the boy and his teacher.

Seer is sitting distractedly at his desk at the back of his classroom when his teacher, Stanley Cunningham (Bruce Norris) asks the children to tell him the name of the United States capital between the years 1790 and 1800. He prompts a response by telling the children that it is the city that they all live in; in unison, they chant the name 'Philadelphia'. Continuing with the theme of local history and its connection to the city's role as the country's former political and legal centre, he asks the class if they know the original purpose of the building they now occupy. Hesitantly, Seer raises his hand. Somewhat surprised by Seer's engagement, the teacher looks to him for an answer. Quietly, Seer explains that it was a building where people were hanged. Despite denials from his teacher, Seer continues, describing in graphic detail the way in which people were pulled from the clutches of their families and loved ones and dragged to their deaths.

Confronted by Seer's insistence as to the veracity of his story, the teacher, with his patience tested, coolly explains that the building used to be a courthouse, populated with lawyers and judges, implying, therefore, that it could not have been a place of death. Seer counters this assertion by telling the teacher that it was precisely these officers of the courts that carried out the killings. At this point, the conversation breaks down. Seer accuses the teacher of 'looking at him' in a way he does not like, whilst the adult's ability to speak is terminated through what we know to be the return of a childhood stutter. This coda illustrates vividly the potential destruction of the symbolic, expressed here in language, that its contact with the abject (it is the dead that have furnished Seer with this knowledge) can bring.

This naming of law as a force for injustice, understood as the absence of ethics, is reinforced further by the nature of the ghosts who visit Seer. Taken together, they are representative of those whose horrendous deaths, evidenced in the abject nature of their injuries, occurred either as a direct consequence of the raw power of judicial action, or whose suffering law has refused to recognise. Hence, throughout the film we hear a spirit pleading for release from incarceration after being falsely accused of the theft of his master's horse; we see the spectacle of a family hanging from the rafters of the school/courthouse, with the deceased dressed in the clothes of 18th century independent artisans, the woman's eyes seemingly imploring Seer; a woman whose cut wrists evidence the taking of her own life after unremitting spousal abuse; we see an adolescent boy, whose horrific head injuries were caused by playing with his father's guns, stored within his reach; we see the ghost of a child murdered by her almost unimpeachable, blonde, suburban, middle class mother; and a recently deceased cyclist, a victim of a drunk car driver. In this way, Shyamalan establishes the law's responsibility for both its denial of justice and the existence and exclusion of the abject.

This notion of the legally derived origins of the abject is overlaid with the notion of the ethical. As the film progresses, the purposes of the ghosts' visits become clear. By narrating to him the unique circumstances of their tragic lives and deaths, they finally have someone to whom they can acknowledge their unique and tragic fate;

their difference that has remained unrecognised by and in law. Once unburdened, they are then able to find the eternal peace that awaits them. It is Seer's gradual realisation of their need, and his acceptance of the responsibility demanded by the ethical obligation of alterity, that saves him from mental and physical destruction. By responding in the correct manner to the obligation of ethics, both Seer and the abject that issued this command survive the incursion in a way that grants peace and tranquillity to each.

Far from reconfiguring the relationship of the law with the abject, this result means that the boundary between the human and the non-human has been re-drawn according to the pre-existing status quo. The most telling illustration of this return to order occurs when the ghost we see visiting Seer (the cyclist killed by a drunk driver) stands outside the closed window of the car in which he and his mother are sitting at precisely their moment of reconciliation with each other. This positioning represents the fact that each domain, the symbolic and the abject, has now returned to its own pre-ordained place and that, despite all the inversions and revaluations, 'the central ideological project of the popular horror film [as the] purification of the abject' (Creed, 1986, p 53) has been obtained.

The structure of the film, then, turns on the untimely and potentially explosive intrusion of the abject into the symbolic, and the attempts to defuse the threat inherent within this transgression. The film radicalises the revaluation of these terms in two ways: first, it presents them as Manichean struggles between good and evil; and, secondly, it brings together the abject and the ethical as the excluding, constituting moment of law. Perhaps not surprisingly, the conclusion of this radicalisation of terms is a correspondingly radical version of the return to the status quo, in this instance, through the almost theological tropes of reconciliation and redemption.

Yet, whilst the individuals who have suffered from the horrors of modern life find personal redemption and reconcile themselves to their fate, the conditions that give rise to them, including the realm of law, remain unaltered and, in the final analysis, unchallenged. The paradox of this resolution of the film's central dilemma is that what began as a critical enterprise culminates, ultimately, in a return to the status quo. This paradox, in turn, is an expression of a methodology that inverts the values of concepts without subjecting them to deeper critique; it is one that is complicit in its own counter regime of erasure.

Erasure

Alongside her comments on the structure and the ideology of the horror film, Creed notes that:

> [A]bject things are those that highlight the 'fragility of the law' and which exist on the other side of the border that separates out the living subject from that which threatens its extinction. *But abjection is not something of which the subject can ever feel free – it is always there, beckoning the self to take up its place, the place where meaning collapses.* The subject, constructed in and through language, is also spoken by the abject, the place of meaninglessness – thus, the subject is constantly beset by abjection which fascinates desire but which must be repelled for fear of self-annihilation. (Emphasis added, Creed, 1986, p 48)

In this quote, Creed notes the inherent and intricate relationship that exists between the abject and the symbolic. Despite appearances to the contrary, the abject can never be truly expelled, but rather acts as a siren to dissolution, buried within the heart of the symbolic. Repulsion and annihilation, in other words, are implicated within each other. Like the return of the status quo, the radicalised nature of *The Sixth Sense* brings to the fore aspects of erasure that remain latent and unacknowledged in the more subtle and discreet theorising of Douzinas and Warrington. It is to this potential of destruction and erasure, as it appears in the film, that I will now turn.

Shortly after he becomes aware of the needs of the restless spirits, Seer is visited by the ghost of a young girl (Mischa Barton). The nature of the scene acts to reinforce and crystallise many of the themes previously discussed. At first sight, the appearance of the child is in keeping with the traditional image of the abject; a frightening intrusion that is to be feared and expelled. However, unlike previously seen ghosts, the length of her time on screen during which she enters into dialogue with Seer, alongside her evident childhood and vulnerability, emphasises Shyamalan's revaluation of the abject from evil to goodness and innocence.

Equally, she comes to embody the conflation of the abject with the ethical. On the one hand, the nature of her 'physical' appearance – a wan, pale, vomiting, female corpse – embodies Creed's definition of the abject (Creed, 1986, p 48). On the other hand, she comes to Seer because of a particular need to narrate to him something about her death that would otherwise remain untold and escape recompense of justice. And, having fled from her disturbing first appearance, Seer returns and indicates his acceptance of the responsibility that lies at the heart of the ethics of alterity. Surviving this initial contact, he asks whether she has something to tell him. As she is about to answer, the image on the screen fades to black.

Seer arrives at the dead girl's house after her funeral has taken place. Through snippets of conversation it is widely believed that the child had died of a two-year battle against cancer, an illness with which her younger sister (Samantha Fitzpatrick) has recently also been diagnosed. Unnoticed, Seer walks through the group of mourners and, making his way upstairs, hesitantly enters the deceased's darkened bedroom. Slowly walking around the room, he locates and picks up a small puppet. Suddenly, indicating the presence of the abject, a hand reaches for his leg and trips him. From her refuge under her bed, the ghost of the dead child silently passes Seer a closed wooden box.

Carrying the box in front of him as if it contained a holy relic, Seer returns downstairs and approaches a man sitting alone. Once he has established that it is the girl's father (Greg Wood), Seer hands him the box, explaining that his daughter, Kyra, wanted to tell him something. Contained in the box is a video cassette. Kyra's father runs the tape immediately. The following scenes are intercut between the television occupying the frame of the entire screen and frontal shots of head and shoulders of the father framed by the armchair in which he sits, riveted.

Framed at either end by brief periods of static, the recording begins with a playful puppet show that is hurriedly dismantled when the girl's mother (Angelica Torn) enters the room. With the camera still running and secreted on a shelf, Kyra quickly clambers back into an unmade bed and feigns sleep.

Figures 11a–e: *The Sixth Sense*, **Shyamalan, 1999.**

The girl's mother is shown placing a tray with a clear glass bowl of soup near the video camera. Vanishing from view she returns opening a bottle of 'Raid'. She adds two spoonfuls to the soup and stirs it in. Taking the tainted mixture over to her daughter, she encourages her to drink it and not complain that it tastes 'funny'. The girl drinks it obediently, intimating the powerlessness of her position. After a short conversation with her mother in which it is established that the poisoning of her lunch is a regular occurrence, the shot dissolves into another short burst of static that fills the entire screen. Wearing an expression of incomprehension and rage, the father walks over to his wife who, alone amongst the mourners, had had her back to the unfolding events. With the camera closing in on his face, he accuses her with the statement that 'you had kept her sick'. Looking around the room, the mother turns to speak, no words come and she retreats to silence.

At first sight, it appears as if the justice the child has sought, the recognition of the harm that has befallen her, has been delivered. The murderer has been identified, and, as we learn in the next scene, the child has found her rightful peace. However, contained within this apparently neat solution is an identifiable series of erasures that culminate in the nihilism of dissolution that underpins the return to the status quo. These points can be elucidated through reviewing this sequence of the film not through the point of view of the ethical abject, but through the prism of the legal symbolic.

In her discussion of courtroom dramas or 'trial movies', Carol Clover (2000) notes the correspondence between the legalistic nature of United States social relations and the relations that exist between a trial movie and its audience. Her thesis turns on the idea that the citizen/viewer is sutured into the respective relations in the role of juror (cf Sibley, 2001). Corresponding to the way in which this interpolation expresses the main tenets of liberal ideology, Clover notes the way in which '[the trial movie] positions us not as passive spectators, but as active ones, viewers with a job to do' (Clover, 2000, p 246).

On the one hand, then, this positioning as juror permits the citizen/viewer a site from which to critically assess the 'evidence' presented to them through the law and law film of which they are a part. On the other hand, however, is the fact that these same processes refrain from calling into question the existence or unity of the juror. Regardless of the ideological nature of this inclusion, it is still the case for Clover that, inherent within both law and films of trials, is the presence of a critical subject, a subject who, 'stud[ies] exhibits and demeanour, speculates on motive, consider[s] other candidates, [and] wrestle[s] with the presumption of innocence of the title [*Presumed Innocence*]' (Clover, 2000, p 250). In bypassing the law, therefore, the ethical command is implicated in the erasure of the active subjectivity within which it is inscribed.

In achieving this erasure of law and legal subjectivity, the ethical 'trial' of the mother is constituted through a series of breaches of the legal symbolic by the ethical abject. In turn, these breaches are governed by the rules of the face-to-face in which the absolute claim to truth of the one party is mirrored by the absolute denial of subjectivity with the other:

> In the face-to-face, I am fully, immediately and irrevocably responsible for the other who faces me. A face in suffering issues a command. A decree of specific performance: 'Do not kill me', 'welcome me', 'Give me Sanctuary', 'Feed me'. The only possible answer to the ethical imperative is 'an immediate respect for the other himself ... because it does not pass through the natural element of the universal, and through respect, in the Kantian sense of the law'. (Derrida quoted in Douzinas and Warrington, 1994, pp 164–65)

This point is clearly in evidence in the meetings between Seer and the ghost of the dead girl. What is most interesting, however, is the way in which the video tape itself comes to take on the characteristic of the face that in the jurisprudence of alterity issues the decree of obligation to the other.

The video tape's distinctive extra-legal origins and its power to momentarily but absolutely erase its 'other' are clearly announced. It is announced first by its enclosure within a sealed wooden box presented to Seer from the hands of the dead girl, and, secondly, by the book-endings of static that frame the images caught by the camera. Moreover, the tape and the origins it contains is not merely a surrogate for the face of the girl, but rather becomes the face of Kyra herself (and it is here worth noting the similarity between the name Kyra and the Greek word Antigone uses for 'beloved head, face', *Kara* (Douzinas and Warrington, 1994, p 57)). This subsumption turns on the tape's metamorphosis from an instrument of representation of past events to the presentation of a face that is reduced to nothing other than its own suffering, death and injustice. It is as a *presentation* of the events themselves, therefore, that it obtains the power and force of an unmediated and unquestionable truth. And, as the truth of the face and the face of truth, it cannot but demand absolute acquiescence to its demands for ethical justice.

This breach of the legal symbolic by the presentation of the abject ethical contains within it the destruction or erasure of the legal subject. Faced with the presentation of an unmediated and immediate truth, the critical functions of the juror are rendered redundant. Expressing the characteristics of the veracity and authenticity of the abject ethical itself, the video tape and its images appear as something external to the world of legal relations. As a consequence of its extra-legal existence, it remains outside those relations that suture the viewer as juror. In its place, in the space in which the ethical obligation maintains momentary dominance, the viewer is transformed from active juror to passive spectator, a transformation expressed in Shyamalan's intercutting between the images on the tape and the increasingly intimate close-up of the father's move from disbelief to complete and unquestioning acceptance of what is being shown.

As the recipient of the truth, the accusation made by the father against the mother becomes impossible to answer. In the face of the face of the other, a face that is nothing other than her suffering, death and injustice, the one accused is forced into silence. The space in which her legal subjectivity is made meaningful and through which it can be articulated is, like all those that are caught in the Medusa-like power of its gaze, frozen and erased by the tyranny of the ethical claim to absolute truth and certainty. The question that immediately presents itself, of course, is where is there for this other silent other to narrate her story and to whom?

Conceptualising law and film; law and ethics

In many ways, the momentary erasure of law, along with the inability of these critical works to offer a sustained and sustainable challenge to legal relations, are the product of the radicalisation and the reification of both the concept of law and of its putative 'others'.

Understood in this way, it becomes apparent that the limits of critique are present within the individual concepts that, when paired together, constitute the relationship of law and ethics and law and film. In this way, the domination of ethics by law that has been identified at the climax of *The Sixth Sense* can be traced back into the singular concepts of ethics and law themselves. This point emerges through an examination of the concept of law present in both *Justice Miscarried* and *The Sixth Sense*.

In both works, law is presented in terms of a radicalised version of legal positivism (Douzinas and Warrington, 1994, pp 3–5).[4] A central tenet of positivism is the insistence on the sharp demarcation between law and other disciplines, including, by definition, ethics. Intimately connected to this premise, therefore, is the presentation of law as self-generating and self-propagating. These themes of positivism reappear in a critical variant through Douzinas and Warrington's insistence on the 'autonomy of law' and through the connected idea that law is constituted precisely through the exclusion of ethics.

This idea of the absolute separation of law from ethics is reinforced by locating each concept in distinct and incompatible realms. Thus, whilst positivism is agnostic as to the ground of the (excluded) ethical, its critical counterparts exhibit

---

4   For a general discussion of legal positivism, see Freeman, 2001; Morrison, 1995; and Penner, Schiff and Nobles, 2002.

no such equivocation. In diagnosing the ground of law, both Douzinas and Warrington and *The Sixth Sense* simultaneously pronounce the ground of ethics. For Douzinas and Warrington, law is rooted in the realm of consciousness, the legal symbolic, whilst ethics is said to emanate from the realm of the unconscious, the site of the ethical abject. *The Sixth Sense* replicates this division through its grounding of law in the sphere of the profane and ethics in the sphere of the spiritual or supernatural.

Correspondingly, whilst positivism remains silent as to the respective *values* of law and ethics, its critical counterpart shares no such inhibitions. On the contrary, both Douzinas and Warrington and Shyamalan imply that the values of the concepts of law and ethics – injustice and justice, respectively – are an integral part of the concepts themselves. It is in presenting these values in a reified manner, that is, as if they are the natural attribute or property of the concepts themselves, that the disjuncture at the level of form is replicated and reinforced as the level of substance.[5] It is as a consequence of this radicalism and reification of positivist conceptions of law through which law and ethics are not only denied any connection, but are placed in a relation of absolute and irresolvable hostility, that the domination of one over the other, of law over ethics, that is present in relations *between* law and ethics, is also built into the very concept of law adopted and adapted by positivism's critical counterparts.

A similar situation presents itself when viewed from the point of view of film, through its claim to an unmediated access and capturing of an 'objective reality'. Here film replicates many of the tendencies identified in both positivism and the reified presentation of the value of the concepts.

Both the critical power of *The Sixth Sense* and *Justice Miscarried* turn on the radicalised notion of an 'objectivity' through which the 'other' of law is said to offer a true and accurate picture of its adversary, a picture, moreover, that is hidden or masked by the 'bad conscience' of law's own self-representation. It is precisely this claim to truth that is captured in the subsumption of the video camera into the face and suffering abject and ethical other, thereby conflating, and reifying, the visual with the ethical. Again, as in the domination of the 'trial scene' discussed above, it is this radicalised and reified concept of realism that in vouchsafing the veracity of its own presentation leaves no room for equivocation, which is the very stuff of law and legal trials.

In conclusion, then, it is the case that the critical intent of the interdisciplinary study of film and law is undermined by co-joining concepts, each of which has the domination of the other residing at its core. It is a domination that will continue as long as radicalism is confused with critical engagement.

---

5   For a discussion of 'reification' see Rose, 1978.

Chapter 9

Endless streets, pursued by ghosts
Angus MacDonald

Three synopses

Synopsis one: a film where a killer is on the loose

The police want to catch him. So do the criminal underworld, because the police investigation is interfering with 'everyday' criminal business. The two sides race against each other. The criminals catch the killer first but the police intervene before the criminals can kill him.

Is this *M* (1931)? It is a plausible interpretation, and the foundation for interpretations, which then present the criminals as stand-ins for the Nazis, the police for the Weimar Republic, and the whole film a prophetic allegory of what happens when corruption captures the institutions of state. This version of the plot of the film concerns the double hunt for a child killer. The hunt is double because, as well as the police hunt, there is a criminal hunt. We assume the normality of the police hunt and the abnormality of the criminal hunt. The latter is motivated primarily by a wish to put an end to the disruption of ordinary criminal activity which the police hunt is causing. It is not that the child killer disrupts the criminal milieu, it is that the police reaction to the child killer disrupts the criminal milieu, by way of raids on nightclubs and demands for papers. There is no co-operation between police force and criminal milieu. Indeed, the criminal milieu is motivated by a wish to catch the child killer, partly due to its perception that the legal process will be too 'squeamish' to impose the only 'final solution' to the problem, which is the death penalty, a solution the criminals' leader is willing to carry out.

In comparing how the police and the criminal milieu carry out their parallel hunts, we might expect a contrast between the law-bound police activity and the vigilante activity of the gang. It doesn't work. To work, it would have to make a clear contrast between the methods of the police, bound by procedural propriety, proportionality and legality,[1] and the criminal mob, driven only by self-interest, fear and prejudice. Instead, we see the police enter and search premises without warrant, entrap an interviewee with false allegations, and bend to political pressure in their campaign. The criminal mob, on the other hand, when they capture the killer, show an odd and unexpected regard for legal procedure: the killer is preserved alive, appointed a 'lawyer', subject to a 'trial', and allowed to deliver a speech of explanation of his actions. Whilst these procedures may be parodic, that they occur at all should cause pause for thought. The criminal mob do not capture institutions of state, they impose upon themselves, at least temporarily, the restraint of law. That they supersede this restraint in ultimately deciding upon death for the killer is not done by means of a distortion of the legal process, but by its suspension,

---

1 All standards appropriate to public bodies in judicial review.

on the point that the killer is not responsible for his actions, and therefore a different calculus must be applied.

This is the calculus of self-interest: he must be killed because he is a threat to others: his victims, and the smooth running of business. The criminal mob were at first motivated by a wish to catch him before the authorities, precisely out of a contemptuous assessment that the authorities would sooner or later release him, in their liberality, and that only death would ensure their own interests. However, their resort to legal procedure shows an acknowledgment of legitimacy. The final scenes of some cuts of the film show that the criminals were under an illusion as to the liberality of the legal process. It in fact has no qualms about the killer's innocence, as we see the judiciary don the black cap of the death penalty. The criminals need not have worried! The legal establishment shares their priorities!

If fundamental values and respect for human rights do not distinguish the forces of criminality from the forces of law, then the notion of a competition between the two sides is weakened. Besides, although the criminals are aware of the need to get to the killer before the police, the police are uninformed and puzzled by what the criminals are up to. They do not know that they are in a race. Turn then to another synopsis, defining the two sides by methods, not values.

Figure 12: *M*, Lang, 1931.

Synopsis two: a killer on the loose in a modern city

Which is the most efficient method for catching the killer, the approach of the police, or of the underworld? What knowledge of the city is available to each? A competition comes into play between abstract and concrete knowledge.

The film plays out a narrative set in a city. We first have to get to know the places of the film: the city. We see a tenement, a courtyard, a stairwell, streets, a café, an abandoned factory, a police office, a nightclub, a rented room, a toyshop window, an office block, an attic storage space, an underground basement. These spaces make up a city, and M poses the epistemological question, how is it possible to have any knowledge of these spaces, this city? The answer given is relativist: there are multiple knowledges of the city.

At first the film seems to organise all knowledges into a polarity: the abstract knowledge of those who know the city from above, and the concrete knowledge of those who know the city from below. The official police knowledge of the city, corresponding to the first category, is based on maps and records and other documents. The knowledge of the city of the criminal milieu, corresponding to the second category, is based on a presence in the streets, an activity requiring watching and listening to the city. There is a polarisation of points of view from which the city can be observed. There is the point of view of law and there is the point of view of the forces in an urban milieu which resist law. Schematically this amounts to the point of view from above and the point of view from below. M dramatises this schema.

Indeed, a reading of the film might make a dialectical contrast between the master police and the servant criminal: whereas the master has an ideal knowledge of the city, the criminal has a material practice in the city. With Kojeve (1980), we might expect the superior knowledge of the servant to triumph, but the police and the criminal do not have this kind of relationship.

Instead, this appealing interpretation lays the foundation for a contrast between the knowledge of the city open to the forces of detection, and to the forces of surveillance. The police proceed by looking for clues, such as attempting to locate the place where the note was written against a rough grained wood surface, correlating this with the addresses of those who fit the psychological profile, or at least those who have psychological records. The police use access to the state archives and to premises in order to conduct their search. At the outset, when they 'don't have a clue', they disturb the criminal underworld by raiding bars and scrutinising identity papers. They use the authority the law gives them, in other words. The criminal underworld do not look for clues, they look for the man. They do not have access to records of the past events, but they do have inconspicuous access to the streets, via the beggars. They will catch the man if and when he strikes again, they are ready, and they are organised: this is a very corporate criminal world, with co-ordination between sectors of the industry managed at the highest level.

The dualism must not be over-emphasised, for example, a contrast between the abstract overview of the police and the real presence on the streets of the criminals, between Icarus and Dedalus, founders on the resort of both forces to maps of districts. It is the criminals who embody Foucault's panoptic surveillance (Foucault,

1979), observing all unnoticed, while the police use targeted interventions to generate more information.

Again, the attempted dualism breaks down. The criminals use maps. The police use informers. Their methods are not so distinct. What they have in common transcends the differences. What is most strikingly held in common is a distance from the 'ordinary citizens' of the metropolis. Whether shown as mothers, men in bars, or crowds on the street, the ordinary people are not aligned with the police any more than they are with the criminals. They are subject to sudden panics and accusations and distrusts. They see the killer everywhere in innocent actions. They are more of a hindrance than a help to the official investigation. As only a connection to the community would distinguish the forces of authority from the outlaw forces, and as this connection is lacking, an equation of the two forces arises.

To reach the third synopsis, let us return to the watching and listening briefly referred to. The situation of the city is connected to sight, to sound and triangulated with worry. Benjamin, in *The Arcades Project* (1999), quotes Simmel:

> Therefore the one who sees, without hearing, is much more ... worried than the one who hears without seeing. This principle is of great importance in understanding the sociology of the modern city. Social life in the large city ... shows a great preponderance of occasions to *see* rather than to hear people ... Before ... the nineteenth century, men were not in a situation where, for minutes or hours at a time, they could or must look at one another without talking to one another. (p 433)

The dominance of the gaze over speech in the modern city: why should this induce worry? What knowledge of the city does the voyeur gain, and how does it compare to the knowledge obtained by the listener? The voyeur by necessity employs an objectifying gaze, the listener eavesdrops upon, or even (notice how Simmel runs, hearing people talking to one another) engages in communication. The voyeur stands outside of the space constituted as a visual field, the listener/speaker is in the aural field. We have here another trope of the alienation effect of the modern city, how it produces an apartness in a crowd, the destructive effect of the city upon traditional community. The voyeur is outside while inside, seeing while knowing that he does not know what goes on with those others he observes. The listener/speaker, by contrast, is engaged in constructing an understanding in communication.

When, a little further on in *The Arcades Project*, Benjamin quotes Caillois on the manner in which the urban detective novel has transposed the forest setting and the figure of the hunter in Fenimore Cooper, 'where every broken branch signifies a worry or a hope, where every tree trunk hides an enemy rifle or the bow of an invisible and silent avenger' (p 439) into the city, once again the visual and unease combine. The detective/hunter is engaged in a semiotic quest, making meaning from signs. The both invisible and silent opponent has left behind traces, which are visible rather than audible: the broken branch. It is possible that the tracker may also be engaged in extracting signal from noise, and so making meaning from sound as well as sight, but it is notable that it is the trope of visibility which dominates in the task of finding clues. Barthes too connects the gaze to unease: '... the gaze *seeks*: something, someone. It is an *anxious* sign' (emphasis added, Barthes, 1985, p 238). The sights and sounds of the city, and the making of meaning from them, are best captured in a medium which combines the visual and the aural, like the cinema; and perhaps best at the moment when the addition of sound to image was still a novelty, in the early days of sound cinema. The exploitation of novelty leads to films which thematise sound and image and their relationship, amongst them, *M*. In *M*, there are many levels at which opposites duel, and the duel between the sight and sound is only the most abstract. Two attempted synoptic duels have been investigated: one more.

Synopsis three: the competing knowledges of the city belong not to institutions but to the senses

Sight and sound compete to instruct the observer and listener as to the activity of the city and the whereabouts of the killer. The film innovates in its secession from the presumed terrain of film, in its resort to sound as much as to sight in the construction of knowledges (Jay, 1993). The significant turning points in the film are all sonic events. We hear children playing while the mother waits for her child; the mother's voice calling for her child down empty stairwells; the killer talking to the first child before we see him. We never see a killing. The killer is detected by sound once: the blind beggar hears him whistle a tune heard at the time and place of an earlier killing. Alerted, he dispatches a boy to follow the killer by sight. The killer is marked by the 'M', yet evades capture. The killer is given away by sound again: trying to scrape his way out of the storage space where he hides, his noise is heard by the criminals. The police cannot see him. They follow his traces, but never catch up with him. The killer confesses his malady: he hears voices in his head, which make him kill. And, the mob gives him a hearing. It is sound which drives him, sound which identifies him, and sound which betrays him.

The working through of a dualism on the visual plane gives way to noise, from which a harmonious resolution is imposed by violence. The film is a melodrama: a play with music. The specificity of the relation of sound to image is the specifically cinematic feature of this work. It is through a focus on this aspect that a thematic reading of figures and discourses can be proposed which actually arises from the material of the film rather than being imposed by the purely narrative element.

The emphasis on sound alongside vision is symptomatic of the layered and limited duels in the film, which are actually symbiotic relations: the police and the criminals, the detective work and the surveillance, the sight and the sound. These binaries do not so much compete as collaborate to narrow down the zone of liberty of the killer until he is trapped: they operate as a pincer movement, moving in on him from both sides, until he is cornered. Their collaboration is clarified in the closing scenes, where the appearance of the law does not save the killer from a lynching, but merely ratifies the same decision. This unsatisfactory resolution is then overdetermined by the closing shot of certain cuts of the film: the mourning mothers. Lang and Harbou are both on record as considering this the moral of the tale: 'Mothers, look out for your little ones' (Lloyd, 1983, p 32).

M articulates (in both senses: enunciates and connects) figures and discourses of state, society, economy, desire, law, public sphere. The overriding dualism dramatised is, however, that of the competition between the police and the underworld to catch the child killer. This 'competition' is also a form of

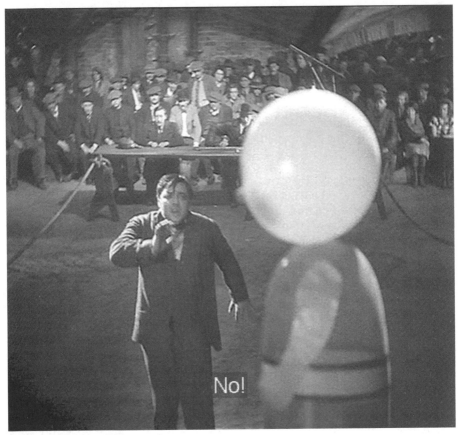

Figure 13: *M*, Lang, 1931.

co-operation. The goal is the same: the elimination of the disruptive figure of the killer from the smooth running of both law and crime. The film therefore articulates law and crime in a way far more subtle than a simple opposition. There is a structured opposition of points of view between that of the police and that of the criminal gang. Yet what is noteworthy is the anti-visuality of this opposition. We hear rather than see the killer's first 'appearance'. The police track traces – notably the pencil-written note and the grain of the windowsill – but they do not have sightings. Of the gang's beggars on the lookout, it is a blind beggar who hears the killer's whistle which is crucial to his capture. The film's very title comes from the exception: when he is seen, he is marked with a chalked 'M', but on that occasion he evades capture.

Thus, the killer, the random element at large in the city, evades detection and surveillance. It is the killer's noise which betrays him. The dramatisation the film offers baffles point of view. Instead of an image of points of view scouring the landscape to detect their quarry, which is what the film at first seems to offer, a better parallel would be the effort to detect recurrent patterns of significant sound in a complex recording. In this way, notions of above and below fail, at best replaced by perspectives of foreground and background.

It then becomes significant that there is silence in the background, the absence of an element against which this drama is being played out: the absence of a virtuous community. There is an avenging community turning on innocents, but the absence of an even neutral community produces the equivalence of police and gang. The film is full of silences and absences, starting from the absence of the child victim, and ending with the elimination of the killer.

The absence of community evacuates the legal process of specific content, of values, and makes it a value-indifferent form, and therefore it is not as shocking as it should be that this form is appropriated by the gang as easily as by the judiciary. The process in both cases also shows the subversion of law by policy, with rejection, in both cases, of the insanity plea in favour of the utilitarian death penalty.[2] In both cases, law exceeds its domain and produces an illegitimacy. It is anything but reassuring when the mothers (as mournful furies) appear after the legal process to insist above all on a new regime of surveillance.[3]

Having been absent from the whole film, the closing moments rush in law, family and community to shore up a conclusion which comes too late: their absence earlier, the society in which each was suspect to all, where police were no more legitimate than lynch mob, where state, figured by the government minister, appears only to bow to populist hysteria, determines the situation. If the end seems to close ranks against the scapegoat (Girard, 1986), it is a closing of ranks which has abandoned any interest in distinguishing the legitimacy of its methods or its values from those of the criminal milieu, a milieu which can indeed, along with the rest of this disconnected society, more like a Hobbesian condition of nature (Hobbes, 1968), return to criminal business as usual.

'M' speaks of running along endless streets pursued by ghosts. Ghosts, we can speculate, which he hears but does not see. He speaks of the ghosts of his victims and their mothers. The crowd of ghosts pursues, but never catches him because the streets are endless. These ghosts are what we do not see in the film: community and legality. Absent or turned to vengeance. They are drowned out by the voices urging killing. The voices in 'M''s head, the voices of the criminals and the voices of the mothers. All who want to kill. As Girard says, 'The murderers remain convinced of the worthiness of their sacrifices' (Girard, 1986, p 212). These murderers include 'M', the murderer, but, figure for a vengeful community, 'M' the mother also.

---

2 I am disagreeing here with Kaes, 2000, who argues that 'we do not learn the verdict' (p 75). The judges clearly don the black caps appropriate to death sentences.

3 It could be argued that the mothers are mournful and not vengeful, a contrast to, and not a confirmation of, vengeance elsewhere. I incline towards the view that they endorse the vengeance expressed earlier on behalf of mothers by the women in the criminal gang. Remember that the furies that abjure vengeance inaugurate law. Law is not inaugurated in M.

Five rules

Deleuze (1994) says the task of philosophy is the creation of concepts (p 5), and in his work on cinema he seeks to create concepts appropriate to the medium. His concepts of cinema do not fit into any of the dominant schools of film theory: they are neither concepts of auteurism, nor are they pertinent to the structural and semiotic analysis of film, which has been so influential in recent decades. Instead, he creates concepts of the narrative forms taken by cinema, in a manner that seems more indebted to Mitry (1998) than to either Sarris (1996) or Metz (1990). To Deleuze, the classical film consists of a structure (Situation Action Situation (SAS)) and what he terms the 'movement-image', and *M* is the 'perfection' of this form. The Deleuzian schema is used as a frame here.

Deleuze's study of cinema (1986) 'sets out ... to isolate certain cinematographic concepts' (p ix), by which is meant 'types of images and the signs which correspond to each type'. Deleuze distinguishes the movement-image from the time-image, and subdivides the former into the perception-image, the affection-image and the action-image. Deleuze's work returns to Bergsonian phenomenology, and thus rejoins the phenomenologically inspired theorisation of cinema developed by Mitry (1998) which was rather left behind with the rise of structuralist/semiotic understandings of the task of film theory (Metz, 1990). The current argument will pursue only the notion of the action-image.

Deleuze has given us an analysis of the centrality of the duel to a certain type of cinema, the cinema of the action-image. He itemises five laws of action-image cinema. In the Deleuzian schema, action-image cinema is a form in which what is at stake is the relation between 'milieux and modes of behaviour, milieux which actualise and modes of behaviour which embody' (Deleuze, 1986, p 141). The milieu acts on the character, throws him a challenge, and constitutes a situation in which he is caught. The character reacts in his turn (action properly speaking) so as to respond to the situation. To modify the milieu, or his relation with the milieu, he must raise his mode of being to the demands of the milieu. Out of this emerges a restored or modified situation, a new situation. The large form is the development from situation to transformed situation via the intermediary of action: SAS.

For this form, Deleuze identifies five laws. The first law of the action-image is of the situation as an ensemble defining the structural relations of places and moments. The second law governs the passage from situation to action. The third law concerns the place and moment of action, of the binomial. The fourth law is: the binomial is a polynomial. The fifth law is: there is a big gap between the situation and the action to come, but this gap exists only to be filled.

The first law 'concerns the action-image as organic representation in its entirety' (p 151). It offers well-defined oppositions in a structural organisation. It is '[a] spiral of development which includes spatial and temporal caesuras'. Deleuze gives as an example the milieux established in the opening shots of *M*: 'the courtyard of the building in town, the landing and the kitchen of an apartment in the building, the journey from the apartment to the school, the posters on the walls, people's excitement ...' (p 152).

From this opening situation, the second law operates to identify a narrative thread emerging from the labyrinth of the ensemble – the particular story to be told out of the infinite possibilities. In *M*, 'two points emerge from this milieu, then two lines of action which ... form a pincer to grab the criminal: the line of the police and the line of the underworld ...' (p 152).

The third law addresses the moment of the action, which will transform the situation: 'there must be a moment where two terms confront each other face-to-face and must be seized in an irreducible simultaneity' (p 153). This is where the application of his schema to *M* begins to falter: if the two terms are the police and the criminals, this *never* happens – unless we take the climactic appearance of the police in the cellar where the criminal trial is being conducted to instantiate it. This is not particularly plausible, as it occurs too late in the film to perform the pivotal function attributed to this moment. The duel, in these terms, cannot be between the police and the criminals. It could only be between the police plus the criminals and 'M', and even then, no irreducible simultaneity brings the three together, an ambiguity noted in Deleuze's next prevarication.[4] For *M*, Deleuze asks:

> In *M*, is the real duel between M and the police or society, or rather between M and the underworld, which does not want him? Does not the real duel remain elsewhere? Finally it might be external to the film, although internal to the cinema. In the scene of the underworld tribunal, the bandits and the beggars vindicate the rights of the crime habitus or mode of behaviour, crime as rational organisation, and criticise M for acting through passion. To which M replies that this is what makes him innocent: he cannot do otherwise, he only acts through impulse or affect, and at precisely this moment, and only at this moment the actor acts in an Expressionist way. Finally is not the true duel in *M* between Lang himself and Expressionism? It is his farewell to Expressionism. It is his entry into realism ... (p 153)

Deleuze claims that the fourth law requires that 'a dovetailing of duels in each other occurs', where 'the binomial is a polynomial' (p 153). This principle is crucial in allowing the expansion of analysis out of the narrative framework, remarking on the cinematic form yet even going beyond this limit.

There is some imprecision in Deleuze's analysis here. If the binomial, the juncture of two laws is indeed actually a polynomial, a juncture of many laws, then the search for the *real* duel, for the *true* duel, is surely misplaced. And if the multiplicity of duels can be external to the film, yet internal to the cinema, then the sequence of duels should include the duel between sight and sound. Yet why should the developing spiral of duels cease at the boundaries of cinema? The polynomial process exceeds cinema, and the film allegorises social relations as well as aesthetic. The duel between police and underworld (and Deleuze slips when he elides 'the police or society') is also a duel between state and society, one where the object becomes not the criminal but the law. All these duels are co-existent as the film is not realist but representational and the representational is also allegorical.

---

4   Deleuze argues that the real duel is here revealed as that between the criminals and 'M', but concedes that ambiguity remains, as the arrival of the police will destabilise the situation.

The stakes of the fourth rule are reinforced by the fifth rule, which returns us to the relation between situation and action. Action does not occur *in* a situation but on the other side of a gap between situation and action, a gap (p 155), a delay, which requires the duration of the film in order to establish this relation. Also, a gap within which the allegorical meaning of even a realist film is generated.

Allegory/critique

Can we claim that any film can give us an understanding of law? If a particular film addresses a particular legal issue, the pedant's first question will be, did the film get the law 'right'? This sets up an opposition between the real of the law and the fantasy of the law, and if the pursuit of veracity is invoked, then the fantasy must cede to the real. This prescribes for a film with a legal theme a realist aesthetic, and indeed many do adopt the mode of the realist narrative: the trial movie, for example, where we see the playing out of a thriller narrative, where the court's verdict is also the plot's resolution, telling the viewer whodunit. But this is a self-denying ordinance, for if a film about law can only tell us anything about law as long as it is *realistic*, then why resort to a film at all in the attempt to understand law? Why go to the Odeon when the Old Bailey keeps a public gallery open? In any case, the realist film can never satisfy the pedant's retort. It will never quite get the law *right*. At the least it will telescope the action of days into a few hours; most likely it will distort rules of procedure and evidence. Better, then, to look to the law film for an understanding of the fantasy of law than of the reality of law. But this does not require us to turn to the fantasy film, only to realise that even the realist film cannot tell us much about law, but only about how law is imagined. This diminishes the relevance of the study of the law film less than might appear, however, as how the law is imagined is a major factor in the real evolution of the law. The public's fear of crime, for example, is acknowledged as a real factor in decisions about policing, even when that fear is factually groundless. Less obviously, the public's imaginary relationship to the institutions of state defines the real parameters of debate about, for example, the UK's relationship to the rest of Europe, thought in terms of the risks to 'our' sovereignty. This also does not mean that study of the law film becomes only a sociology, reducing the study of a law film to its impact on the particular culture pertinent to its time and place of origin.

Deleuze's rules can be used to produce the three synopses outlined above, with a little modification. The structure of an analogy is a double relation: a correspondence between two things because of a third element that they are considered to share, and is a form of inference: that if two things agree in at least one respect, then they may agree in other respects.

In *M*, the narrative structure is precisely this: a presentation of the correspondence between two things, the police force and the criminal milieu, because of the shared element, the wish to catch the child killer. This simple equation, police force equals criminal milieu, has been the basis of interpretations of *M* as an allegory for the rise of Nazism, showing what happens when a criminal gang usurps the legitimate function of maintaining social order. The film is sufficiently ambiguous, however, to have been received warmly by at least some Nazis as an apologia for the death penalty as 'social hygiene'.

It is the analogical relation which must be analysed. *M* does not simply embody an equation of the police force with the criminal milieu; the criminals are like the police as regards the child killer: whether there are further similarities remains to be established. Moreover, it is not so much the undertaking of the police function by the criminal milieu which is anomalous (we know, after all, many crime fiction detectives whose deepest camaraderie is with criminals, both seeing themselves as outside normal society), as the curious assumption by the criminal milieu of the adjudication process. The film's allegorical character eclipses its realism at the point at which the criminal gang constitutes itself as a court of law for the purpose of a trial. As sound cinema replaced silent cinema, and a stylised realism replaced expressionist allegory, it seemed as if the explicit allegorical style of filmmaking, such as Lang practised in *Metropolis*, was now inappropriate. This new concreteness can obscure the continued practice of large-scale allegory built upon units of analogy, which is to be found in *M*.

The analogical structure (a correspondence between two things because of a third element that they are considered to share) develops as a narrative structure and a cinematic structure. It is by analogy and not by duel that the key relationships in *M* are built. The critical scholarship of film studies, auteurist, structuralist or semiotic, provides a series of formal aesthetic schema by means of which film material may be analysed. The critical scholarship of law, dialectical, postmodernist, deconstructive or ethical, likewise provides a series of perspectives by means of which legal material may be analysed, not even to discuss the legalities of film, or the cinematicity of law. Is film abetting an understanding of law, or vice versa? Here it is the former: to provide an understanding of law by means of an analysis of one particular film. The film, *M*, contains a range of legally relevant tropes: the criminal, the police, the investigation of the crime, the fear of the crime in the community, the trial. The way the film presents these tropes leads to a glimpse of an understanding of law not otherwise available. Whether this glimpse reveals something substantial about law is a question for a different investigation: here and now, what has been done is the construction of the glimpse by an analysis of the construction of the film. There is sufficient scope in the film material to allow an allegorical reading of its narrative and its form.[5] The alternative would require preliminary proofs of the truth of the film's portrayal of law, this itself requiring, first of all, proof of the film's truthful portrayal of reality, and thus an investment in the aesthetics of realism. If we take *M* as allegory, and examine how the film imagines law, we can avoid such dead ends.

The film has been analysed at length, both as allegory and as documentary, without, even so, any agreement as to what exactly is allegorised or documented. A particular historical murderer is documented. The rise of fascism in Germany is allegorised. In reaching these conclusions, the role of law in the film's construction has been treated as mere means towards the desired narrative. What *M* does with law (and with film) is the issue examined here.

---

5 See also Pasolini's theory of poetic cinema in Nichols, 1976, pp 542–58.

By modifying the functioning of Deleuze's rules, in the direction of recognising more complex relations than duels, relations of analogy, where what links two parties is their common relation to a third element, the productivity of his polynomial method is extended. It, finally, allows connections to be made between the relationships within the narrative, within the cinematic form, and even to the activity of critical analysis performed upon the film:

> ... most languages do not dissociate [stereotypes of persecution]. This is true of Latin and Greek, for example, and thus of French or English, which forces us constantly in our study of stereotypes to turn to words that are related: *crisis, crime, criteria, critique*, all share a common root in the Greek verb *krino*, which means not only to judge, distinguish, differentiate, but also to accuse and condemn a victim. ... It implies an as yet concealed relationship between collective persecutions and the culture as a whole. (Emphasis added, Girard, 1986, p 22)

This etymology, then, has been retraced here, from a binomial kernel in the film's concrete and abstract duels and analogies outwards. The crime of 'M', the crisis of the city, the accusation and condemnation of the victim, the criteria of Deleuze and the critique concealed in the allegory revealed alongside the surface realism of the film. In this way, hopefully, nothing has been superimposed upon the film beyond a working out of the consequences of its structure. By demonstrating how the film creates concepts, which then reach beyond its limits, something is also said about the concepts of law, not by juxtaposition of one against the other, but by clarification of the process of representation of law, or more precisely, non-representation of law, which happens in the film. For although representation of crime, imagining crime (Young, 1996), is a widespread cultural activity, glimpsing the representation of law is more elusive. As Deleuze says of the fifth rule of action-image cinema, so it is equally valid to say of the moving image of law, that 'organic representation is ruled by this last law of development: *there must be a big gap between the situation and the action to come, but this gap only exists to be filled*, by a process marked by caesuras, as so many retrogressions and progressions' (emphasis added, Deleuze 1986, p 156). The caesuras and retrogressions of the film are the moments when law fails to appear. In *M*, law is never where it should be. In showing the consequences of an absence of law, the film does not provide an image of law, but nonetheless imagines law.

Chapter 10
'Into the blue': the cinematic possibility of judgment with passion

Alison Young

This chapter is broken into two parts.[1] In the first part, my concern is with the written texts of law; in the second, it is with a visual, cinematic text. The theme of both parts is nevertheless with the interpretation of HIV and its relation to the process of judgment, its force as a limit or liminal case in revealing the imaginary order of judgment. In substance, this chapter will concentrate upon the reading of cases concerning the judgment of the gay man before the law. Although focusing on the appearance of the gay man in judgment, the implications of my argument might well extend to the painful oscillation between negation and derogation in the legal imagination suffered by many marginalised groups. The intent of this chapter is not to advocate any kind of withdrawal from the legal sphere, any opting out of legal discourse. Rather, my intent is to find hopefulness in paradox: it is only in the disappearance of images that the compassionate envisioning of the other can take place.[2]

And then, in response to the pain and passion of the lover/the other, what might ideally be asked of the judge is compassionate judgment: judgment with passion, a connection to law's lost emotional body. And it is in the immaterial judgments of cinema that reflections of an ethics of judgment in law might be glimpsed.

To this end, I begin by emphasising a largely unremarked feature of modern judgment – namely, the legal recognition of phantasy as a distinct order of reality. The specific phantasy in question involves a narrative of abuse variously thematised in terms of homosexual sex and HIV infection. This phantasy is set in motion in an attempt to gain exemption from the ordinary responsibilities of legal subjecthood. I explore the judicial response to this move – namely, a narrative of the betrayal of trust between men. My argument in the first half of the chapter will be that the modern textuality of law has been occupied by a visual order of representation: to the extent that judgment has not been reduced to the anaesthetic product of administration, judgment becomes an aesthetics of appearance which returns law to the horizon of 'our' values.

---

1 An extended version of this chapter was presented at the Symposium on *Cultural Studies and the Law: Beyond Legal Realism in Interdisciplinary Legal Scholarship*, Yale Law School, April 2000, and at the 10th Annual International Conference of the Law and Literature Association of Australia, Sydney, July 2000. An extended version of this argument can be found in Young, 2001 and 2003. My thanks to Peter Rush for his thoughtful conversations throughout the writing of this article.

2 For other evocations of ethical or compassionate judgment, see Glass, 1997; Goodrich, 1990.

The second part of the chapter turns this understanding of judgment on its head. The resource for this task is the cinema of Derek Jarman, specifically his film *Blue* (1993). This text comprehends the judgment of HIV/AIDS as an aesthetics of disappearance. Paradoxically, the visual text is iconoclastic. As Jarman will put it, our prayer or plea must be to be *delivered from image*. My gloss on the visual text draws this iconoclastic process into relation with an ethics of alterity and the materials for reconstructing judgment.

HIV and the legal aesthetics of appearance

(a) Legal phantasies

In *Green v R* (1997), the accused, Malcolm Green, had been convicted of murdering his friend Don Gillies, the local real estate agent. It was well known, by Green and in the small town in which they lived, that Gillies was gay. One night, Green and Gillies ate dinner and watched television together. They drank a considerable amount of alcohol and at least one of them used amyl nitrate. Green stayed the night. At some point, Green beat Gillies, and killed him by stabbing him with scissors and bashing his head against the bedroom wall. Green tried to clean up the blood, failed, and called the police.

At the trial, the prosecution case was that Green had killed Gillies pursuant to a premeditated plan to kill, and that his defence story was an invention. The defence claim was that Gillies had made persistent homosexual advances to Green, which had prompted in Green an image of his father beating his mother and sexually assaulting his sisters, causing him to lose self-control and kill Gillies. He was convicted of murder, unsuccessfully appealed against the conviction to the Court of Criminal Appeal of New South Wales, and then successfully appealed to the High Court of Australia. His case was sent back for re-trial; at the second trial, Green was acquitted of murder and convicted of manslaughter on the grounds of provocation, receiving a sentence of 10 years' imprisonment.

The case, then, is one of a number of so called 'homosexual advance' cases: in a series of Australian and North American cases, heterosexually identified male defendants have argued that an alleged homosexual advance provides a basis for the defence of provocation (and sometimes self-defence).[3] It has become increasingly common in homicide trials in Australia. For example, between 1993 and 1995 in New South Wales, 13 murder trials saw the homosexual advance defence invoked. Of those trials, two resulted in acquittals; two in jury verdicts of murder; three in verdicts of not guilty of murder but guilty of manslaughter; eight resulted in pleas being accepted to a lesser charge such as manslaughter and one case was dismissed (Attorney General's Department, New South Wales, 1996).

Successful attempts to enter evidence about a homosexual advance can be seen in the following cases. For example, one accused said an elderly man invited him for a

---

3 See Australian cases such as *R v Pritchard* (1990); *R v Stiles* (1990); *R v Grmusa* (1990); *R v Preston* (1992); *R v Whittaker* (1993). The homosexual advance defence has received much attention, judicial and academic, in Anglo-American jurisdictions: eg, see Howe, 1997; Mison, 1992; Moran, 1996.

drink in his house; he accepted. The old man grabbed his buttocks and made an indistinct comment. The accused beat him with a garden gnome, then stabbed him to death. He was found guilty of manslaughter rather than murder and received a three-year sentence of imprisonment. In another case, the defendant, while riding his bike along a cycle path, saw a man in a dress waving his penis and shouting at him. The defendant beat the man to death. He was found not guilty of murder and guilty of manslaughter (Marr, 1999, p 60). Although straightforward claims that the accused killed in direct response to a homosexual advance have been successful, defence lawyers soon realised that an argument based on homosexual advance would be more persuasive if it could be tethered to some additional feature.

However, the case of *Green* (1997) is distinctive for linking homosexual advance to a *phantasy* of abuse (as opposed to any actual experience of abuse). During police questioning, Green said two crucial things. The first arose soon after he arrived at the police station: 'He told the police: "Yeah, I killed him, but he did worse to me." When asked why he had done it, the appellant said: "Because he tried to root me"' (quoted in Kirby J, *Green* (1997), p 700). Green thus constructed himself in the now classic manner as the object of a homosexual advance, wherein the possibility of homosexual anal intercourse is viewed as worse than death. However, later in the interrogation, Green also added the following, 'In relation to what had happened this night I tried to take it as a funny joke but in relation to what my father had done to four of my sisters it forced me to open more than I could bear' (quoted in Toohey J, *Green* (1997), p 667). Green was asked at trial to explain what he meant by this. He explained:

> Well, it's just that when I tried to push Don away and that and I started hitting him it's just – I saw the image of my father over two of my sisters ... and they were crying and I just lost it ... Because of those thoughts of me father just going through me mind ... About [him] sexually assaulting me sisters ... (quoted in Toohey J, *Green* (1997), p 667).

In short, the defence that was persuasive for the High Court and for the jury at the re-trial comprised two elements: one, a homosexual advance by a male friend; and two, an image of heterosexual and incestuous abuse. As McHugh J stated: 'The sexual, rather than homosexual, nature of the assault filtered through the memory of what the accused believed his father had done to his sisters, was the trigger that provoked the accused's violent response' (*Green* (1997), p 683).[4] In the arguments of the defence, accepted by the majority of the High Court, these two elements are fused so that Gillies' actions become characterised as sexual abuse by a father figure. Only on the basis of the displacement of homosexuality and its replacement with abuse by a father figure does the judiciary bind the objectivity of what has now become 'sexual abuse' with a subjective phantasy.

---

4   In respect of the homosexual advance, the prosecution did not concede that there had been such an advance. At most, there had been amorous or sexual touching by Gillies, which the accused could easily have rebuffed. As Kirby J remarked in his dissenting opinion in the High Court: 'if every woman who was the subject of a "gentle", "non-aggressive" although persistent sexual advance ... could respond with brutal violence rising to an intention to kill or inflict grievous bodily harm on the male importuning her, and then claim provocation after a homicide, the law of provocation would be sorely tested and undesirably extended' (*Green* (1997), p 719).

In respect of the image of the abuse that the accused said he experienced, the prosecution argued that it was concocted or irrelevant. But the reality of this image of abuse was endorsed in the High Court, and endorsed in a distinctive way. All the judges noted that the accused did not witness directly the sexual abuse of his sisters; all noted that whether or not such abuse occurred is immaterial. What was important is that the accused was told of the abuse and told by his mother and sisters. What the accused heard from the lips of others became a visual scene that he played in his head. The accused became, as described by his lawyer and the High Court judges, a person carrying around 'mental baggage'[5] with the image of abuse a burdensome prosthesis. Gillies' sexual overtures – a touching of Green on the hip as they lay in bed together – animated this prosthesis so that, the defence argued, in killing Gillies, Green was killing the image (of his father). As McHugh J (dissenting in the Court of Criminal Appeal) confirms, 'He sees the advance through the spectacles of what his father had done to his sisters' (Green (1996), p 30). The validity of Green's substitution mechanism is affirmed by the High Court's determination to reconstruct the victim as a 'father figure', as Brennan CJ comments:

> The real sting of the provocation could have been found not in the force used by the deceased but in his attempt to violate the sexual integrity of a man who had trusted him as a friend and father figure ... and in the evoking of the appellant's recollection of the abuse of trust on the part of his father (Green (1997), p 665).[6]

The victim, then, in his sexual touching of Green, betrayed the trust between friends, between men.

The case of Green, then, marks the recognition by law of the visual force of phantasy. More than this, however, it recognises a visual phantasy that exists through a conversion of oral familial stories into the realm of the visual.[7] The force of such phantasy cannot be evaluated by reference to an empirical reduction: there is no derivation of the image from the father's behaviour as seen by Green (in fact, Green had not seen his father for approximately 12 years). And it cannot be reduced to the symbolic order of law: this is not homophobia per se (although the majority in the Australian High Court and the minority in the Court of Criminal Appeal cannot restrain themselves from commenting on the moral reprehensibility and horror of an amorous homosexual encounter).[8] In short, phantasy emerges here as a space of

---

5 In transcript of application for special leave to appeal to the High Court, Green (1996), p 9, per defence counsel and Gummow J.

6 McHugh J also describes Gillies as 'a person whom the accused looked up to and trusted' (Green (1997), p 683). In the Court of Criminal Appeal, Smart J commented on 'the deceased's betrayal of the relationship of trust, dependency, friendship and the abuse of his hospitality' (quoted in Kirby J's opinion, Green (1997), p 704). In applying for special leave to appeal to the High Court, defence counsel argued: 'He said ... there were flashes of his father over his two sisters, at the time he lost self-control, that he kept hitting him because he felt trapped. The evidence ... would establish a clear connection between his relationship with the deceased as a father figure and his own sense of betrayal in relation to his relationship with his father' (Green (1996), p 2).

7 In contrast, see the provocation cases R v Moffa (1977) and R v Tuncay (1998), which emphasise that words must be of a violent or extreme character in order to be provocative.

8 See, eg, the comments of Smart J in the Court of Criminal Appeal, where he states: 'Some ordinary men would feel great revulsion at the homosexual advances being persisted with in the circumstances ... They would regard it as a serious and gross violation of their body and their person ...' (quoted in the judgment of Brennan CJ, Green (1997), p 665).

the imaginary: it is the specular phantasy of law. As Lacan emphasises, phantasy has a protective quality for the subject: Lacan compares the scene of phantasy to a frozen image on a cinema screen, as if the film had been stopped in order to avoid showing a traumatic scene (Lacan, 1994, pp 119–20).[9] Phantasy fixes and immobilises a threat or trauma, which can then be excluded from representation. The tales told in law become specularised as a visual phantasy, which can screen out or guard against the threat embodied by the object of law – here, portrayed as the gay man.

(b) Killing the image

The following case shows how the law's recognition of the visual phantasy of the gay man as a betrayer of the trust between men can be given additional force through its reconfiguration with HIV. The case also shows the judiciary actively participating in the defendant's phantasy of the gay man. In *Benjamin Bruce Andrew and Peter Clive Kane* (1999), also involving the murder of a gay man, the phantasy again involves the narrative of abuse and betrayal by the gay man, but it is conjoined with the imagined embodiment of the gay man as a repository of HIV infection. In this case, two 16-year-old boys killed a man called Wayne Tonks. They were prosecuted for murder: the jury found Peter Kane guilty of murder and Benjamin Andrew guilty of manslaughter.

At the trial, Andrew argued that, several weeks earlier, he had been forced to have sex with Tonks, and that he became increasingly aggrieved over this. Andrew had come into contact with Tonks by finding his name and phone number in a public toilet. Andrew was being teased at school for possibly being gay; he said at trial that he wanted to ask Tonks, whom he did not know, for advice. It turned out that Tonks was a schoolteacher, albeit at a different school and with his identity as a gay man unknown to family and colleagues. Andrew went to Tonks' apartment in the early hours of one morning; they drank alcohol, they watched a porn video; Andrew alleged that he was then forced to have anal sex with Tonks. Some time later, he became convinced that he was infected with HIV and obtained an HIV test (pp 11 and 15). Tonks was not HIV positive and the accused did not test positive. In a state of anxiety about the encounter he had had, Andrew, with his friend Kane, returned to Tonks' apartment equipped with baseball bat, duct tape and a plastic bag: they had agreed beforehand that Andrew would verbally abuse Tonks and if necessary hit him (p 11).

The sentencing judge commented that it was plain that Andrew's aim was 'to avenge himself on the victim by inflicting ... bodily injury serious enough to expunge what ... was his firm conviction that he had been subjected to vile and degrading conduct wholly unprovoked by, and wholly unwelcome to, him' (pp 18–19). Together, Andrew and Kane beat Tonks with the baseball bat, bound, gagged and blindfolded him and left him with the plastic bag fastened over his head, so that he later suffocated. While Kane was convicted of murder, Andrew was convicted of manslaughter by reason of provocation.

---

9 On phantasy and the structure of attachment more generally, see Laplanche and Pontalis, 1986.

His defence had succeeded in ways similar to those played out in *Green*. In both cases, gay sex is identified with sexual abuse. In both cases, sexual abuse is then hitched to a phantasy – of familial abuse in *Green* and of HIV infection in *Andrew and Kane*. In both cases, the salience of the phantasies is that they are elements in a legal narrative of the betrayal of trust between men (in *Andrew and Kane*, Tonks is judicially constructed as the teacher, the older man, the paternal figure of trust, who should have given advice, but who instead exacted anal intercourse). And finally, in both cases, this legal narrative of betrayal produces an anti-portrait of the dead gay man. Where in *Green*, however, this specular image belonged to the defendant and was recognised by the judges, in *Andrew and Kane*, the sentencing judge himself participated in the perception of the victim as the embodiment of infective abuse. Sully J considered the event described by Andrew and his phantasy of infection as being significant in understanding the 'objective criminality' of Andrew (1999, p 7).

This objective criminality is measured against an imagined portrait of the dead man. As with many cases of homophobic murder, the judge noted that the dead cannot speak; others speak to the court on their behalf. Sully J characterised this 'body of material' representing the deceased as 'damaging as it inevitably was in its illumination of the character and lifestyle of the dead man' (p 7; see also p 14). The oral tales told by witnesses were transformed into a judicial image of the identity of the victim. In this conversion, law attaches an intention or desire to the dead. Tonks was described by Sully J as having 'a clandestine but active homosexual lifestyle' and 'a particular attraction towards teen-aged boys and young men. He actively sought out homosexual encounters with such partners, doing so by a number of methods of which one was to solicit, in effect, by leaving appropriate invitations and personal details inscribed on the walls of public toilets' (pp 6–7). Sully J glossed this 'lifestyle' as follows:

> It could scarcely be doubted that there are many people – and, more probably than not, a clear majority of people – in contemporary Australian society for whom the kind of lifestyle that the late Mr Tonks is shown to have followed would be morally reprehensible, physically repellent and socially subversive. All the more reason to emphasise in the strongest and most uncompromising of terms that a person who follows that lifestyle, even if that lifestyle entails the committing of serious criminal offences, does not become on that account an outlaw whose life is simply forfeit to anybody who feels strongly enough to take it in fact. The paramount purpose of the rule of law is to uphold in principle and to shield in practice the absolute and fundamental sanctity of human life: all human life. (p 7)[10]

A compromise is being effected here, evidenced in the acceptance of the defence of provocation, the leniency recommended by the jury, and the judge's endorsement of leniency in a reduced sentence of six years imprisonment. The compromise is between the moral principle of the sanctity of all human life (which has no exceptions, which cannot be sacrificed in ideal or in practice) and the subjective legitimacy, for law, of killing those who are its practical exceptions: the abusive and infectious outlaws whose necessary and contradictory inclusion within legal discourse shores up the moral principle of the legal sanctity of life.

---

10 This echoes the comments of Smart J in the Court of Criminal Appeal in *Green*, when he describes the 'great revulsion' that 'some ordinary men' would feel at a homosexual advance (quoted in the judgment of Brennan CJ, *Green* (1997), p 665).

Into the blue: the aesthetics of disappearance

My reading of these two cases has shown that judgment in legal texts is predicated upon an aesthetics of appearance – a conversion of writing into a specular image. Moreover, that aesthetics subjects the appearance of gay sex and HIV positivity to the horizon of 'our values': the values of the 'ordinary' person, of the territorial nation state, the values and law of the living. In reading these cases, I have sought to show the carceral effects of imagination: the image of the gay man conjured in each judgment freezes and frames the victims Gillies and Tonks. And at the same time, the defendants – Green and Andrew – are retrospectively empowered to act in response to that image, to act without the constraints which normally enjoin against killing or against discrimination. My aims in this second part of the chapter are to reject law's judgment of the gay man or the HIV positive gay man through an invocation of appearance (of the image), and to argue instead that we might look towards the aesthetics of disappearance achieved in certain cultural texts. Such texts – exemplified here by *Blue* (1993) – help us forestall the closure of community effected by the legal aesthetics of appearance and open the processes of judgment to the proximate others dwelling in law. In the written texts of law, HIV is made to appear through a phantasy of abuse (leading to the legitimated annihilation of the personae of infection), while the visual texts of culture approach the representation of HIV through an image of disappearance, or disappearing images.

A comparative reading of the legal and cultural texts of HIV allows us to ask what understanding of judgment could take account of the suffering and fleshly body. In *Andrew and Kane* (1999), judgment proceeds from the sense of betrayal imagined in the transmission of HIV. The judge projects anger and vengeance in response to such an imaginary event, and makes it an *a priori* condition for any judgment of the gay man. In the cultural text that this chapter examines, HIV transmission is more than any phantasy, it is bodily reality. Derek Jarman's film *Blue* offers an approach to the other and a means to approach the image as if it were the body of the other, without vengeance or anger. In contrast to the self-righteously violent judgment of law, in this cinematic text can be found a relation of compassionate judgment.

Blue, a film made by Derek Jarman, the British artist, filmmaker, writer and gardener, who died of AIDS in 1994, is structured around a liminal moment between appearance and disappearance. The film is at once a meditation on colour and also a film without a moving image.[11] For 75 minutes, the screen is filled with cobalt blue, while voices, sounds and music enact scenes, read poems, toll bells and provide an aural landscape for that which cannot be seen. *Blue* gives up the glamour and the visual charge of cinema, although its abstractions, however, are still rooted in narrative: a narrative of pleasure (sunshine on a warm summer day, sex with a good looking stranger, dancing in nightclubs), of anger (at AIDS activism,

---

11 The chapter 'Into the Blue' (Jarman, 1995) represents the text of the film *Blue*. Quotations of lines from the film can be found in that text. The film's image is motivated by Jarman's admiration of Yves Klein, of whom Jarman writes, 'The great master of blue – the French painter Yves Klein. No other painter is commanded by blue ...' (1995, p 104). On the film, see Lombardo, 1994; Schwenger, 1996; Smith 1993.

at the double bind of AIDS drug trials), of grief (for lost friends already dead from AIDS), of mourning and the contemplation of one's own death. Of the film, Lombardo (1994) writes, 'With a violent leap, the most bodyless film ever produced projects the human body in its most cruel and unspeakable presence: pain, illness, suffering at the borderline between the physical and the mental, the conscious and the unconscious, life and death' (p 133). *Blue* is a judgment of death, of the inscription of bodily pain: the pain of radical otherness, of the loss of self and the loss of the other.

Jarman was losing his sight as a result of cytomegalovirus (CMV). *Blue* allows us to imagine sightlessness and the rehearsal of imminent but still uncertain death. Rehearsal becomes the main modality of existence, '[t]he worst of this illness is the uncertainty. I've played this scenario back and forth each hour of the day for the last six years' (Jarman, 1995, p 109). Rehearsal and repetition: with every opening succeeded by a moment of closure, as the narrative plays on and out towards its end. To that extent, *Blue* has a perfectly circular, or perhaps spiralling, structure. The opening lines of *Blue* evoke an awakening to vision:

> You say to the boy open your eyes
> When he opens his eyes and sees the light
> You make him cry out. Saying
> O Blue come forth
> O Blue arise
> O Blue ascend
> O Blue come in (p 107)

'Blue' is thus marked as the space of subjectivity and relationality, a gesture which intensifies with the subsequent passage, 'Blue of my heart/Blue of my dreams/ Slow blue love/Of delphinium days' (pp 107–08). In *Blue*'s closing poem, having moved through details of illness, treatment and decline, the final line re-writes 'blue' as the space of subjectivity, relationality and death, 'I place a delphinium, Blue, upon your grave' (p 124). 'Blue' is not only the colour of the screen that captivates the gaze of the spectator; it also names and marks the site to which the oral speech is destined or transmitted (in a juridical terminology, it is *justice*). And *Blue* always moves towards death. The key motifs of the opening minutes are given a melancholic finality as Jarman reads the closing lines:

> Our name will be forgotten
> In time
> No one will remember our work
> Our life will pass like the traces of a cloud
> And be scattered like
> Mist that is chased by the
> Rays of the sun
> For our time is the passing of a shadow
> And our lives will run like
> Sparks through the stubble.
> I place a delphinium, Blue, upon your grave. (pp 123–24)

In some ways, the film makes literal the difficulties inherent in the struggle to portray the unpresentable that is HIV, the virus that cannot be seen, the illness that for years has no symptoms other than invisible antibodies present in the blood. As

Haver (1996) evokes, the struggle to represent the relation of the self to the loss of self occasioned by AIDS, 'signals what will henceforth be the impossibility of language, communication, and sociality' (p 124), an impossibility inscribed as a narrative of melancholia, desire and mourning. David Wojnarowicz, another artist who died from AIDS, spoke angrily of the pain of being frozen in the image: 'Sometimes I come to hate people because they can't see where I am. I've gone empty, completely empty and all they see is the visual form ... I'm a Xerox of my former self ... I am disappearing. I am disappearing but not fast enough.'[12]

Blue engages with the paradoxical acceleration of invisibility in the image imposed upon marginal groups (often those who have become synonymous with the transmission of HIV): gay men, injecting drug users, whiteness' racial others, prisoners. Jarman's film can thus be understood as an activist intervention, from an artist who for years had been sickened by the endless parade of stereotypes deployed by the British media when depicting gay sexuality and when depicting HIV/AIDS.[13] As Jarman asks in *Blue*, 'How are we to be perceived, if we are to be perceived at all? For the most part we are invisible' (p 113).[14] Jarman is all too aware that visibility can be a projection, an image constructed around a condensation of fearful signifiers.[15] He notes that HIV infection invokes, 'All the old taboos of/ Blood lines and blood banks/Blue blood and bad blood/Our blood and your blood/I sit here and you sit there' (p 121), linking social class, racial and sexual segregation, and homophobia in the overcoded signifier of blood which works to effect a paradoxical visual invisibility.

Both intensely figurative (representing blue as sexual desire, sadness, melancholy, serenity and so on) and also utterly literal in that it presents to us no image other than a blue screen, *Blue* is a cinematic work that rejects kinesis, the moving image. It has no personae in the sense of actors or characters, places or scenes. It thus removes the object of the gaze by providing instead a visual object, which remains unmoving. *Blue* is thus strangely paradoxical: film is the art of the moving image, while *Blue* is a film whose image does not move. Attachment to the image is interrupted by the immobile image of blue. While the spectator seeks in vain for something to look at, the film insists rather that we listen and remember. Jarman tells us, 'In the roaring waters/I hear the voices of dead friends ... My heart's memory turns towards you ...' (p 108). *Blue* detaches the spectator from the screen and attaches the viewer to the voice. In this process, we are removed into an audience of voices, into an ethical relation that allows a response to the suffering other.

The scene of a judgment with passion

Jarman's displacement of visual personae is not simply a consequence of filmmaking after the advent of blindness, but rather:

---

12 Text from the artwork, *Untitled* (1992), by David Wojnarowicz.

13 See the account in Peake, 1999, esp Chapter 27; and Parkes, 1996, p 137.

14 See also the discussion of visibility, nationality and queer politics in the cinema of AIDS (including Jarman's *Blue*) in Smith, 1993.

15 Further on the metaphorisation of HIV/AIDS and its consequences, see Sontag, 1991; Watney, 1989; Young, 1996.

> In the pandemonium of image
> I present you with the universal Blue
> Blue an open door to soul
> An infinite possibility
> Becoming tangible. (p 112)

Caught in the tension between the tyranny of the image and the desire to make images, Jarman enjoins us:

> For accustomed to believing in image, an absolute idea of value, [the] world had forgotten the command of essence: Thou Shalt Not Create Unto Thyself Any Graven Image, although you know the task is to fill the empty page. From the bottom of your heart, pray to be delivered from image. (p 114–15)

Thus, Jarman uncovers the attachment to the visual order that is entailed when phantasy seizes the imagination. His injunction – 'pray to be delivered from image' – substitutes 'image' for 'evil' in the conventional invocation. A plaintiff before the court was archaically said to 'pray' to the court for relief. One of my aims in this chapter has been to trace this indelible, if illegible, prayer as the vocation of judgment. As *Green* and *Andrew and Kane* make clear, judgment proceeds by means of a series of configurations, personae or images of infection which fix and immobilise the subject of HIV and gay sex. The written texts of law reconstruct the event (the 'real') of HIV in the order of vision, where judgment is governed by the desire to see, and in 'seeing', to have done with HIV.[16] The vision of law remains an aesthetic in which an inscribed image breaks the link between the eye and the pain of the other.

Nevertheless, it is still possible that the eye of the law could be made to flicker from the mark to the pain of the other in law, for the stilled voice to listen or hear, for the upright hand that holds the rule to waver. Jarman reminds us that law has not been totally occupied by the modern textuality. There is a site through which judgment can take place, reconstructed around the aural and corporeal scenes of attachment. *Blue* interrupts the idolatry of modern textuality by reasserting the melancholy claims of speech, as the moving image inscribes the other in the ear of the spectator. The transmission of law in the moment or scene of judgment takes place, as a response to the other, through the corporeal and audible inscription of the pain and passion of the lover. Legal judgment may be dominated by modern textuality and the order of the visual, but the texts of culture show that there are materials (which operate through memory, incorporation, hearing) available through which to respond in judgment to the proximate other: the materials of voice, touch and memory, materials for compassionate judgment in proximity with the fragmented bodies of law's suffering others.

---

16 The Aristotelian account of the will to knowledge as a desire to see, constructs the juridical moment of metaphysics as the pronunciation of judgments on the correctness of the world. Minkinnen, 1999, notes the aporetic and agonising nature of this will or desire when remarking that, 'Justice constitutes the desired object (*to orekton*) of a "first philosophy" of law, but in the judgments of correctness that a mortal man is capable of, such justice is forever delayed. For the ownmost essence of things, that is, justice in itself, or the future that will come to be, is a matter fit only for infinite gods' (p 47).

PART 3
REGULATION:
HISTORIES, CULTURES, LEGALITIES

Not harmless entertainment: state censorship and cinema in the transitional era[1]

Lee Grieveson

Lexington police officers were directed by the Commissioner of Public Safety to sit amongst the audience to control 'demonstrations' and 'enthusiastic outbursts' when *The Birth of a Nation* (1915) played the city's opera house in early 1915, marking a curious conjuncture of film, highbrow culture and state authority (Waller, 1995, p 158). Likewise, police in Boston sought to prevent black people from buying tickets to the film when it played the Tremont Theatre, though the concern here was less about the audience's enthusiasm and more about their anger at the film's racism, and was consistent with a broader policing of racially bifurcated public space (Cripps, 1977, pp 59–60). Inside, Pinkerton detectives were scattered throughout the auditorium to stop demonstrations against the film like those that had taken place when the film was shown in the Liberty Theatre in New York City. Protestors had thrown eggs at the Liberty's screen at the moment when a black man was shown chasing a young white woman with the intention of raping her (*New York Times*, 15 April 1915, p 1; *New York Times*, 18 April 1915, p 15; see Mast, 1983, p 129). In other locations, the governmental policing of the film and of audiences led to the film being banned. Local censor boards, councils or mayors refused to allow the film to be seen in cities like Cleveland, Wilmington, Del, St Louis, Topeka, Louisville, and San Antonio (Fleener-Marzec, 1980, pp 66–73, 94–99). Likewise, the film was at least initially banned by state-wide authorities in Illinois, Michigan, Kansas and Ohio.[2] In Ohio, censors rejected the film in accordance with the remit of the state censor board established in 1913 that had granted the board authority to pass films of a 'moral, educational or amusing and harmless character' and to ban films that were 'sacrilegious, obscene, indecent or immoral'.[3] The film was, they

---

1   A version of this chapter also appears in Keil and Stamp, 2004. Reprinted by permission of the University of California Press. My thanks to the Arts and Humanities Research Board for a grant that enabled me to carry out the research for this article. Thanks also to the archivists and librarians at the Illinois Regional Archives Depository, Ronald Williams Library, Northeastern Illinois University; Chicago Public Library; Ohio Historical Centre; Pennsylvania State Archives; Rare Books and Manuscripts Division, New York Public Library; Academy of Motion Picture, Arts and Sciences, Margaret Herrick Library, Los Angeles; and the Institute for Advanced Legal Study at the University of London. My thanks also to Charlie Keil for helpful editorial input and to Peter Kramer for a characteristically insightful reading of an earlier draft.

2   *Chicago Defender* (22 May 1915), cited in Gaines, 2001, p 233; see Fleener-Marzec, 1980, pp 265–68; *Record of Proceedings of the Industrial Commission of Ohio, Department of Film Censorship*, 6 January 1916, General Correspondence 1916–56, Box 50,736, Ohio Historical Centre (hereafter OHC).

3   House Bill No 322, 80th General Assembly, Ohio, 1913, in *General Assembly: Legislative Service Commission, Bills and Acts, 1835–1996*, Box 3552, OHC.

said, 'not harmless'.[4] Epoch appealed, but the board restated their opinion that the film 'was harmful and not of a harmless character'.[5]

Local and state boards banned *The Birth of a Nation* in line, principally, with public nuisance and public disorder legislation, registering concerns about the responses of both black and white audiences and, more broadly, about the policing of vulnerable *and* potentially dangerous audiences as seen so vividly in Lexington, Boston and New York City. Integral to the regulation of cinema and audiences was the rendering of the potentially 'harmful' cinema 'harmless', a transition that I take to be one of the most important of the so called 'transitional era'.[6] Important to this, no doubt, was the censorship of content like the incendiary images of race hatred visible in *The Birth of a Nation*, and also the shaping of filmic discourse into a narrative discourse intertwined with prevailing standards of morality (Staiger, 1995, pp 55–115; Gunning, 1988 and 1991, pp 151–87). Even more substantively, though, regulatory discourses, practices and institutions in this period were linked to important debates about the social functioning of cinema: debates about how cinema should function in society, the uses to which it might be put, and thus effectively about what it could or would be. Here the issues revolved principally around conceptions of the cultural functions and relative weighting of 'entertainment' and 'education', played out frequently through discussions about narrative, but also about the merits of fiction, non-fiction, indexicality and 'realism'. Was it possible for cinema to represent issues of broader political import? Was cinema simply a commercial entertainment medium? Could cinema be a part of a public sphere of political debate or was it to be configured differently?

Located in this context, *The Birth of a Nation* can stand as a useful starting point for an account of these debates about the function of cinema and their effects on censorship practices. The film was made to coincide with the 50-year anniversary of the Civil War, and was positioned by its producers and supporters as an intervention into broader public debates about the nation's history and about race and the necessity of racial hierarchies. It was widely praised by many precisely for this public intervention. Vice crusader, Reverend Dr Charles Parkhurst wrote, 'This drama is a telling illustration of the possibilities of motion pictures as an instrument of history' (Parkhurst, 1971, pp 102–03) and the National Board of Censorship, a self-regulatory censorship body, passed the film with minor cuts because of its 'historic significance'.[7] Likewise, the film's director, DW Griffith, asserted that the

---

4 *Record of Proceedings of the Industrial Commission of Ohio, Department of Film Censorship*, 6 January 1916, General Correspondence 1916–1956, Box 50,736, OHC.

5 *Record of Proceedings of the Industrial Commission of Ohio, Department of Film Censorship*, 11 January 1916, General Correspondence 1916–1956, Box 50,736, OHC.

6 Cinema historians have argued that the period poised between the end of an earlier 'cinema of attractions' or 'exhibitor-led' industry from around 1907 and the establishment of 'classical Hollywood cinema' from around 1915–17 is best labelled 'transitional', and this has become a crucial part of the historiographical scaffolding of American cinema. A particular configuration of visual grammar and narrative discourse was established in the period, complemented by a number of new institutions, including the emergence of feature films, the star system, picture palaces, and new studios and systems of distribution. See here, eg, Bordwell, Staiger, and Thompson, 1985, pp 85–231; Keil, 2001.

7 'A Statement in Regard to the General Committee Meeting Held at the Liberty Theatre on 1 March at 2.30 pm', National Board of Review of Motion Pictures Collection, Rare Books and Manuscripts Division, New York Public Library (hereafter NBR).

film was true in its historical detail and he backed this up by offering to pay the President of the National Association of Coloured People $10,000 if he could find a single historical inaccuracy in the film (Schickel, 1984, p 294). Later, after the controversy over the film, Griffith privately published a pamphlet called *The Rise and Fall of Free Speech* in which he argued that film as 'the pictorial press' deserved the constitutional guarantees of free speech enshrined in the First Amendment and in state constitutions. If people 'muzzle the "movies"', Griffith wrote, they will 'defeat the educational purpose of this graphic art', for '[c]ensorship demands of the picture makers a sugar-coated and false version of life's truths'. The central contention here was that film could make visible the 'truths of history' or contemporary social problems 'while at the same time bringing diversion to the masses' (Griffith, 1915). Many people of different political persuasions argued for a similar sense of cinema's potential role in the public sphere.

Even so, state attention in the early teens to a series of controversial films about 'white slavery', contraception, venereal disease and labour/capital and race problems suggested that such a stance on the social role of cinema was increasingly contested.[8] Concerns about the potential effects of films on public order and on audiences (made up of what was widely seen as the 'light-minded' of the 'lower middle classes') led many to argue for the necessity of a separation of the referential and the entertaining dimensions of cinema, and hence the drawing of a distinction between mainstream cinema as a purveyor of 'harmless' entertainment and the social role of the press.[9] Looked at like this, then, the response of the municipal and state boards in banning *The Birth of a Nation*, and, as we shall see, other films, was less a judgment simply of individual films and more a judgment of the possible social role of cinema and its place in the public sphere; that common space in which members of society meet through a variety of media and discuss matters of common interest.

Legal decisions further mandated the gathering sense of the correct social functioning of cinema, culminating in a crucial Supreme Court decision in early 1915 on the validity of state censorship that was binding on the legal system throughout the nation. Legislating the legal status and function of cinema, the decision also insisted on the necessity of a split between the referential and pleasurable or entertaining functions of cinema. Even though the Supreme Court justices seemed to like *The Birth of a Nation* when it was screened specially for them – apparently the Chief Justice had been a former Klan member – the decision they rendered effectively disallowed the conception of the function of cinema that Griffith shared with many others.[10] Cinema was now to be conceived of as a business with a public role distinct from that of the press, becoming the only

---

8 On the debates about white slave films and other sex problem films, see Grieveson, 1997; Stamp, 2000, pp 41–101; Stamp, forthcoming. On labour filmmaking in the period and the ensuing controversies, see Ross, 1998.

9 Letter from Assistant Secretary of the National Board of Censorship to the Moral Feature Film Company, 22 December 1913, Box 171, NBR.

10 Edward D White, the Chief Justice of the Supreme Court, is reported by Thomas Dixon to have told Dixon he was a Klan member and to have asked him if the film told 'the true story of that uprising of outraged manhood'. See Schickel, 1984, p 270.

medium of communication in the history of the United States subject to legal prior restraint.

Legal discourse is, as Pierre Bourdieu has observed, a peculiarly performative discourse (Bourdieu, 1987). Legal decisions thus enabled additional state intervention, effectively narrowing the definition of the function of cinema further by validating the stance that defined cinema as harmless entertainment to remove it from the contentious sphere of the political. Accordingly, what follows considers the formation and operation of municipal and state censor boards in the transitional era, before shifting to an account of the legal decisions following the censor board directives that reached the federal level in the Supreme Court, and that had considerable effect on the shaping of cinema thereafter. Such an examination will allow me to attend to a crucial but under-explored dynamic in the transition to what has been called 'classical Hollywood cinema', supplementing important work on the interrelation of the mode of production and representation with attention to the mode of regulation. This entails shifting attention away from the formal developments important in the transitional era towards an account of the establishment of a set of distinctions and definitions that were critical to the establishment of the discursive formation of mainstream cinema.

'Limited means'

Late in 1907, a police censor board was established in Chicago, emerging as the first functioning censor board in the United States and paving the way for the plethora of municipal and later state boards that followed. The board was established after a number of reports were undertaken and published on the new phenomenon of nickelodeons, that were in turn followed by a series of public discussions in the city about moving pictures and nickelodeons, including a 'crusade' against them by the *Chicago Tribune*.[11] In the midst of these debates, an ordinance was proposed to the Chicago City Council that would require police censorship of all films to be shown in the city. It was initially regarded as an unusual extension of regulatory powers. 'The question involved in this ordinance is a novel one', Assistant Corporation Counsel Cassels wrote to the proposer, Aldermen Uhlir, for the ordinance 'is in advance of the usual legislation regulating and controlling places of amusement' and work on the police power of the states suggested that it 'may be regarded as prohibited by the spirit of the Constitution'.[12] Cassels, though, proceeded to downplay this potential constitutional problem by suggesting that 'amusements' could not be protected on free speech grounds and, furthermore, by pointing to pre-existing legislation that allowed the city council '[t]o license, tax, regulate, suppress and prohibit' amusements. Nickelodeons could, it was argued, be inscribed into these pre-existing regulatory powers because they could be defined as 'amusements', and moving pictures could thus not claim the protection of the free speech guarantees of the First Amendment and state constitutions.

---

11 *Chicago Tribune*, 3 May 1907, p 2; see Grieveson, 1999.
12 Memorandum from Assistant Corporation Counsel Edwin H Cassels to Alderman Joseph Z Uhlir, 24 June 1907, p 3, quoted in Lindstrom, 1998, p 32.

Clearly this stance on the legal definition of the nascent cinema was widely supported, for the bill was voted on and overwhelmingly passed on 4 November 1907. A board of censors drawn from the police force was set up to view all films to be shown in the city and to prevent 'the exhibition of obscene and immoral films ... of the class commonly shown in mutoscopes, kinetescopes, cinematographs and penny arcades'.[13] Exhibitors or film exchanges had now to submit an application for a permit to screen a film for exhibition and then send a copy of the film to the police board of censors to be screened. A number of other municipal boards emerged from this moment, including ones initially in Detroit, Cleveland, Butte, Montana and later in the 1910s and early 1920s in Lexington, Kentucky, San Francisco, Kansas City, Portland, Oregon, Seattle, Dallas, Gainesville, Texas, Pasadena, Palo Alto, California, Camden, New Jersey and others.[14]

Extant records suggest the Chicago board focused particularly on films suggesting or representing sexual impropriety and/or political corruption. Exhibitors or distributors seeking a permit for the film *She Never Knew* (1916), for example, were told to 'transfer marriage ceremony to scene before showing baby'.[15] Likewise, *Sappho* (1913) was rejected because it included 'immoral scenes and adultery'; *Satan's Pawn* (1915) was rejected 'because it features a wife's infidelity'; *Forbidden Fruit* (1916) was banned because it showed an illegitimate child; and a host of films showing white slavery were banned, including *Smashing the Vice Trust* (1914), *The Eagle* (1915), *Nobody Would Believe* (1915), *The Heart of New York* (1915), *The Bridesmaid's Secret* (1916), *It May Be Your Daughter* (1916) and *Protect Your Daughter* (1918) (IRAD, Boxes 65a, 68, 72). Late in 1914, a film called *Forcing the Force* (1914) was rejected, 'because of its slur on the police force' in the form of a story about how an 'entire police force made love to two lady policewomen and neglect [*sic*] their duties', showing a concern again about sexuality, but also now about the representation of the police that was not surprising for a board made up of police officers (IRAD, Box 72). Visible also in relation to a host of other films that reflected poorly on the police, like *The Cooked Goose* (1914), *The Gilded Kid* (1914), *The Hostage* (1914) and *Some Cop* (1914), the actions of the board segued here into broader political concerns and interventions. Important here also was the excision of scenes of miners 'rioting' from *The Mainspring* (1917), the excessive regulation of the films of the black filmmaker Oscar Micheaux, and the banning of a number of films representing the then European conflict in 1914 and 1915 (IRAD, Boxes 72, 65b, 66a, 65b).[16] In these interventions, the board made important judgments on the possible

---

13 *Proceedings of the City Council of the City of Chicago*, 4 November 1907, 3052.

14 *Moving Picture World*, 7 September 1907, 422; *Moving Picture World*, 21 September 1907, 454; *Moving Picture World*, 7 December 1907, 645; *Moving Picture World*, 14 December 1907, 665; *Views and Film Index*, 14 December 1907, 3; *Moving Picture World*, 21 September 1907, 454; *Moving Picture World*, 14 December 1907, 665; *Motion Picture News*, 6 June 1914, 39–40; Waller, *Main Street Amusements*, 139–43, 505; Cannon, 1920; Oberholtzer, 1922, pp 117–18.

15 Illinois Regional Archives Depository, Ronald Williams Library, Northeastern Illinois University, Box 65a (hereafter IRAD).

16 The review of *The Mainspring* in *Moving Picture World* suggests the miners were actually striking: *Moving Picture World*, 2 December 1916, 1344. On the broader censorship problems besetting Micheaux, see Regester, 1996.

public role of cinema, particularly evident in relation to films that touched upon questions of sexuality like the white slave films or on controversial themes of race and political corruption.

Late in 1908, a legal case sought to work out the constitutionality of the police censor board and in doing so drew questions of morality and political import together with those of public role and social function. Exhibitor Jake Block had been denied a permit for two films, *The James Boys in Missouri* (1908) and *Night Riders* (1908), and had appealed the decision to the Illinois Supreme Court. Lawyers working for Block argued that the censorship ordinance unconstitutionally discriminated against the exhibitors of moving pictures, making a distinction between moving pictures and other forms of commercialised amusements. In particular, they argued that the ordinance drew an unfair distinction between cinema and the theatre, for whilst the films were disallowed, 'certain plays and dramas were being performed in certain playhouses in the city of Chicago of which the pictures were reproductions of parts' (*Block v City of Chicago* (1909), p 1013). Leading on from this, the lawyers launched a further intriguing line of defence: the films, they claimed, were based on the 'American historical experience' and thus could not be challenged on the grounds of immorality and obscenity. From this perspective, the basis of the films in historical actuality, that is, in non-fictional discourse, protected them from concerns about morality and obscenity.

Early in 1909, Chief Justice James H Cartwright dismissed these claims in the Illinois Supreme Court. It was the purpose of the law, Justice Cartwright asserted, 'to secure decency and morality in the moving picture business, and that purpose falls within the police power', that power defined as the right (and duty) of the states to protect the health, morals, and safety of their citizens (*Block v City of Chicago* (1909), p 1013). Even though the ordinance focused solely on moving pictures, Cartwright further observed, it did not necessarily license other immoral representations and, furthermore, there is something specific to the regulation of moving pictures – the audience. Low admission prices, Cartwright claimed, meant that nickelodeons:

> ... are frequented and patronised by a large number of children, as well as by those of limited means who do not attend the productions of plays and dramas given in the regular theatres. The audiences include those classes whose age, education and situation in life especially entitle them to protection against the evil influence of obscene and immoral representations (*Block v City of Chicago* (1909), p 1013).

'Limited means' effectively translated here as lower class immigrant groups; those groups that were commonly seen to make up the majority of the audience of nickelodeons and who also formed, the *Chicago Tribune* had suggested in the midst of fears about labour unrest and criminal activity in the city, 'the early stage of that dangerous second generation which is finding such a place in the criminals of the city' (*Chicago Tribune*, 15 April 1907, p 1).[17] Vulnerable but also potentially dangerous audiences frequented nickelodeons more than the theatre, Justice

---

17 On the broader concerns about criminality and immorality in Chicago, see George Kibbe Turner, 'The City of Chicago: A Study of the Great Immoralities', *McClure's*, 28 April 1907; and Harring, 1983, pp 228–33.

Cartwright suggested, and so distinctions between the public roles afforded cinema and theatre needed to be carefully drawn and policed.

Leading on from this, Cartwright responded also to the claim that the films depicted 'experiences connected with the history of the country' by observing that, even if that was so, it did not follow that they were 'not immoral' since they 'necessarily portray exhibitions of crime' (*Block v City of Chicago* (1909), p 1016). Even though it is almost certain that the two films under consideration replayed historical actuality through fictional conventions, that they were only retrospectively discursively positioned as straightforward representations of historical actuality, the decision took that positioning at its word and disallowed it.

Linking cinema to the theatre and to non-fictional discourse – at least, the ostensibly non-fictional discourse of history – seemed to offer a way for Block to circumvent the powers of the police censor board. Yet these alliances were denied by the state Supreme Court which insisted on a clear distinction between film, theatre and history amidst fears about the effects of films on audiences and public order. Cartwright's decision had important ramifications for the definition of the uncertain social function of cinema, seemingly suggesting that mainstream cinema be disengaged from public debates about (for example) the history of the country, and that it should occupy a fundamentally delimited place within the public sphere. Important precedents were set in a number of ways here, paving the way for the proliferation of municipal and state censor boards from this moment on, and for future legal decisions on the public role of cinema.

'Immoral, sacrilegious, indecent and obscene'

Like the board in Chicago, the first state-wide censor board set in place in Pennsylvania in 1911 was established with a clear distinction in mind between moving pictures on the one hand and the press and the stage on the other. Initial discussions described the proposed bill as an:

> ... attempt to keep motion pictures attuned to public opinion and not necessarily in harmony with productions of the stage or newspapers, but rather to restrict the motion pictures to such as would afford clean entertainment or amusement and to eliminate everything which would tend to debase or inflame the mind to improper adventures or false standards of conduct.[18]

Likewise, following the precedent of the board in Chicago, the Pennsylvania board was also set up to censor 'immoral and obscene films'.[19] No film could be sold,

---

18 Pennsylvania State Board of Censors, Rules and Standards, passed 19 June 1911, Pennsylvania Session Laws for 1911, 1067–69, Pennsylvania State Archives, Box 3 (hereafter PSA). The board was established in 1911 but did not actually start functioning until 1914, initially because no appropriation of money was made in the Bill and subsequently because producers sought a legal challenge to the Bill. *Motion Picture News*, 6 June 1914, 23; *Moving Picture World*, 3 January 1914, 25–27; *Motion Picture News*, 9 May 1914, 21–24; *Motion Picture News*, 16 May 1914, 21–22.

19 *Journal of the House of Representatives of the Commonwealth of Pennsylvania*, Part IV (1911), 3905–06; *Journal of the Senate of the Commonwealth of Pennsylvania*, Part IV (1911), 3078; *Philadelphia Inquirer*, 20 June 1911, 2; *Smull's Legislative Handbook and Manual of the State of Pennsylvania* (Harrisburg: WS Ray, 1914), 66.

leased, lent or exhibited in the state until it had been inspected by the board and films would not be passed if they were seen to be 'sacrilegious, obscene, indecent or immoral' or if they tended 'in the judgment of the board to debase or corrupt morals'.[20]

Other states took this formulation as a precedent, including Ohio in 1913, Kansas in 1914 and Maryland in 1916. The state legislature in Ohio vowed to disallow films that were 'sacrilegious, obscene, indecent or immoral,' and would similarly not allow 'an indecent subject, nor [one] representing lust'. Boards in Kansas and Maryland employed similar language, setting out to disapprove of films 'such as are cruel, obscene, indecent or immoral, or such as tend to debase or corrupt morals' and those that are 'sacrilegious, obscene, indecent or immoral'.[21] Immorality and obscenity were keywords for practically all the municipal and state censor boards, then, as the declared reasons for the necessity of state interventions focused in the main on questions of sexuality. Here the history of moving picture censorship connects to a broader history of sexuality, particularly in relation to anxieties about the governance of individual bodies and the social body of a mass public.[22]

One of the first acts of the Pennsylvania state censor board was the banning of the white slave film, *Smashing the Vice Trust*, because of concerns both about the dissemination of images of urban vice to smaller towns and broader concerns about the kind of public role that cinema might take. Like other white slave films, *Smashing the Vice Trust* was presented by its producers – though seemingly disingenuously – as a moral lesson and as an intervention into the broader public debates about white slavery, based, the *Variety* reviewer noted, on 'newspaper stories' and including scenes featuring New York District Attorney Whitman.[23] White slave films like *Traffic in Souls* (1913) and *The Inside of the White Slave Traffic* (1913) had occasioned considerable debate about the public role of cinema, in particular whether it was acceptable for cinema to represent pressing but distressing public problems. Earlier debates within the self-regulatory National Board of Censorship had produced a complicated stance that leant toward the acceptance of a delimited social role for cinema, but that still held out the possibility of cinema functioning as 'propaganda' for pressing social issues.[24] Like the censor board in

---

20 *Journal of the Senate of the Commonwealth of Pennsylvania*, Part 1 (1916), 73. For subsequent accounts of the function of the Pennsylvania board, see Oberholtzer, 1922; Aronson, 1998; Saylor, 1999.

21 House Bill No 322, 80th General Assembly, Ohio, *General Assembly: Legislative Service Commission, Bills and Acts, 1835–1996*, Box 3552, OHC; *Journal of the House of Representatives of Ohio* (Columbus, Ohio: The FJ Heer Printing Co, 1913), 854; Senate Bill 367, *Kansas Senate Journal* (1913), 136; Maryland: Laws, 1916, c 209, 411–16. On the formation and subsequent function of the Ohio Censorship Board, see Brychta, 1952.

22 On this configuration generally, see Burchell and Gordon, 1991. The relations between morality, governance and the regulation of cinema are outlined in more detail in Grieveson, 2004.

23 *Variety*, 20 February 1914, 23. *Variety* regarded the film as a cheap imitation of *Traffic in Souls*.

24 *Moving Picture World*, 23 December 1916, 1792; Grieveson, 2004, pp 166–71. The board was effectively split over how to deal with the white slave films and, later, *The Birth of a Nation*. Its inability to resolve its stance on the social function of cinema drew considerable criticism and this was one of the reasons behind the impetus for the creation of other municipal and state boards. For more on this, see Grieveson, 2004, Chapter 6.

Chicago, the Pennsylvania board took a clearer stance here in banning all white slave films, predicated on the fact that from the outset the board conceptualised film as having a distinct social role from that of the theatre and the press. Even if the film was strictly a 'propaganda' film produced for social betterment, it should not be allowed, for that role was beyond the one allotted to mainstream cinema.

Ellis Paxson Oberholtzer, longtime member of the Pennsylvania board, published a book length treatment of the censorship question in 1922, which made clearer the logic underpinning the board's decisions. He argued, in particular, that an educational remit was beyond the cinema as a 'place of amusement', and that films about political issues, including in particular those relating to sexuality, were necessarily 'contrary to public policy' (Obertholtzer, 1922, pp 35, 41). The municipal board in Minneapolis expressed similar logic in ruling that, 'as a general proposition the so-called educational and propaganda film for commercial use is to be condemned ... People go to the movies for recreation, amusement'.[25] Other decisions to ban films entirely by the boards in Pennsylvania and Ohio followed this logic about the public role of cinema. Hence the film *Where are My Children?* (1916), covering the issues of abortion and contraception, was banned in Pennsylvania (PSA, Box 10). The prologue to the film *Prohibition* (1916) was excised in Pennsylvania because it included a display of a number of public figures, including senators, who supported the temperance cause and so made a political statement that ran contrary to the board's conception of the social role of cinema (PSA, Box 2).[26] Likewise, *The Iron Hand* (1916), telling a story of political corruption, was rejected in Pennsylvania, whilst *Stacked Cards* (1914) and *Tracking the Government* (1914) were banned in Ohio because of 'scenes showing collusion between prostitute, policeman and corrupt politicians' and showing a 'judge dividing ill-gotten money with moonshiners' respectively (PSA, Box 3; OHC, Box 50, 736). *The Strike at Coaldale* (1914), showing miners striking in Ohio, and *By Man's Law* (1913), critiquing Rockefeller's greed and manipulation of the police, were also banned in Ohio (Ross, 1998, pp 109–10). Important to the decisions of the municipal and state boards, then, was a careful policing of the public role of cinema, evident most clearly in the films that were banned outright and that entered either into broader political debates about sexuality and morality like *Smashing the Vice Trust* or *Where Are My Children?* or about other political questions like temperance, the civil war or official corruption. Like investigative journalism or 'muckraking', these films sought to engage in public debates about pressing issues, sometimes no doubt for the commercial benefit that it was thought would accrue – but this public role was actively discouraged by state intervention.

Important here also in the state intervention into the definition and functioning of cinema were the distinctions drawn between the social role of cinema and that afforded to art, evident from Corporation Counsel Cassell's dismissal of the police power problems in regulating cinema in 1907, to Justice Cartwright's decision drawing a distinction between theatrical and filmic representations of historical

---

25 Letter of Robbins Gilman to Executive Secretary, National Board of Review, 23 November 1916, Box 103, NBR.
26 *Moving Picture World*, 17 April 1915, 399.

events in early 1909, and to the establishment of the Pennsylvania board in 1911. In this context, the banning of a number of films based on novels, operas and plays helped further define the public role of cinema. *The Kreutzer Sonata* (1915), for example, told a story based on a novel by Leo Tolstoy (and a play based on that) that ends with murder and suicide and was deemed unacceptable by censors in Pennsylvania and accordingly banned.[27] Likewise, the film *Carmen* (Fox, 1915), based on a story that was also a successful opera, was banned in Pennsylvania, as were the films *Sealed Lips* (Equitable Motion Pictures, 1915) and *The Easiest Way* (Clara Kimball Young Film Corp, 1917), based on a novel and play respectively (PSA, Box 3). The novels and the play on which *The Birth of a Nation* was based were considerably less controversial than the film. Long accepted in post-romantic cultural theory as a force of limited cultural negation like that seen in the conclusion to *The Kreutzer Sonata*, the social role of art was evidently distinct from that afforded to cinema (Burger and Burger, 1992).

Important though these decisions were in relation to the individual films and the economic viability of their producers, their real importance lies more in the way in which the underlying logic they manifested influenced the self-definition of the film industry and, then, the production of films. The delimited public role of cinema was becoming ever more clear to those involved in the industry. Films representing controversial issues of white slavery, eugenics or birth control, like *Is Any Girl Safe?* (1916), *The Black Stork* (1916), *Birth Control* (1917), *The Hand That Rocks the Cradle* (1917) and others were increasingly condemned in the trade press for being 'too preachy'.[28] Edward Weitzel of *Moving Picture World* argued that 'the family photoplay theatre, in the opinion of the writer, is not the proper place' for the consideration of 'serious ethical questions' and should therefore be reserved for 'amusement and recreation', not 'propaganda'.[29] *Moving Picture World* condemned *The Black Stork*, about eugenics and 'defective' babies, noting that, 'The place to exploit [the subject] is not the moving picture theatre'.[30] Likewise, the screenplay writing manuals that began to appear in the teens, further disseminating industry practice, frequently told prospective authors to avoid propaganda and controversy. '[H]eart interest must predominate', the authors of a manual called *Writing the Photoplay* suggested, and '[t]hat form of journalism which is best known as muckraking is also out of place in the picture' (Esenwein and Leeds, 1913, pp 243–44). Aspiring writers were told, 'one may not use the screen for the aims of the proselyte', to avoid tragedy and 'morbidness', and to aim for a form of 'art' that says 'something worthwhile in a beautiful way' (Dimick, 1915; Van Buren Powell, 1919; Palmer, 1924).[31]

---

27 PSA, Box 3.

28 *Wid's*, 31 May 1917, 349. Economic issues were critical here, of course, for the industry was increasingly becoming a national and indeed global one and the mainstream industry was developing oligopolistic strategies of creating barriers to entry and of marginalising maverick producers whose films could damage the long-term profitability of the industry.

29 *Moving Picture World*, 2 June 1917, 1458. Likewise, a survey of exhibitors by the National Board showed that exhibitors tended to steer away from 'sex pictures' and demanded instead films that were suitable for family audiences. Box 145, NBR.

30 *Moving Picture World*, 24 February 1917, 1211, cited in Pernick, 1996, p 124.

31 On the dissemination of censorship standards, see Hale Ball, 1913; Lord Wright, 1922; Aber Hill, 1924.

Increasingly, then, the effort to shift cinema from harmful to harmless became concentrated in pushing cinema away from an engagement with the public sphere of political debate or cultural negation, rendering cinema ostensibly apolitical, as a provider of 'harmless entertainment'. Legal decisions about the validity of state intervention further supported these definitions of the public role of cinema.

'A pretence to worthy purpose'

Lawyers for the interstate film exchange, Mutual Film Corporation, challenged the Ohio state censorship ordinance in late 1913, gaining a temporary injunction against the state censorship board and so halting its work after just two months of censoring activity. Counsel for Mutual, Walter N Seligsberg, argued in the District Court of the United States for the Northern District of Ohio that the censorship law imposed unconstitutional burdens on interstate commerce and thus had invidious effects on property rights (*Mutual Film Co v Industrial Commission of Ohio et al* (1914)).[32] Linked to this was a secondary argument about free speech rights, predicated on the definition of motion pictures as 'publications'. This was in line with a previous Supreme Court decision that held that a painting was a publication and was so protected by state and federal constitutions guaranteeing people the right to speak freely and publish their sentiments. Legislators in Ohio had no right to abridge or restrain the freedom of publication, Seligsberg argued, and so '[u]nless this court is prepared to say that Ohio could pass a law providing for the censorship of newspapers and magazines, it cannot sustain the censorship of motion pictures' (*Moving Picture World*, 27 December 1913, p 1527). The same arguments were mounted by Mutual's lawyers slightly later, in separate cases challenging the constitutionality of the Chicago police censor board and the Pennsylvania and Kansas state boards.[33]

The decision rendered in April 1914 in the Ohio case denied Mutual's case, though in line with the Ohio Attorney General's arguments that the censorship law fell within the police power abrogated to the states, a precedent that was quoted in the subsequent denial of Mutual's cases in Chicago, Pennsylvania and Kansas.[34] Judges in the various cases noted that the police power extends 'to the making of regulations promotive of domestic order, health, morals and safety' and could be defined as the 'principle of self-preservation of the body politic', indeed as the 'chief function of government'.[35] Even though lawyers for Mutual had described moving pictures as 'harmless', the judges acted from the position that, 'it does not matter that the subject in the main is harmless; it does matter, however, if something

---

32 *Moving Picture World*, 27 December 1913, 1526–27; *Motion Picture News*, 18 April 1914, 17–18.

33 *Mutual Film Corp v City of Chicago*, 224 F 101 (USCCA Ill 1915); *Buffalo Branch, Mutual Film Corp v Breitinger*, 250 Pa 225 (1915); *Mutual Film Corp of Missouri v Hodges*, 236 US 230 (1915). See Wertheimer, 1993.

34 *Mutual Film Corp v Chicago* (1915) 139 CCA 657, 224 Fed 201; *Buffalo Branch, Mutual Film Corp v Breitinger*, 250 Pa 225 (1915); *Motion Picture News*, 18 April 1914, 17–18.

35 *Mutual Film Corp v Industrial Commission of Ohio et al*, 215 *Federal Reporter* (September–October 1914), 141; *Moving Picture World*, 27 December 1913, 1527; *Buffalo Branch, Mutual Film Corp v Breitinger*, 250 Pa 231–32; *Motion Picture News*, 18 April 1914, 17–20, 44.

associated with it that [*sic*] is harmful' (*Mutual Film Corp v Industrial Commission of Ohio et al* (1914), p 141). The free speech argument was denied on the grounds that corporations were not citizens and thus not included in constitutional guarantees of free speech. Even if they were, there is a clear distinction, the judges asserted, between the press and moving pictures. 'Counsel overlook a broad distinction between the things they describe in their bills and the objects with which they make comparison', the judges noted, for moving pictures are aimed principally at 'furnishing entertainment and amusement' (*Mutual Film Corp v Industrial Commission of Ohio et al* (1914), pp 142–43).

Lawyers for Mutual duly filed an appeal with the Supreme Court and the court agreed to hear the cases together in January 1915. The legal strategy adopted by Mutual here differed from before though, for now the free speech questions were given precedence over those involving the restraint of trade. Lawyers for Mutual argued that the company was entitled to invoke the protection of the state constitutional guarantees of free speech and freedom of publication, because moving pictures were publications and thus 'constitute part of "the press" of Ohio within the comprehensive meaning of that word' (*Mutual Film Corp v Industrial Commission of Ohio* (1915), p 236). This was defined by the lawyers with the help of a suitably inclusive dictionary definition as 'a means of making or announcing publicly something that otherwise might have remained private and unknown' (*Mutual Film Corp v Industrial Commission of Ohio* (1915), p 243).[36] Leading on from this, a description of the 'use, object, and effect of motion pictures' by the lawyers was heavily skewed towards a sense of cinema's educative social function:

> They depict dramatisations of standard novels, exhibiting many subjects of scientific interest, the properties of matter, the growth of the various forms of animal and plant life, and explorations and travels; also events of historical and current interest – the same events which are described in words and by photographs in newspapers, weekly periodicals, magazines, and other publications, of which photographs are promptly secured a few days after the events which they depict happen (*Mutual Film Corp v Industrial Commission of Ohio* (1915), p 232).

Like the arguments mounted within the film industry about the white slave and other 'sex problem' films and *The Birth of a Nation*, the critical argument here was about the proposed social function of cinema and its positioning in the cultural topography of America.

Lawyers for the state boards countered these arguments by arguing that 'uncensored pictures were detrimental to the morals and perversive of true education' and should be restrained according to the police powers abrogated to the states (*Mutual Film Corp v Industrial Commission of Ohio* (1915), p 251). It was this latter argument that carried most weight with the Supreme Court Justices, for the decision rendered in late February 1915 denied Mutual's claims and their conception of the function of cinema. No doubt moving pictures had 'many useful purposes as graphic expressions of opinion and sentiments, as exponents of

---

36 Lawyers did not argue for First Amendment guarantees here, but relied on the state constitutions' guarantees of free speech because it was not clear that the First Amendment was binding on the states.

policies, as teachers of science and history' and could be 'useful, interesting, educational and moral', Justice Joseph McKenna wrote in the court's unanimous verdict:

> [b]ut they may be used for evil, and against that possibility the statute was enacted. Their power of amusement, and, it may be education, the audiences they assemble, not of women alone nor of men alone, but together, not of adults only, but of children, make them the more insidious in corruption by a pretence of worthy purpose. Indeed, we may go beyond that possibility. They take their attraction from the general interest, eager and wholesome it may be, in their subjects, but a prurient interest may be excited and appealed to (*Mutual Film Corp v Industrial Commission of Ohio* (1915), p 242).

Moving pictures were 'a business, pure and simple' that was in fact 'capable of evil', even more so when they 'pretended' to worthy purpose as films like the white slave films and *The Birth of a Nation* had done (*Mutual Film Corp v Industrial Commission of Ohio* (1915), p 242). Entertainment, for the justices, was a category distinct from ideas and a boundary line between the two needed to be affirmed and policed. Keeping separate the referential from the prurient, the justices' comments made clear that their scepticism about referentiality was not simply a denigration of 'prurient films', even if the concerns were frequently intertwined.[37] The logic of their argument suggested that the 'pretence to worthy purpose' in film should be avoided, that cinema should be linked to fictional goals and non-practical ends.

The *Mutual* decision was a vital one that was binding on the entire legal system and that governed the validity of state censorship and the legal prior restraint of moving pictures until the Supreme Court reversed the decision in *Burstyn v Wilson* (1952) (see Jowett, 1989). The consequences of the decision were both specific and wide-ranging, including the mandating of increased state regulation of cinema alongside a long-lasting and performative definition of the function of mainstream cinema as 'entertainment' that should be divorced from the 'pretence of worthy purpose'. The decision effectively cemented the delimitation of cinema's role in the public sphere evident in earlier debates and legal decisions. In this sense, a critical line in the sand was drawn here, divorcing the role of mainstream cinema from a function similar to the press or art and linking it to the goals of harmless and culturally affirmative entertainment. These distinctions and definitions were crucial to the establishment of the discursive formation of mainstream cinema, setting in place a set of basic assumptions and norms about the identity and parameters of that cinema that henceforth became hegemonic.

Conclusion

Legal decisions effectively backed up the judgments of municipal and state censors and together they marked out the margins of what was acceptable in cinema, establishing the terrain of classical Hollywood cinema as that necessarily of harmless entertainment divorced from the broadly defined political. In the process, these decisions marked a delimitation of the public role of cinema and indeed of the

---

37 Eg, a legal decision in 1922 following the logic of the *Mutual* decision denied that newsreels could be likened to the press: *Pathé Exch v Cobb* (1922).

public sphere of what Charles Taylor has recently called 'metatopical common space', that broad space in which members of society meet through a variety of media and discuss matters of common interest (Taylor, 2002). Regulatory interventions extended the remit of governance in a liberal democracy and limited public discourse. Griffith's plea for First Amendment rights, shared by others of different political persuasions, was effectively a plea to be included in this common space – though it was a plea that was ultimately refused. *The Birth of a Nation*, so frequently regarded as the birth of classical Hollywood, was in this sense a curious and complex birth, for the film manifested a conception of the function of cinema that concomitant censorship decisions refused. *Intolerance* (1916), following in the footsteps of *The Birth of a Nation* and *The Rise and Fall of Free Speech*, does not then mark simply a formally excessive deviation from classical norms – as the standard film historical narrative suggests – but together the two films mark a *functionally excessive* sense of mainstream cinema.[38]

Even so, this refusal of an engaged public role for cinema was not inevitable but was contingent. Cinema could be different and revisions were possible in changed political circumstances, evident almost immediately after the *Mutual* decision, when events in the wider geo-political sphere culminated with the entry of the United States into the World War that led to a revised governmental sense of the possible public role of cinema. Immediately upon entry into the war, a Committee on Public Information was established by President Woodrow Wilson to help shape public opinion to support the war effort. Wilson and the head of the Committee, George Creel, called upon the film industry to undertake a propagandistic role in this context and the film industry worked closely with the so-called Creel Committee, supporting the production of short instructional films, longer feature films, encouraging film stars to rally to the war effort and exhibitors to use the space of cinemas as communal meeting sites (DeBauche, 1997, pp 104–36).

Important though this reconfiguration of the relation between state and cinema was, it was partial and short-lived. Increased concerns during wartime about free speech, population strength, governance and national security spilled over into an increased surveillance of cinema, visible, for example, in the new banning of *The Birth of a Nation* in a number of states where it had previously been shown because of its possible effects on race relations, in heightened concerns about films about birth control, and in the prosecution of at least one filmmaker under the terms of the 1917 Espionage Act (Fleener-Marzec, 1980, p 265).[39] The definition of the public role of cinema was re-enforced in the immediate post-war period. One example can exemplify this. *Fit to Fight* (1918) was produced during the war period by the government to educate soldiers about the dangers and effects of venereal disease. Re-titled *Fit to Win*, the film was released to a wider audience in the immediate post-war period but was caught up in considerable controversy, including the

---

38 Philip Rosen has summarised this trope of film history thus: 'The classical cinema has a genius father (Griffith), a first-born (*The Birth of a Nation*) and a magnificent freak (*Intolerance*)' (Rosen, 1984, p 22).

39 See *Message Photoplay Co v Bell*, 167 NYS 129 (1917); *Moving Picture World*, 22 December 1917, 1786; *Moving Picture World*, 29 December 1917, 1947; *Moving Picture World*, 11 May 1918, 865; *Moving Picture World*, 25 May 1918, 1145; Wood, 1990, p 296.

emergence of a Catholic-led campaign against the film that foreshadowed the later actions of the Catholic Legion of Decency.[40] *Moving Picture World* asserted that the film 'does not belong in a family theatre to be shown to a mixed audience of men and women' and the film was banned in New York City, a decision upheld by the US Circuit Court of Appeals.[41] Evidently representations of the effects of sexuality could be imperative to state power in times of war, but were quickly re-branded as 'obscene' in the context of the resumption of normal business for the film industry in the immediate post-war period. Censorship was again tied to broad concerns about sexuality and the governance of populations. Even though the war period showed the malleability of the definition of the public role of cinema, then, the dominant framework set in place in the pre-war period was quickly re-established after the war and henceforth underpinned the definition and operations of classical cinema.

Excluded from the mainstream, alternative conceptions and practices of cinema flourished in the margins. Exploitation cinema, propaganda, documentary and the avant-garde all emerged in this context, following the definition of the constitutional status of mainstream cinema and demonstrating not only stylistic deviations but, more critically, functional differences (Kuhn, 1988, pp 45–48; Schaefer, 1999).[42] The critical distinction set in place in regulatory discourses and practices between entertainment and various alternatives was predicated on diverging conceptions of the function of cinema; this meta-generic categorisation – one of the most important in film history – was critical to the establishment of the terrain of classical Hollywood cinema and its alternatives. In this sense, the study of censorship in the transitional era is crucial for our understanding both of the effects of censorship as a broad discursive and practical logic – tied to the broader sphere of the governmental – and also for our efforts to precisely map the nature of the transition to classical Hollywood cinema. The narrowing of the definition of the function of cinema and its place in the public sphere was crucial to the formative shaping of American cinema.

---

40 *Variety*, 21 February 1919, 71; *Moving Picture World*, 24 May 1919, 1167; *Variety*, 18 July 1919, 46; Schaefer, 1999, pp 27–36.

41 *Moving Picture World*, 12 April 1919, 276; *Exhibitor's Trade Review*, 14 June 1919, 104, cited in Schaefer, 1999, p 29.

42 On the emergence and connections between documentary and avant-garde practices and institutions, see, eg, Wolfe, 1995; Nichols, 2001.

Chapter 12
The natives are looking:
cinema and censorship in colonial India
M Madhava Prasad

The Indian Cinematograph Committee (ICC) report of 1928 offers an insight into the ways in which British colonial rule in India felt threatened by cinema. The British were concerned about what the native population might be seeing through this new and popular medium. Cinema could potentially destabilise the existing relations of power between Britain as ruler and its subjects, and disrupt existing relations of governance, through its portrayal of Europeans and Indians. The question the report was to address, therefore, was how cinema in India should be censored, but before that the Committee needed to understand how films were actually being viewed. As a historical document on the regulation of cinema, the report of the Committee (henceforth the RICC) is invaluable. It not only provides one of the earliest surveys on the power of cinema and its effects in India, but it also explores the impact of this new cultural medium on relations between the British and Indian nationalists.

The ICC began its project in 1927, to 'report on the system of censorship of cinematograph films in India and to consider whether it is desirable that any steps should be taken to encourage the exhibition of films produced within the British Empire generally and the production and exhibition of Indian films in particular' (RICC, Vol 1, 1928, p xi). The Committee was set up by an order of the government of India's Home Department (Political), on the recommendation of the Council of State in India. The government had been careful to provide representation for the two communities that, according to the by then well-established colonial common sense, constituted the principal population segments of the subcontinent: Hindus and Muslims. The Committee was headed by Diwan Bahadur T Rangachariar, CIE, Vakil, High Court, Madras. The other members of the Committee were the Honourable Khan Bahadur, Sir Ebrahim Haroon Jaffer, Kt; Colonel JD Crawford, DSO, MC, MLA, Mr KC Neogy, MLA, Vakil, High Court, Calcutta; Mr AM Green, ICS, Collector of Customs and Member of Bombay Board of Film Censors; Mr J Coatman, MLA, Director of Public Information. The decision to give the Chair to an Indian was a noteworthy symbolic gesture.[1] The terms of reference were as follows:

(1) to examine the organisation and the principles and methods of the censorship of cinematograph films in India;

(2) to survey the organisation for the exhibition of cinematograph films and the film-producing industry in India;

---

1 The three 'European' members who represented different interests of the ruling race in the colony together appended a minute of dissent to the final report, demonstrating a degree of solidarity that was not always in evidence during the proceedings of the Committee.

(3) to consider whether it is desirable that steps should be taken to encourage the exhibition of films produced within the British Empire generally and the production and exhibition of Indian films in particular; and to make recommendations.

The third term of reference, the report explains, is a direct consequence of a resolution passed at the Imperial Conference of 1926 (RICC, Vol 1, 1928, p xii) seeking to extend the policy of Imperial preference to the film industry. The order in which the terms of reference were presented, however, was designed to de-emphasise the question of Imperial preference and highlight the issue of censorship.

In the only detailed consideration of the Committee's proceedings available, Brian Shoesmith[2] has pointed out that in 1927, several other countries – Australia, England, France, Germany and Japan – had conducted similar inquiries to gauge the impact of film on society, and in particular to find ways to protect national markets against Hollywood's dominating presence (Shoesmith, 1988–89, p 74). The Indian inquiry was also motivated by similar concerns, but here the dyarchic colonial regime then in place gave an interesting twist to the proceedings. For in the colony it was not only a question of the influence of cinema in general, but of the impact of American cinema. Further, it was not just a question of its impact on everybody, but of the impact on the natives in particular.

Calls for stricter censorship had been voiced since 1913 in England and India (Shoesmith, 1988–89, p 77), and in 1918 the Cinematograph Act was put in place in response to widespread concern. In 1921, a 'cinema expert' by the name of W Evans had been sent to India to report on the film industry in that country. Evans had recommended stiffer censorship rules and better implementation, but Evans' mission and subsequent discussions in England and India showed that it was by no means a settled issue. The colonial structure's anomalous co-existence with the idea of a comity of nations contributes to the peculiar tonality of the discussions about films in the colonies, and in particular in India. This is in part because while in other colonies the audiences for film were predominantly Europeans, in India the natives were also rushing to experience this new form of amusement in large numbers.

The need for special attention to censorship of cinema was explained in the following terms at the beginning of the RICC:

> There are two reasons for differential treatment of the cinema. One reason is that the cinema appeals to a much wider audience. The number of persons who witness a successful play is infinitesimal compared with the vast numbers who witness a successful film. The second reason is that the film has a special and peculiar appeal. It has to achieve its effect visually, without the aid of the spoken word. The result is an exaggeration of physical expression and suggestive action. Every device is employed in order to intensify the visual impression, such as the well known device of the 'close-up', and thus a peculiarly direct and vivid impression is produced upon the mind of the spectator. (RICC, Vol 1, 1928, p 1)

According to the head of the Committee, Rangachariar, who examined a number of the articles warning that 'much harm was being done in India by the widespread exhibition of Western films', published in the British press following Evans' report:

---

2 Brian Shoesmith has given a detailed account of the politics behind the setting up of the commission and the fate of its recommendations, (Shoesmith, 1988–89). See also Barnouw and Krishnaswamy, 1980.

The general trend of them is that, owing to difference of customs and outlook, Western films are misunderstood and tend to discredit Western civilisation in the eyes of the masses in India ... The majority of the films, which are chiefly from America, are of sensational and daring murders, crimes, and divorces, and, on the whole, degrade the white women in the eyes of the Indians. (RICC, Vol 1, 1928, p 3)

Rangachariar noted that questions were also raised in Parliament (RICC, Vol 1, 1928, p 4). In 1926–27, further 'drastic criticism' was made by the British Social Hygiene Delegation after a visit to India. They claimed that throughout India, 'the evil influence of the cinema was cited by educationists [sic] and the representative citizens as one of the major factors in lowering the standard of sex conduct, and thereby tending to increase the dissemination of disease' (reported in RICC, Vol 1, 1928, pp 4–5). In Burma, the National Council of Women advised that sex and crime pictures should be banned. In India, in the Legislative Assembly, questions were raised about the extent and nature of censorship. Indian members like Honourable V Ramadas Pantulu and Honourable Rao Saheb Dr U Rama Rao agreed with the British view and called for measures to restrict or prevent the screening of films likely to have a bad influence. HG Haig, Home Secretary, agreed: 'The censor has to decide not only what is tolerable from a Western standpoint in the representation of western manners but what is tolerable from an Eastern standpoint, or even what is tolerable from the standpoint of probable error or misrepresentation.' He continued, more British films might be better, but, 'a still greater improvement would lie in a considerable extension of the production of Indian films, showing Indian stories in an Indian setting' (reported in RICC, Vol 1, 1928, p 7).

In pursing its investigations, the Committee issued 4,325 copies of a questionnaire, of which 320 were received back with answers. Three hundred and fifty-three witnesses were examined, of whom 114 were Europeans/Anglo-Indians/Americans. Of the remaining 239 natives, the papers of the Committee record the following ethnic profile: 157 Hindus and 82 non-Hindus (38 Muslim, 25 Parsi, 16 Burmese, two Sikhs and one Christian). There were 35 women in all, 16 Europeans, and 19 Indians, Parsi and Burmese. The ethnic composition of the witnesses was a matter of great importance to the entire enterprise, for it was precisely a matter of finding a way in which the 'privacy' of ethnic groups in India could be protected against the cinema's tendency to make everything public. In his summation, Rangachariar noted:

The majority of the European witnesses who take the view that film misrepresentation does harm, seem to consider that this misrepresentation lowers Western, especially European, civilization, in the minds of Indians, and that therefore the effect is injurious to Europeans. In some cases they consider that the result is also injurious to Indians. Those Indian witnesses, however, who agree that Western life is misrepresented, consider that the misrepresentation is *definitely harmful to Indians* because it either induces them to ignore what is good in Western civilization or to copy what is bad. (Emphasis added, RICC, Vol 1, 1928, p 111)

In order to show that there was no danger of misrepresentation of western life demoralising spectators, Rangachariar cites an incident that he witnessed in a theatre in Madras:

The white heroine in every reel was being persecuted by a cosmopolitan band of villains whose leader was an Oriental and whose rank and file comprised other Orientals.

> Whenever the white hero made a timely appearance or the heroine escaped from the toils, spontaneous applause broke forth, and on one occasion when the screen showed the heroine about to fall into the hands of her Oriental persecutor an excited voice cried out in Tamil: 'Look out, Miss, look out!' No more convincing argument could be adduced to show that the sympathies of Indian audiences are not alienated or seriously affected by the portrayal on the screen of a life that is strange to them, always provided that an appeal is made to their human emotions. (RICC, Vol 1, 1928, pp 111–12)

These questions of representations and misrepresentations arise in a context where relations between a ruling race and a 'subject race' are suddenly restructured by the entry of a third element: the institution of cinema, already dominated by the American product. Britain had free trade with the rest of the world, but wanted a different regime, of Imperial preferences,[3] to be enforced in its colonies. The anxieties expressed by various sections of British public opinion, as well as members of the British Parliament, came as a handy excuse to propose preferences. It is not that the need for Imperial preference led to the invention of a threat from American cinema, since this threat of perception was in existence long before the Imperial Conference. Imperial preference was seen by some as a solution to the problem posed by American films, since British films, produced in a climate of stricter moral values, were considered more healthy, less prone to presenting the 'seamier side' of European life.

The social hygienists might already have been the inspiration behind the questions frequently raised in the British Parliament about the possible relation between American cinema and declining native respect for its rulers. Gandhi's views on cinema, which he expressed rather bluntly in a two-line response to the Committee's questionnaire,[4] may also have been indirectly influenced by the hygienist movement in Britain, which must have been an important influence during his time in England. In a memorandum following their visit, the British Social Hygiene Delegation noted, 'In every province that we visited, the evil influence of the cinema was cited by educationists [sic] and the representative citizens as one of the major factors in lowering the standard of sex conduct and thereby tending to increase dissemination of disease' (reported in RICC, Vol 1, 1928, pp 4–5). From all accounts this appears to have been a crackpot delegation, but its alarmist claims, which were later discredited by the very people who were cited as sources of information by the delegation, may have played an important role in pushing the government to order the inquiry. In India, the Council of State and the Legislative Assembly discussed the issue. Sir Haroon Jaffer (who was later to be included in the inquiry Committee) expressed concern about the low quality of films that were circulating in India, and the Home Secretary agreed with him that, 'gross misrepresentations of Western morals, of Western culture, and Western civilisation ... have not infrequently found their way into cinema exhibitions' (RICC, Vol 1, 1928, p 6). Thus the terms of reference of the future committee were based on

---

3 These preferences related to trade in all kinds of goods, cinema being a relatively minor element.

4 This was Gandhi's reply: 'Even if I was so minded, I should be unfit to answer your questionnaire, as I have never been to a cinema. But even to an outsider, the evil that it has done and is doing is patent. The good, if it has done any at all, remains to be proved.' (RICC, Vol 4, 1928, p 56)

the solutions that had already been decided upon by the rulers. The report notes that the Home Secretary had already expressed a hope that more British films would find their way to India, to improve the quality of the fare available to the audiences in the colonies. The colonial officer clearly felt obliged to suggest that British films were of a better quality than the American imports, but he also knew that it was difficult to sustain such an opinion when everybody, even in England, knew that the British films were no match for the Hollywood product.

American cinema contained scenes set in nightclubs, highlighting the lives of women of loose morals and the like. But, even the more normal aspects of western life, such as couples kissing or hugging or dancing 'in public' were equally a cause for worry, because the uneducated native was gaining access to views of the private lives of the ruling race. Cinema, and in particular 'close-ups', provided a view of the white woman's body to all and sundry; even the most impoverished Indian could, for a small fee, walk in and look at the bodies of white women and their amorous activities. The repeated reference to 'close-ups' shows a preoccupation with the public exposure that white people's private lives were susceptible to: one witness suggested that much of the harm could be prevented by simply cutting out the close-ups. It was a question, quite simply, of a collapse of order and hierarchy, an alarming levelling of rulers and ruled.

Throughout the volumes of evidence, one theme is repeated again and again: it is not the educated Indians, who are familiar with cultural differences and can be relied upon to appreciate the films in a proper manner, it is the illiterate masses and what impressions they will form of the ruling race, that is at issue. Encouragement to Indian cinema, especially to mythologicals, is seen by many as one way of keeping the 'low class of Indians' away from theatres that show Western films. Rangachariar, for his part, tried to reassure the ruling race that the illiterate were far from getting the wrong ideas about white women. His anecdote, referred to above, is revealing: the Indian spectator sympathises with the white hero and heroine to the extent of crying out to the heroine to escape and seems not to regard colour as a basis for identification. This spectator is in no danger of being alienated, Rangachariar explains, with unintentional irony. Giving evidence of one kind of alienation, he reassured the white residents of India that another kind of alienation – disenchantment with the Empire – was unlikely.

Cinema thus put the social order of British India into an ideological crisis, at a time when it was hardly seen by more than a small fraction of the population. The nationalists among the witnesses were fully aware of this, and resolutely refused to say that American films were doing any harm to Indians. Various versions of the problem were presented:

(1) the image of British women will suffer;

(2) the minds of gullible Indians will be corrupted;

(3) all races should be treated with respect, there should be no bad images of Indians in Western films any more than there should be bad images of Westerners in films screened in India.

On all these fronts, the nationalists remained firm: the minds of Indians were not so weak as to be corrupted by a few films; if the image of British women suffered, it is not the fault of Indians, it is the British who are making these films; and so on.

Other subsequent committees, set up by the government of free India to inquire into the film industry, repeat many of the ideas of the RICC and tend to pose the problems in the same way, with the same terms and concepts. In this way, the report has had a lasting impact on thinking about cinema in India.

Beyond this, the true value of the document lies in the four volumes of evidence, including the written answers to the questionnaire as well as the full details of the oral examinations conducted. It is a text of tremendous historical value, documenting a dramatic confrontation between two or more different conceptions of the nature of the Indian polity and culture in a colonial state. In the next section, I discuss some aspects of the report that concern the disruptive role played by cinema vis-à-vis the existing colonial relations of governance and social relations between the three most important ethnic groups in the colony: Hindus, Muslims and 'Europeans'.

The Chairman of the Committee, in his words to 'the first European gentleman' to give evidence, posed the crucial question in these terms: 'We have heard complaints from European gentlemen and ladies that the exhibition of western life to an Easterner produces a lowering effect concerning the European' (RICC, Vol 1, 1928, p 41). J Stenson, Supervisor, Bombay Entertainments Duty Act, replied that this was not his view. He did not think it a serious issue. The Chairman persisted:

> We have all different ideas of decency; for instance, we have different notions of decency and the Europeans have different notions of decency, and as long as the Europeans live here we do not expect them to give up their notions of decency, and their manners unless there is something extraordinarily indecent in the pictures shown. We often hear these complaints, but when pressed to a point they are not able to tell us where the trouble actually lies, and I seek your assistance in this matter. (RICC, Vol 1, 1928, p 41)

Stenson responded by declaring that he could not answer the question. The Chairman persisted, and pointed out that there were 'certain things in your mode of life' which Indians would not care to adopt and vice versa, but that was no reason to judge these things immoral. Stenson responded that he found nothing objectionable among Indians. On further questioning by other members, Stenson agreed that, 'Western films as shown today, including all these cabaret scenes and scenes of the underworld, are a definite misrepresentation of western life' (RICC, Vol 1, 1928, p 43). However, it was suggested that in Bombay at any rate, the 'people in the cheaper seats' who are the main cause for concern were not seeing these films in large numbers, firstly because there were very few 'four-anna' seats in the theatres showing western films. Only the educated Indians could go to see these films and they were 'not likely to be seriously deceived'. Committee member, Mr Green, summed it up in the following terms, 'the people who would misunderstand them do not see them' (RICC, Vol 1, 1928, p 44). At the very beginning, the tone of the Committee's proceedings was set.

However, the theme of the unwelcome gaze of the uneducated Indian keeps coming back. Thus RK Mhatre, Assistant Director of Public Health, in his written statement suggested: 'Western films are greatly misunderstood by the uneducated Indian as evidenced from their behaviour at the cinema theatres. Innocent action such as embracing or kissing are hissed and jeered at through their ignorance of Western social life and customs' (RICC, Vol 1, 1928, p 50). In his oral deposition, Mhatre confirmed his views, but averred that the remedy was not censorship but to 'raise the educational standard' (RICC, Vol 1, 1928, p 55). Others consider that a bad impression about Western culture was being created by the Europeans in India, some of whom lead 'bad lives', and not just by the films (RICC, Vol 1, 1928, p 209).

An interesting encounter occurred between the Chairman and a journalist with nationalist leanings, R Venkataram. The journalist was firmly against censorship based on the misrepresentation thesis, and argued for a 'widening in our outlook of mind', which provoked the Chairman to ask:

Q: Would you like Indian ladies to be shown in the way Western ladies are shown?
A: You can't help it.
Q: I mean in Indian pictures; would you like a Madrassi lady – a Madrassi Brahmin lady – shown in an Indian picture dressed in a Western costume?
A: If she were so shown I would not object to it.
Q: On what grounds would you not object to it?
A: Because these things are happening in real life.

The nationalist refused to budge on his principles. Evidencing increasing frustration the Chairman persisted with his line of questioning:

Q: Supposing they depict Rangachariar [referring to himself] without a turban, in a hat?
A: What would be wrong?
Q: Supposing your character was being portrayed as addressing a public meeting without a Gandhi cap and khaddar dress, and you were dressed in a Bond Street costume ... do you think it would be right?
A: I do not know what a Bond Street costume is. If somebody took a fancy to represent me in full English costume I would not object to it. (RICC, Vol 1, 1928, pp 542–43)

The issue comes down to individual representation, where Rangachariar tries to highlight the absurdity of representing a man who wears a turban in a hat. Of course, from a biographical point of view, this raises problems, but what has happened meanwhile is that Rangachariar has turned a question of cultural representations applicable to complex social formations into one of individual representation.

The difference between the two broad viewpoints that are opposed to each other throughout these proceedings hinges on two different conceptions of the polity. Nationalists like Venkataram proceed on the assumption that Indians are modern individuals, (future) citizens of a democratic country, whereas the conservative opinion takes the colonial polity as the natural and durable state of affairs. The nationalist objects to misrepresentation of 'Orientals' in Hollywood films, but sees no evidence of objectionable misrepresentation of white people in them. A European subject, Major W Ellis Jones, MLC, insisted that the 'class of film depicting so-called "Society Life" in Europe and America ... are harmful to young people of all races and must convey to the uninformed Indian an entirely false view of the woman of these continents' (RICC, Vol 1, 1928, p 306). He recommended that 'such low cabaret scenes should be deleted' (RICC, Vol 1, 1928, p 309). Jones also claimed that his educated Indian acquaintances wanted such films to be banned. Here a commonality of interest between Indians and Europeans begins to appear: while Europeans are against exposing European women (through their representations) to the uneducated Indian gaze, it is also proposed that the educated Indians are also not comfortable with the general availability of such views. In other words, a paternalist compact between right-thinking Europeans and Indians is hinted at.

Faced with a situation where its own skills of voyeuristic observation and reformist intervention, the former in any case, have suddenly become available for the native to use against it, the colonial authority was clearly on the defensive. What Partha Chatterjee (1993) has called the 'rule of colonial difference', on which colonial power rested, required the preservation of the 'alienness of the ruling group' (p 10), its transcendence of the social order over which it exercised power. Chatterjee has also shown how, on the other hand, the nationalists also sought to separate the public domain of politics (where colonial power held sway), from the socio-cultural 'inner world' which would be out of bounds for the colonial gaze. The nationalists won for themselves the freedom to interpret modernity in their own way by insisting on this demarcation of spaces.

Chatterjee places this development in the mid to late 19th century and tracks the theme in particular reference to the 'women's question' (pp 116–34). It is not coincidental, therefore, that it is precisely the image of the white woman in the eyes of the natives that precipitates a brief reversal of historical roles. With the advent of cinema, an unexpected situation develops, where the colonial authorities find themselves identifying with their ethnic origins, something they did not have to do before. Under the impact of cinema, the British seem to lose their footing in the universal as it were. If earlier British authorities could, without damage to their despotic status, undertake social reform informed by universal values, now the native, a colonised subject, was occupying the universalist position of viewing offered by Hollywood cinema, an intolerable situation for the logic of colonial difference.

Sometimes, the compulsions of colonial representationalism would generate some unusual modes of thinking symptomatic of the untenable, indefensible nature of the colonial presence. Major Jones, continuing with his oral evidence, explained a remark in his 'Written Statement', where he had objected to the depiction of 'kept women' in an Indian film:

Q: (Chairman): Do you mean to say that there should be no play or drama or story in which kept women should be referred to?
A: What I really intended to convey was that as far as possible they should be of the same race. If the film was produced by the Indians it should be all Indians. If they are produced by Englishmen they should be all Englishmen. If they are produced by Madrassis they should all be Madrassis. There should be only one race engaged in it, I mean the actors and actresses of films.

The witness is objecting to what he perceives as an unacceptable mingling of races, a sort of miscegenation. However, it is not merely a question of appearances, racial mixing *in* the film text, but of the reality behind the text:

Q: You say a female character was taken by an Englishwoman in life?
A: Yes. The film was produced in Calcutta. It was a local product.
Q: (Mr Green): Do you say that she was represented on the screen as an Englishwoman?
A: No.
Q: As a Bengali herself?
A: Yes. She was represented as an outside woman altogether.
Q: She was dressed as a Bengali?
A: No. She was dressed as an ordinary outside Indian woman.

Q: (Chairman): She was dressed as an Indian?
A: Yes.
Q: She was not represented as a European?
A: No.
Q: She consented to take that part. She was not represented as an Englishwoman?
A: I have an objection to showing to the general public a film of that nature.
Q: If she was represented as an Indian what is your objection? I thought it comes within your meaning that they should have the same race. You would bar English actresses taking the part of Indian girls?
A: Yes.

Under pressure, Jones gives an explanation that equates European interests with those of native communities, demanding the same ethnic autonomy that they later claim for themselves:

Q: On what ground would you ban it?
A: On the same ground as I would protest against a Madrassi woman being employed with a Bengali man. I think the people of the race would object. They do object. We know in India they object very strongly to their women acting with men of other races ... Indians object to it very strongly and we object on the same basis.
Q: Do you object to Frenchmen taking the part of Englishmen on the stage?
A: We are of the Western race. The Bengalis, the Madrassis, and the Rajputs think of themselves separately.

Finally to Committee member Mr Green's question:

Do I understand you to object to a European actress appearing in an Indian film even if she acted so well that she would not be recognised on the screen as a European? (RICC, Vol 1, pp 310–13)

Jones replies with an emphatic 'yes'. Jones represented 'cotton', that is, the community of European cotton planters. His objection, as the Chairman restates it, is 'generally to any race representing another race'. For a colonial polity to survive as a stable formation, there must be no neutral currency through which coloniser and colonised can interact. Democracy would have been one such currency, which one stream of British opinion understandably opposed (Chatterjee, 1993, pp 16–18). Cinematic representation also threatened to function precisely as such a currency, where the substance (European blood) is hidden behind the mask (representation of Indian womanhood). Even if the representation is so perfect as to conceal any hint of European origins, it is still a problem because for Jones it is not a question simply of representations, it is a matter of actual social/sexual relations. Here realism functions as a moral-political norm. Secondly, Jones' testimony also points to the way in which the European community perceived itself as one of the many communities of India: the Rajputs, the Madrassis, the Bengalis, etc. Thus it is by analogy with these communities,[5] and their strict enforcement of endo-sociality, that Jones makes a case for the Europeans' right to their racial separateness.

---

5 These were not actually existing communities in any real sense, they were rather, national cultures with further internal divisions. Usually, when a Madrassi community was referred to, it was the Brahmin or upper caste groups.

HW Hogg, Secretary of the Punjab Boy Scouts Association, summed up the dangers posed by reference to an example of films which show 'a white woman being easily led astray say by an Arab ... a white woman leading a loose idle life ... that is bound to lower the respect of Eastern races for white women of the Western races' (RICC, Vol 2, 1928, p 69). Where 'a small number of English people' live amidst a large number of Indians, Hogg explains (hinting at more sinister possibilities), women 'living in isolated stations where very often law and order is not maintained ... the dignity and the respect which is due to a woman ... would certainly be lowered' (RICC, Vol 1, 1928, p 70). Among the natives, there were several who agreed with this point of view. Thus Diwan Bahadur from Punjab objected to foreign films which showed revolutions, because he was confident that grievances 'can be redressed without having recourse to revolution or rowdyism', to which the Chairman replied, 'You are very optimistic that way' (RICC, Vol 2, 1928, p 141).

The underlying logic of Major Jones' reservations is far more tellingly revealed in the repeated discussions of the question of kissing. The common refrain, which begins to be used by many people in these proceedings, and which was repeated until recently as an explanation, was that Indians do not kiss in public and therefore that they should not be shown doing so. In addition, this was also used to explain why the native spectator might end up with a low opinion of Europeans, whom he sees on screen, kissing. Rangachariar exposes the faulty logic of the claim, pointing out that while the image of kissing is shown in public, the act itself is depicted as taking place in private.[6] This difference, which seems obvious to us, is imperceptible to people then: kissing in public means being seen in public kissing. It is another version of Major Jones' argument, which sees, in the images on screen, not a set of cinematic signifiers strung together to tell a tale, but the actual people behind it, who acted out those scenes so that they may be displayed in public. The logic of the colonial social order is revealed here: ideally, there must be no public space as such, the social fabric must consist entirely of the communities each with its separate, closed social order, its moral and cultural leaders, and its rules of conduct. The inner life of one community must not be made public, made visible to the gaze of an individual from another community. Cinema comes in the way of such a conception of colonial society. Its realistic images of private life cause an acute sense of violation of the right of communities to privacy in a polity organised as a series of discrete mutually exclusive units. Before the advent of cinema, it was only the native communities which sought to protect their 'inner domain' from the reformist/universalist interventionist gaze of the British rulers.

With the advent of cinema, the modern suddenly comes loose from its presumed immanence to white society. It is the nationalists who suddenly occupy centre stage as harbingers of a modern future, who dismiss British and Indian conservatives alike as representatives of a passing order. Thus the nationalist Lala Lajpat Rai was uncompromising in his rejection of proposals for censorship and Imperial preference. He also told the Committee, in no uncertain terms, that in his opinion

---

6 For a more detailed consideration of the ban on kissing (with reference to independent India), see Prasad, 1998, Chapter 4.

Imperial preference was the actual intention behind the whole enterprise. Asked about cabaret scenes, underworld scenes and scenes that 'tend to lower the Western womanhood in the estimation of our people here', Rai replied:

> I don't want the youth of this country to be brought up in a nursery. They should know all those things, because then they will be better able to resist those things when they go out. They should see all those things here and they will be able to understand better all the points of modern life. (RICC, Vol 2, 1928, p 201)

An exchange followed. The Chairman asked whether 'knowledge of other portions of the Empire' is not essential. Rai replied:

> I think knowledge of the world is essential ... I don't know if there is any special reason why we should know more of the Empire than of the rest of the world ... You will pardon me, Mr Chairman, I have no use for the Empire at all. The Empire treats us as helots everywhere, and therefore I have no affection for this Empire. My point of view cannot agree with those who love this Empire. (RICC, Vol 2, 1928, p 202)

No danger to morality is posed by such films because if Indians are to get educated in Western morals (which the West wants us to learn), then it is necessary for us to watch such films.

A ban on American films was not a realistic option for a number of reasons. First, being a schizophrenic entity, British political authority could not have adopted colonial trade practices towards a free country like the USA. Secondly, British films were no match for the racier American product, even in the eyes of the ordinary British residents of India, who would certainly have objected to a ban. It would have been very difficult to impose a restrictive policy of showing the films only to white people. Most importantly, the nationalist gaze was taunting the colonial regime for its political backwardness, the hollowness of its claims to participate in the Enlightenment. The RICC reveals to us the irresolvable dilemma faced by the colonial authority in the cultural domain, in the face of a new cultural technology which the ideology of colonialism had not anticipated.

In place of a ban, and a blanket imposition of Imperial preference, therefore, the Committee's report contains some compromise proposals. One proposal put forward to the Committee by Mrs VG Coulson, a representative of the Bengal Presidency Council of Women, focuses upon a cinematic device, the close-up. 'Avoid close-ups as much as possible. That is the main thing' (RICC, Vol 2, 1928, p 925). The close-up, Mrs Coulson argued, brings the image of the Western woman too close to the viewer, who experiences a sense of possession of the image, and by extension, the woman herself. But the Chairman wanted to know why only the Indians should be deprived of such an illusion of possession. 'The close-ups', he explained:

> ... are in evidence everywhere. In England also it is in evidence very largely. How is it then that the English society does not revolt against it? May I put to you how the Indians view it? The thing is done in the West. It is not we who misrepresent them, but it is the Westerner himself who represents himself or herself in that light, and why don't they tap the very source of mischief without coming here and asking to put a stop to it?' (RICC, Vol 2, 1928, p 926)

The Chairman's questions here expose a weakness in the argument of the conservatives. The witness cannot claim ethnic solidarity with those who produce these films, but the images give the impression that the women on screen and the white women in India belong to the same race. On the other hand, the Europeans in India do want to identify with the 'white race' as far as the situation in India is concerned. There is no racial leadership which can be appealed to, to stop the production of objectionable films: the white race's *imaginary* unity is not complemented by a *symbolic* unity. Unlike the Madrassis, the Rajputs and the Bengalis, who appear to function as communities with a recognised leadership, the British in India could claim to belong to a community called Europeans, with an identifiable position of authority to which complaints could be addressed. Coulson's comments suggest that since neither she nor the colonial authorities could intervene to change the free market to suit the needs of colonial moral order, the Indians who ordered the films should be asked to desist.

Another proposal, to encourage Indian film production, provided the only instance when all the diverse interests represented in the entire debate seem to arrive at some kind of consensus. The RICC notes that the Home Secretary had already given expression to this, 'But it seems to me that a still greater improvement would lie in a considerable extension of the production of Indian films – showing Indian stories in an Indian setting' (RICC, Vol 1, 1928, p 8).

The RICC bears witness to a singular moment in world history when a colonial order encounters in cinema a threat to the social order that was built up by a consensus among the elite leadership of the different communities. Cinema exposes these communities to the gaze of a non-denominational public, but perhaps it also exposes the falsity of the claims of the leadership that such communities exist at all. The gaze of the film spectator comes to haunt the conservative desire for closed community spaces, and in the most interesting development of all, many European groups find themselves seeking the very communal right to non-interference from outside that the nationalists had demanded from them. But cinema, a product at the forefront of a newly aggressive American capitalism's global drive, harbinger of a new logic of universality, cannot be held to account, it will not abide their question. They try to inveigle the Indian community leaders into a pact that could save them all, but the nationalists stand firm against such a compact. Censorship guidelines end up reflecting the concerns of the conservatives on both sides, and for several decades after Independence, the Indian state would continue with the same censorship rules informed by the same colonial logic, for the nationalists, with power in their own hands, began to find comfort in the conservative opinion they had so firmly opposed.

Chapter 13
Rethinking regulation:
violence and 1967 Hollywood
J David Slocum

This chapter seeks to expand the concept of 'regulation' for the study of violence in Hollywood cinema by examining the specific historical moment of the US release of, and subsequent controversy over, *Bonnie and Clyde* (1967). It will open with an historical overview of cultural regulation as an intervention between political economy and the field of cultural production and consumption. A range of possible critical meanings and interpretative strategies will then be identified, from statutory control and official censorship to the circumscription of normative cultural and psychic processes in audience engagement with cultural productions. The aim here is to explore the integration of cultural regulation into an interdisciplinary sociology of popular media that casts light on such concerns as the social control of deviance, the deployment of specific cinematic forms and practices, and the circumscription of the production of knowledge about film violence and popular cinema generally.

Regulation has been traditionally understood as a variant of censorship, in so far as both involved the legal and institutional suppression of speech or other expression. Legal statutes, codes and prohibitions commingled with institutional or industry guidelines, the formal and organised position-taking of public interest or reform groups, and perhaps religious interdictions, define standards for expression and communication based in tenets of morality or concerns about social stability or national security. This definition of standards for possible or socially acceptable expressive practices results in constraints being placed on others. Viewed more politically, the production and circulation of speech and public expression were subject to the sovereignty of a beneficent and representative state and its allied economic interests. Shaped by moral, legal, and institutional instruments, in other words, media practices (meaning, familiarly, standards for content) are shaped so as to protect the values of the social and cultural status quo. In broad terms, the prevailing discourse in the US thus engenders focus on the reach, sway, or quantity of these instruments, that is, on this sovereignty over individual or corporate producers of expression. The usual questions become those of 'regulation versus de-regulation', the appropriateness of industrial 'self-regulation', or the scope of legal regulation over specific content areas, especially as an intrusion upon constitutionally guaranteed rights to expression.

Being suggested here is an expanded conception of regulation as a cultural process of privileging certain media forms, institutions and content, and marginalising and repressing others. Regulation seen this way becomes a constant rather than a more-or-less proposition: it is an ongoing process that establishes and reinforces norms and deviance in media and social practice. Crucially, such regulation polices those categories by also determining what is subject to active, acceptable deliberation and what is marginalised or silenced (Post, 1998, pp 1–12). Rather than being a suppressive, 'top-down' exercise of governmental or institutional control over cultural production, this orientation sees power as dispersed across a range of discursive and political practices. The traditional legal and institutional instruments noted earlier participate in this process, though as instances and enactments of an ongoing process more deeply rooted in political economy and the maintenance of prevailing social, moral and institutional authority. As such, regulation of the cultural field proceeds by the interaction of structures of social and economic relations, including those governing the formation of social institutions and individual subjects *and* relatively autonomous practices enabling transformations to occur.

Cultural regulation

Antonio Gramsci, the Italian writer imprisoned between 1929 and 1935, adapted and complicated Marx's ideas about the relationship between economy and culture. Gramsci was the first to suggest, albeit generally, intervening modes of regulation between economic production and the culture of consumption. He advanced the notion that increasingly standardised practices of economic institutions – the automobile assembly line perhaps most conspicuously, but, for the present discussion, also the Hollywood mode of production – constrained the cultural forms they produced and the practices they allowed. In other words, the institutionalisation of cultural production was, for Gramsci, itself a process that largely appropriated and contained forms that opposed as well as sustained dominant relations of social power. Social and moral controversies over meanings thus became occasions *both* for the retrenchment of institutional power *and* the concealment of the very process by which oppositional forms were re-appropriated or repressed (Gramsci, 1971).

It was not until the last three decades of the 20th century that a number of strands of critical work converged to address this relationship more consistently. One of these strands, emergent in the cultural and linguistic turns of the late 1970s and 1980s, moved to embrace Gramsci and a broader Marxian orientation as guiding the analysis and contextualisation of cultural production and circulation. Around the same time, historians began revisiting earlier years, often the 1930s, in particular, in which bureaucratisation seemed to define politics and the consolidation of media institutions like Hollywood. A third strand was the development of economic regulation theories, by Michel Aglieta (1979, 1987), among others, who asserted that every form of production requires a complementary form of consumption. Such complementarity requires a mode of moral and social regulation that is maintained and preserved through state, educational, and media institutions. According to this view, moral regulation operates in part to establish certain behaviours, identities, and practices as natural or normal, and to mark others as unnatural or deviant. The result is an identifiable correspondence between historically specific regimes of production and consumption *and* the cultural forms and practices that operate within and also sustain them (see also Corrigan and Sayer, 1985; Ray and Sayer, 2000).

The specific history in play here covers roughly the past four decades. During that period of great changes in the critical field, the recognition and study of power was reconceived as more dispersed than had been previously imagined. Michel Foucault, in particular, seminally called for the eschewal 'of the model of Leviathan in the study of power' in favour of multiple mechanisms of power and resistance. Foucault sought to 'escape from the limited field of juridical sovereignty and state institutions, and instead base our analysis of power on the study of techniques and tactics of domination' (Foucault, 1977, p 102). Later in the period, dramatic changes in material conditions, epitomised by the end of the Cold War, appeared to punctuate such a call to look beyond state power to more variegated discursive models.

In fact, after 1989, fervent efforts to comprehend and advance changes in Eastern European societies prompted a renaissance of the notion of 'civil society'. Originally developed by Locke and Ferguson in the late 17th century to refer to that realm of institutions and associations beyond the economy or the state, the term was pejoratively associated with market capitalism by Marx in the mid-19th century. Today, following the writing of Jeffrey Alexander (1998a), John Keane (1988) and others, the term has taken on new meaning. Civil society is a historically specific complex of institutions, customs and discourses; it is a sub-system of society that includes media and communications institutions and is charged with the moral regulation of that society. Much of this regulation concerns the ongoing negotiation of boundaries between social order and disorder – that is, between legitimate and illegitimate violence or proper and improper expression.

Tying together theories of economic regulation and civil society is a shared focus on the broader dynamics and social structures that exist among the state, economy, and more everyday, culture-building institutions like media (Bobbio, 1988). Again, the precise roles of the state or of non-institutional or non-traditional realms are subject to debate. Yet my claim here is that it is crucial (for a fuller understanding of media regulation and, more specifically, as will be discussed, film violence) to broaden our view of the social field and to acknowledge the many mechanisms and structures that shape given media practices and inform specific instances of media regulation. Of special importance is the field of cultural production, so regularly, as with Hollywood, the subject of public debates and controversies over film content, but rarely included in more integrated models of media or its regulation. Public discourse that addresses the morality or 'values' of content in terms of scandal and controversy thus can be seen as often to displace attention to economic, institutional and governmental concerns as to address them directly.

How does this cultural field operate? Sociologist Jeffrey Alexander writes, 'the language that forms the cultural core of civil society can be isolated as a general structure and studied as a relatively autonomous symbolic form' (Alexander, 1998b, p 99). That language constitutes a binary – for Alexander, a 'bifurcating' – discourse in which elements are opposed in terms of their serving democratic or non-democratic purposes. Pure, autonomous and rational motivations for individual and social action in this way contrast the polluted, dependent and hysterical. It is the contest between putatively democratic and non-democratic individuals, groups and behaviours that gives form and shape to civil society; the binary structure marks the boundaries of acceptable expression and positions its constituents vis-à-vis prevailing society and its norms. In the process, the language of celebrating democracy and demonising non-democracy inscribes cultural productions and media while establishing social legitimacy.

This symbolic form helps to illuminate the preoccupation with violence in media policy and public debate. While numerous reasons have been adduced for media violence, many are variations on John Fiske's (1989) suggestion that it appears as a cultural response to perceived social pressures (pp 134–37). The precise correspondence between media violence and actual behaviour or even perceptions is, of course, the rub of most critical accounts. Cast in binary terms, social pressures are polluting and non-democratic threats to democracy and prevailing order; violence in media is likewise perceived as a break from norms of cultural production and conventional narrative storytelling. Shared is the language of opposition, non-conformity and threat. Making that language all the more resonant is the widespread cultural connotation of violence as a violation of rational norms for social association or narrative construction. Violence in this way stands as an aberration in actual behaviour and cultural practice, a break against which legitimate standards might be clarified and oppositional elements confirmed.

I introduce violence at this point to underscore the important critical reformulation of regulation and, more explicitly, censorship that has taken place over the last 40 years. No longer is censorship viewed as the unidirectional legal suppression of speech by the state: that traditional monopoly of power is now seen as having been dispersed and operating across multiple institutional and everyday practices. Such operation recurs, indeed, throughout our everyday lives by continually marking the boundaries of free expression. In the words of Pierre Bourdieu (1988), the structure of the cultural field itself circumscribes 'both access to expression and the form of expression' (p 137). Censorship becomes productive, constructing knowledge and establishing the practices that help to define us as social subjects. It is no longer an exceptional practice aimed at curbing putatively deviant expression, like that featuring violence, but a normative one constituting the shape and media of expression.

In the United States in the 20th century, civil society and especially its component media institutions have quite effectively produced and communicated consistent norms for expressions of violence in media. Using Ronald Jacobs' (1998) words, 'the semiotic code is organised around the sacred signs of rational and controlled motivations, open and trusting relationships, and impersonal, rule-regulated institutions' (p 140). The predominant symbolic form in which these signs circulate is narrative storytelling, which helps individuals and groups to understand their progress in moving toward democratic values and away from those opposed. 'The basic plot of civil society', Jacobs notes plainly, 'is the story of integration, participation, and citizenship' (p 140) and, we might add, the active repudiation of threats to community and individual rights. The regulation of media violence relies on presuppositions of rational law and society underwritten by a discourse of liberty, as well as the continuity of a delimited semiotic code and symbolic forms. Put differently, public discourse on media violence tends to negotiate the moral norms of media content while avoiding interference in institutional media practice or close scrutiny of the frameworks through which they are understood (Bok, 1994, 1998). Especially lacking is any serious reconciliation of the putatively democratic accountability of media systems with imperatives of the marketplace (Schudson, 1992; Garnham, 1992).

Violence is an especially resonant topic for the exploration of an expanded conception of regulation. Its centrality to the operation of civil society, as posited by Alexander and Jacobs, turns on its role in the integration of participants and their ongoing social relations. The contestation of boundaries of order and disorder in society entails a negotiation *both* of the legitimacy of certain forms of violence *and* of specific media producers. Who is authorised to employ violence and in which circumstances? Likewise, for media producers, who may legitimately represent violent action, and in which forms? The answers to these questions draw attention to the formation and operation of social institutions and subjects. At the same time, they also raise further questions about the prevailing public and critical discourses about violence. Who, for example, are the stewards of the predominant discourse of violence in society or media? My suggestion is that by analysing the cultural field – encompassing corporate and governmental institutions, the economics involving producers and consumers, systems of symbolic capital, and cultural forms themselves – it is possible to address better how 'violence' itself is defined and knowledge about it produced.

Hollywood cinema and the discourse of film violence

Cinema studies scholarship has been uneven in its responses to these questions. Critical attention to the history of regulation of film violence in the US remains mostly focused on specific historical periods, either the 1930s or the 1960s. For those periods, research generally considers the links between evolving formal regulatory instruments and social factors, and the putative 'effects' of film-going on viewers, during those years. Little, if any, comparative, trans-historical or cross-cultural work has appeared. More familiar in the study of cinematic regulation is research into the place and meaning of sexuality in cinema in these and other periods. The very primacy of social efforts to contain and repress representations of sexuality rather than violence calls attention to the need to interrogate how such priorities and boundaries are culturally set. Of the analyses that have been undertaken, many provide instructive illuminations not only of the relationship between legal, institutional and statutory instruments governing film violence and cultural regulation, but of the mechanisms of institutional power and processes of legitimisation relevant to violent images and narratives as well. Among the specific concerns raised by these works are criminalisation, pacification, the legitimacy of state authority (and its use of physical force) and the civilising process.

Historical research undertaken on early cinema is illustrative. Annette Kuhn's *Cinema, Censorship and Sexuality* (1988) was pathbreaking in its sustained reading of early British cinema through a Foucauldian lens. Censorship here was rethought and ostensibly prohibitive activity viewed as renegotiations of power productive not only of meanings within films, but the discourses surrounding them. Likewise for the early US cinema, Shelley Stamp (1999) developed the notion of a 'dance of interlegitimation' involving the film industry, self-professed reformers, traditional stewards of social morality, commercial interests, and the viewing public. Her exploration of 'vice films' like *Traffic in Souls* (1913) and *Inside the White Slave Traffic* (1913) speaks directly to cultural contests over images of physical threat, harm, injury and death. These contests, she argues, helped to shape early narrative and aesthetic practices by legitimising the presentation of public concerns like white slavery through 'fictional' individual morality plays, rather than ambiguously documentary productions that would more problematically point to more widespread cultural and economic causes (Budd, 1985).

Lee Grieveson's work probes the relationship between emerging norms of narrative filmmaking, on the one hand, and the legitimisation of US cinema itself as a respectable institution in the cultural field during the first two decades of the 20th century, on the other (Grieveson, 2001). Grieveson develops a notion of 'policing' that undergirds both textual inscriptions of racism, imperialism, and nationalism *and* the positioning of cinema as a social space of cultural consumption. Also looking at *Traffic in Souls*, he complicates the notion of an emergent classicism by connecting the evolution of film form and narrative with the construction of a viable commercial movie industry. The resulting 'heterogeneous' classicism illustrates the inextricable links between forms of expression and access to them (Grieveson, 1997).

Almost certainly the best known episode of US media regulation is that of motion pictures in the late 1920s and early 1930s. Coinciding with the introduction of sound technology and the Great Depression, this episode features public outcry over the sexual permissiveness of 'fallen women' films or Mae West and the glorification of criminality in gangster movies. Concerns mounted over the possible effects of viewing these movies, particularly the possible imitation in actual behaviour of what occurred on-screen by children, but also by 'vulnerable' ethnic groups and workers. Regulation during the classical or studio period seldom addressed 'violence' directly (the word itself did not appear in the original Production Code). The attention of reformers and, increasingly, social scientists to what we might construe as violence was chiefly devoted to representations of criminality or other violations of social morality. Also importantly, and had occurred with the earlier 'vice' films, an important outcome of these cultural and institutional negotiations was the consolidation of narrative or formal strategies, like the imposition of proper, moral endings for dealing with controversial representations.

I have argued elsewhere that the evolution across the 20th century of film industry and public discourses about movie violence corresponds with, and contributes to, key moments in the institutionalisation of popular cinema (Slocum, 2000). Besides sound and economic depression, social instability and questions about official authority, and the growth of administrative institutions, particularly in the state, the 1930s were surely years during which the consolidation of the film industry as a social institution was at issue. By 1934, the film industry had established means for self-regulation of content through the Motion Picture Production Code enforced by an office run by Will H Hays. At the time and for decades following, the film industry itself and later chroniclers lent detail to, but mounted no substantive critique of, this recounting of the Code's emergence. Only more recently, as film historian Richard Maltby (1991) argues, have these 'official' accounts been criticised for following the narrative structure of a Hollywood melodrama, with Will Hays as a crusader fighting the turpitude of filmmakers and finally triumphing in the name of moral decency and popular will. One conclusion is that Hollywood marketed this earlier history of regulation in order to affirm its concern for prevailing social values, and to protect and consolidate its own commercial enterprise.

Regulation here entails contested standards of social morality, changing film form and practices, and the evolution of Hollywood corporatisation and its relations with the government and other institutions. Beyond these dynamics of the cultural field, though, are those of the critical field that explain how the idea of regulation is approached, shaped and contained, and how prevailing conceptions of regulation enter into historical, popular or critical understanding. In terms of violence, a ready example is the privileging of public and industry discourse about criminality as a standard for Hollywood's engagement (and why not, for instance, the often physically cruel or injurious treatment of the working class or of Blacks). Related is the issue of periodisation and how the focus on certain historical episodes, and the particular cultural contests taking place during them, amount to an implicit process of classification, emphasis and exclusion. While a layered exploration of the events and cultural negotiations of the 1930s can be instructive, it is also necessary to ask about other forms of violence, that is, of physical harm, pain, or death, or their threat, that may be regularly excluded from active considerations of criminality. These marginalised or repressed forms may turn on issues of race, economic exploitation or empire building, for example, and may be made more visible through comparison of one period with another – say, by looking to earlier representations of modern society or subsequent images of war. Again, the task is not to diminish a critical field that produces fuller accounts of criminality in the 1930s, but to expand that field by comparison with cultural negotiations over different forms of violence prevailing at other times.

The second great period of historical attention to Hollywood violence is the late 1960s and early 1970s. Converging with the breakdown of longstanding aesthetic and narrative norms, changing technologies, industrial structures and modes of production, and shifting audiences and social contexts, the appearance of unprecedented visual images of violence and death have underscored for many a major change or break in the history of motion pictures (Bordwell, Staiger and Thompson, 1987). As a result, US cinema of the 1960s is seen in alignment with the efflorescence of New Hollywood, in which various aspects of classicism are subverted by formal innovation and narrative exploration, alternative modes of production, and institutional participation in the counterculture. The end of the Production Code, the fragmentation of audiences (and the continuing emergence of a clear-cut youth audience), an increasingly decentralised mode of production and the incorporation of alternative filmmaking practices (including editing techniques and the development of new special effects such as squibs) could be offered as explanation for changes on-screen. As well, the social and cultural contexts, such as the controversial war in Vietnam, continuing urban unrest and racial strife, and their coverage on television, contribute importantly to the contemporary cinematic imagination and process of institutionalisation.

These social factors, especially, are typically adduced in accounts of film violence during the period that feature attention to protracted images of physical brutality and bloodshed. These images are presented spectacularly through the use of special effects and imaginative editing, often with a less serious, even cavalier or mocking tone different from earlier cinematic portrayals of pain and death, and raising questions about what effects they will have on viewers. But these images also speak more generally to the status and role of cinema in social life. As Robert Sklar (1987–88) has argued:

> ... the issues and perspectives of American filmmaking changed fundamentally during the decade of the 1960s, in tandem with the widespread transformations of American society, but certainly not merely as a 'reflection' of them. Films' links to society were dialectical rather than reactive: they catalysed and disseminated viewpoints as much as they absorbed and responded to them. (p 53)

The challenge for historians has been to identify and prioritise those viewpoints and to elucidate the cinematic processes engaging them. Formal developments did take place at the time, perhaps most importantly those conducing to what Paul Monaco (2001) has called 'the cinema of sensation', and industrial changes did reorient how Hollywood cinema operated as a social institution (see also James, 1989). Also in the foreground was the question of whether violence was more than an aberration to be policed or repressed. Besides marking standards of moral and institutional legitimacy or criminalising putatively deviant social behaviour, in other words, the cinema of the 1960s probed the potential of violent actions and media images to liberate or effect fundamental social change.

Crises of legitimacy for mainstream cinema and the social norms it represents also occurred in the 1980s and 1990s as the convergence of new media technologies was contested within the broader cultural field. In Britain, the 'video nasties' debate put changing media formations in sharp relief; in the US during the same period, 'censorship' controversies or 'panics' worked through complex cultural politics of identity. In both cases, as Martin Barker argues, the 'effects lobby' continued to drive critical and public discourse on film and media 'violence', thereby circumscribing discussion on the topic and repressing attention to a wider range of relevant histories and social mechanisms (Barker, 1984; Barker and Petley, 1997; Slocum, 2004). Also of concern, though not so directly addressed, were the consequences of the trans-nationalisation of media technologies, which emerged as a feature of late- and post-Cold War global economic and cultural expansion, and recast political and economic relations domestically and around the world.

Such episodic summaries draw critical attention to the multiple mechanisms imposed by structures of the cultural field that accord legitimacy to specific practices or institutions. Those mechanisms, as noted earlier, involve forms of expression and the social, economic and discursive access to them, thereby potentially enabling both the reproduction and transformation of social relations over time. The call here is for a broader understanding of how given cultural fields are structured and therefore potentially reproduced historically, while simultaneously allowing for the translation of those structuring principles into practices that effect change in cinema and society.

Hollywood, 1967

Reconciling structural determinism and transformative autonomy in these terms is a longstanding problem for sociologists attempting to theorise the historical functioning and evolution of social institutions and order. Likewise, for explanations of the cultural field, a persistent challenge is the integration of formal, symbolic and institutional patterns, which emphasise the continuity and reproduction of existing social relations, with everyday, cultural or creative practices that can alter and eventually reconstitute them. However, approaching film violence, closer attention has traditionally been paid to analyses of exceptional moments of transformation or transgression than the putatively stable structures or broader cultural fields against which they militate. Not unimportantly, this emphasis on exceptional moments helps to reproduce the underlying assumption that violence itself should be viewed as a violation of ethical or behavioural norms rather than as a constitutive, structuring element of social relations.

The foremost illustration of this problem of reconciliation in Hollywood history remains the productions of the 1960s and early 1970s. In part, this historical emphasis reflects a broader historiographic preoccupation of film scholars with the breakdown of earlier, classical Hollywood cinema and the innovations of an emergent 'New Hollywood' or post-classical cinema. Bordwell, Staiger and Thompson's canonical *Classical Hollywood Cinema* (1987) closes in 1960 with concurrent modifications to stylistic and narrative norms, technology, modes of production and other industry practices. Their model, it should be emphasised, conceives of a classicism that turns on standardisation and an acceptable, indeed necessary, degree of ongoing differentiation. But a persistent concern with the model is its formulation of an identifiably stable, unified or dominant classicism against which what follows might be defined. Murray Smith has raised questions concerning the historical plausibility of models opposing stability or equilibrium, and change or transition. He calls for close historical attention to the overlapping and interdependent factors determining Hollywood's past – as well as those shaping our retrospective accounts and analyses of that past (Smith, 1998). Models privileging beginnings, endings and classical unities may be schematically helpful, that is, but also demand greater nuance and historical grounding.

Smith's concerns about the general formulation of classicism might usefully be voiced in more specific regard to violence in the 1960s. Bordwell, Staiger and Thompson (1987) say little explicitly about the topic. Their most sustained attention appears in a short chapter on 'The Bounds of Difference', which discusses the assimilation of the European avant-garde and the *film noir* and ties such differentiation from (and subversion of) norms back to the changing mode of production, rather than to political or social contexts (pp 70–84). This is in keeping with the study's overall focus on formal, stylistic and industrial practices rather than social and or wider historical determinants. It also foregrounds the necessary, if limited, differentiation of narrative and aesthetic practices that enabled 'classical' cinema to operate and provide varied products to its audience – and, according to Bordwell, continued, with modifications after 1960, to inform Hollywood production. My suggestion here is both to complicate the notion of a turning point in the representation of film violence in the early 1960s, mainly by expanding attention to the cultural field in which specific representations appeared *and* to problematise the perceived stability or coherence of a long-term classical period preceding it.

For the public at the time, and for film scholars, historians and policy makers since, the defining break and controversy over film violence occurred with the release and *cause célèbre* of *Bonnie and Clyde* in 1967 (Friedman, 2000a, 2000b; Toplin,

1996). That year witnessed an explosion of interest in cinematic and social violence in America, and a concern that images themselves foreground violent action. Gore and mayhem on-screen appeared to increase, as physically injurious or deadly behaviours of criminals, but also individuals not so readily categorisable, were presented with a host of stylistic innovations: rapid and concussive editing, innovative camera work often involving unconventional angles and multiple film speeds, special effects like squibs, and discordant musical accompaniment. Also typically examined have been other aspects of the cultural field that defined film violence at the time and, as importantly, during the preceding decade. Broader institutional and social contexts are typically adduced as relevant to the shaping of cinema of the 1960s or of New Hollywood. For filmmakers, the introduction of a substantially revised Motion Picture Production Code in September 1966 (calling for 'restraint' in depictions of violence), the fragmentation of audiences, an increasingly decentralised mode of production, as well as the incorporation of alternative filmmaking practices, could be offered as explanation for changes. As mentioned earlier, the controversial war in Vietnam, continuing urban unrest and racial strife, and their coverage on television were also seen to explain stylistic innovations and alterations in the behaviours imaged on-screen. Revisiting contemporary responses to the bloody fare of 1967, Hoberman (1998) recognises the efforts to link the carnage and changed attitudes represented in Hollywood productions with broader preoccupations about America as an exceptionally violent society. Hoberman is right to allow, in his conclusion, 'that public attitudes toward violent imagery are historically determined' (p 141).

Yet the nature of linkages between the cinematic and social, between images on-screen and the tumultuous events underway outside the theatre, remains powerfully circumstantial and speculative, and so the calculus of Hoberman's determination is obscure. At the heart of the obscurity is an emphasis on certain kinds of images of brutality, the tones informing them, and the effects these might have on viewers. Each of these concerns had important precursors that typically dropped out of public discourse at the time and continue to be neglected in historical accounts of the period produced since. Appearing in 1960, Hitchcock's *Psycho* (1960) is sometimes held up as the film that inaugurated a new process of viewing popular movies by remaking the pleasures – for Linda Williams, the 'regimes of visual and visceral "attraction"' – wrought by Hollywood (Williams, 2000). Earlier films, too, from *film noir* to revisions of existing genres like the Western and the domestic melodrama in the 1950s (consider *The Searchers* (1955) and *Rebel Without a Cause* (1955)), have occasionally been held up as redefinitions of more traditional or classical standards of violent representation (Alloway, 1971). Likewise, redefining standards, though typically neglected in considerations of gore and mayhem in the early 1960s, were productions like *The Manchurian Candidate* (1962) and those in the popular James Bond franchise, which began the same year, and consistently employed an increasingly light and even cavalier or cynical tone while presenting brutal action on-screen.

Critical reactions to *Bonnie and Clyde* in 1967 ranged from condemnation of immoral excess to celebration of trend-setting artistry. Sometimes, as in the case of reviews that appeared in *Time* and *Newsweek*, critical appraisals involved public reversals from one stance to the other. More often, and heatedly, the critics used the film as the basis for comments about the status of violence in cinema and across society. The most famous confrontation occurred between Bosley Crowther, the lead movie critic of *The New York Times*, and therefore among the most important public voices on film, and Pauline Kael, then a young Berkeley freelancer. Crowther saw Penn's film as not only pointless, but also lacking in taste. When challenged by readers, Crowther grew more strident in his assertions that such a vision of brutality, humour and inaccurate history was irresponsible and contributed to social instability, and even the increasing violence on American streets. Kael drafted a 9,000 word manifesto that appeared in *The New Yorker* (where she would soon assume a regular position and become the most influential film reviewer of the succeeding two decades). It celebrated *Bonnie and Clyde's* presentation of subjects hitherto excluded from treatment in motion pictures which, she claimed, were understood by much of the public as being central to their contemporary experience. The contrast between Crowther and Kael captured the confrontation between more traditional approaches to the seeming utility or tastefulness or even values implicit in images on-screen, and a new recognition of the violent nature of contemporary society and media alike.

In fact, the panic sparked by the film's innovative visualisation of eroticism and bloodletting, its unmistakable violation of physical bodies, and its presentation of ideas long suppressed by Hollywood, was as much over the social role of media themselves, movies, of course, but also print and the more general media landscape. This concern was, as ever, partly economic: audience demographics were changing, growing younger, and foreign and independent cinemas were forcing acknowledgment of a break between art and commerce. In a society increasingly rent racially and generationally, film violence became an issue around which to argue for or against the often brutal means employed to maintain the prevailing social order. *Bonnie and Clyde* was a cultural event, in part, because it afforded such a direct and public juxtaposition of those supporting and criticising the prevailing social order, morality and status of cinema as a recuperative cultural form institutionalised to represent that society and morality.

Indeed, while introducing his study of the censorship and regulation of popular films and pornography at the time, Jon Lewis (2000) has observed that, at such moments, 'film content is mostly beside the point' (pp 6–10). Industrial and economic retrenchment, he argues instead, are the primary drivers of media events and the recasting of regulation that results. While Lewis' account focuses on the serious challenge to Hollywood's authority over American filmdom from hard-core pornographic movies between 1968 and 1973, we might hazard a similar proposition about the status of Hollywood as social and corporate institution, as purveyor of cultural productions containing violent images. Instead of only closely analysing specific 'graphic' images of such productions as *Bonnie and Clyde* or *A Clockwork Orange* (1971), or even tracking the demise of the Production Code and rise of the ratings system, we must attend to the concatenation of discursive, disciplinary and institutional practices that shaped the representation and reception of violence.

Neither the institutional role of Hollywood nor the process of 'mediating' contemporary violent events, in other words, is straightforward. Many have rightly viewed stylistic and narrative innovations in films of the time, including the imaging of violence, as key expressions of Hollywood's participation in the counterculture. Yet the aestheticisation of violence can also be seen as relating cinematic and social activity in several ways. Arguing that such images could, for example, distance cultural productions from contemporary society, Todd Gitlin (1980) has written that, 'In the bloody spring of 1968, it was easy to lose a sense of the real. Increasingly the cultural artefacts, like the movement itself, were taking for granted a context of political extremity' (p 200). The larger point is that questions about institutional relations or 'mediation' are subject to the same complex contests or 'struggles' over meanings that have been acknowledged to shape the historical reception of Hollywood movie content. Following her work on *Classical Hollywood Cinema*, Janet Staiger has written perceptively that these struggles over meanings – of individual films, of popular cinema, and, here, of social values and understanding of violence itself – do not abide facile connections between cinema and society or history, or straightforward research questions or policy making (Staiger, 1992, 2000). Illuminating this struggle, however, can revise the questions posed about the place and function of movies in individual lives and across civil society.

Returning to *Bonnie and Clyde*, a possible revision might be to approach the cinematic event both as historically specific and, less conventionally, as being inflected by ongoing cinematic and social concerns not so readily historicised to 1967 or 'the Sixties'. These interventions and events, in other words, were aspects of a wider regulatory process that responded to historically and culturally inflected concerns such as racial demonisation, criminalisation, and the attributes of governance. Among these would be the ascendance of science-based and research-driven models of media 'effects', ultimately supported by behaviouralist and social learning theories, which informed both 'official' debates about the social function of cinema and the pathologising of certain forms of social behaviour. Such models have deep roots in the rise of social science research in the 1920s and 1930s, but became institutionalised and the basis of 'official' knowledge produced about media and social behaviour in the decades following World War II.

In question should also be the further concern of how cinematic, institutional, and social changes are themselves understood and effected. For historians and other analysts of society and politics, 'the Sixties' remain a crucible for understanding social and political narratives of order and disorder, stability and change. The appearance of violence can serve as a key marker for situating Hollywood (or other) cinemas in this changing civil society that itself was being tested and altered by events. Put in the terms of structures of stability and agents of change, the preoccupation with 1967 and 'the Sixties' effectively brackets more far-reaching questions raised about civil society, by emphasising the exceptional and transgressive quality of individual historical moments and events.

Historicising regulation beyond *Bonnie and Clyde*

In 1967, the release of, and critical debate over, *Bonnie and Clyde* catalysed a series of attempts by filmmakers to develop, and in the process engage audiences with, new forms of bloodletting in popular film. That historical moment drew on a range of existing forms and practices for presenting violence that had been sustained, though also variously disrupted, in the two decades following the end of World War II. The institutional and critical eruptions over violence in US cinema in 1967 were, as is often the case in accounts of Hollywood regulation, twofold. Innovative aesthetic, behavioural and political forms *did* appear, especially in volume and variety, that broke from the more stable and largely naturalised (that is, unacknowledged or concealed) violence that had inscribed mainstream cinema. At the same time, the public discourse about film violence also changed markedly, linking alleged excesses on-screen to events outside the theatre; in Vietnam, in city streets strewn with riot, and with a society increasingly defined, for many, by bloodletting. The tracking of putatively violent images since has consequently turned on this *sui generis* moment of origin, which emerged from the widespread social and political turning point of the 1960s and early 1970s.

My proposal here is that the apparent transgressions in 1967 Hollywood partook in a more long-standing process of institutionalising new forms of imagining physical injury, pain and death. This is not to say that they were entirely co-opted and reintegrated by dominant social or cultural institutions. Yet even as disruptive forms of violence drew attention to the relations of power entrenched in conventional film narratives and various social and political practices, much of the critique or opposition became institutionalised. This 'takeover of form', as Bourdieu puts it (1984, p 213), is perhaps most familiar in post-1960s US cinema in the overt redeployment of stylistic innovations in the representation of violence in the slasher and action film of the last three decades. Just as important, however, were a range of typically concealed practices of violence that have sustained Hollywood cinema through their imagining of inequitable social relations: the persistent representation of the rape of women, for example, or the violence against African-Americans arguably fundamental to US films (Projansky, 2001; Guerrero, 2000). Such a view suggests that the seemingly singular cinematic developments of 1967 might constructively be approached as one in a series of moments in which the regulation of violence reshapes Hollywood cinema as an institution that contributes symbolically to the maintenance of inequitable social relations.

Despite the greater diversity of voices, today's critical and public discourse about violence (in cinema and society) continues in many ways to delimit focus on the seemingly singular crucible of screen violence in 'the Sixties' rather than opening up consideration of other, earlier forms of violence and the cultural fields in which they circulated. In particular, little public or even scholarly attention is paid to the forms of systemic or structural violence that shed light on relationships between economic conditions and cultural developments. As a way of rethinking regulation, this focus on forms and effects of violence is potentially especially telling, as violence can be seen as a primary mode of representing social relations and the ongoing renegotiations of their legitimacy. The 'effects' debate today continues to be illustrative: controversies, often heated, persist over the relevance and meaning of research into film and media effects on behaviour, but those very debates limit questions of social effects to demonstrable, individual behavioural modification rather than broader influence on attitudes, prejudices and everyday social practices. Francis Couvares (1996, p 11) wrote that our question should 'become not whether but which censorship' operates at a given moment to affirm and define the predominant view of reality or, at least, the legitimate boundaries of expression.

Likewise, for on-screen violence, we need to shift the focus from whether social and behavioural effects are appropriate for public and critical engagement, to which types of influence gain prominence and authority in public and media discourse, and why.

The focus on *Bonnie and Clyde* and the transformation of Hollywood violence in 1967 remains illuminating but also limiting, constraining the critical field and, by extension, conceptions of violence, its meaning and influence. Yes, Penn's production was an important, even seminal moment in the history of Hollywood film and film violence. And yes, the contemporary debates that emerged around it, particularly concerning cinema's relations with society and influence on behaviour, continue to be instructive when revisited. But a fuller understanding of regulation must be as much about continuities as transformations, as much about structural or orienting principles as agents or moments of change. Part of the challenge faced in accounts of film violence is to avoid unproblematically reproducing the privilege accorded certain stylistic forms, behavioural and narrative norms, historical backdrops and research priorities. Particularly acute, for example, is the problem of periodisation and the location of the 'origins' of film violence in the 1960s: the fixation on the period, especially on a handful of individual films (typically beginning with *Bonnie and Clyde*) that are seen to carry almost its entire cultural freight, can actually repress analysis of other relevant historical or conceptual contexts. One alternative strategy posited here is to destabilise the notion of classical unities or stable starting points by which transgressions can be evaluated. Following Janet Staiger, we might profitably broaden the struggles over the meaning and influence of violent films to cinemas beyond Hollywood, across historical periods, even perhaps across national cinemas.

Those very struggles should be seen as more than arcane scholarly endeavours. They should also be understood as constituting more than a novel introduction of critical and political ideas about cultural consumption, social institutions and civil society, into discussions about cinema. It is, precisely, an attempt to attract attention to the mostly naturalised and concealed forms of violent social relations inscribing Hollywood movies and, therefore, to the mostly unexamined parameters of critical and public debates about cinematic regulation. To rethink regulation means to expand conceptions of censorship beyond statutes, laws and prohibitions and to engage the broader, if still importantly constraining, links between institutional development, civil society and the cultural field. Undertaking such a shift is particularly important when addressing violence, because on-screen renditions of interpersonal conflict or of physical injury, pain and death so richly stylise social and institutional relations. Rethinking thus requires us as critics and citizens to confront the fact that our very interventions and efforts contribute to shaping a critical field that itself plays a role in enabling and maintaining social relations and the institutional exercise of power.

Chapter 14
Cultural 'patronage' versus cultural 'defence': alternatives to national film policies

Bill Grantham

It is as if there are two TRUTHS: one that is dull, flat, boring, at least in the eyes of those who daub it with falsity; the other ...

(Emphasis provided, Bresson, 1997)

Film policy is not much younger than the cinema. In 1915, the United States government, using its nascent antitrust laws, succeeded in breaking the camera and projector cartel that had sought to corner the production, distribution and exhibition market in that country (*United States v Motion Picture Patents Co* (1915)).[1] Looming beyond its shores, the United States started collecting information from its overseas consulates on the exhibition, distribution and popularity of American films as early as 1916 (Jarvie, 1992, p 276). In 1917, the French Interior Ministry created a 'commission charged with studying the best conditions for the regulation and protection of cinematography' (Leglise, 1969, p 61). That same year, a group of German army officers, dismayed at the successful propaganda films made by the Allied powers with which they were at war, persuaded their Chief of Staff, General Erich Ludendorff, to request the official creation of the film company that would become known as Universum-Film AG, or Ufa (Kreimer, 1994, p 18). The 1920s and 1930s saw the first wave of government imposed quotas in Europe and elsewhere, mainly aimed at limiting the entry of American films into domestic markets (Grantham, 2000, pp 46–53). Since these first initiatives, the wave of film policies has never broken. At the global, multilateral and bilateral levels, via treaties and memorandums of understanding, and through interventions at virtually every other governmental and administrative level – national, regional, state, county and even city and town – policies and supporting machinery have been put in place to promote, stimulate and protect cinema production and the cultural values of such production.[2]

---

1 An appeal (1918) was dismissed on the basis that patents cannot be acquired or combined for the purposes of unlawful restraint of trade.

2 Eg, see at the global level: 'Special Provisions Relating to Cinematograph Films', General agreement on Tariffs and Trade: Text of the General Agreement, 1986, p 8, Geneva: GATT; multilateral: Council Decisions (95/563/EC) and (95/564/EC) (together establishing the EU's Media II programme); bilateral: Films Co-Production Agreement between the Government of Australia and the Government of Canada, 23 July 1990, Canberra: Australia Treaty Series No 37; national: *Loi du 25 octobre 1946 portant création d'un Centre national de la Cinématographie* in Leglise, Vol 2, *Entre deux républiques 1940–1946*, p 203 (creating the French national cinema regulator, the CNC); regional: 'Background to the Northern Ireland Film Commission', Belfast: NIFC, available at www.nifc.co.uk/aboutus/background.html, accessed on 15 December 2002; local: 'The Providence Film Commission', Providence, Rhode Island: PFC, available at providenceri.com/film/frame.html, accessed on 15 December 2002.

What are all these policies for? In fact, many things.[3] The focus here will be on those policies whose declared aims are either exclusively cultural, or which include, as a substantial portion of their rationale, the expression of cultural goals.

Such cultural policies can have substantial impact in international relations, particularly those concerning trade. For instance, in 1993, during multinational negotiations to extend the General Agreement on Tariffs and Trade (GATT) to include, among other things, intellectual property services, and to create the World Trade Organisation, the entire project almost foundered on a bitter disagreement between the United States and the European Union over whether the new treaty should include a 'cultural exception' that would allow certain forms of protection for national film and television industries. Only a last minute climb-down by the United States prevented the collapse of the proposed structure for all world trade. In other words, the stakes of cultural policy can be very high indeed.

It is unarguable that film is 'an economic commodity as well as a cultural good' (Moran, 1996, p 1). When both of these elements are recognised, the cultural impact of film is often linked to the promotion of economic objectives. In the 1920s, policy makers developed the idea that 'trade follows the film': that Brazilians would build American-style bungalows or Europeans buy US fashions, because they had seen them in the cinema. And today, American cultural policy types like to advance Oliver Wendell Holmes' concept of the 'marketplace of ideas' to connect liberalised cultural markets, into which Hollywood films would have free access, with the asserted international appeal of American cultural production.

Outside America, however, the play between commodities and culture is not always acknowledged in policy making. Often, they are expressed as opposite. For example Jacques Delors, then president of the European Commission, declared in 1989, at the moment when Europe imposed quotas on the importation of non-European (essentially, American) television programmes, 'Culture is not a piece of merchandise, like other things ... I say to the United States, "Have we the right to exist, to perpetuate our traditions?"' (Greenhouse, 1989, p D20). This type of observation is commonplace both in its substance and its rhetorical form, particularly in Europe. It posits, first, a threat, a commercial threat with a cultural impact, and then invokes a right of self-defence. However, the argument for film policies is sometimes presented the other way round, as an essentially industrial intervention, which incidentally yields a cultural benefit. For example, the European Commission explained the policy basis of its 'support of the audiovisual industry', the MEDIA Plus programme (the third phase was launched in 2001), in the following terms:

Faced with a new environment marked by the *de facto* globalisation of the methods of exploitation, the European audiovisual content industry, because of its fragmentation, is not yet fully able to stand up to the growing worldwide competition. The Commission's

---

3 I will not address the 'film commission' role of attempting to attract film production by promoting the cinegenic qualities of the town or region in question and removing local administrative and bureaucratic obstacles from the paths of the filmmakers. See, eg, the account of the successful efforts of the Wexford Film Commission to persuade the producers of *Saving Private Ryan* to recreate the Normandy landings on the beach at Curracloe, in Mooney and Eustace, 1998, pp 22–26.

proposals are intended to establish optimum conditions based on a coherent strategy and clear objectives, with a view to overcoming these difficulties and allowing European operators to position themselves as best possible in these new markets *while exploiting European cultural diversity*. (Emphasis added)[4]

There is a particular significance to what might otherwise seem to be a chicken-and-egg argument regarding the industrial and cultural bases of film policy. The idea of a purely industrial intervention to support a commercial sector such as the audiovisual industry is generally, or at least theoretically, offensive to the international trade order. After all, the 144 countries that are members of the World Trade Organisation (WTO)[5] have stated that they are 'desirous of ... entering into reciprocal and mutually advantageous arrangements directed to the substantial reduction of tariffs and other barriers to trade and to the elimination of discriminatory treatment in international trade relations'.[6] Even if, during the Uruguay Round talks that culminated in the creation of the WTO, the United States failed in its attack on European audiovisual quota regimes, neither did the EU succeed in obtaining a 'cultural exception' to international trade regulation. Given this, it is at least arguable, almost as a *reductio ad absurdum*, that if a film policy were purely industrial – that is, in some way had no cultural element at all – such a policy would be illegal pursuant to international trade law.

That is not, in fact, the argument that I wish to make here. I point it out since it is one way of explaining that film policies need a grounding point in cultural politics, but not merely for cultural reasons. Even if the cultural aspect of such policies were merely window dressing, it would nonetheless be an essential element of an industrial policy that would otherwise look much like a market-distorting subsidy or other trade barrier, and accordingly disfavoured.

The rhetoric of cultural defence does have a market theory, of course: that the market power of the United States will kill national film industries and therefore kill national cultures. As the French director, Bertrand Tavernier, put it, the 'Americans want to treat us like they treated the redskins ... If we're very good, they will give us a reservation' (Rollat, 1993, p 18). It is an important rhetorical position, a rallying point for the principle of cultural 'defence'. An example from outside the film industry helps clarify the point. If everybody agrees, say, that McDonald's is a bad

---

4 Communication from the Commission to the Council, the European Parliament, the Economic and Social Committee and the Committee of the Regions concerning a proposal for a programme in support of the audiovisual industry (MEDIA Plus – 2001–2005, 14 December 1999, p 2 (COM [1999] 658 final)).

5 As of 1 January 2002. As of 15 December 2002, Armenia had additionally been accepted as a WTO member, 29 further nations were negotiating membership and two others were seeking to open negotiations. Information available at www.wto.org/english/thewto_e/acc_e/acc_e.htm and related links.

6 Agreement Establishing the World Trade Organisation, at Marrakech on 15 April 1994, Preamble, Geneva: WTO. Of course, the current anti-globalisation movement has caused some Western nations to moderate the fervour for free trade and open markets that characterised – rhetorically, at least – international trade politics in the 1980s and early 1990s. Moreover, the multiple and mutual allegations of protectionism – of aerospace manufacture, bananas, meat products, textiles and the agricultural sector, among others – continue to threaten to poison the relations among the economically powerful trading blocs. None of this appears to have dissipated or diluted the arguments over cultural protection and trade.

thing, there may still be honest divergence about how you confront it, whether through market action (eating elsewhere) or 'direct action' in the anarchist sense (looting it). Naturally, such direct action may carry a stronger rhetorical punch, as witnessed by the 40,000 supporters of the French farm campaigner José Bove who rallied at his trial for trashing a McDonald's restaurant in the Aveyron (Anon, 2000). Mr Bove's sense of the power of symbols travels in both directions. While demonstrating against the WTO in Seattle in 1999, he held a chunk of Roquefort cheese in his hand. Roquefort, which had been subjected to punitive US tariffs in a dispute over European restrictions on the importation of genetically modified foods, is not only French and Aveyronnais, it is in a sense *the* French cheese, eaten by Julius Caesar and cited by Pliny, prized by Charlemagne and protected throughout the ages by kings (Rance, 1989, pp 178–79). McDonald's and Roquefort, as skilfully manipulated by Mr Bove, metonymically polar, are an almost perfect statement of cultural 'defence'. However, if you decide to consume 'French' food, say in an ordinary Paris café, you find French people paying to eat bad French dressing made by French agribusiness giants and poured from French jars by French waiters onto flavourless French salad greens force-raised by French market gardeners in French greenhouses. This disastrous salad bespeaks a cultural problem, alright, but McDonald's is only a small part of it. Nevertheless, this type of culinary outrage provides little political traction for the premise that culture requires defending: focusing on the bad thing that is McDonald's – weirdly, a form of the Other in French symbology – is the *sine qua non* of a cultural 'defence' argument.

Something similar has happened to the cinema in Europe and elsewhere. For more than 75 years, since the first quotas were imposed, Europeans have been defending their cinematic culture from outside threats. On a purely cultural level, this has always seemed to be an empirically suspect proposition. In 2000, the leading contenders for the best director prize during the annual film awards season leading up to the Oscars included Lasse Hallström (*Chocolat*, 2000), Giuseppe Tornatore (*Malena*, 2000), Ridley Scott (*Gladiator*, 2000), Ang Lee (*Crouching Tiger, Hidden Dragon*, 2000), Nick Park (*Chicken Run*, 2000), Steven Daldry (*Billy Elliot*, 2000), Guy Ritchie (*Snatch*, 2000) and István Szabó (*Sunshine*, 2000). The films that they directed were set in France, Italy, China, England and Hungary. The films' stars were French, Italian, Australian, Chinese and English, with just a smattering of Americans. If one was considering the impact on culture, you might have expected the United States to seek a reopening of the Uruguay Round in order to obtain its own cultural exception and right to defence against an onslaught of foreign influences. Despite this, in Europe we still tend to believe that it is *our* culture – the culture of Eisenstein, Lang, Dreyer, Clair, Renoir, Buñuel, Hitchcock, Powell, Rossellini, Wajda, Bergman, Truffaut, Godard, Fassbinder, Wenders, etc – that needs defending. And it is this belief that shapes our film, our policies, which is indeed their *raison d'être*.

So, how are our film policies faring? In recent years, the predominant sentiment has appeared to be panic. In those countries that provide substantial regulatory and financial support for the domestic film industries, such as Australia, Canada, France, Germany, Ireland and the UK, studios and production houses have veered wildly from running at full capacity to near standstill. The early years of this decade have seen the collapse or near collapse of major, high cost electronic media investments in all of the major territories: Vivendi in France (Carney, 2002, p A18), ITV Digital in the UK (Larsen, 2002), Helkon ('Helkon', 2002), Kirch Gruppe in Germany ('KirchPayTV', 2002), Telepiú in Italy (Bianchi, 2002) and Quiero TV in Spain (Beresford, 2002). More significantly, the film industries, politicians and public in these same places are all asking the same question: where are the good films? In Britain, the windfall of lottery money, which has so far pumped nearly £140 million into the domestic film industry, has led to a flood of production, much of which cannot find distribution outlets, in many cases, it appears, fortunately so.[7]

However, taking an industrial view of film policies, assessing the success of a particular intervention regime according to the box office success of the films supported, seems to miss the point, if the aim of the policies is truly to make a cultural difference. But this illustrates the film policy maker's 'Catch-22'. If you support commercially successful films, you are probably giving your money to the productions that do not need it, but if you support commercially unsuccessful films, you may be giving the money to productions that nobody wants, or that are vulnerable to political claims to that effect. For example, the Film Council in Britain allocated nearly £2.6 million to Mira Nair's version of *Vanity Fair* (a co-production of Granada Film Productions and USA Films), and nearly £3.5 million to Robert Altman's *Gosford Park*, while the EU's current Media Plus programme allocated €888,000 toward the European distribution of *Bend It Like Beckham*, a proven hit in its home country.[8] In a similar vein, the old Media II programme gave cash to such high budget blockbusters as *Ridicule* and *Le Comte de Monte Cristo*, which had little trouble finding their audiences in many countries (European Commission, 2000, p 10). In the light of such substantial support for likely successes, it is at least worth inquiring whether such investments are a way of manufacturing an appearance of institutional success for an otherwise unfocused, or wrongly focused, policy. In making this observation, I am not arguing that giving money to popular entertainment is a mishandling of public funds. I am, instead, simply suggesting that the decision to favour popular entertainment (and therefore probably undeserving of such support in the strictly financial sense) is driven more by a need to justify the support mechanism rather than an intrinsic and viable policy goal.

What a real film policy, as opposed to a merely industrial or self-protective strategy, could seek to achieve is a means by which cultural objectives can be supported, and even realised, through ensuring proper stewardship of public money and resources, while substituting a different measure for the money-standard when gauging the goals, value and success of such a policy. While this is not the place to state in detail what such means might be, it is possible to suggest what they might resemble. Until some time in the 1980s, governments, particularly in Europe, believed in public broadcasting as a means of delivering a rich mix of

---

7   For data on lottery grants, see Film Council, 2002, pp 52–53. Three 'franchise' companies were given access to a total of £96.65 million lottery funding. For more details of Film Council Lottery Awards see www.filmcouncil.org.uk/aboutus/?p=1017229237138 and related links.

8   For Film Council grants see fn 7 above. For Media Plus allocations, see Media Distribution, 'Results of Deadline 19/07/2002 – Call 21–2001', available at http://europa.eu.int/comm/avpolicy/media/results/21014.pdf, accessed on 16 December 2002.

cultural content to audiences of varying size, ranging from the mass (major football matches) to the minuscule (a Stockhausen night on the classical radio station). For a variety of reasons, ideological, political, cultural and financial, these governments began to abandon, or lose faith, in the public broadcasting ethos around 20 years ago, and both the prestige and cultural centrality of these institutions has generally waned.

This is not to suggest that public cinema policy should be entrusted to public broadcasters, although these have at times been a factor in the emergence of important films, such as the new German cinema of the 1970s. Instead, it is to propose, as an analogy to what is needed, a type of public institution that is financially responsible (because it has to be), but which internally has substituted the money-standard for a different criterion of success. Prestige and critical respect may constitute one such measure. In other words, the essential goal of a culturally orientated film policy should be public service, not industrial or institutional development. One benefit of this approach is a certain clarity: the institution would not be placed in the impossible position of trying to second-guess the marketplace (looking for hits) while paying lip service to a different and oppositional mission.

Of course, there are obvious risks. Public institutions can become bloated and complacent, beset by infighting and often by a loss of fundamental vision. (So too can private corporations.) Unless adequately supervised and controlled, they may tend towards expansionism and gigantism. And because they depend ultimately on forms of political sponsorship, they are vulnerable both to political pressure and to extra-institutional criticism that is not always disinterested. But at a time when cultural 'defence' really means using culture as a fig leaf either for questionable industrial goals or for institutional self-protection, a shift in emphasis towards cultural 'patronage' of a more old-fashioned type becomes a rather attractive alternative. How our publicly supported cultural impresarios might function is a matter for further discussion.

Chapter 15
How the movie moguls learned to stop worrying and love the new technologies: copyright and film

Fiona Macmillan

Copyright, creativity and culture

I have argued in other places (Macmillan, 1998; Macmillan, 2002a; Macmillan, 2002b) that copyright's relationship to the concepts of creativity and culture, with which it is often rhetorically associated (Waldron, 1993, p 853), is most accurately viewed as an instrumental rather than a fundamental one.[1] In other words, rather than encouraging and protecting cultural output on the basis that it has a fundamental and non-economic value as an expression of human creativity, copyright has been well used as an instrument for promoting trade in the cultural output that comes within its purview. Thus, copyright deals with works in relation to which it subsists as products or commodities, the importance of which is reflected in their impact on trade rather than in any non-economic value they may enjoy. One of the best examples of this type of approach to copyright (and to intellectual property as a whole) arose in the context of the negotiation and conclusion of the World Trade Organisation (WTO) Agreement on Trade Related Aspects of Intellectual Property Rights (the TRIPs Agreement).

The conclusion of the TRIPs Agreement was, of course, driven by the United States. As Michael Blakeney has shown (1996, Chapter 1), the US used two tools in particular to drive the negotiations. First, it took on the burden of convincing the GATT[2] Council that intellectual property rights were relevant to GATT. In 1983 and 1984, evidence was submitted to Congressional hearings by US trade associations on the economic loss which the members of those associations suffered internationally as a consequence of the non-enforcement or absence of intellectual property laws.[3] Amongst other things, evidence was presented at these hearings that the video industry was losing $6 billion annually (p 2). The second tool used by the US to drive the TRIPs process was the amendment in 1984 to s 301 of the Trade Act of 1974 to make intellectual property protection explicitly actionable under s 301 (p 4). This was followed by the introduction in the Omnibus Trade and

---

1 The fundamental/instrumental distinction drawn here is taken from the World Commission on Culture and Development, 1996. For a further discussion and application of that distinction in the context of copyright, see Macmillan, 1998 and Macmillan, 2002a.

2 GATT stands for General Agreement on Tariffs and Trade.

3 *Possible Renewal of the Generalised System of Preferences – Hearing Before the Subcommittee on Trade of the US House of Rep Comm on Ways and Means*, 98th Cong 1st Sess (1983); and *Unfair Foreign Trade Practices, Stealing American Intellectual Property: Imitation is Not Flattery*, 98th Cong 2nd Sess (1984): both cited in Blakeney, 1996, p 2 ff.

Competitiveness Act of 1988 of 'Special 301', enabling the US Trade Representative to put countries failing to protect US intellectual property on a watch list with a view to investigation and possible trade retaliation (p 5).

For those who would want to see copyright bolstering the fundamental rather than the instrumental role of culture, some comfort might be taken from the fact that the TRIPs Agreement refers to the trade related aspects of intellectual property and thereby suggests that there may be some other aspects. But it is cold comfort. The truth is that, at least in the Anglo-American model of copyright law, we had already gone a long way down the instrumental/trade related road before the US did us the favour of bringing it all out into the open. We have done this by using copyright as a tool for the commodification of the creative works to which it relates. There are four interdependent aspects of copyright law that have been essential to the commodification process and to copyright's consequent instrumental approach to culture and creativity. The first and most basic tool of commodification is the alienability of the copyright interest. A second significant aspect of copyright law making it an important tool of trade and investment is its duration. The long period of copyright protection increases the asset value of individual copyright interests (Towse, 1999, pp 98–99). Thirdly, the strong commercial distribution rights,[4] especially those which give the copyright holder control over imports and rental rights, have put copyright owners in a particularly strong market position, especially in the global context. Finally, the power of the owners of copyright in relation to all those wishing to use copyright material has been undermined by a contraction of some of the most significant defences to copyright infringement. Of particular note in this respect are the repeated assaults on the cogency and practical utility of the fair dealing and public interest defences to copyright infringement.

It may be possible to justify a degree of commodification by reference to the need for creators to be remunerated in order to encourage them to create[5] and by reference to the need for cultural works to be disseminated in order to reap the benefits of their creation. This latter point would fit in with the argument that an important aspect of copyright is its communication role (Van Caenegem, 1995). Whether some degree of commodification is essential to the integrity of copyright law or not, the point is that we have allowed the process of commodification to take over copyright without adequately considering the costs and consequences of this commodification.

The acquisition of private power in the film industry

(a) Global rights, global distribution, global dominance

A consequence of commodification of copyright is the way in which it permits the build up of private power over cultural output (see Bettig, 1996, esp Chapter 3; and

---

4 See especially the TRIPs Agreement, Arts 11 and 14(4), which enshrine rental rights in relation to computer programs, films and phonograms; WIPO Copyright Treaty 1996, Art 7; and WIPO Performances and Phonograms Treaty 1996, Arts 9 and 13.

5 See, however, Towse, 2001, especially Chapters 6 and 8, in which it is argued that copyright generates little income for most creative artists. Nevertheless, Towse suggests that copyright is valuable to creative artists for reasons of status and control of their work.

Towse, 1999). The way in which the distribution rights attaching to copyright might be used by a multinational to carve up the international market (Macmillan, 1998) is a small part of a much bigger story about the way in which commodification can lead to global domination of a market for cultural output. The capacity to achieve a position of global power is a combination of the international nature of intellectual property rights, the fact that many of the corporations owning the rights operate on a multinational level, and the fact that many of the media and entertainment corporations are conglomerates which display a high degree of horizontal integration by operating in a number of different areas of cultural output (Towse, 1999, pp 97–98). Some are also vertically integrated with a high degree of control over the entire distribution process.

All these industry features are characteristics of the market for the production and distribution of film. Corporations owning the lion's share of the world's copyright interests in films are multinational conglomerates, the activities of which are characterised by substantial horizontal and vertical integration. The major US studios are particularly important players in this context. Their oligopoly is built upon the dominance that US corporations have held over the international film industry from its inception.[6] Some idea of the early grip that the US film industry achieved over the international market for film may be gleaned from Sklar's (1993) estimate that between 75% and 90% of films shown in most countries between the First and Second World Wars were US films (pp 94–95). Since that time, the oligopolistic nature of the market for filmed entertainment has been accentuated through a series of horizontal and vertical mergers.

The fashion for horizontal and vertical mergers and acquisitions in the media and entertainment sector began in the 1970s. It seems that one force driving these mergers is the desire to increase the level of corporate ownership over copyright interests. As Smiers (2002, p 120) puts it:

> The best way to acquire rights on huge quantities of entertainment and other artistic materials is through mergers. Synergy is the rationale for media conglomerates snatching up as much copyrighted material as they can. (See also Bettig, 1996, pp 40–42.)

Such activity is not only stimulated by the significant asset value of copyright interests,[7] it also reflects strategic business concerns. Bettig (1996) describes mergers and acquisitions in the media and entertainment sector as 'a process of reorganisation around core and related lines of business along with an effort to establish alliances across national boundaries with market dominant firms in other countries' (p 37). This process has been reflected in the activities of media and entertainment corporations such as Viacom Inc (which owns Paramount Communications Inc), Time Warner Inc, News Corporation Ltd and Walt Disney, so

---

6   On the history of the penetration by US corporations in international film markets, see Guback, 1985.

7   It was reported, eg, that Chrysalis, the music and broadcasting group, raised £60 million against its music publishing catalogue, which comprised 50,000 copyrights valued for the purpose of the securitisation at £150 million and generating a revenue stream of £8 million per year: 'Chrysalis in £60m fundraising', *The Times*, 9 February 2001.

that the activities of these corporations involve diversified lines of business including film and television production and distribution, international ownership of cinema chains, broadcasting, cable networks, music and book publishing.[8] Beginning in the late 1980s, there has also been a trend on the part of corporations that were primarily engaged in the production of technology used in the distribution of media and entertainment content to merge with or acquire interests in corporations producing that content. So, for example, Sony Corporation acquired Columbia Pictures Entertainment in 1989; and Matsushita Electric Industrial Company acquired MCA, the parent company of Universal Pictures, in 1991. The most significant recent example of this tendency towards the integration of corporations owning rights over content and distribution of filmed entertainment and those owning rights over the technology of distribution is the merger of AOL and Time Warner. Not only do these mergers increase the concentration of copyright ownership in the media and entertainment sector, they also place the ownership of the patent rights over the distribution technology in the same hands.[9] This process of concentration seems to be leading inexorably to the conclusion that, 'a handful – six to ten vertically integrated communications companies – will soon produce, own and distribute the bulk of the culture and information circulating in the global marketplace' (Bettig, 1996, p 38).

Copyright has been one essential tool in the orchestration of this global oligopoly because of the long period of control that it gives its owner over the distribution of content. The copyright monopoly, allied with the vertical integration of the market for filmed entertainment, has allowed the major media and entertainment corporations to dominate, not only the market for first run cinema, but also the markets that have been created as a consequence of the development of new technologies for the distribution of filmed entertainment. That is, the same oligopolistic market structure controls the market for television feature films, cable transmission of films, videos and (now) digital versatile disks (DVDs) (Bettig, 1996, pp 39–42). The video market, now being superseded by the market for DVDs, has been a particularly significant market for the major media and entertainment corporations. Bettig (1996) estimates that in the early 1990s the video market for sales and rentals accounted for 35–45% of the global revenues of the filmed entertainment industry (p 40). In 1992, six major filmed entertainment corporations accounted for 77% of the total revenue of the North American video market. These were: Disney (21.3%), Warner Home Video (18.1%), Fox Video (14.1%), Columbia Tri-Star Home Video (9.7%), Paramount (7.3%) and MCA/Universal Home Video (6.6%) (p 40). Making allowances for the processes of merger and acquisition that have characterised the media and entertainment sector, more or less the same majors dominate the video market in Europe. For example, in 1987, the video rental market in the UK was dominated by four US corporations: Warner (21.6%),

---

8 For an example of this, see Bettig's description of the process of integration by Paramount Communications Inc (Bettig, 1996, pp 37–38).

9 Thus returning us, strangely enough, to the origins of the filmed entertainment industry, which grew out of a need to exploit patents over cinematograph technology: see further, eg, Vaidhyanathan, 2001, pp 87–93.

CBS/Fox (18.5%), CIC Video, handling distribution for MGM/UA, Universal and Paramount (12.7%), and RCA/Columbia (11.6%). By 1992, CIC Video had increased its share of the rental market to 20%. So far as the video sale market in the UK was concerned, in 1992 Warner and Disney held approximately 50% of this market between them (Bettig, 1996, pp 210–14). With the exception of Italy, in which there was a significant market in pirated videos, the story is more or less the same in the rest of Europe. In Spain, for example, four of the US majors (RCA/Columbia, CBS/Fox, CIC and Warner), accounted for 70% of the video market in 1990 and they managed to increase this dominance to 78% by 1991. It is perhaps worth noting, finally, that the introduction of the WTO TRIPs Agreement in 1995 is likely to have increased the market dominance of the major filmed entertainment corporations in countries where a significant portion of the video market was taken by the sale or rental of pirate videos.

(b) The role of technology

Technological development has an important role to play in the consideration of the relationship between copyright and the filmed entertainment sector. Bettig (1996) has argued that successive technological developments, such as cable television (Chapter 5) and the development of the domestic video recorder (Chapter 6), have produced crises for the filmed entertainment sector as the new technologies threatened their control over the distribution of filmed entertainment. Copyright law, which is the key to the control of distribution, is intimately bound up with these developments because they raise questions about either the scope or the enforceability of copyright.

A recent controversy, which has created alarm in the ranks of the filmed entertainment industry and has seen the majors jumping to the defence of their distribution monopoly, was the release of the DeCSS (Decrypted Content Scrambling System) source code. This source code allows the copying of DVDs and their transmission via the internet. Not only did the eight US majors of the filmed entertainment industry take an action against the publishers of sites that had disclosed the code, they also commenced proceedings against *Copyleft* for reprinting the code onto a T-shirt.[10] Of the three internet site publishers pursued by the film industry majors, two negotiated consent decrees. The third, who goes by the underground name of Eric Corley,[11] had published the code in his online journal, *2600: The Hacker Quarterly*, and chose to defend the case. On 17 August 2000, US District Court Judge Lewis Kaplan handed down a decision preventing *2600* from continuing to publish the DeCSS code on its website (*Universal City Studios Inc v Shawn C Reimerdes* (2000)). This decision, which may resonate in European jurisdictions as a result of Art 6 of the Copyright in the Information Society Directive, has now been affirmed on appeal (*Universal City Studios Inc v Corley* (2001)).

Judge Kaplan's original decision was based on a provision of the Digital Millennium Copyright Act (s 1201, Title 17 of the US Code). This Act forms part of the amended US Copyright Act of 1976. The Act, in s 1201(a)(1), prohibits the

---

10 See *The Wizard*, 7 August 2000, www.wizardfkap.com/page6.html and www.copyleft.net.
11 In homage to the character of the same name in George Orwell's *Nineteen Eighty-four*.

circumvention of technological measures controlling access to a copyright work. Section 1201(a)(2) prohibits a person, amongst other things, offering to the public or providing 'any technology, product, service, device, component or part thereof' that:

(a) is primarily designed for the purpose of circumventing a technological measure;
(b) has limited commercially significant purpose other than circumvention of a technological measure; or
(c) is marketed with personal knowledge of use in circumventing a technological measure.

Corley was held to have breached this section. This was despite the fact that s 1201(c) of the Act provides that nothing in the section limits the rights of free speech for activities using consumer electronics, telecommunications or computing products, nor the rights of fair use with respect to copyright works. Taking the matter of free speech first, there is a reasonable argument to be made that merely posting and linking the DeCSS code, as opposed to making use of it, is purely expressive. If this is so, then injuncting such behaviour raises serious free speech concerns.[12] The US Court of Appeals for the Second Circuit accepted that the decryption code was constitutionally protected speech. However, it held that the right of the copyright holder to protect its property must be balanced against the right to free speech and that, as a result, the restraint imposed by the circumvention provisions of the Digital Copyright Millennium Act was not an undue restraint on speech.

So far as the issue of fair use/fair dealing is concerned, the consequences of the case are also serious. The Court of Appeals noted that Corley was not claiming to have made a fair use of the copyright material. However, it did observe that fair use does not involve a right to access to copyright material 'in order to copy it by the fair user's preferred technique or in the format of the original' (*Universal City Studios Inc v Corley* (2001), p 71). Overall, the Court of Appeals seems to have brushed aside the combined result of its determinations on the free speech and fair dealing issues. If the publication and use of the DeCSS code is not permitted, it will not be possible to copy any part of a film on DVD. Consequently, the right to engage in a fair use/fair dealing with the film, for example, for criticism or review, is meaningless. Thus, the effect of this case is to strengthen considerably the rights of the filmed entertainment corporations over their output and fatally undermine the cogency of the fair use/fair dealing defence. The case does more than merely maintain the exclusive distribution rights of the majors.

Hot on the heels of the decision of the Court of Appeals in the DVD case is a case that explores the legitimacy of film sharing software for the distribution of film over the internet. The complaint in *Metro-Goldwyn-Mayer Studios Inc v Grokster Ltd* (2001) was filed on behalf of the film studios making up the Motion Pictures Association of America (MPAA) in November 2001. It makes up one part of two closely associated actions, the other filed as a class action on behalf of all music publishers represented by the Harry Fox Agency (*Leiber v Consumer Empowerment BV* (2001))[13] against the

---

12 'Studios Score DeCSS Victory', *Wired News*, 17 August 2000.

13 The two cases have now been consolidated: see *Metro-Goldwyn-Mayer Studios Inc v Grokster Ltd* (Hearing Transcript, 4 March 2002) and *Leiber v Consumer Empowerment BV* (Hearing Transcript, 4 March 2002).

same defendants in respect of the same activities. The activities complained of relate to peer to peer file sharing software provided by the defendants, which it is alleged amounts to, 'a 21st century piratical bazaar where the unlawful exchange of protected materials takes place across the vast expanse of the internet' (*MGM v Grokster* (2001), para 1) or a 'cybernetic Alice's Restaurant [where] the menu is our protected content' (*MGM v Grokster* (2002), p 8) – either way, a copyright infringement. The software in question, variously known as KaZaA, Grokster or Morpheus (but referred to as Morpheus hereafter), can be downloaded by the user from the defendant's website. Once the user has logged on to the defendant's server, it is connected to a so-called 'supernode', a more powerful computer operated by another user. Search requests are sent to the supernode, which searches the computers of other users in the Morpheus network and compiles search results. The user then selects and downloads the files that it wants directly from the other user.

The plaintiffs in the Morpheus case appear to have accepted that the issue is not about the software *per se*,[14] but rather about the behaviour of the defendants in relation to the use of the software (*MGM v Grokster* (2002), pp 6–9). That is, they argue that the defendants are 'knowingly and systematically, participating in, facilitating, materially contributing to, and encouraging' (*MGM v Grokster* (2001), para 52) infringing behaviour of the users. Concerns that the entertainment industry is not attempting to use copyright law in a fashion that is anti-innovation should not, however, be regarded as being allayed. The line between accepting the lawfulness of the programme, but not of its distribution, is a rather blurry (if not completely meaningless) one. This is particularly so when there is a good argument to be made that distribution is the only thing the defendants have actually done. The defendants draw the attention of the users to their obligations under copyright law.[15] Unlike the famous Napster program, the Morpheus program does not rely on a central server system to hold an index of all available files on the network.[16] This was central to the decision of the Central District Court of California granting summary judgment to the defendants and denying it to the plaintiffs (*Metro-Goldwyn-Mayer Studios Inc v Grokster Ltd*, 25 April 2003).[17] Needless to say, the plaintiffs are appealing this decision (*Metro-Goldwyn-Mayer Studios Inc v Grokster Ltd*, 16 July 2003). If the studios (and music publishers) are successful in this appeal, we may not be a million miles away from the proposition that innovations in the use of the internet have to be approved by the entertainment industry before the rest of us can enjoy them. Some may even think that the mere fact that the entertainment industry uses its deep pockets to take such overreaching actions in order to protect its distribution monopoly means that we are already there.

---

14 The legality of which would appear to be protected on the basis that it has substantial non-infringing uses pursuant to the authority of *Sony Corp v Universal City Studios Inc* (1984).

15 Although the plaintiffs argue that bulletin boards maintained by the defendants acknowledge that the software is for infringing purposes: complaint in *Lieber v Consumer Empowerment BV* (2002), para 66.

16 The plaintiffs are, of course, downplaying this difference between Napster and Morpheus, referring to it as being merely 'architectural': Hearing Transcript in *MGM v Grokster* (2002), p 10.

17 This Order on Motion relates only to the Grokster and Morpheus software: no order is made in relation to the KaZaA software.

(c) The exponentiality of power

Despite the concern engendered by the new technologies, the general rule appears to be that the position of power that is enjoyed by media and entertainment corporations is self-reinforcing. By having such considerable power they are able to acquire more. Put simply, this is a consequence of the interdependence in most Western economies between the public and private sector. The economic health of nations is dependent on the success of the corporate sector (Macmillan Patfield, 1993, pp 299–300). This puts corporations in the position to demand of government that it take steps to protect their interests and thereby to reinforce their positions of private power.[18] It is important in this context not to forget that it was the US corporate sector that the US government was seeking to protect when it engaged in its various strategies to force the progress of the TRIPs Agreement. Not only has the US government protected the media and entertainment corporate sector, its actions have allowed the sector substantially to increase their stranglehold over international cultural output protected by copyright (Capling, 1996, p 23; Drahos, 1995). The fact that the government is so willing to act in the interests of the corporate sector – even if for its own reasons – shows the power that the sector wields.[19] It is not unreasonable to suggest that the power of the private sector compares with that of government (if not exceeds it) (Chayes, 1959, reprinted 1980). One significant difference is that the power of government, at least in democratic societies, is legitimated through accountability mechanisms such as elections and the rules of administrative law (Macmillan Patfield, 1995, pp 7–15). The private sector has a free hand to use power in a way that government can only dream about.

The significance of private power

(a) Cultural filtering and homogenisation

How does this copyright facilitated aggregation of private power affect society and its development process? The control over film distribution that is enjoyed by the major media and entertainment corporations means that these corporations can control to some extent what films are made, what films we can see, and our perception of what films there are for us to see. The expense involved in film production and distribution means that without access to the deep pockets of the majors and their vertically integrated distribution networks, it is difficult, but not impossible, to finance independent filmmaking and distribution. This, naturally, reduces the volume of independent filmmaking. The high degree of vertical integration that characterises the film industry, in particular, the ownership of cinema chains, means that many independent films that are made find it difficult to make any impact on the film going public. This is mainly because we do not know they exist. The control by the media and entertainment corporations of the films

---

18 Not to mention the fact that the economic power of the media and entertainment sector gives it deep enough pockets to fend for itself in problematic cases like *Universal Studios v Corley* (2001) and the Morpheus litigation.

19 Bettig (1996) argues that the copyright laws follow the logic of capital.

that are made is also a consequence of their habit of buying the film rights attached to the copyright in novels, plays, biographies and so on. There is no obligation on the film corporations to use these rights once they have acquired them but, of course, no one else can do so without their permission. Similarly, the film corporations may choose not to release certain films in which they own the exclusive distribution rights, or only to release certain films in certain jurisdictions or through certain media. All these things mean that the media and entertainment corporations are acting as a cultural filter. Not only might we regard this cultural filtering by the corporate sector as a matter of intrinsic concern, it also has the consequence that much of the cinema offered for our consumption has 'about as much cultural diversity as a McDonald's menu' (Capling, 1996, p 22).[20] This copyright facilitated cultural homogenisation presents the film corporations with a problem in relation to the promotion of their output, which is the problem of how to distinguish and promote essentially homogenous products. The industry's answer to this problem has been, in large part, to employ the concepts of the blockbuster film and the film star.

The blockbuster film is generally a film of a particular genre, often the 'action' or 'epic' genre, known for its particular ability to attract a mass audience. (In fact, it is arguable that the very existence of the types of genre giving rise to the blockbuster is a reflection of the homogenisation of the film industry.) Typically, these types of films are expensive to produce. The logic of capital investment is that they should be heavily promoted in order to provide a return. What makes a genre film a 'blockbuster', therefore, is heavy investment in the production and, especially, in the promotion of the film. Investment of this type is only possible in an oligopolistic industry where the excess industry rents create the ability to absorb loss. More importantly, heavy investment in production and in promotion makes particularly good sense in a legal environment where there is the type of monopoly control conferred by copyright over the distribution of the film. Due to the degree of vertical integration in the film industry, the blockbuster film typically hits all the major cinema chains in any country at the same time in order to secure maximum market impact and saturation. This, needless to say, cuts down the range of cinema available to movie-goers.

A variety of promotional tools are used in the construction of the blockbuster. One of these is its association with a celebrity/star. Often a type of chicken-and-egg situation occurs where the blockbuster is also promoted as a 'star vehicle'. Thus, the blockbuster is part of the creation of stardom, while stardom is part of the creation of the blockbuster.[21] The construction of the star has been an integral part of both the homogenisation and the differentiation of filmed entertainment (Gaines, 1991, esp pp 36–39; DeCordova, 1991; Balio, 1985, p 114; Coombe, 1998, Chapter 2). This chapter has argued that the drive for the acquisition of copyright-

---

20 Capling is, in fact, referring here to the similar phenomenon in the popular recorded music industry, but the sentiment also seems apposite in the present context.

21 In both these forms of promotion, but especially the star system, copyright is not the only intellectual property that is used. The role of trade marks and personality rights is of particular importance. For interesting discussions of this intersection of legal rights with the culture of film, see Gaines, 1991, Chapter 7, and Coombe, 1998, pp 88–100.

based monopolies has been essential to the creation of the film industry structure. The star system, in its turn, has been essential to the commercial effectiveness of that structure from the very early days of cinema production. According to Gaines:

> In the period from 1919 to 1935, which was characterised by increasing concentration of capital in the industry and marked by the vertical integration of the major studios, the star, the established director, and the story were the keys not only to cornering distribution markets but also to securing capital from outside investors. (1991, p 36)

This analysis is valuable in understanding the interrelationship of a number of factors in the production and development of the film industry. It tends, however, to underplay the role of the copyright monopoly, not only as a magnet for capital, but also as a device for the control of distribution. Nevertheless, markets in which the copyright monopoly could play its full and dominating role had to be developed. This has been the role of promotion and differentiation and, accordingly, of the star system. One consequence of this overwhelming significance of the star/celebrity system is the extent to which it creates pressures for homogenisation in society in general. Coombe (1998) has shown how even the creation of alternative identities on the basis of class, sexuality, gender and race is constrained and homogenised through the celebrity or star system (pp 100–29).

(b) Loss of the commons

The way in which the film industry controls and homogenises the way in which we construct images of our society and ourselves is reinforced by its assertion of control over the use of material assumed by most people to be in the intellectual commons. The irony is that the reason people assume such material to be in the commons is that the copyright owners have force-fed it to us as receivers of the mass culture disseminated by the mass media. The more powerful the copyright owner, the more dominant the cultural image, but the more likely that the copyright owner will seek to protect the cultural power of the image through copyright enforcement. The result is that not only are individuals not able to use, develop or reflect upon dominant cultural images, they are also unable to challenge them by subverting them (Chon, 1993; Koenig, 1994; Macmillan Patfield, 1996, pp 219–22). This is certainly unlikely to reduce the power of those who own these images.

As an example of this type of concern, Waldron (1993, p 853) uses the case of *Walt Disney Prods v Air Pirates* (1978). In this case, Walt Disney successfully prevented the use of Disney characters in *Air Pirates* comic books. The comic books were said to depict the characters as 'active members of a free thinking, promiscuous, drug-ingesting counterculture' (p 753).[22] Note, however, that the copyright law upon which the case was based does not prevent this depiction only, it prevents their use altogether. Waldron (1993) comments:

> The whole point of the Mickey Mouse image is that it is thrust out into the cultural world to impinge on the consciousness of all of us. Its enormous popularity, consciously

---

22 Quoting Wheelwright, 1976, p 582.

cultivated for decades by the Disney empire, means that it has become an instantly recognisable icon, in a real sense part of our lives. When Ralph Steadman paints the familiar mouse ears on a cartoon image of Ronald Reagan, or when someone on my faculty refers to some proposed syllabus as a 'Mickey Mouse' idea, they attest to the fact that this is not just property without boundaries on which we might accidentally encroach ... but an artifact that has been deliberately set up as a more or less permanent feature of the environment all of us inhabit. (p 833, footnote omitted)

Coombe (1998) describes this corporate control of the commons as monological and, accordingly, destroying the dialogical relationship between the individual and society:

Legal theorists who emphasise the cultural construction of self and world – the central importance of shared cultural symbols in defining us and the realities we recognise – need to consider the legal constitution of symbols and the extent to which 'we' can be said to 'share' them. I fear that most legal theorists concerned with dialogue objectify, rarefy, and idealise 'culture', abstracting 'it' from the material and political practices in which meaning is made. Culture is not embedded in abstract concepts that we internalise, but in the materiality of signs and texts over which we struggle and the imprint of those struggles in consciousness. This ongoing negotiation and struggle over meaning is the essence of dialogic practice. Many interpretations of intellectual property laws quash dialogue by affirming the power of corporate actors to monologically control meaning by appealing to an abstract concept of property. Laws of intellectual property privilege monologic forms against dialogic practice and create significant power differentials between social actors engaged in hegemonic struggle. If both subjective and objective realities are constituted culturally – through signifying forms to which we give meaning – then we must critically consider the relationship between law, culture, and the politics of commodifying cultural forms. (p 86)

If copyright has any hope of answering a criticism this cogent, then a key aspect of copyright law is the fair use/fair dealing defence. It is this aspect of copyright law that permits resistance and critique (Gaines, 1991, p 10). Yet the fair dealing defence is a weak tool for this purpose and becoming weaker. A crucial flaw in the fair use defence as a tool of resistance and critique was exposed in the famous 'String of Puppies' case, *Rogers v Koons* (1992). In this case, Koons' use of an image in a photograph of a couple holding seven puppies as the basis of a sculpture failed to escape copyright infringement. Koons argued that he was entitled to the protection of the fair use doctrine on the basis that his work was a parody for the purpose of criticising the banality of popular cultural images (Bowrey, 1994, esp pp 311–16). It was held, however, that the fair use defence only applies where the infringing work has used a copyright work for the purpose of criticising that copyright work, rather than for the purpose of criticising society in general. Recent developments in the context of the digital reproduction, which are well illustrated by *Universal Studios v Corley* (2001), tend to remove the utility of the defence altogether.

(c) Copyright and development?

The utilitarian/development justification for copyright is overwhelmingly familiar. The general idea underlying this rationale is that the grant of copyright encourages the production of the cultural works, which is essential to the development process.[23] However, the consequences of copyright's commodification of creativity, as described above, seem to place some strain on this alleged relationship between copyright and development. This argument may be illustrated by reference to the World Commission on Culture and Development's (1996) concept of development as being about the enhancement of effective freedom of choice of individuals ('Introduction'; and see Sen, 1999). Some of the things that matter to this concept of development are 'access to the world's stock of knowledge ... access to power, the right to participate in the cultural life of the community' (World Commission, 1996, 'Introduction'; see Macmillan, 1998; Macmillan, 2002a). The edifice of private power that has been built upon a copyright law that seems to care more about money than about the intrinsic worth of the cultural product it is protecting has deprived us all to some extent of the benefits of this type of development. As Waldron (1993) comments, '[t]he private appropriation of the public realm of cultural artifacts restricts and controls the moves that can be made therein by the rest of us' (p 885). It seems worth noting briefly that increases in the duration of copyright protection, such as that which has occurred in the European Union countries[24] and in the United States[25] are hardly helping.

Things look no better if we focus on the World Commission on Culture and Development's (1996) fundamental approach to culture, which is the handmaiden of its wide concept of development. A fundamental approach to culture means valuing cultural output as an end in itself, a commitment to diversity and multiculturalism, and the control of power in the form of cultural domination (Analytical Chapter 9). Not only has copyright failed to effect these things in relation to cultural output in the form of filmed entertainment, it is arguable that it has effected their opposite. Since copyright law dominates the production and distribution of filmed entertainment, its failure to take a fundamentalist approach to this very dominant form of cultural product may be regarded as a factor in our failure to achieve development in the wide sense. What is more, the unaccountable and self-reinforcing power of the media and entertainment conglomerates suggests that this process of development failure is accelerating.

---

23 For a good example of a statement of this rationale, see the Preface, World Intellectual Property Organisation, 1978:

Copyright, for its part, constitutes an essential element in the development process. Experience has shown that the enrichment of the national cultural heritage depends directly on the level of protection afforded to literary and artistic works. The higher the level, the greater the encouragement for authors to create; the greater the number of a country's intellectual creations, the higher its renown; the greater the number of productions in literature and the arts, the more numerous their auxiliaries in the book, record and entertainment industries; and indeed, in the final analysis, encouragement of intellectual creation is one of the basic prerequisites of all social, economic and cultural development. (See, Waldron, 1993, pp 850 ff; Macmillan Patfield, 1997.)

24 As a result of Council Directive 93/98/EEC, 1993 OJ L290/9.

25 As a result of the Bono Copyright Term Extension Act 1998.

Could copyright do better?

(a) Limiting commodification?

The question of whether copyright could do better is a question about the extent to which commodification is essential to the concept of copyright. The idea that the copyright interest is and should be assignable goes hand in hand with the Anglo-American conception of copyright as primarily an economic, and thus assignable, right (Bently, 1994, esp pp 980–81). This is important because, as argued above, assignability of the copyright interest appears to be necessary in order to commodify cultural and creative output. Even though the first owner of copyright is generally the person identified by copyright law as 'the author', that person may license or assign their right to others. In the context of film, this generally means that all the different 'authors' or copyright owners, the work of whom makes up the finished product of the film, must license or assign their interest to those who 'author' the film. Thus, the novelist upon whose work the film is based, the authors of the screenplay, the composer of the soundtrack, and so on, must all participate in a sort of a commodification of their copyright work. Of course, there are some people whose efforts are essential to the finished product, but whose authorship is not recognised by copyright law. Such people include, for example, actors and editors. Ultimately, the work of all these people coalesces into another copyright work, 'the cinematograph film'. Limiting the assignability of copyright works would have some impact on commodification. This would, however, fly in the face of the common law conception of copyright and is likely to be regarded as an untenable solution.

This does not mean that commodification cannot be assailed on other fronts. It has been argued in this chapter that the degree of commodification of cultural products that has been created through the copyright instrument is not purely a consequence of assignability. Other aspects of copyright law that have a part to play are the strong distribution rights attached to copyright and the long period of copyright protection. Placing limits on the exclusive distribution rights and reducing the period of copyright protection would address some of the concerns raised in this chapter about the processes and consequences of commodification. It also appears to be the case that such alterations to the law would involve less conflict with the essential nature of Anglo-Saxon copyright law than attempts to limit the alienability of the copyright interest.

In the early life of English copyright law, much of the justification for increases in duration and in the exclusive rights of the copyright holder appears to be a manifestation of the influence of romantic conceptions of the author and the author's right to control the work (Bently, 1994, p 979 ff).[26] Given that the process of commodification divorces the author from his or her work (Gaines, 1991), so that the author has become a somewhat marginalised figure in copyright law, extensions of the copyright interest based upon the figure of the author seem to have little justification. Furthermore, the current fruits of long duration and strong distribution

---

26 See reference to Wordsworth's support for Sergeant Talfourd's famous campaign to extend the duration of copyright. See also Vaidhyanathan, 2001, Ch 2.

rights are, as argued in this chapter, so unpalatable that there are good reasons grounded in public interest to look at these issues again.

(b) Counterbalancing rights?

It is often suggested that the provision of counterbalancing rights would do much to break down the power of the commodifiers. The rights being referred to here are moral rights and performers' rights. These rights are not a cure for the displacement of the author in the copyright system, rather they are a response to such a displacement (Gaines, 1991, p 26). As is well known, the introduction of both types of rights has been strenuously resisted by the media and entertainment sector. Opposition of this sector to moral rights was one of the reasons for the reluctance of the US to join the Berne Convention on the Protection of Literary and Artistic Works. The US film industry opposed moral rights, fearing that they would interfere with industry practices such as the alteration of screenplays, the release of the studio's rather than director's cut and the 'colourisation' of black and white films (Bettig, 1996, p 222). The US eventually joined the Berne Convention as part of the process of securing the WTO TRIPs Agreement. The TRIPs Agreement incorporates all of the substantive provisions of the Berne Convention except, of course, Art 6bis, its moral rights provision.

The story with respect to the introduction of performers' rights is somewhat similar. Performers represent an area of creativity that is not well recognised by copyright law. As with moral rights, the media and entertainment industry, especially that part of it concerned with film production and distribution, has resisted an attempt to bring performers into the copyright fold through the introduction of performers' rights. Essentially, the industry sees such rights as conferring an undue amount of power on performers, whose relationship with the studios is currently governed by contract. When the WIPO Performers and Phonograms Treaty of 1996 was negotiated, the US (representing the interests of Hollywood) engaged in an aggressive diplomatic strategy to ensure that the Treaty should not apply to audiovisual performances. The end result of the diplomatic wrangling over this issue was that the Treaty text protects only audio performances. Unhappiness over this outcome, especially in the European Union camp, led to the adoption by the Diplomatic Conference of a *Resolution Concerning Audiovisual Performances*.[27] This Resolution called for the competent WIPO governing bodies to decide on a schedule for preparatory work for a Protocol to the Treaty dealing with audiovisual performances. The Resolution called for the adoption of this Protocol by 1998. To date no such Protocol has, however, been agreed. All this means that to date the film industry remains untouched, not only by any Treaty requirement, but also by any clear international consensus that performers' rights are desirable.

If we are going to keep copyright as an economic right, then counterbalancing the power of the commodifiers with unassignable moral and performers' rights seems to be a reasonable idea. It is unclear, however, what weight such rights might

---

27 Diplomatic Conference on Certain Copyright and Neighbouring Rights Questions (Geneva, 2–20 December 1996), *Resolution Concerning Audiovisual Performances*, WIPO Doc CRNR/DC/99, 20 December 1996.

have given the extent of power enjoyed by the media and entertainment corporations. Both moral rights and performers' rights may be waived, that is, they can be bought off, if not bought. The uneven bargaining positions of the film industry and many participants, such as screenwriters, actors and directors, mean these waivable rights are inherently weak. In addition, there is a concern that where moral rights are enforced, they might also lead to the stultification of creativity.[28] For example, the right of integrity might interfere with fair dealing with a copyright work for the purpose of criticism or review.

(c) Fair dealing defences?

Copyright's central tool for securing the public domain and protecting the intellectual commons has been the fair use/fair dealing defence. This defence has, however, been subject to continual erosion (see Bently, 1994, p 979 ff). In *Rogers v Koons* (1992), the fact that the fair use doctrine did not entitle Koons to engage in an act of cultural pastiche and parody is of concern if one thinks that copyright law should be about the promotion of cultural activity and diversity. It is of serious concern if one subscribes to the postmodernist view that modern cultural products are all about pastiche or parody or both,[29] whether consciously referential or not. Optimists may argue that subsequent decisions on both sides of the Atlantic in cases like *Campbell v Acuff-Rose Music Inc* (1994) and *Time Warner Entertainments Company LP v Channel 4 Television Corporation plc* (1994)[30] repair or mitigate some of the damage that *Rogers v Koons* has done to the vitality of the fair dealing/fair use defence as a weapon for securing the intellectual commons. However, the more likely result of this mishmash of case law is to create confusion about the scope of the defence. The outcome of this confusion is to make users of copyright works reluctant to rely on the fair dealing/fair use defences with a consequent increase in the power of the copyright owner over the work in question.

Even an optimist could hardly be sanguine about recent developments concerning the application of the fair dealing/fair use defences in the digital context (Van Caenegem, 1995). The pressures that gave rise to the WIPO Copyright Treaty of 1996 have spawned a series of pieces of domestic or regional legislation that tip the copyright power balance even more strongly in favour of the commodifiers.[31] The legislation in question is designed to strengthen the position of copyright owners in the face of the perceived threat to copyright as a consequence of digitisation and new forms of communication technology, such as the internet. One of the ways in which these pieces of legislation typically seek to shore up the position of copyright holders is by removing or reducing the existence or practical utility of the fair dealing or fair

28 See Smiers, 2002; Vaidhyanathan, 2001, pp 160–62, who take the view that performers' rights could also have this effect.
29 This is somewhat of an oversimplification. See further, eg, Hutcheon, 1989; Polan, 1993. With respect to postmodern art and copyright law, see Bowrey, 1994; Wood, 1996; Rimmer, 1998.
30 For a fuller discussion of these cases in the context of the relationship between copyright and free speech, see Macmillan Patfield, 1996, pp 226–30.
31 See, eg, the Digital Millennium Copyright Act, the Australian Copyright Amendment (Digital Agenda) Act 2000, and the European Parliament and Council Directive on the harmonisation of certain aspects of copyright and related rights in the Information Society, COM (1999) 250 final.

use exemptions (Macmillan, 1999; Vaidhyanathan, 2001, Chapter 5). This point could hardly be better illustrated than by *Universal Studios v Corley* (2001).

(d) Thinking holistically?

This chapter has raised questions about whether the contraction of the public domain as a result of copyright's commodification of creativity and culture may be addressed by methods such as weakening the exclusive rights of the copyright holder, reducing the duration of copyright, introducing counterbalancing interests, and reinvigorating the fair dealing and public interest defences. Perhaps, however, given the spiralling power of the media and entertainment sector, even these solutions are not enough on their own. The *Report of the World Commission on Development and Culture* (1996) recommended the promotion of media competition, access and diversity at an international level (International Agenda, Action 5). It also suggests an international clearing house for national media and broadcast laws. These types of things are essential to reducing the power that the media and entertainment corporations exercise over cultural output. Clearly, being serious about making inroads into private corporate power means thinking about the role of media and competition law. However, this very small leap across boundaries is not enough on its own. If we want to legitimate the power of the corporate sector then we have to look for ways of making private power more publicly accountable. The area of law that needs work here if we are to have accountability in any structured and comprehensive fashion is, of course, corporate law. Thinking across intellectual property law, media law, competition law and corporate law sounds like a tall order, but it has been the failure of legislators, regulators, lawyers, academics and other commentators to do just that which has brought us the present era of cultural homogenisation and domination.

Chapter 16
A more developed sign: the legal mediation of things

Celia Lury

Introduction

A common way to describe the transmission of culture is in terms of mediation (McLuhan, 1997) or re-mediation, a process in 'which one medium is itself incorporated or represented in another medium' (Bolter and Grusin, 1999, p 45). But what exactly is a medium? And what is the relation between a text, artwork or cultural product and a medium? This chapter draws on an empirical study of the global culture industry[1] that mapped the movements of a number of cultural objects (Lash and Lury, forthcoming), focusing on the role that the law plays in the transmission of culture. In the first half it presents an account of some of the ways in which the chosen objects moved, and then in the second half draws attention to the role of the law in creating the qualities of the objects that move, the things of mediation. The concern in both halves is to draw attention to mediation as an active, productive process, as a performance or event, and to address how it is that the (legal) mediation of things may contribute to the global flows of disjuncture and difference (Appadurai, 1996).

The seven objects we chose to study are a subset of those produced by the culture industry (Adorno and Horkheimer, 1982; Adorno, 1991), namely such activities as publishing, film, television, art, advertising, fashion, and sport. They are the films *Trainspotting* (1996) and *Toy Story* (1995); the Wallace and Gromit animation series from Aardman Productions; the art movement, 'YBAs' or Young British Artists; two global retail products, Swatch and Nike; and Euro '96, the European football championship. In each case, we were concerned with the movements of our chosen objects. If, for instance, we follow a particular film back in time and forward along its trajectory: what are the key components of the story? How are pivotal transactions managed? What apparently tangential issues divert, recast and redirect the initial project? Throughout, how is the object transformed, and how does it transform, from stage to stage, medium to medium, context to context? The methodology adopted in this study, that of the biography of objects (Kopytoff, 1986), was designed to enable a questioning of the enduring identity of the objects of study even as they move. As an approach, the notion of biography does not privilege one moment in an object's life, its production, distribution or reception. It is tempting either to run these three moments together or to give undue prominence

1 The study was an ESRC funded project. It was conducted by Deirdre Boden, Scott Lash, Celia Lury, Vince Miller, Dan Shapiro and Jeremy Valentine. This chapter draws on discussions within this group, the project findings and the collectively authored report submitted to the ESRC. I would like to thank Elena Loizidou, Emma Sandon and an anonymous reader for their helpful comments on an earlier version of this chapter.

to one or other of them. In each case, the result is more or less the same. A delicately balanced sequence of relationships is obscured, to be replaced by a simplistic set of reductions, ignoring transformations in the objects as they circulate through networks, trajectories, or cycles of production, promotion and reception, processes of mediation and re-mediation. Our hope was that as a consequence of the attention the biography of an object draws to the temporality of the thing or, rather more grandly, its differentiation in time, it would be possible to avoid seeing the object as the outcome by which predefined attributes acquire a fixed reality. Instead, the methodological focus was on the object as a process in which the objectivity emerges in time,[2] in mediation.

The rise of a highly mediated culture has of course been widely considered as a characteristic of the global culture industry. It is commonly described as a flow of multiple materials, in which the integrity of individual works or products is called into doubt by their subsumption within the flow. In his influential account of television, Raymond Williams (1974) argues that flow is a sequence or serial assembly of units characterised by speed, variability and miscellaneity. He notes the historical decline of intervals between programmes in broadcasting; or rather, he draws attention to a fundamental re-evaluation of the interval. No longer dividing discrete programmes, no longer an interruption or silence, the interval is part of a flow, in which the true sequence is not the published sequence of programme items, but a series of differently related units, some larger and some smaller than the programme. As Williams argues, the fact of flow means that the viewer's experience of any particular item, 'given our ordinary organisation of response, memory, persistence of attitude and mood' (p 95), is affected by those preceding and following them. In their study of the James Bond phenomenon, Tony Bennett and Janet Woolacott (1987) describe the proliferation of ancillary products as textual meteorites shooting off from an inter-textual chain, with each story being written onto as well as over the earlier story, creating a paradigmatic narrative build up. Writing in relation to video, Frederic Jameson argues that the multiple materials that comprise the 'constant stream, or "total flow" of multiple materials' (1991, p 86) in contemporary culture can be understood as shorthand signals for a distinct type of narrative. He further argues that the intersections of materials within the total flow cannot be understood by means of interpretation. Within this specific type of narrative:

> ... no single sign ever retains priority as a topic of the operation; ... the situation in which one sign functions as the interpretant of another is more than provisional, it is subject to change without notice. ... signs occupy each other's position in a bewildering and well nigh permanent exchange. (p 87)

---

2 Our assumption – although it was only formulated in this way in retrospect – was that while the materiality of an object is one of its defining characteristics, there may not only be differences *over* time in the objective presentation of materiality, but also differences *in* time. For us, tracking the biography of our objects meant that we could begin to consider not only the temporal sequencing of production, distribution and consumption, but also consider processes of objectification in terms of duration (Bergson, 1991).

Jameson further notes that, 'no product seems identifiable, not even the range of generic products designated by the logo in its original sense, as the badge of a diversified multinational corporation' (p 87).

But the findings of the study described here do not support the view that it is impossible to identify objects in the multiple mediated movements that are characteristic of the global culture industry. Instead, the study suggests that objects are variably constituted in mediation, specifically in the movements of translation and transposition (to be discussed further below). In the co-ordination, organisation and integration of these movements, the study further demonstrates that the law plays a vital role. In short, in studying the biography of the selected objects, we came to the view that it is the practices of the law, specifically those relating to copyright and trade mark, that enable the identification and ownership of moving things in the global culture industry. As such, the study suggests that the law may be considered as a performative medium among other media.

Translation and transposition

Let me begin this argument by mapping the biography of *Trainspotting*. In the study, we tracked the film's movements, conducting interviews in the theatre and literary scenes in Edinburgh, with publishers and Film Four in London, and distributors, exhibitors and journalists in São Paulo and Rio de Janeiro. We documented its reception in advertisements, posters, newspaper reviews and conversations in the USA, Switzerland, Austria, Germany and France. In the interviews, the origin of *Trainspotting* was typically located in a literary short story, 'Trainspotting at Leith Central Station' by Irvine Welsh, circulating in Edinburgh in 1992 in the context of an explosion of New Scottish Writing. Encouraged by Jonathan Cape's Deputy Publishing Director, Welsh extended the story to novel length. Cape's parent firm, Random House, adopted the manuscript, and 3,000 copies were published as a Secker paperback in 1993. Positive reviews encouraged republication as a Minerva paperback. The book obtained a cult following as the literary expression of the 'E' generation, spawning a series of imitators. In 1994, the book sold 300,000 copies. Then, in 1996, the book about 1980s Scottish heroin culture was translated into a hallucinogenic visual style and Britpop soundtrack for a late 1990s cinema audience. This is the moment in the biography at which the integration of the object is such that it comes to be recognised as separate, discrete and external. Or, to put this in another way, it is the moment at which the object acquires a sufficient density of internal relations to emerge from its context and produce its own past, its own origin. More succinctly, this is the moment in which the object acquires integrity as an artistic or cinematographic work. But this integration should not be seen to produce a static object. Rather, the object continues to be organised or organises itself, in a series of events.

Optioned to Figment Films, and co-produced with Channel 4, the cinema distribution rights to *Trainspotting* were bought by Polygram Filmed Entertainment and released in all the territories they owned at the time: Australia, Belgium, Holland, Canada, France, Germany, Ireland, Spain and the UK. Initially shown on 57 screens in the UK, in the West End and Scotland, distribution was extended to 248 screens nationwide by March, from where the film went on to successful runs in

Europe and the USA (in which territories it had been sold to Miramax). The promotion of the film property, which, as is now common in the film industry, cost more than the production of the film itself, negotiated potential conflict between controversial content and the desired mass audience through careful deployment of PR and above-the-line advertising. Making use of the considerable number of images taken by a photographer, whom they had arranged to be on set everyday, Polygram were initially able to manage the appearance of a promotional package in a very controlled way. As a representative of Polygram says in interview:

> So in fact what we did was to choose loads of different sets of photography and said right the first set of photography we are going to let out are these shots. Then to the women's mags we're gonna give out this set of photography, to the men's mags we're gonna give this set of photography, to the national press we're gonna keep this set and nobody but the national press can use it. Then we're gonna have a special set of photography of Ewan McGregor, a special set of Robert Carlisle and we were absolutely rigid in our strategy and then everybody had a completely different photograph to the media than had broken before.

Additionally a 'teaser trailer' was shot on a day taken out of shooting in order that its release could coincide with both the release of a video of *Shallow Grave* (a previous film by the director and producer of *Trainspotting*) and the occasion of university students' freshers' fairs. The timing of the distribution of the film was decided by Polygram on the basis of an internally conducted analysis of when, in any year, '18' films were historically most successful (which, they found, is just after Christmas). Television advertising was not agreed until the film was showing, and broadcasting of advertising was then linked to the results of weekly cinema exit polls, and used strategically to boost attendance once it began to fall.

Most remarked in these movements was the event of the poster. Indeed, for some people, the poster eclipsed the film. As the Polygram representative says: 'We created the campaign for the world. We didn't realise it at the time, cos we just thought it's a film about drugs, about heroin, who's gonna go and see it?' Polygram were only able to monitor a fraction of the resulting copies of, improvisations on, the design template of the poster that proliferated at this time (and still continue). These adaptations included an accountancy recruitment promotion poster, advertisements for Adidas trainers and Starlight Express, window displays in the fashion chain store French Connection, and amateur posters advertising student housing among many others. Polygram threatened some of the companies who appropriated aspects of the poster design with legal action for breach of copyright. For most, however, the only financial penalty was to make a 'voluntary' financial payment in the form of sponsorship of the football team that is part of a drug rehabilitation unit featured in the film. In any case, in some kind of happy ending to the life of this object, the owners of the copyrighted literary property were able to capitalise on these illicit appropriations, as the cover of the novel was redesigned according to the same template, helping lift sales to 800,000.

One of the notable things about the movements of the poster described here is that they did not require (or help produce) the integrity of *Trainspotting* as an artistic or cinematographic work. Instead, it is specific, qualitative characteristics, rather than any kind of aesthetic unity, which enables movement. Or, to put this in another way, certain characteristics or qualities become the intensive ordinates of movement. Furthermore, this movement does not occur in relation to a fixed origin. Let me give some more examples to illustrate this further. The elements of the poster that were most frequently reproduced by the many imitators included: the colour orange, chosen 'cos we knew orange was gonna be the fashion colour, where-ever-you-looked lipstick'; the timetable lay-out; and the use of photographic portraits, a device whose initial rationale was described by Polygram in the following terms:

> ... we went through the script and we identified all the characters and the key characteristics of each of the characters, so you know the aggressive one had to be fairly in your face, Sick Boy was obsessed by James Bond ...

Additionally, the second album of *Trainspotting* music included not only songs featured in the film as well as tracks mentioned in the novel but not featured in the film, but also songs that had been considered but not included in the film (as well as not even being mentioned in the novel). Other features that enabled movement included items of clothing, such as a style of short-sleeved T-shirt worn by the character played by Ewan McGregor, which became fashionable in association with the film (even though the style long pre-existed the film). Here then the object's movements have multiple origins, some actual, some virtual.

In mapping even this apparently simple biography, it becomes clear that there are elements of complexity in the object's movements. At least two general principles of transformation, of mediation may be identified. The first is translation, an organisational process in which the object moves as a book to a film to video to television and so on. In these movements, while there are significant translations in cultural form across media, the object itself develops and maintains an aesthetic integrity, a unity of sorts, and moves within and across relatively fixed, stable territories. This movement, which maintains and preserves the integrity of an artistic work, occurs in an indexical or motivated relation to an origin typically understood in terms of authorship, creativity and sometimes to a specific place, a regional or national culture. The second process, in which the movement of the object does not require or presume its artistic integrity, may be described as one of transposition. This is a term adopted from Eisenstein's description of the caricaturist and fabulist, La Fontaine, in his account of the special characteristics of (early) Disney cartoons. Eisenstein says of La Fontaine:

> He does not copy. ... He does not transcribe what he has seen. He condenses and he deduces. He *transposes*, and this is the most precise word; for he transports into one world what he has seen in another, into the spiritual world, what he has seen in the physical world. The zoologist and orator attempt, by means of enumeration and grouping, to give us an ultimate sensation; he [the fabulist] installs himself from the very first in this sensation in order to develop further ones within us. (Emphasis provided, 1988, p 39)

Transposition is a process in which it is the intensive features of the object, rather than any kind of aesthetic unity, that enable movement. It is as if the object moves in an iconic relation to itself, in 'a self-reflexive use of reference that, in creating a representation of an ongoing act, also enacts it' (Lee and Lipuma, 2002, p 195). The movement of the object enabled by transposition is thus characterised by multiplicity, and an associative discontinuity of events. And while the movement transposition affords may be constrained by territorial boundaries, its reach or extension is not so much a matter of the overcoming of distance from an origin, but rather of the multiplication of origins.

The installation of sensation

A couple of other examples of (partial) biographies will illustrate these two principles of mediation further. They are those of Wallace and Gromit and *Toy Story*, the first being a series of three animated, 30 minute features featuring a claymation man and dog, directed by Nick Park of Aardman Studios. The second is the first feature length computer animated feature film and a co-production between the new and old companies, Pixar and Disney. In relation to these two biographies, it is the narrative internal to the product that is accorded most significance by the product's creators in explaining its global success. In the case of *Toy Story*, the story co-creator comments that, 'If the story isn't there, all the breakthrough computer graphics in the world piled onto it won't matter. You'll have made a piece of passing fashion' (quoted in Lasseter and Daly, 1996, p 52). The screenwriter also believes that while we laugh at Buzz, the toy space ranger who is one of the two main characters, the dramatic effect is tied to the narrative development of the other principal character, the sheriff doll Woody. It is Woody's development, he believes, that underpins the film as a whole:

> Woody is the person who needs to learn the lesson of the movie. Buzz has to learn that he is really a toy and he's a little full of himself. But Woody is the one who needs to learn about friendship and trust and dealing with potential loss. He's the guy who needs to be redeemed. (Quoted in Lasseter and Daly, 1996, p 42)

However, mapping the biography of *Toy Story* reveals that the narrative, conventionally an important source of aesthetic unity, was not the only factor to sustain the movement of the film. Indeed, a conflict between the narrative needs of drama and the explosive needs of the comic is one that structures accounts of the film's production.

In reports of the making of the Wallace and Gromit series, the difficulties of reconciling narrative with the graphic elements of the films are also acknowledged. So, for example:

> Many aspects of the story sprang directly out of Nick [Park]'s sketches – such as that drawing of a penguin in a milk bottle. A writer usually constructs a story as a series of events that lead to an inevitable climax. Working with Nick was challenging in that the climax was the first – or only – detail in place. The puzzle was how to arrive at that conclusion: there is a penguin in a milk bottle – how did he get there? (Sibley, 1998, p 14)

Or again, as the script editor comments:

> Nick talks and thinks through the pencil ... and the seeds of these films are all in Nick's sketchbooks. At story-meetings, he would often say: 'I've got this bit of an idea and it kind of looks like this ...' and, of course his drawings are so full of life that you could see the potential in the idea. But the first thing that needed to be done was to develop some crazy rationale that could allow these various images to co-exist in a narrative space and then to refine it and refine it. (Quoted in Sibley, 1998, p 18)

While both objects employ a narrative that contributes to character development, in both cases it is continually compromised by the demands of gesture and the comic. It is repeatedly either side-stepped or brought to a halt while 'something explosive' takes over. Additionally, small details, catchphrases such as 'Cracking toast, Gromit', or even the upward movement of Gromit's eyebrows, work in a similar way; they punctuate rather than motivate the action. As two of our 'audience' respondents comment:

A: Gromit's the one who makes the breakfast.
B: Sort of like raises his eyes and goes – 'Oh no, not again'.

Similarly, while it seems that it was the intention of *Toy Story*'s producers that the needs of drama should predominate (that the audience should identify with Woody), what was apparent in the reception of the film was that it was Buzz Lightyear (the character whose subjective development, such as it is, is to learn that he is a toy) who was the focus of enthusiasm and interest. This was true not only for the young children who were a significant part of the targeted market, but also amongst their parents, notably their fathers. One sign of this interest was the demand in the UK for Buzz toys for Christmas 1996, following the release of the video by Disney in the autumn. The demand was so great that it outstripped supply, and stayed high following the release of an 'improved' model of Buzz: Disney stores sold more over the Christmas 1997 period than they had the previous year.

So although the imperatives of narrative may dominate the production of the films themselves, there is also another dynamic at work here. And to some extent at least, it seems to cut across the movement established as a consequence of the dominance of a narrative in sustaining the aesthetic unity of the product. This dynamic relates to the ways in which both gesture and the comic, while disconnecting characters from narrative, open up the object to the possibility of transposition. So, for example, while the characters are tied to the films through the internal development made possible by a narrative, their gestures work to disengage them from their narrative role and constitute them instead as exemplary of a type, true to themselves whatever situation they find themselves in. And it is these gestures that underpin many kinds of merchandise, including the Wallace and Gromit calendar discussed here:

B: ... it's like the calendar, it's keeping the characters [from the Wallace and Gromit trilogy] in character in a different situation.
A: I was going, I must admit ... the, the calendar for this year I do think that's a, looks a clever/
B: And it's, it's original. Creative.
A: Yea I've no doubt they're linking it to, to classic films and, and the/
B: Preston [another dog character] is King Kong/
A: Yea.
B: And it's stuff like that and you know and they put the porridge gun trying to get him and that.
A: Yea I think it's, it's that sort of, I mean that really is sort of you know branching out into, to, to different cultural references but,
B: There's a bit from Cleopatra and stuff yea.
A: Yea and it's, it's, it's which characters they choose to, to play whatever and I think they've got a scene from *The Great Escape*. The one, you know at the end of it where

Steve McQueen's trying to jump over the barbed wire fence and it's obviously, it's Wallace and Gromit in the motorcycle but it/

B: With the sidecar. ... 'I don't think it's going to get over.'

A: ... and I think that sort of given that there hasn't been a film that sort of extends their, their, their sort of life beyond you know they're, they're still there and you can almost imagine them being involved in these other great films.

More generally, affective gestures, catchphrases and intensive details have, in Eisenstein's terms, the power to install sensation in such a way as to develop further; they are the means of transposition. Of course, the importance of the process of transposition in these two biographies may relate to the capacity of animation to represent a principle or abstract concept in itself and this may be what makes characters such as Woody and Buzz, Wallace and Gromit especially suitable for merchandising. But while the process of transposition may be most visible in relation to animated films, the exploitation of intensive features, of qualities or sensation, characterised the movement of all our other products as well, although at different points in their biographies and to a greater or lesser extent.

Certainly, it is the merchandising tie-ins that make animation one of the most lucrative sectors of the film industry. Both examples discussed here exploited this possibility extensively through a complex set of licensing arrangements.[3] *Toy Story* was able to benefit from Disney's tightly integrated global distribution operations including the Disney television channels and Disney retail stores. In 1995 alone, profits from tickets, merchandise and videos from *Toy Story* were over $500 million (as a result of the deal struck with Disney, Pixar was only to receive a tenth of the profits). The BBC, which owns the worldwide merchandising rights for Wallace and Gromit, subcontracted to around 55 licensees in the UK, who in turn produced about 300 different products for the films. Internationally, the BBC either makes use of its own offices or contracts the services of a licensing and merchandising agency, such as, in this case, Fording Union Media for the USA. As a company representative puts it, 'We don't create products; ... we create opportunities for companies to create products'. She further explains that it is the first medium of exposure that typically comes to define the core attributes of the property, 'Like if it's TV it's usually pretty close to the TV show story line. If it's a movie, it's probably stills from the movie'. However, a book is often seen as the richest medium from which to develop the representation of a property:

---

3 Before *Star Wars*, merchandise was used primarily to promote movies; for most makers of films for adults it had no sustained value apart from the films. But the *Star Wars* trilogy brought in about $1.3 billion in worldwide box office sales and more than $3 billion more in licensing fees. In short, with *Star Wars* merchandise became a business: 'it inaugurated modern merchandising as we know it – the Warner Bros Store, Power Rangers, the seventeen thousand different "101 Dalmatians" products that Disney has licensed so far ...' (Seabrook, 1997, p 40). George Lucas, the director of *Star Wars*, describes himself as 'trying to rethink the art of the movies – it's not a play, not a book, not music or dance. People were aware of that in the silent era, but when the talkies started they lost track of it. Film basically became a recording medium'. In contrast, he suggests that in *Star Wars*, the literary elements of narrative and of plot are subordinated to the visual elements: 'I'm a visual filmmaker ... I do films that are kinetic, and I tend to focus on character as it is created through editing and light, not stories. ... I was always coming from pure cinema – I was using the grammar of film to create content. I think graphically, not linearly.' (Lucas quoted in Seabrook, 1997, p 45.)

If it's a book it's – it's just whatever creative process that people go through for a book, it's usually closest to the property itself. You'll get ... you can't tell a story through a T-shirt usually, or through a coffee mug or through cufflinks, so that's why those products are great and they say something about the property but they don't say a lot about the property. But a book can. A book can tell a story.

In the case of Wallace and Gromit, for example, the relationship between Wallace and Gromit as developed in the narrative is defined as most important, 'you can try to do that through images but you won't get the same emotion'. Nevertheless, the merchandising was designed to convey the relationship of man and dog, frequently depicting the two principal characters together in a characteristic pose. Significantly though, a further factor in the successful representation of the properties was identified as the detail, the ornament, all that was extraneous to the narrative:

I mean the music in the videos is as important as the wallpaper in the videos, as important as what Wallace is saying to Gromit and the fact that Gromit's not answering but he's answering with his eyes. There's so many different things that go on in every single video that the whole thing's unique.

The study presented here thus suggests that the movement of global cultural products needs to be understood in terms of two processes of mediation, translation and transposition. It also suggests that significant alteration, or *modulation*, takes place in the movement of objects across media. So, for example, characters do not necessarily carry their narrative scheme within them like a genetic code. While shards of narrative undoubtedly circulate in the flow of the media, sometimes condensed in the form of a character, the character, and other elements such as catchphrases, gestures and ornamental details, may also circulate as intensities of sensation, qualities or affect. Furthermore, such intensities enter into and disrupt the time and space in which they occur. So, for example, as discussed earlier, *Trainspotting* moves as a consequence of both 'legitimate' promotional posters and 'illegitimate' posters making use of the same design template. It also moves as a soundtrack, which includes tracks that do not appear in either the film or the book. The video for *Toy Story 2* promotes itself through the inclusion of what are described as 'out-takes' but which, given that the film is not a recording, can only be alternative or virtual in-takes. The ability of intensities of sensation to act as ordinates of movement suggests that it is not always necessary for producers to attempt to fix a single, originary point of creation in an object's biography to enable and regulate its movement in a highly mediated culture. Instead, creation may be multiple, constituted within the many and various re-formations of the object that arise in the process of mediation. But in what sense then is such an object identifiable? To address this question, let me turn to a discussion of the law.

The legal mediation of things

Discussions of intellectual property law have for some time played a significant part in the analysis of the culture industry, especially in terms of the relation of the law of copyright to notions of authorship and creativity (Gaines, 1991; Rose, 1993; Coombe, 1998; Lury, 1993, 2002; Frith, 1988; Barron, 2002). It has been widely argued that it is in copyright law that the author is constituted as the (prior) origin of the artwork, with the consequence that the artwork is seen legitimately to exist in relation to a subject that precedes it. This relationship is an important part of what constitutes the integrity and originality of the work or cultural product in law. It is also, as is illustrated above, the basis on which movement of the artwork has been, and continues to be, legally and commercially regulated. But the current study provides a new vantage point from which to look at these debates, suggesting that the author's labour is simply one, historically privileged, form of the mediation of things.[4] A further implication of the findings outlined above is that while there is continuing legal support for this form of mediation in the functioning of copyright, it is increasingly supplemented by another form, that of transposition. And in this regard, trade mark law is of increasing importance.

Let me try then to outline the specificity and significance of this form of mediation by discussing the law of trade marks in a bit more detail. First, consider the current legal definition of a trade mark as 'any sign capable of being represented graphically which is capable of distinguishing the goods or services of one undertaking from those of other undertakings' (Trade Marks Act 1994, s 1(1)). The notion of sign at issue here may be usefully elaborated via a discussion of the semiotics proposed by Charles Sanders Peirce (1978) and developed in the writings on cinema by Gilles Deleuze (1986, 1989). Semiotics, as elaborated by Peirce, is a study of signs which restores the immanence of movement to the logic of the image, sign and narration. It draws on a notion of the image in general – the image – as a mobile material, as universal variation, the identity of matter with movement and light (Rodowick, 1997). According to Peirce, the image is not a unified or closed whole, but rather an ensemble or set of logical relations that are in a state of continual transformation.[5] That these logical relations are what constitute signs is made clear in his well-known definition of a sign as:

> ... something which stands to somebody for something in some respect or capacity. It addresses somebody, that is, creates in the mind of that person an equivalent sign, or perhaps a more developed sign. That sign which it creates I call the interpretant of the first sign. The sign stands for something, its object. It stands for that object, not in all respects, but in reference to a sort of idea, which I have sometimes called the ground of the representamen. (Peirce, 1978, p 99)[6]

From the perspective of such a semiotics, the law is implicated in the mediation of things in so far as it has a role in the development of the sign. And, as the definition of trade mark given above suggests, this role in developing the sign involves deciding whether and how a sign recognised as a trade mark is capable of distinguishing goods or services.

---

4 I would like to thank Elena Loizidou for this phrase.

5 Another way of saying this is that sign and object are not immediately given entities but 'abstract elements of a sign continuum' (Rochberg-Halton, 1986, p 86).

6 'A sign ... consists of the triadic representation of some object (in the broader grammatical sense) to an interpreting sign, or interpretant, and thus intrinsically involves communication. Because it also takes time to occur and is framed within a normative community of interpretation, a sign is by this definition a sign-process, a communicative act. And because the interpretant is itself a sign, it also "addresses" another interpretant, in a continuing process of interpretative communication.' (Rochberg-Halton, 1986, p 28.)

Let me elaborate this claim a little further. I have suggested that the definition of the developed sign outlined above may help explain what might be at issue in trade mark law. The significance of this definition for understanding what I have called transposition is perhaps made clearer in Deleuze's formulation of one particular kind of sign, that is, the movement-image. This kind of sign is not analogical in the sense of resemblance: 'it does not resemble an object that it would represent'. Rather, the movement-image, 'is the object; the thing itself caught in movement as continuous function. The movement-image is the modulation of the object itself' (Deleuze, 1989, p 27). From this perspective, just as a shot in cinema is the mobile section of the duration of an object, so may the sign that is registered as a trade mark be seen. As a section of duration the intensive ordinates of movement described above may be turned on the one hand towards their object, and on the other towards an expanding whole of relations that changes in time (a medium). In this turning outwards, what is crucial is how movement is organised as intervals in relation to the sign or, to put this the other way around, how the sign is differentiated by the interval. As noted above, in contemporary media culture, the interval is no longer an interruption or silence; it is no longer a part of any segment as the ending of one and the beginning of another, but is rather part of a flow. As such, intervals may make links, including associative links, not links of metaphor or metonymy, but what Deleuze describes as 'relinkages of independent images', 'one image plus another'. In these linkages, the object may be identified in the development of a sign or mark, and through such identification, the law may make of the sign an object of property claims. The object thus becomes a new kind of property not by the legal arrest of the flow, but as a consequence of the role of the law in the development of signs. The development of these signs is not a matter of interpretation, but of intensity, of association, and of linkage.

A number of recent shifts in trade mark law underpin the role of the law in this regard. Three such shifts will be identified here.[7] The first concerns the kind of signs recognised in law as capable of being trade marks. In the USA, the Lanham Act of 1946 has for a long time provided protection for a diverse range of symbols, including among other things, sounds, smells, numeric radio frequencies and alphanumeric telephone numbers. But in the UK, it was not until the 1994 Act that smells, sounds, colours, gestures or movements, as well as catchphrases, names and three-dimensional shapes could be registered as intellectual property. This first shift thus expands the kind of signs that may be the subject of trade mark law, increasing the range of the qualitative intensities of the signs recognised in law.

A second change is the movement away from a 'confusion' definition of infringement (as to the origin of the product) toward a broader 'dilution' definition, which precludes all unauthorised uses that would lessen (or take advantage of) the mark's distinctiveness. It used to be the case that trade mark infringement would only be found where the use of a protected mark by someone (X) other than its owner (Y) was likely to cause consumers to be confused as to the origin of the product to which the mark was attached. The issue was whether consumers would

---

7 I am grateful to Anne Barron for information relating to the changes in trade mark law discussed here.

think that X's product actually came from Y. Now it is increasingly being suggested, with varying degrees of success, that if X's use of Y's signs on its product causes consumers to be reminded of Y on seeing X's product, even while knowing that X and Y are distinct traders, infringement has occurred. In other words, what is emerging is legal protection for the use of a sign that does not have to rely on a privileged relation to an origin (as is the case with the object of copyright), but is developed through the creation of associations. The development of such signs is becoming established as the exclusive prerogative of the trade mark owner: associations created by other producers can be legally prevented.

This second shift, partial and uneven though it is, is the increasingly important basis of the legal identification of things in movement, and is therefore worth discussing a little more fully.[8] There have been a number of cases relating to an ambiguous phrase in the Trade Marks Act 1994 (TMA) which specifies grounds for the opposition of a trade mark registration (or founding an infringement action) which are of relevance here. The ground in question is, 'identical marks on similar goods and services, with the proviso that there exists a likelihood of confusion on the part of the public which includes the likelihood of association with the earlier mark' (s 5(1)). This wording was new to the TMA 1994 and comes from Art (1)(b) of the European Trade Mark Directive. It is usually accepted that 'likelihood of confusion' means the likelihood that the public will be confused as to the origin of the mark. However, some EC Member States, notably those represented in the Benelux court, have argued that the addition of the words, 'including a likelihood of association' extends the protection given to trade marks beyond their function as indicators of origin. They argue that it now includes protection of their reputation, which might be diluted by 'mere association' with another mark even when the public is not confused as to origin. Consider, for example, the case *Claeryn/Klarein* (1975). Claeryn was a well-known alcoholic (gin) drink and Klarein a toilet cleaner/detergent. There was no argument that the public would believe the two products originated from the same source. What the drinks maker argued was that if the 'Klarein' mark continued to be used, the public would associate the two products and the reputation of the 'Claeryn' mark would suffer. The Benelux court in which the case was heard accepted that there was a likelihood of association, although not confusion as to source, and the drinks maker won the case.

However, one of the first UK cases to consider the meaning of the proviso, *Wagamama v City Centre Restaurants* (1995), provided an alternative ruling. The plaintiff was the proprietor of the mark 'Wagamama' for a chain of successful Japanese restaurant services, and operated a London restaurant under this name. The defendant operated an Indian restaurant under the name 'Rajamama', later 'Raja Mama'. The plaintiff sued for infringement, arguing both infringement as to trade origin as well as likelihood of association. Laddie J accepted that there was a likelihood of confusion but rejected the argument that the likelihood of association imported the non-origin concept of dilution into UK law. Instead, he took the view that 'likelihood of association' derived from previous case law by which marks are

---

8 In outlining this shift, I draw on a number of very helpful sources, including Davis, 2001; Panesar, 2001; and Cornish, 1999.

'associated in the sense that one is an extension of the other or that they are derived from the same source'. In this ruling then, the likelihood of association introduced in the TMA 1994 was held to be contained within the concept of 'likelihood of confusion'. Significantly, this decision was explained by Laddie J in terms of an unwillingness to create a new type of monopoly, a type 'not related to the proprietor's trade but in the trade mark itself'.[9]

Ultimately it was the European Court of Justice (ECJ) that had to decide whether the broad Benelux or the narrow UK interpretation of 'likelihood of association' was to stand as the correct interpretation of the Trade Mark Directive. The issue was considered in the case of *Sabel v Puma* (1998). Puma was the registered proprietor of two German trade marks comprising bounding puma and leaping puma devices, registered in respect of jewellery and leather goods. Puma opposed the registration of Sabel's sign of a bounding cheetah device with the name 'Sabel' for leather and clothing goods. The German Supreme Court decided that the marks were not sufficiently similar to give rise to likelihood of confusion as to origin, but that the similarity of the 'semantic' content of the marks might give rise to a likelihood of association. When this ruling was tested at the higher court of the ECJ, it was decided that the likelihood of association was not sufficient grounds for Puma to oppose registration of the Sabel mark. However, while this case may be seen as supporting the narrow interpretation of the proviso, the terms of this court's decision are not clear-cut.

On the one hand, it ruled that a likelihood of association was merely one element of a likelihood of confusion as to origin, not a separate ground for opposition. On the other hand, it also ruled that likelihood of association must be appreciated 'globally', taking into account numerous factors. These include the recognition of the trade mark on the market, the association which can be made between the registered mark and the sign and between the goods and services identified. The ruling continues:

> That global appreciation of the visual, aural or conceptual similarity of the marks in question must be based on the overall impression given by the marks, bearing in mind, in particular, their distinctive and dominant components. The wording of Article 4 (1)(b) of the Directive ... ["there exists a likelihood of confusion on the part of the public ..."] shows that the perception of the marks in the mind of the average consumer of the type of goods or services in question plays a decisive role in the global appreciation of the likelihood of confusion. The average consumer normally perceives a mark as a whole and does not proceed to analyse its various details.
>
> In that perspective, the more distinctive the earlier mark, the greater will be the likelihood of confusion. It is therefore not impossible that the conceptual similarity resulting from the fact that two marks use images with analogous semantic content may give rise to a likelihood of confusion where the earlier mark has a particularly distinctive character, either *per se* or because of the reputation it enjoys with the public. (Quoted in Cornish, 1999, p 493)

So while this ruling suggests that the likelihood of association is not a separate factor in finding conflict, it does recognise that the likelihood of association helps to

---

9   He goes on to note that this 'could be likened to a quasi-copyright in the mark' a comparison which indicates an emerging convergence between copyright and trade mark.

define the scope of the likelihood of confusion.[10] This is a broadening of the grounds of conflict which now include the distinctiveness of the earlier mark, understood in terms of its reputation and the likelihood that the public might associate the two marks. What is increasingly important from the legal point of view, then, is less what is 'in' the sign that is protected than the relations it opens on to, how it may be linked, grouped and interconnected. In this regard, it is the time of perception (or duration) the sign presents, its 'organisation of response, memory, persistence of attitude and mood' (Williams, 1974, p 95) that is at issue in judgments of distinctiveness. In short, the second shift indicates that the properties of transposition, in which intensive associations are the ordinates of movement, are coming to be more closely protected, giving owners more exclusive rights of movement.

In a third change to the action of trade mark law, there has been an expansion in the range of goods and services that the developed sign may take as its object. Until recently, the originator of a mark was unlikely to be able to control the use of a mark in relation to products in different trade classifications of goods, since it was held there was unlikely to be confusion as to the origin of trade. However, following the so-called Ninja Turtles case, *Mirage Studios v Counter-Feat Clothing* (1991), the application of a mark across classes of goods can now be prevented by the originator of the sign, under the law of passing off, if that originator has a business selling the right to use the sign. The plaintiffs licensed the reproduction of fictitious cartoon characters, the 'Teenage Mutant Ninja Turtles', but did not manufacture any goods themselves. The defendant made drawings of turtle characters using the concept but not copying the plaintiffs' drawings, and licensed them for use on clothing. The plaintiffs sued for copyright infringement and passing off. The court held that there was a case to answer in passing off on the grounds that the public would be aware of the licensing industry and would assume a connection between the plaintiffs and the defendant. This third shift thus secures legitimacy in law for the more or less unlimited transference of the sign so fundamental to licensing and the associated practice of merchandising.[11]

Coda

To sum up then, the study of the biographies of selected objects of the culture industry indicates that their movements can be understood in terms of two processes of mediation, those of translation and transposition. It further indicates that the interconnected uses of copyright and trade mark organise these processes in ways that actively contribute to the movements of objects across the media. Thus, it is suggested that contemporary intellectual property law not only provides protection for the relatively fixed thing that is an artwork and is the object of interpretation (in copyright), but it also recognises, creates, something more open-

---

10 Returning to *Sabel*, the ECJ held that neither of the marks was particularly distinctive, and their use did not give rise to a likelihood of confusion.

11 It seems to indicate an internal reversal within trade mark law: 'While unfair competition law is based on the prohibition against palming off one's goods as the goods of another, licensing itself is essentially a "passing off".' (Gaines, 1991, p 214.)

ended, something in a process of constant transformation (in trade mark). To elaborate this claim, it has been argued that trade marks may usefully be seen as examples of the more developed signs that are described by Peirce and by Deleuze. From the perspective of this semiotics, a series of recent shifts in trade mark law increases the range of intensities of the signs recognised in law, extends the terms of exclusive ownership and control to signs created through association, and supports the unlimited transference of signs. In short, the study suggests that trade mark law is growing in relevance to the global culture industry in so far as it makes a fundamental contribution to the global movement of things through its role in development of the sign. This does not, however, imply a loss of the object as such, of objectivity, but rather involves the legal privileging of particular object characteristics, through the making objective of intensities of sensation, qualities or affect. It may thus be described as legal objectivity in a post-medium condition (Krauss, 1999). Or to put this another way, the mediation of the law increasingly makes possible an exclusive monopoly of not simply a static sign, but of a sign that is an entry into, an opening onto, a flow of things.

Bibliography

Aber Hill, W, *Ten Million Photoplay Plots*, 1924, Los Angeles: Feature Photodrama

Adorno, T and Horkheimer, M, *Dialectic of Enlightenment*, 1982, New York: Continuum

Adorno, T, *The Culture Industry: Selected Essays on Mass Culture*, 1991, London and New York: Routledge

Aglieta, M, *A Theory of Capitalist Regulation*, Fernbach, D (trans), 1979, London: New Left Books

Aglieta, M, *A Theory of Capitalist Regulation: The US Experience*, Fernbach, D (trans), 1987, London: Verso

Aldgate, A and Richards, J, *Britain Can Take It: The British Cinema in the Second World War*, 1986, Oxford: Blackwell

Alexander, J, 'Introduction: civil society I, II, III: constructing an empirical concept from normative controversies and historical transformations', in Alexander, J (ed), *Real Civil Societies: Dilemmas of Institutionalization*, 1998a, Thousand Oaks, CA: Sage, pp 1–19

Alexander, J, 'Citizen and enemy as symbolic classification: on the polarizing discourse of civil society', in Alexander, J (ed), *Real Civil Societies: Dilemmas of Institutionalization*, 1998b, Thousand Oaks, CA: Sage, pp 96–114

Alexander, W, *Film on the Left: American Documentary Film from 1931–1942*, 1981, Princeton: Princeton UP

Alloway, L, *Violent America: The Movies, 1946–1964*, 1971, New York: Museum of Modern Art

Althusser, L, 'Ideology and ideological state apparatuses', in *Lenin and Philosophy and Other Essays*, Brewster, B (trans), 1971, London: New Left Books, pp 127–88

Andrews, N, 'For Wilde read shy' (1997) *Financial Times*, 16 October

Ang, I, *Watching Dallas: Soap Opera and the Melodramatic Imagination*, Couling, D (trans), 1982, London: Methuen

Anon, *Just Out. Complete. The Life of Oscar Wilde as Prosecutor and Prisoner*, 1895, London

Anon, *Human Rights Season, Programme Notes*, 1968, London: National Film Theatre

Anon, 'The French farmers' anti-global hero' (2000) *The Economist*, 8 July

Appadurai, A, *Modernity at Large: Cultural Dimensions of Globalization*, 1996, Minneapolis and London: University of Minnesota Press

Arendt, H, *Eichmann in Jerusalem: A Report on the Banality of Evil*, 1963, New York: The Viking Press

Arendt, H, *On Revolution*, 1990, London: Penguin

Aronson, MG, '"All love making scenes must be normal": Pennsylvania movie censorship in the progressive era', in Stabile, CA (ed), *Turning the Century: Essays in Media and Cultural Studies*, 1998, Boulder, Con: Westview Press, pp 75–99

Attorney General's Department (New South Wales), *Review Of The 'Homosexual Advance' Defence*, Discussion Paper, 1996, Sydney: Department of the Attorney General

BC, 'The trials of Oscar Wilde' (1960) *The Daily Cinema*, 25 May, p 946

Baker, 'Review of "*The Trials of Oscar Wilde*" and "*Oscar Wilde*"' (1960) *Films and Filming* 6(10) July, 23–24

Balio, T (ed), *The American Film Industry*, revised edn, 1985, Madison: Wisconsin UP

Barker, M, *The Video Nasties: Freedom and Censorship in the Arts*, 1984, London: Pluto. Also published as Barker, M, *The Video Nasties: Freedom and Censorship in the Arts*, 1984, London: Barone Center, Harvard University

Barker, M and Petley, J (eds), *Ill Effects: The Media/Violence Debate*, 1997, New York: Routledge

Barnett, H, *Constitutional and Administrative Law*, 1995, London: Cavendish Publishing

Barnouw, E and Krishnaswamy, S, *Indian Film*, 2nd edn, 1980, New York: OUP

Barron, A, 'Copyright, art and objecthood', in McClean, D and Schubert, K (eds), *Dear Images: Art, Copyright and Culture*, 2002, London: Ridinghouse and ICA, pp 277–309

Barthes, R, *The Responsibility Of Forms*, 1985, New York: Hill and Wang

Bartlett, N, *Who Was That Man? A present for Mr Oscar Wilde*, 1988, London: Serpent's Tail

Bartlett, R (ed), *The Mabo Decision*, 1993, Sydney: Butterworths

Bataille, G, *Literature and Evil*, Hamilton, A (trans), 1973, London: Calder and Boyars

Baudelaire, C, 'A philosophy of toys', in Mayne, J (ed), *The Painting of Modern Life and Other Essays*, 1964, London: Phaidon Press

Benjamin, W, *Illuminations*, Zohn, H (trans), 1973, London: Fontana

Benjamin, W, *The Arcades Project*, Eiland, H and McLaughlin, K (trans), 1999, Cambridge, Mass and London: Belknap Press

Bennett, T and Woolacott, J, *Bond and Beyond: Career of a Popular Hero*, 1987, London: Routledge, Kegan Paul

Bently, L, 'Copyright and the death of the author in literature and law' (1994) 57 MLR 973

Beresford, M, 'Spain's Quiero TV set to join pay-TV victims' (2002) *Dow Jones International News*, 4 April

Bergman, P and Asimow, M, *Reel Justice: The Courtroom Goes to the Movies*, 1996, Kansas City: Andrews and McMeel

Bergson, H, *Matter and Memory*, Paul, NM and Palmer, WS (trans), 1991, New York: Zone Books

Berlant, L, *The Queen of America Goes to Washington City: Essays on Sex and Citizenship*, 1997, Durham and London: Duke UP

Berlant, L, 'Collegiality, crisis and cultural studies' (1998) *Profession* 119

Berlant, L, 'The subject of true feelings: pain privacy and politics', in Ahmed, S, Kilby, J, Lury, C, McNeil, M and Skeggs, B (eds), *Transformations: Thinking through Feminisms*, 2000, London: Routledge, pp 33–47

Berlin, I, *Four Essays on Liberty*, 1969, London: OUP

Berman, H, *Law and Revolution: The Formation of the Western Legal Tradition*, 1983, Cambridge, Mass: Harvard UP

Bettig, R, *Copyrighting Culture: The Political Economy of Intellectual Property*, 1996, Boulder: Westview Press

Bianchi, FG, 'News Corp buys Vivendi's Telepiu for EUR893M' (2002) *Dow Jones International News*, 1 October

Black, DA, *Law in Film: Resonance and Representation*, 1999, Chicago: Illinois UP

Blakeney, M, *Trade Related Aspects of Intellectual Property Rights*, 1996, London: Sweet & Maxwell

Bloxham, D, *Genocide on Trial: War Crimes Trials and the Formation of Holocaust History and Memory*, 2001, Oxford: OUP

Bobbio, N, 'Gramsci and the concept of civil society', in Keane, J (ed), *Civil Society and the State: New European Perspectives*, 1988, London: Verso, pp 73–100

Bok, S, 'TV violence, children, and the press: eight rationales inhibiting public policy debates', Discussion Paper D-16, April 1994, The Joan Shorenstein Barone Center, Harvard University

Bok, S, *Mayhem: Violence as Public Entertainment*, 1998, Reading, Mass: Addison-Wesley

Bolter, JD and Grusin, R, *Remediation: Understanding New Media*, 1999, Cambridge, Mass and London: MIT Press

Bordwell, D, Staiger, J and Thompson, K, *The Classical Hollywood Cinema: Film Style and Mode of Production to 1960*, 1985, London: Routledge. Also published as Bordwell, D, Staiger, J and Thompson, K, *The Classical Hollywood Cinema: Film Style and Mode of Production to 1960*, 1987, New York: Columbia UP

Botting, F and Wilson, S, 'Homoeconopoesis I', in McQuillan, M (ed), *Deconstruction: A Reader*, 2000, Edinburgh: Edinburgh UP, pp 263–72

Botting, F and Wilson, S, 'Morlan', in Zylinska, J (ed), *The Cyborg Experiments*, 2002a, London and New York: Continuum, pp 149–67

Botting, F and Wilson, S, 'This is not a presentation' (2002b) 44(3) *Critical Quarterly* 27–36

Bourdieu, P, 'Delegation and political fetishism' (1984), in Thompson, J (intro), *Language and Symbolic Power*, Raymond, G and Adamson, M (trans), 1991, Cambridge, Mass: Harvard UP, pp 203–19

Bourdieu, P, 'The force of law: toward a sociology of the juridical field' (1987) 38 *The Hastings Law Journal* 38–70

Bourdieu, P, 'Censorship and the imposition of form' (1988), in Thompson, J (intro), *Language and Symbolic Power*, Raymond, G and Adamson, M (trans), 1991, Cambridge, Mass: Harvard UP, pp 137–59

Bourne, S, *Brief Encounters: Lesbians and Gays in British Cinema 1930–1971*, 1996, London: Cassell

Bowrey, K, 'Copyright, the paternity of artistic works, and the challenge posed by postmodern artists' (1994) 8 *Intellectual Property Journal* 285

Branagh, K, *Beginnings*, 1989, London: Chatto and Windus

Bresson, R, *Notes on the Cinematographer*, Griffin, J (trans), 1997, Copenhagen: Green Integer Books

Brogan, H, *The Pelican History of the United States of America*, 1988, London: Penguin

Brooks, P and Gewirtz, P (eds), *Law's Stories: Narrative and Rhetoric in the Law*, 1996, New Haven: Yale UP

Brown, W, *States of Injury*, 1995, Princeton: Princeton UP

Brychta, I, 'The Ohio Film Censorship Law' (1952) 13(2) *Ohio State Law Journal* 350–411

Budd, M, 'The National Board of Review and the Early Art Cinema: *The Cabinet of Dr Caligari* as affirmative culture' (1985) 26(1) *Cinema Journal* 3–18

Burchell, G and Gordon, C (eds), *The Foucault Effect: Studies in Governmentality*, 1991, London: Harvester Wheatsheaf

Burger, P and Burger, C, *The Institutions of Art*, Kruger, L (trans), 1992, Lincoln: Nebraska UP

Butler, J, *The Psychic Life of Power: Essays in Subjection*, 1997, Stanford: California UP

Caillois, R, *Mind, Play, and Games*, Barash, M (trans), 1962, London: Thames and Hudson

Camus, A, *The Rebel*, 2000, London: Penguin

Cannon, L, *Motion Pictures: Law, Ordinances, and Regulations on Censorship, Minors and other Related Subjects*, 1920, St Louis Public Library

Capling, A, 'Gimme shelter!' (1996) February/March, *Arena Magazine*, 21

Carmen, I, *Movies, Censorship and the Law*, 1967, Michigan: Ann Arbor

Carney, BM, 'Messier days at Vivendi' (2002) *Wall Street Journal*, 2 July, p A18

Cartnell, D, *Interpreting Shakespeare on Screen*, 2000, Basingstoke: Macmillan

Chase, A, 'Towards a legal theory of popular culture' (1986) *Wisconsin Law Review* 527–69

Chase, A, *Movies on Trial: The Legal System on the Silver Screen*, 2002, New York: The New Press

Chatterjee, P, *The Nation and Its Fragments*, 1993, Delhi: OUP

Chayes, A, 'The modern corporation and the rule of law', in Mason, ES (ed), *The Corporation in Modern Society*, 1959, reprinted 1980, New York: Atheneum, pp 25–45

Chibnall, S and Murphy, R, *British Crime Cinema*, 1999, London: Routledge

Chon, A, 'Postmodern "progress": reconsidering the copyright and patent power' (1993) 43 *DePaul Law Review* 97

Christie, I, *A Matter of Life and Death*, 2000, London: British Film Institute

Clover, CJ, 'Judging audiences: the case of the trial movie', in Gledhill, C and Williams, L (eds), *Reinventing Film Studies*, 2000, London: Arnold, pp 244–64

Cohen, AK, *Delinquent Boys: The Culture of the Gang*, 1955, Glencoe: Free Press

Cohen, S and Young, J (eds), *The Manufacture of News: Social Problems, Deviance and the Mass Media*, 1981, London: Constable

Cook, P, 'Neither here nor there: national identity in Gainsborough costume drama', in Higson, A (ed), *Dissolving Views: Key Writings on British Cinema*, 1996, London: Cassell, pp 51–65

Cook, P and Bernink, M (eds), *The Cinema Book*, 2nd edn, 1999, London: British Film Institute

Coombe, R, *The Cultural Life of Intellectual Properties: Authorship, Appropriation and the Law*, 1998, Durham and London: Duke UP

Corner, J, 'Presumption as theory: "realism" in television studies' (1992) 33(1) *Screen* 97–102

Cornish, WR, *Cases and Materials on Intellectual Property*, 1999, 3rd edn, London: Sweet & Maxwell

Corrigan, P and Sayer, D, *The Great Arch: English State Formation as Cultural Revolution*, 1985, Oxford: Blackwell

Couvares, F, 'Introduction', in Couvares, F (ed), *Movie Censorship and American Culture*, 1996, Washington, DC: Smithsonian Institution Press, pp 1–15

Creed, B, 'Horror and the monstrous feminine – an imaginary abjection' (1986) 27(1) *Screen* 44

Cripps, T, *Slow Fade to Black: The Negro in American Film 1900–1942*, 1977, New York: OUP

Crowl, S (ed), *Cambridge Companion to Shakespeare on Film*, 2000, Cambridge: CUP

Crowther, B, 'Oscar Wilde', in *The New York Times Film Reviews 1959–1968*, 1970a, New York: New York Times and Arno Press, pp 3195–96

Crowther, B, 'The Trials of Oscar Wilde', in *The New York Times Film Reviews 1959–1968*, 1970b, New York: New York Times and Arno Press, pp 3196–97

Davis, G, 'Taming Oscar Wilde: queerness, heritage, and stardom', in Griffiths, R (ed), *British Queer Cinema*, forthcoming, London: Routledge

Davis, J, *Intellectual Property Law*, 2001, London: Butterworths

DeBauche, LM, *Reel Patriotism: The Movies and World War I*, 1997, Madison: Wisconsin UP

DeCordova, R, 'The emergence of the star system in America', in Gledhill, C (ed), *Stardom: Industry of Desire*, 1991, London: Routledge, pp 17–29

De Grazia, E and Newman, R, *Banned Films: Movie Censors and the First Amendment*, 1982, New York: Bowker

Deleuze, G, *Cinema 1: The Movement-Image*, 1986, London: Athlone

Deleuze, G, *Cinema 2: The Time-Image*, 1989, London: Athlone

Deleuze, G, *What Is Philosophy?*, 1994, London: Verso

Denvir, J (ed), *Legal Reelism: Movies as Legal Texts*, 1996, Urbana: Illinois UP

Derrida, J, *The Post Card*, Bass, A (trans), 1987, Chicago: Chicago UP

Dicey, AV, *Introduction to the Study of the Law of the Constitution*, 9th edn, 1965, London: Macmillan

Dimick, HT, *Photoplay Making*, 1915, Ridgewood, NJ: The Editor Company

Dorsett, S, 'Civilisation and cultivation: colonial policy and indigenous peoples in Canada and Australia post-*Wik*' (1995) 4 *Griffith Law Review* 214–38

Douglas, L, *The Memory of Judgment: Making Law and History in the Trials of the Holocaust*, 2001, New Haven: Yale UP

Douzinas, C and Nead, L (eds), *Law and the Image*, 1999, Chicago: Chicago UP

Douzinas, C and Warrington, R, *Justice Miscarried: Ethics, Aesthetics and the Law*, 1994, London: Harvester Wheatsheaf

Douzinas, C and Warrington, R, 'Antigone's law: a genealogy of jurisprudence', in Douzinas, C, Goodrich, P and Hatchamovitch, Y (eds), *Politics, Postmodernity and Critical Legal Studies: The Legality of the Contingent*, 1994, London and New York: Routledge

Drahos, P, 'The visual artist in the Global Information Economy' (1995) 14 *Communication Law Bulletin* 1–42

Drexler, P, 'The German courtroom film during the Nazi period: Ideology, aesthetics, historical context', in Machura, S and Robson, P (eds), *Law and Film*, 2001, Oxford: Blackwell, pp 64–78

Dumm, T, 'Toy stories: downsizing American masculinity' (1997) 1(1) *Cultural Values* 81–100

Dworkin, A, *Pornography: Men Possessing Women*, 1981, London: Women's Press

Dworkin, R, *Taking Rights Seriously*, 1977, Cambridge, Mass: Harvard UP

Dworkin, R, *A Matter of Principle*, 1985, Cambridge, Mass: Harvard UP

Dworkin, R, *Law's Empire*, 1986, Cambridge, Mass: Belknap Press

Dyer, R, 'Victim: hegemonic project', in Dyer, R (ed), *The Matter of Images: Essays on Representation*, 1993, London: Routledge, pp 93–110

Dyer, R, *Heavenly Bodies: Film Stars and Society*, 1987, London: British Film Institute

Dyer, R, *Se7en*, 1999, London: British Film Institute

Dyer, R, *Stars*, 2001, London: British Film Institute

Dyer, R, *The Culture of Queers*, 2002, London: Routledge

Edgeworth, B, 'Tenure, allodialism and indigenous rights at common law: English, United States and Australian land law compared after *Mabo v Queensland*' (1994) 23 Oct/Dec *Anglo-American Law Review* 397–433

Eisenschitz, B, *Nicholas Ray: An American Journey*, 1993, London: Faber & Faber

Eisenstein, S, *Eisenstein on Disney*, Leyda, J (ed), Upchurch, A (trans), 1988, London: Methuen

Eisenstein, S, 'Judith', in *Mémoires 2*, 1980, Paris: Union Générale d'Éditions, pp 195–244

Eliot, TS, *Complete Poems and Plays*, 1969, London: Faber & Faber

Elley, D, *Variety Movie Guide*, 1994, London: Hamlyn

Ericson, RV, *Visualizing Deviance: A Study of News Organization*, 1987, Toronto: Toronto UP

Ericson, RV, *Representing Order: Crime, Law, and Justice in the News Media*, 1991, Toronto: Toronto UP

Esenwein, JB and Leeds, A, *Writing the Photoplay*, 1913, Springfield, Mass: Home Correspondence School

European Commission Report, *Results Obtained under the Media II Programme (1996–2000) from 1.1.96–30.6.98*, 2000, Brussels: European Commission

Fedorov, N, *What Was Man Created For?*, 1990, Lausanne: L'Age L'Homme/Honeyglen

Felman, S, 'The return of the voice: Claude Lanzmann's *Shoah*', in Felman, S and Laub, D (eds), *Testimony: Crises of Witnessing in Literature, Psychoanalysis, and History*, 1992, London: Routledge, pp 204–83

Fish, S, 'Boutique multiculturalism or why liberals are incapable of thinking about hate speech' (1997) 23(2) *Critical Inquiry* 378–95

Fiske, J, *Understanding Popular Culture*, 1989, Boston: Unwin Hyman

Fleener-Marzec, N, *DW Griffith's "The Birth of a Nation": Controversy, Suppression, and the First Amendment as it Applies to Filmic Expression, 1915–1973*, 1980, New York: Arno Press

Foucault, M, *The History of Sexuality, Volume 1: An Introduction*, Hurley, R (trans), 1976, London: Penguin

Foucault, M, 'Two lectures' (1977), in Gordon, C (ed), *Power/Knowledge: Selected Interviews and Other Writings, 1972–1977*, Fontana, A and Pasquino, P (trans), 1980, New York: Pantheon, pp 78–108

Foucault, M, *Discipline and Punish*, 1979, London: Peregrine Books

Freeman, M (ed), *Lloyd's Introduction to Jurisprudence*, 2001, London: Sweet & Maxwell

Freud, S, 'The uncanny', in *Collected Papers*, Riviere, J (trans), 1924–50, Vol IV, pp 368–407. Also published as Freud, S, 'The uncanny', in *Art and Literature, Vol 14: The Pelican Freud Library*, Strachey, J (trans) and Dickson, A (ed), 1990, London: Penguin, pp 335–77

Freud, S, *On Metapsychology: The Theory of Psychoanalysis, Vol 11: The Pelican Freud Library*, Strachey, J (trans) and Richards, A (ed), 1984, London: Penguin

Friedan, B, *The Feminine Mystique*, 1965, London: Penguin Women's Studies

Friedman, L, 'Law, lawyers and popular culture' (1989) 98 YLJ 1579–1606

Friedman, L, *Bonnie and Clyde*, 2000a, London: British Film Institute

Friedman, L (ed), *Arthur Penn's 'Bonnie and Clyde'*, 2000b, New York: CUP

Frith, S, *Music for Pleasure: Essays in the Sociology of Pop*, 1988, Cambridge: Polity

Frye, N, *Anatomy of Criticism*, 1957, Ewing, New Jersey: Princeton UP

Gaines, J, *Contested Culture: The Image, the Voice and the Law*, 1991, Chapel Hill and London: North Carolina UP and British Film Institute

Gaines, J, 'Introduction: "the real returns"', in Gaines, JM and Renow, M (eds), *Collecting Visible Evidence*, 1999, Minneapolis: Minnesota UP, pp 1–18

Gaines, JM and Renow, M (eds), *Collecting Visible Evidence*, 1999, Minneapolis: Minnesota UP

Gaines, JM, *Fire and Desire: Mixed-Race Movies in the Silent Era*, 2001, Chicago: Chicago UP

Garnham, N, 'The media and the public sphere', in Calhoun, C (ed), *Habermas and the Public Sphere*, 1992, Cambridge, Mass: MIT UP, pp 359–76

Gibson, PC, 'Film costume', in Hill, J and Gibson, PC (eds), *The Oxford Guide to Film Studies*, 1998, Oxford: OUP, pp 36–42

Gillers, S, 'Taking *LA Law* more seriously' (1989) 98 YLJ 1607–23

Girard, R, *The Scapegoat*, 1986, Baltimore: Johns Hopkins UP

Gitlin, T, *The Whole World is Watching: Mass Media in the Making and Unmaking of the New Left*, 1980, Berkeley, California: California UP

Glass, A, 'The compassionate decision-maker' (1997) 3 *Law/ Text/ Culture*, 162–93

Gledhill, C, 'Genre and gender: the case of soap opera', in Hall, S (eds), *Representation: Cultural Representations and Signifying Practices*, 1997, London: Sage, pp 337–87

Gledhill, C, 'Rethinking genre', in Gledhill, C and Williams, L (eds), *Reinventing Film Studies*, 2000, London: Arnold, pp 221–43

Godden, L, '*Wik*: legal memory and history' (1997) 6 *Griffith Law Review* 122–43

Goodrich, P, *Languages of Law: From Logics of Memory to Nomadic Masks*, 1990, London: Weidenfeld & Nicolson

Goodrich, P, 'Poor illiterate reason: history, nationalism and common law' (1992) 1 *Social and Legal Studies* 7–28

Goodrich, P, *Oedipus Lex: Psychoanalysis, History, Law*, 1995, Berkeley, California: California UP

Goodrich, P, *Law in the Courts of Love: Literature and Other Minor Jurisprudences*, 1996, London: Routledge

Gorbman, C, 'Film music', in Hill, J and Gibson, PC (eds), *The Oxford Guide to Film Studies*, 1998, Oxford: OUP, pp 43–50

Goux, J-J, 'Subversion and consensus: proletarians, women, artists', in Goux, J-J and Wood, PR (eds), *Terror and Consensus: Vicissitudes of French Thought*, 1998, Stanford: Stanford UP, pp 37–53

Gramsci, A, 'Americanism and Fordism', in *Selections from the Prison Notebooks*, Hoare, Q and Nowell-Smith, G (eds and trans), 1971, London: Lawrence & Wishart, pp 277–318

Grantham, B, *'Some Big Bourgeois Brothel': Contexts for France's Culture Wars with Hollywood*, 2000, Luton: Luton UP

Greenfield, S and Osborn, G, 'Lawyers in film: where myth meeting reality' (1993) 43 NLJ 1791–92

Greenfield, S and Osborn, G, 'Where cultures collide: the characterisation of law and lawyers in film' (1995) 23 *International Journal of Sociology of Law*, 107–30

Greenfield, S, Osborn, G and Robson, P, *Film and the Law*, 2001, London: Cavendish Publishing

Greenhouse, S, 'Europe reaches TV compromise; US officials fear protectionism' (1989) *New York Times*, 4 October, p D20

Grieveson, L, 'Policing the cinema: *Traffic in Souls* at Ellis Island, 1913' (1997) 38(2) *Screen* 149–171

Grieveson, L, 'Fighting films: race, morality and the governing of cinema 1912–1915' (1998) 38(1) *Cinema Journal*, 40–72

Grieveson, L, 'Why the audience mattered in Chicago in 1907', in Stokes, M and Maltby, R (eds), *American Movie Audiences from the Turn of the Century to the Early Sound Era*, 1999, London: British Film Institute, pp 75–87

Grieveson, L, 'A kind of recreative school for the whole family: making cinema respectable, 1907–09' (2001) 42(1) *Screen*, 149–71

Grieveson, L, *Policing Cinema: Movies and Censorship in Early Twentieth Century America*, 2004, Berkeley, California: California UP

Griffith, WD, *The Rise and Fall of Free Speech*, 1915, Los Angeles: private publisher

Grolleau, CG, *The Trial of Oscar Wilde from the Shorthand Reports*, 1906, Paris: privately printed

Guback, T, 'Hollywood's international market', in Balio, T (ed), *The American Film Industry*, revised edn, 1985, Madison: Wisconsin UP, pp 463–80

Guerrero, E, 'Black violence as cinema: from cheap thrills to historical agonies', in Slocum, J (ed), *Violence and American Cinema*, 2000, New York: Routledge, pp 211–25

Gunning, T, '"Now you see it, now you don't": the temporality of the cinema of attractions', in Abel, R (ed), *Silent Film*, 1996, London: Athlone, pp 71–84

Gunning, T, 'From the opium den to the theatre of morality: moral discourse and film process in early American cinema' (1988) 30 *Art and Text*, reprinted in Grieveson, L and Kramer, P (eds), *Silent Cinema Reader*, 2003, London: Routledge, pp 163–72

Gunning, TDW, *Griffith and the Origins of American Narrative Film: The Early Years at Biograph*, 1991, Urbana: Illinois UP

Hale Ball, E, *The Art of the Photoplay*, 1913, New York: Veritas

Hammond, P, 'Georges, this is Charles' [on early trick films] (1981) 8/9 *Afterimage*, 30–48

Harper, C and Americhrist, 'Child at risk', Landover Baptist (1999), www.ananova.com/news/story/sm_227926.html?menu=news.quirkies

Harring, SL, *Policing a Class Society: The Experience of American Cities, 1865–1915*, 1983, New Brunswick, New Jersey: Rutgers UP

Harris, DJ, *Cases and Materials on International Law*, 1998, London: Sweet & Maxwell

Hausner, G, *Justice in Jerusalem*, 1966, New York: Harper & Row

Haver, W, *The Body Of This Death*, 1996, Stanford: Stanford UP

Hegel, GWF, *Philosophy of Right*, Knox, TM (trans), 1945, Oxford: Clarendon

'Helkon Media AG files for insolvency proceedings' (2002) *Dow Jones International News*, 2 August

Hendrick, K, 'War is mud; Branagh's Dirty Harry V and the types of political ambiguity', in Boose, LE and Burt, R (eds), *Shakespeare the Movie*, 1997, London: Routledge, pp 45–60

Henry, S and Milovanovic, D, *Constitutive Criminology: Beyond Postmodernism*, 1996, London: Sage

Heuston, RFV, *Essays in Constitutional Law*, 2nd edn, 1964, London: Stevens

Higson, A, 'Re-presenting the national past: nostalgia and pastiche in the heritage film', in Friedman, L (ed), *British Cinema and Thatcherism: Fires were Started*, 1993, London: UCL Press, pp 109–29

Higson, A, *Waving the Flag: Constructing a National Cinema in Britain*, 1995, Oxford: OUP

Higson, A (ed), *Dissolving Views: Key Writings on British Cinema*, 1996, London: Cassell

Hobbes, T, *Leviathan*, 1968, London: Pelican

Hoberman, J, '"A test for the individual viewer": *Bonnie and Clyde*'s violent reception', in Goldstein, J (ed), *Why We Watch: The Attractions of Violent Entertainment*, 1998, New York: OUP, pp 116–43

Holland, M, *Irish Peacock and Scarlet Marquess: The Real Trial of Oscar Wilde*, 2003, London: Fourth Estate

Howe, A, '"More folk provoke their own demise": homophobic violence and sexed excuses – rejoining the provocation law debate, courtesy of the homosexual advance defence' (1997) 19 *Sydney Law Review* 336

Huizinga, J, *Homo Ludens*, Hall, RFC (trans), 1949, London: Routledge and Kegan Paul

Hurley, A, *Diners, Bowling Alleys, and Trailer Parks: Chasing the American Dream in Postwar Consumer Culture*, 2001, New York: Basic Books

Hutcheon, L, *The Politics of Postmodernism*, 1989, London: Routledge

Hutchings, P, *The Criminal Spectre in Law, Literature and Aesthetics: Incriminating Subjects*, 2001, London: Routledge

Indian Cinematograph Committee, *Report of the Indian Cinematograph Committee 1927–1928* (Volumes 1–5) #65279, 1928, Calcutta: Government of India Central Publication Branch

Ivison, D, 'Decolonising the rule of law: Mabo's case and post-colonial constitutionalism' (1997) 17 *Oxford Journal of Legal Studies* 253–79

Jacobs, L (ed), *The Wages of Sin: Censorship and the Fallen Woman Film 1928–1962*, 1992, Madison: Wisconsin UP

Jacobs, R, 'The racial discourse of civil society: the Rodney King affair and the City of Los Angeles', in Alexander, J (ed), *Real Civil Societies: Dilemmas of Institutionalization*, 1998, Thousand Oaks, California: Sage, pp 138–61

James, D, *Allegories of Cinema: American Film in the Sixties*, 1989, Ewing, New Jersey: Princeton UP

Jameson, F, *Postmodernism, or, the Cultural Logic of Late Capitalism*, 1991, London: Verso

Jarman, D, *Chroma* (1995 edn, first published 1988), London: Vintage

Jarvie, I, *Hollywood's Overseas Campaign*, 1992, Cambridge: CUP

Jay, M, *Downcast Eyes*, 1993, London: California UP

Jowett, G, '"A significant medium for the communication of ideas": the *Miracle* decision and the decline of motion picture censorship, 1952–1968', in Couvares, F (ed), *Movie Censorship and American Culture*, 1996, Washington, DC: Smithsonian Institution Press, pp 258–76

Jowett, GS, '"A capacity for evil": the 1915 Supreme Court *Mutual* decision' (1989) 9(1) *Historical Journal of Film, Radio and Television* 59–78

Julius, A, *Transgressions: The Offences of Art*, 2003, Chicago: Chicago UP

Kaes, A, *M*, 2000, London: British Film Institute

Kairys, D, *The Politics of the Law: A Progressive Critique*, 1982, New York: Pantheon

Kantorowicz, E, *The King's Two Bodies: A Study in Medieval Political Theology*, 1997, Ewing, New Jersey: Princeton UP

Keane, J, 'Introduction', in Keane, J (ed), *Civil Society and the State: New European Perspectives*, 1988, London: Verso, pp 1–31

Keil, C, *Early American Cinema in Transition: Story, Style, and Filmmaking, 1907–1913*, 2001, Madison: Wisconsin UP

Keil, C and Stamp, S (ed), *American Cinema in Transition*, 2004, Berkeley, California: California UP

Kemp, S, '"Myra, Myra on the wall": the fascination of faces' (1998) 40(1) *Critical Quarterly* 38–69

Kincaid, J, *Erotic Innocence*, 1998, Durham: Duke UP

Kipnis, L, 'Film and changing technologies', in Hill, J and Gibson, PC (eds), *The Oxford Guide to Film Studies*, 1998, Oxford: OUP, pp 595–604

'KirchPayTV Files for Insolvency as Kirch Collapse Gathers Pace' (2002) *Dow Jones Business News*, 8 May

Koenig, D, 'Joe Camel and the First Amendment: the dark side of copyrighted and trademark-protected icons' (1994) 11 *Thomas M Cooley Law Review* 803

Kojeve, A, *Introduction to the Reading Of Hegel*, 1980, New York: Cornell UP

Kopytoff, I, 'The cultural biography of things: commoditization as process', in Appadurai, A (ed), *The Social Life of Things: Commodities in Cultural Perspective*, 1986, Cambridge: CUP, pp 64–94

Krauss, R, *'A Voyage on the North Sea'*, *Art in the Age of the Post-Medium Condition*, 1999, London: Thames & Hudson

Kreimer, K, *Une histoire du cinéma allemand: la Ufa*, Mannoni, O (trans), 1994, Paris: Flammarion

Kristeva, J, *Powers of Horror: An Essay on Abjection*, 1982, New York: Columbia UP

Krutnik, F, *In a Lonely Street: Film Noir, Genre and Masculinity*, 1991, London: Routledge

Kuhn, A, *Cinema, Censorship and Sexuality, 1909–1925*, 1988, London: Routledge

Kuzina, M, 'The social issue courtroom drama as an expression of American popular culture', in Machura, S, and Robson, P (eds), *Law and Film*, 2001, Oxford: Blackwell, pp 79–96

Lacan, J, 'The mirror stage as formative of the function of the I as revealed in psychoanalytic experience', in *Ecrits: A Selection*, Sheridan, A (trans), 1977, London: Tavistock, pp 1–7

Lacan, J, *The Four Fundamental Concepts of Psychoanalysis*, Miller, J-A (ed), Sheridan, A (trans), 1977, London: The Hogarth Press

Lacan, J, *The Seminar of Jacques Lacan Book 1*, Forrester, J (trans), 1988, Cambridge: CUP

Lacan, J, *The Psychoses 1955–1956: The Seminar of Jacques Lacan, Book III*, Miller, J-A (ed), Grigg, R (trans), 1993, London: Routledge

Lacan, J, *Le Séminaire. Livre IV. La Relation D'Objet, 1956–57*, Miller, J-A (ed), 1994, Paris: Seuil

LaCapra, D, *History and Memory after Auschwitz*, 1998, New York: Cornell UP

Laplanche, J and Pontalis, J-B, 'Fantasy and the origin of sexuality', in Burgin, V (ed), *Formations Of Fantasy*, 1986, New York: Methuen, pp 5–34

Larsen, K, 'ITV digital licences for sale after pay-TV ops shut down' (2002) *Dow Jones International News*, 1 May

Lash, S and Lury, C, *Global Culture Industries: The Mediation of Things*, forthcoming, Cambridge: Polity

Lash, S and Urry, J, *Economies of Signs and Spaces*, 1996, London: Sage

Lasseter, J and Daly, S, *Toy Story: The Art and Making of the Animated Film*, 1996, New York: Hyperion

Lawrence, R, 'Last night while you prepared for class I went to see Light of Day: a film review and a message for my first-year property students annotated to my colleagues' (1989) 39(1) JLE 87

Lee, B and Lipuma, E, 'Cultures of circulation' (2002) 14(1) *Public Culture* 191–214

Leglise, P, 'Histoire de la politique du cinéma française', Vol 1, *La Troisième République*, 1969, Paris: Filméditions Pierre Lherminier

Leonard, JD (ed), *Legal Studies as Cultural Studies: A Reader in (Post)modern Critical Theory*, 1995, Albany: New York State UP

Levinas, E, *The Levinas Reader*, Hand, S (ed), 1995, Oxford: Blackwell

Lewis, J, *Hollywood v Hard Core: How the Struggle over Censorship Saved the Modern Film Industry*, 2000, New York: New York UP

Liebman, S, '"If this be a man ..." Eichmann on trial in *The Specialist*' (2002) XXVII(2) *Cineaste* 40–42

Lindley, D, *Court Masques: Jacobean and Caroline Entertainments, 1605–1640*, 1998, Oxford: OUP

Lindstrom, JA, '"Getting a hold deeper in the life of the city": Chicago nickelodeons, 1905–1914' unpublished PhD thesis, 1998, Northwestern University

Llewellyn, K, *The Common Law Tradition: Deciding Appeals*, 1960, Boston: Little, Brown

Lloyd, A (ed), *Movies of the Thirties*, 1983, London: Orbis

Loizidou, E, 'Intimate queer celluloid: heavenly creatures and criminal law', in Moran, L, Monk, D and Beresford, S (eds), *Legal Queeries*, 1998, London, New York: Cassell, pp 167–84

Loizidou, E, 'Learning pain: poetry in emotion' (2001) 23(2) *Liverpool Law Review*, 179–85

Lombardo, P, 'Cruellement bleu' (1994) 36(1) *Critical Quarterly* 13

Lord Wright, W, *Photoplay Writing*, 1922, New York: Falk Publishing

Lury, C, 'Reading the self: autobiography, gender and the institution of literacy', in Franklin, S et al (eds), *Off-Center: Feminism and Cultural Studies*, 1991, London: Hutchinson, pp 97–108

Lury, C, *Cultural Rights: Technology, Legality and Personality*, 1993, London: Routledge

Lury, C, 'Portrait of the artist as a brand', in McClean, D and Schubert, K (eds), *Dear Images: Art, Copyright and Culture*, 2002, London: Ridinghouse and ICA, pp 310–29

MacCabe, C, 'Realism and the cinema: notes on some Brechtian theses' (1974) 15 *Screen* 7–27

MacCabe, C, *Performance*, 1998, London: British Film Institute

Machura, S and Robson, P (eds), *Law and Film*, 2001, Oxford: Blackwell

Mackinnon, C, *Toward a Feminist Theory of the State*, 1991, Cambridge, Mass: Harvard UP

Macmillan, F, 'Copyright and culture: a perspective on corporate power' (1998) 10 *Media and Arts Law Review* 71

Macmillan, F, 'Striking the copyright balance in the digital era' (1999) 10 *International Company and Commercial Law Review* 350

Macmillan, F, 'Corporate power and copyright', in Towse, R (ed), *Copyright and the Cultural Industries*, 2002a, London: Edward Elgar, pp 99–118

Macmillan, F, 'The Cruel ©: copyright and film' [2002b] *European Intellectual Property Review* 483

Macmillan Patfield, F, 'Defamation, freedom of speech and corporations' (1993) *Juridical Review* 294

Macmillan Patfield, F, 'Challenges for company law', in Macmillan Patfield, F (ed), *Perspectives on Company Law*, Vol 1, 1995, London: Kluwer, pp 1–21

Macmillan Patfield, F, 'Towards a reconciliation of free speech and copyright', in Barendt, E (ed), *The Yearbook of Media and Entertainment Law 1996*, 1996, Oxford: Clarendon, pp 199–233

Macmillan Patfield, F, 'Legal policy and the limits of literary copyright', in Parrinder, P and Chernaik, W (eds), *Textual Monopolies: Literary Copyright and the Public Domain*, 1997, London: Office for Humanities Communication, pp 113–32

Maitland, FW, *Equity, Also, the Forms of Action at Common Law: Two Courses of Lectures*, Whittaker, WJ (ed), 1909, Cambridge: CUP

Maltby, R, 'The genesis of the production code', in *Prima dei codici 2: Alle Porte di Hays (Before the Codes 2: The Gateway to Hays)*, 1991, Venice: La Biennale di Venezia, pp 60–80

Maltby, R, 'The production code and the Hays office', in Balio, T (ed), *Grand Design: Hollywood as a Modern Business Industry 1930–39*, 1993, New York: Scribner's

Marr, D, *The High Price of Heaven*, 1999, Sydney: Allen & Unwin

Marrus, M, 'History and the Holocaust in the courtroom', in Brayard, F (ed), *Le génocide des juifs entre process et historie*, 2000, Paris: CNRS, pp 25–56

Marshall, G, *Constitutional Theory*, 1971, Oxford: Clarendon Law Series, OUP

Marshall, TH, *Citizenship and Social Class*, 1950, Cambridge: CUP

Marx, K, *Karl Marx: Selected Writings*, McLellan, D (ed), 2000, Oxford: OUP

Mast, G (ed), *The Movies in Our Midst: Documents in the Cultural History of Film*, 1983, Chicago: Chicago UP

McCarthy, K, 'Nickel vice and virtue: movie censorship in Chicago 1907–1915' (1976) 5(1) *Journal of Popular Film* 38

McDonald, P, 'Film acting', in Hill, J and Gibson, PC (eds), *The Oxford Guide to Film Studies*, 1998, Oxford: OUP, pp 30–35

McLuhan, M, *Understanding Media: The Extensions of Man*, 1997, London: Routledge

McNeil, K, *Common Law Aboriginal Title*, 1989, Oxford: OUP

Medhurst, A, 'Licensed to cheek' (1997) 10 (October) *Sight and Sound*, 32

Mellor, D, 'Sketch for an historical portrait of Humphrey Jennings', in Jennings, M-L (ed), *Humphrey Jennings: Film-Maker, Painter, Poet*, 1982, London: British Film Institute, pp 63–72

Merton, RK, 'Social structure and anomie' (1938) 3 *American Sociological Review* 672

Metz, C, *Film Language*, 1990, Chicago: Chicago UP

Metz, C, 'The imaginary signifier' (1976) 16(2) *Screen* 14–76

Millard, S, *Oscar Wilde: Three Times Tried*, 1912, London: Ferrestone Press

Minkinnen, P, *Thinking Without Desire: A First Philosophy of Law*, 1999, Oxford: Hart

Mison, RB, 'Homophobia in manslaughter: the homosexual advance as insufficient provocation' (1992) 80 *California Law Review* 133

Mitry, J, *The Aesthetics and Psychology of the Cinema*, 1998, London: Athlone

Monaco, P, 'Landmark movies of the 1960s and the cinema of sensation', in *The Sixties: 1960–1969, Vol 8: The History of American Cinema*, 2001, New York: Charles Scribner's Sons, pp 168–97

Monk, C and Sargeant, A (ed), *British Historical Cinema: The History, Heritage and Costume Film*, 2002, London: Routledge

Montgomery Hyde, H, *The Trials of Oscar Wilde*, 1948, New York: Dover

Mooney, T and Eustace, S, *Battleground: The Making of Saving Private Ryan in Ireland*, 1998, Enniscorthy: Milestone L Press

Moran, A, 'Terms for a reader: Film, Hollywood, national cinema, cultural identity and film policy', in Moran, A (ed), *Film Policy: National and Regional Perspectives*, 1996, London: Routledge, pp 1–22

Moran, LJ, *The Homosexual(ity) Of Law*, 1996, London: Routledge

Moran, LJ, 'Oscar Wilde: Law memory and the proper name', in Moran, L, Monk, D and Beresford, S (eds), *Legal Queeries*, 1998a, London: Cassells, pp 10–25

Moran, LJ, 'Heroes and brothers in love: the male homosexual as lawyer in popular culture' (1998b) 18 *Studies in Law, Politics and Society*, 3

Moran, LJ, 'Gothic law' (2001) 10(2) *Griffith Law Review* 75–101

Moreton-Robinson, A, *Talkin' Up to the White Woman: Aboriginal Women and Feminism*, 2000, St Lucia, Queensland: Queensland UP

Morrison, W, *Jurisprudence: From the Greeks to Post-Modernity*, 1995, London: Cavendish Publishing

Motha, S, '*Mabo*: encountering the epistemic limit of the recognition of "difference"' (1998) 7(1) *Griffith Law Review* 79–96

Mouffe, C, 'Democratic citizenship and the political community', in Mouffe, C (ed), *Dimension of Radical Democracy: Pluralism, Citizenship, Community*, 1992, New York: Verso

Munby, J, *Public Enemies, Public Heroes: Screening the Gangster from 'Little Caesar' to 'Touch of Evil'*, 1999, Chicago: Chicago UP

NH, 'Trials of Oscar Wilde' (1960) 27 (July) *Monthly Film Bulletin* 95–96

Neale, S, *Genre*, 1980, London: British Film Institute

Neil, S, 'Lie back and think of … widescreen' (1996) 17(2) Feb/March *Eyepiece* 29–33

Nichols, B, 'Documentary film and the modernist avant-garde' (2001) 27 *Summer Critical Inquiry* 581–610

Nichols, B, *Movies and Methods*, 1976, London: California UP

Nichols, B, *Representing Reality: Issues and Concepts in Documentary*, 1991, Bloomington: Indiana UP

Nietzsche, F, *On the Genealogy of Morality*, Ansell-Pearson, K (ed), 1994, Cambridge: CUP

Oberholtzer, EP, *The Morals of the Movie*, 1922, Philadelphia: The Penn Publishing Company

Osborn, G, 'Borders and boundaries: locating the law in film', in Machura, S and Robson, P (ed), *Law and Film*, 2001, Oxford: Blackwell, pp 164–76

Osiel, M, *Mass Atrocity, Collective Memory and the Law*, 1997, New Brunswick: Rutgers UP

PJD, 'Oscar Wilde' (1960) 27 (July) *Monthly Film Bulletin*, 94–95

Palmer, F, *Technique of the Photoplay*, 1924, Hollywood: Palmer Institute of Authorship

Panesar, S, *General Principles of Property Law*, 2001, Harlow: Pearson Education Ltd

Panofsky, E, 'Style and medium in the moving pictures' (originally published 1934), in Talbot, D (ed), *Film: An Anthology*, 1966, Berkeley, California: California UP, pp 34–45

Parkes, JC, 'Et in arcadia … homo: sexuality and the gay sensibility in the art of Derek Jarman', in *Derek Jarman: A Portrait*, 1996, London: Barbican Art Gallery

Parkhurst, C, 'The Birth of a Nation', reprinted in Silva, F (ed), *Focus on 'The Birth of a Nation'*, 1971, Englewood Cliffs, New Jersey: Prentice Hall, pp 102–05

Peake, T, *Derek Jarman*, 1999, London: Little, Brown

Pearlman, M, *The Capture and Trial of Adolf Eichmann*, 1963, New York: Simon & Schuster

Pearson, H, *Oscar Wilde*, 1946, London: Methuen

Pearson, N, '204 years of invisible title', in McRae, H, Nettheim, G, Beacroft, L and McNamara, L (eds), *Indigenous Legal Issues: Commentary and Materials*, 1997, Sydney: LBC Information Services, p 214

Peirce, CS, *The Philosophy of Peirce: Selected Writings*, Buchler, J (ed), 1978, London: Kegan Paul

Penner, J, Schiff, D and Nobles, R, *Introduction to Legal Theory and Jurisprudence*, 2002, London: Butterworths

Pernick, MS, *The Black Stork: Eugenics and the Death of 'Defective' Babies in American Medicine and Motion Pictures Since 1915*, 1996, New York: OUP

Perrin, C (ed), 'In the wake of *terra nullius*' (1998) 4(1) *Law/Text/Culture* 1–34

Playfair, I, *Gentle Criticisms on British Justice*, 1895, London: privately published

Polan, D, 'Postmodernism and cultural analysis today', in Kaplan, EA (ed), *Postmodernism and Its Discontents*, 1993, London: Verso, pp 45–58

Post, R, 'On the popular image of the lawyer: reflections in a dark glass' (1987) 75 *California Law Review* 379–89

Post, R, 'Censorship and silencing', in Post, R (ed), *Censorship and Silencing: Practices of Cultural Regulation*, 1998, Los Angeles: The Getty Research Institute for the History of Art and the Humanities, pp 1–12

Pountain, D and Robins, D, *Cool Rules: An Anatomy of an Attitude*, 2000, London: Reaktion Books

Povinelli, E, 'The cunning of seduction: real being and Aboriginal recognition in settler Australia' (1998) *Australian Feminist Law Journal*, 11 September, 3–27

Prasad, M, *Ideology of the Hindi Film: A Historical Construction*, 1998, New Delhi: OUP

Projansky, S, *Watching Rape: Film and Television in Postfeminist Culture*, 2001, New York: New York UP

Proudhon, PJ, *Selected Writings of Pierre-Joseph Proudhon*, Edwards, S (ed), Fraser, E (trans), 1969, Garden, New York: Anchor Books

Quinn, J and Kingsley-Smith, J, 'Kenneth Branagh's *Henry V* (1989): genre and interpretation', in Monk, C and Sargeant, A (eds), *British Historical Cinema: The History, Heritage and Costume Film*, 2002, London: Routledge, pp 163–75

Rafter, N, *Shots in the Mirror: Crime Films and Society*, 2000, Oxford: OUP

Rafter, N, 'American crime trials: an overview of their development, 1930–2000', in Machura, S and Robson, P (eds), *Law and Film*, 2001, Oxford: Blackwell, pp 9–24

Rance, P, *The French Cheese Book*, 1989, London: Macmillan

Rand, E, *Barbie's Queer Accessories*, 1995, Durham: Duke UP

Randall, R, *Censorship of the Movies*, 1968, Madison: Wisconsin UP

Ransome, A, *Oscar Wilde: A Critical Study*, 1912, London: Methuen

Ray, L and Sayer, A, *Culture and Economy After the Cultural Turn*, 2000, London: Sage

Redhead, S, *Unpopular Culture: The Birth of Law and Popular Culture*, 1995, Manchester: Manchester UP

Regester, C, 'Black films, white censors: Oscar Micheaux confronts censorship in New York, Virginia, and Chicago', in Couvares, F (ed), *Movie Censorship and American Culture*, 1996, Washington, DC: Smithsonian Institution Press, pp 159–86

Rimmer, M, 'Four stories about copyright law and appropriation art' [1998] 3 *Media and Arts Law Review* 180

Rochberg-Halton, E, *Meaning and Modernity: Social Theory in the Pragmatic Attitude*, 1986, Chicago: Chicago UP

Rodowick, DN, *Gille Deleuze's Time Machine*, 1997, Durham: Duke UP

Rollat, A, 'Une pléiade de vedettes à la rescousse' (1993) *Le Monde*, 17 September, p 18

Rose, G, *The Melancholy Science: An Introduction to the Thought of TW Adorno*, 1978, London: Macmillan

Rose, M, *Authors and Owners: The Invention of Copyright*, 1993, Cambridge, Mass: Harvard UP

Rosen, P, 'Securing the historical: historiography and the classical cinema', in Rosen, P and Mellencamp, P (eds), *Cinema Histories, Cinema Practices*, 1984, Frederick, Maryland: University Publications of American, pp 104–21

Rosen RE, 'Ethical soap: *LA Law* and the privileging of character' (1989) *University of Miami Law Review* 229

Rosenfeld, AH, 'Another revisionism: popular culture and the changing image of the Holocaust', in Hartman, G (ed), *Bitburg in Moral and Political Perspective*, 1986, Bloomington: Indiana UP, pp 90–102

Ross, SJ, *Working Class Hollywood: Silent Film and the Shaping of Class in America*, 1998, Princeton, New Jersey: Princeton University Press

Rothwell, I, *A History of Shakespeare on Screen*, 1999, Cambridge: CUP

Runciman, D, 'The politics of good intentions' (2003) *London Review of Books*, 8 May, p 5

Rush, P, 'An altered jurisdiction: corporeal traces of law' (1997) 6(2) *Griffith Law Review* 144–68

Russo, V, *The Celluloid Closet*, 1981, New York: Harper & Row

Ruth, DE, *Inventing the Public Enemy: The Gangster in American Culture 1918–1934*, 1996, Chicago: Chicago UP

Rutherford, J, *The Gauche Intruder: Freud, Lacan and the White Australian Fantasy*, 2000, Melbourne: Melbourne UP

Ryall, T, 'Genre and Hollywood', in Hill, J and Gibson, PC (eds), *The Oxford Guide to Film Studies*, 1998, Oxford: OUP, pp 327–41

Ryan, HB, *The Vision of Anglo America: the US-UK Alliance and the Emerging Cold War 1943–1946*, 1987, Cambridge: CUP

Ryans, T, 'Wilde' (1997) 10 (October) *Sight and Sound* 34

Sarat, A, 'Imagining the law of the father: loss, dread, and mourning in the sweet hereafter' (2000) 34(1) *Law and Society Review* 3

Sarat, A and Kearns, TR (eds), *Law in the Domains of Culture*, 1998, Ann Arbor: Michigan UP

Sargeant, A, 'The content and the form: invoking "pastness" in three recent retro films', in Monk, C and Sargeant, A (eds), *British Historical Cinema: The History, Heritage and Costume Film*, 2002, London: Routledge, pp 15–30

Sarris, A, *The American Cinema*, 1996, New York: Da Capo Press

Sartre, J-P, *Existentialism and Humanism*, Mairet, P (trans), 1973, London: Eyre Methuen

Saylor, RC, 'The Pennsylvania State Board of Censors (Motion Pictures)', unpublished MA American Studies thesis, 1999, Pennsylvania State University at Harrisburg

Schaefer, E, *Bold! Daring! Shocking! True! A History of Exploitation Films, 1919–1959*, 1999, Durham: Duke UP

Schickel, R, *DW Griffith*, 1984, London: Pavilion

Schudson, M, 'Was there ever a public sphere? If so, when? Reflections on the American case', in Calhoun, C (ed), *Habermas and the Public Sphere*, 1992, Cambridge, Mass: MIT UP, pp 143–63

Schwenger, P, 'Derek Jarman and the colour of the mind's eye' (1996) 65(2) *University Of Toronto Quarterly* 419

Seabrook, J, 'Why is the force still with us?' (1997) *The New Yorker*, 6 January, pp 40–53

Segev, T, *The Seventh Million: The Israelis and the Holocaust*, 1993, New York: Hill & Wang

Sen, A, *Development as Freedom*, 1999, New York: Anchor Books

Shale, S (née Gibson), '"I saw it with my own eyes": justice, evidence and inference in the moving pictures', unpublished paper, 1996a, The Art of Justice Conference, Tate Gallery

Shale, S (née Gibson), 'The conflicts of law and the character of men: writing *Reversal of Fortune* and *Judgement at Nuremberg*' (1996b) 30(4) Summer *University of San Francisco Law Review* 91–120

Shapiro, C, 'Women lawyers in celluloid: why Hollywood skirts the truth' (1995) 25 *University of Toledo Law Review* 955–1020

Shaw, CR and McKay, HD, *Juvenile Delinquency and Urban Areas: A Study of Delinquents in Relation to Differential Characteristics of Local Communities in American Cities*, 1942, Chicago: Chicago UP

Sheffield, R, 'Taking exception to six decades on film: a social history of women lawyers in popular culture, 1930–1990' (1993) 14(1) *Loyola of Los Angeles Entertainment Law Journal* 73

Sherwin, RK, *When Law Goes Pop: The Vanishing Line Between Law and Popular Culture*, 2000, Chicago: Chicago UP

Shoesmith, B, 'The problem of film: a reassessment of the significance of the Indian Cinematograph Committee, 1927–1928' (1988–89) 2(1) *Continuum* 74–78

Sibley, B, *Wallace and Gromit: 'The Wrong Trousers'*, storyboard collection, 1998, London: BBC Worldwide Ltd

Sibley, J, 'Patterns of courtoom justice', in Machura, S and Robson, P (eds), *Law and Film*, 2001, Oxford: Blackwell, pp 97–117

Sklar, R, 'When looks could kill: American cinema of the sixties' (1987–88) XVI(1–2) *Cineaste* 50–53

Sklar, R, *Film: An International History of the Medium*, 1993, London: Thames & Hudson

Slocum, J, 'Film violence and the institutionalization of cinema' (2000) 67(3) *Social Research* 649–81

Slocum, J, 'The "film violence" trope: New Hollywood, the "Sixties", and the politics of history', in Schneider, S (ed), *New Hollywood Violence*, 2004, Manchester: Manchester UP

Smiers, J, 'The abolition of copyrights: better for artists, third world countries and the public domain', in Towse, R (ed), *Copyright and the Cultural Industries*, 2002, London: Edward Elgar, pp 119–39

Smith, M, 'Theses on the philosophy of Hollywood history', in Neale, S and Smith, M (ed), *Contemporary Hollywood Cinema*, 1998, New York: Routledge, pp 3–20

Smith, PJ, '*Blue* and the outer limits' (1993) 3 *Sight And Sound* 10

Soifer, A, 'Complacency and constitutional law' (1981) 42(1) *Ohio State Law Journal* 383

Sontag, S, *Aids and its Metaphors*, 1991, Harmondsworth: Penguin

Sparks, R, *Television and the Drama of Crime: Moral Tales and the Place of Crime in Public Life*, 1992, Milton Keynes: OU Press

Staiger, J, *Interpreting Films: Studies in the Historical Reception of American Cinema*, 1992, Ewing, New Jersey: Princeton UP

Staiger, J, *Bad Women: Regulating Sexuality in Early American Cinema*, 1995, Minneapolis: Minnesota UP

Staiger, J, *Perverse Spectators: The Practices of Film Reception*, 2000, New York: New York UP

Stamp, S, 'Moral coercion, or the National Board of Review ponders the vice films', in Bernstein, M (ed), *Controlling Hollywood: Censorship and Regulation in the Studio Era*, 1999, New Brunswick, New Jersey: Rutgers UP, pp 41–59

Stamp, S, 'Taking precautions, or contraceptive technology and cinema's regulatory apparatus', in Bean, J and Negra, D (eds), *Feminist Silent Cinema Reader*, forthcoming, Durham: Duke UP, pp 270–97

Stamp, S, *Movie-Struck Girls: Women and Motion Picture Culture After the Nickelodeon*, 2000, Ewing, New Jersey: Princeton UP

Stark, SD, 'Perry Mason meets Sonny Crockett: the history of lawyers and the police as television heroes' (1987) 42 *University of Miami Law Review* 229–83

Taylor, C, 'Modern social imaginaries' (2002) 14(1) *Public Culture* 91–124

Teicholz, T, *The Trial of Ivan the Terrible: State of Israel v John Demjanjuk*, 1990, New York: St Martin's Press

The Trial of Adolf Eichmann: Record of the Proceedings in the District Court of Jerusalem, Volumes 1–6, 1992–95, Jerusalem: Ministry of Justice, State of Israel

Toplin, R, '*Bonnie and Clyde*: "violence of a most grisly sort"', in *History by Hollywood: The Use and Abuse of the American Past*, 1996, Urbana and Chicago: Illinois UP, pp 127–53

Towse, R, 'Copyright risk and the artist: an economic approach to policy for artists' (1999) 6 *Cultural Policy* 91

Towse, R, *Creativity, Incentive and Reward: An Economic Analysis of Copyright and Culture in the Information Age*, 2001, London: Edward Elgar

Uricchio, W and Pearson, R, 'Dialogue: Manhattan's nickelodeons. New York? New York?' (1997) 36(4) *Cinema Journal* 99–112

Vaidhyanathan, S, *Copyrights and Copywrongs: The Rise of Intellectual Property and How It Threatens Creativity*, 2001, New York: New York UP

Van Buren Powell, A, *The Photoplay Synopsis*, 1919, Springfield: Home Correspondence School

Van Caenegem, W, 'Copyright, communication and new technologies' (1995) 23 *Federal Law Review* 322

Vasseleu, C, *Textures of Light: Vision and Touch in Irigaray, Levinas and Merleau-Ponty*, 1998, London: Routledge

Wade, HWR, 'The basis of legal sovereignty' (1955) *Cambridge Law Journal* 172

Waldron, J, 'From authors to copiers: individual rights and social values in intellectual property' (1993) 69 *Chicago-Kent Law Review* 841

Waller, GA, *Main Street Amusements: Movies and Commercial Entertainment in a Southern City, 1896–1930*, 1995, Washington: Smithsonian Institution Press

Ward, I, *Shakespeare and the Legal Imagination*, 1999, London: Butterworths

Ward, I, *A State of Mind: The English Constitution and the Popular Imagination*, 2000, Stroud: Sutton Publishing

Watney, S, *Policing Desire*, 1989, London: Comedia

Webber, J, 'The jurisprudence of regret: the search for standards of justice in *Mabo*' (1995) 17 *Sydney Law Review* 5–28

Weber, M, 'Politics as a vocation', in Runciman, WG (ed), Matthews, E (trans), *Selections in Translation*, 1978, Cambridge: CUP, p 212

Wertheimer, J, 'Mutual film reviewed: the movies, censorship, and free speech in progressive America' (1993) 37 *The American Journal of Legal History* 212–45

Wheelwright, T, 'Parody, copyrights and the First Amendment' (1976) *US Federal Law Review* 564

White, BJ, *The Legal Imagination*, 1973, Chicago: Chicago UP

Willemen, P, 'On realism in the cinema' (1972–73) 13 *Screen* 37

Williams, C, *Realism and Cinema: A Reader*, 1980, London: Routledge

Williams, C, 'After the classic, the classical and ideology: the differences of realism' (1994) 35 (3) *Screen* 275

Williams, L, 'Discipline and fun: *Psycho* and postmodern cinema', in Gledhill, C and Williams, L (eds), *Reinventing Film Studies*, 2000, New York: OUP, pp 351–78

Williams, R, *Television: Technology and Cultural Form*, 1974, London: Fontana/Collins

Williams, R, 'A lecture on realism' (1977) 18 *Screen* 39

Wolfe, C, 'Straight shots and crooked plots: social documentary and the avant-garde in the 1930s', in Horak, J-C (ed), *Lovers of Cinema: The First American Film Avant-Garde, 1919–1945*, 1995, Madison: Wisconsin UP, pp 234–66

Wolfenden, J, *Report of the Departmental Committee on Homosexual Offences and Prostitution*, Cmnd 247, 1957, London: HMSO

Wollen, P, '*La règle du jeu* and modernity' (1999) 1 *Film Studies* 5–13

Wood, L, 'Copyright and postmodern artistic practice: paradox and difference' (1996) 1 *Media and Arts Law Review* 72

Wood, R (ed), *Film and Propaganda in America: A Documentary History. Vol I: World War I*, 1990, Westport, Connecticut: Greenwood Press

World Commission on Culture and Development, *Our Creative Diversity*, 2nd edn, 1996, Paris: UNESCO

World Intellectual Property Organisation, *Guide to the Berne Convention for the Protection of Literary and Artistic Works*, 1978, Geneva: WIPO

Yates, FA, *The Art of Memory*, 1966, London: Routledge

Young, A, '"Into the blue": the image written on law' (2001) 13 *Yale Journal of Law and the Humanities* 101

Young, A, *Imagining Crime*, 1996, London: Sage

Young, A, 'Murder in the eyes of the law' (1997) 17 *Studies in Law, Politics and Society* 31

Young, A, *Judging the Image: Art, Value, Law*, 2003, London: Routledge

Zizek, S, *The Plague of Fantasies*, 1997, London: Verso

Always, Spielberg, USA, 1989

Bad Lord Byron (The), MacDonald, UK, 1949

Bend It Like Beckham, Chadha, UK, 2002

Between Two Worlds, Blatt, USA, 1944

Billy Elliot, Daldry, UK, 2000

Birth Control, Message Photo-Play Company, USA, 1917

Birth of a Nation (The), DW Griffith, USA, 1915

Black Stork (The), Wharton and Wharton, USA, 1916

Blue, Jarman, UK, 1993

Bonnie and Clyde, Penn, USA, 1967

Bridesmaid's Secret (The), Essanay, USA, 1916

By Man's Law, Christy Cabanne Biograph, USA, 1913

Castle (The), Sitch, Australia, 1997

Chicken Run, Park, UK, 2000

Chimes at Midnight, Welles, Spain/Switzerland, 1966

Chocolat, Hallström, USA, 2000

Citizen Kane, Welles, USA, 1941

Clockwork Orange (A), Kubrick, UK, 1971

Cooked Goose (The), Thanhouser, USA, 1914

Crouching Tiger Hidden Dragon, Lee, USA, 2000

Death Takes a Holiday, Leisen, USA, 1934

Dirty Harry, Siegel, USA, 1971

Eagle (The), De La Mothe, USA, 1915

Eighty-first Blow (The), Gouri, USA, 1974

Fit to Fight (Re-titled *Fit to Win*), Griffin and Milestone, USA, 1918

Forbidden Fruit, Abramson, USA, 1916

Forcing the Force, Eclectic, USA, 1914

Four Horsemen of the Apocalypse, Ingram, USA, 1921

Gilded Kid (The), Edison, USA, 1914

Gladiator, Scott, USA, 2000

Gosford Park, Altman, UK, 2001

Guy Named Joe (A), Fleming, USA, 1944

Hand That Rocks the Cradle (The), Philips, Smalley and Weber, USA, 1917

Heart of New York (The), Wilson, 1915

Henry V, Branagh, UK, 1989

Henry V, Olivier, UK, 1946

Here Comes Mr Jordan, Hall, USA, 1941

Hostage (The), Lasky, USA, 1914

Ideal Husband (An), Korda, UK, 1947

Importance of Being Earnest (The), Asquith, UK, 1952

Inside of the White Slave Traffic (The), Samuel London, USA, 1913

Iron Hand (The), Ulysses Davis, USA, 1916

Intolerance, Griffith, USA, 1916

It May Be Your Daughter, Moral Uplift Society of America, USA, 1916

Is Any Girl Safe?, Jacques Jaccard, USA, 1916

It's a Wonderful Life, Capra, USA, 1946

James Boys in Missouri (The), Essanay, 1908

Kreutzer Sonata (The), Brenon, 1915

Lady Windermere's Fan, Lubitsch, USA, 1925

Le Comte de Monte Cristo, Autant-Lara, 1962

Liliom, Lang, France, 1934

M, Lang, Germany, 1931

Mainspring (The), King, 1917

Malena, Tornatore, Italy/USA, 2000

Manchurian Candidate (The), Frankenheimer, USA, 1962

Matter of Life and Death (A), Powell and Pressburger, UK, 1946

Metropolis, Lang, Germany, 1926

Mr Smith Goes to Washington, Capra, USA, 1939

Muriel's Wedding, Hogan, Australia, 1994

Myra Breckinridge, Sarne, USA, 1970

Native Land, Hurwitz and Strand, USA, 1942

Night Riders, Kalem, USA, 1908

Nobody Would Believe, USA, 1915

On the Waterfront, Kazan, USA, 1954

Oscar Wilde, Ratoff, UK, 1960

Outward Bound, Milton, USA, 1930

Passing of the Third Floor Back (The), Viertel, UK, 1935

Picture of Dorian Gray (The), Lewin, USA, 1945

Prohibition, Reid, USA, 1916

Protect Your Daughter, All Star, USA, 1918

Psycho, Hitchcock, USA, 1960

Rebel Without A Cause, Ray, USA, 1955

Remarkable Andrew (The), Heisler, USA, 1942

Ridicule, Leconte, France, 1996

Sappho, Majestic Motion Picture Company, USA, 1913

Satan's Pawn, Barker and Ince, USA, 1915

Se7en, Fincher, USA, 1995

Searchers (The), Ford, USA, 1955

Seventh Heaven, Borzage, USA, 1927

She Never Knew, Herbert Brenon, USA, 1916

Shoah, Lanzmann, USA, 1986

Sixth Sense (The), Shyamalan, USA, 1999

Smashing the Vice Trust, Progress Film Company, USA, 1914

Snatch, Guy Ritchie, UK, 2000

Some Cop, Philips Smalley, USA, 1914

Specialist (The), Sivan, USA, 1999

Stacked Cards, Kay-Bee, USA, 1914

Star Wars, Lucas, USA, 1977

Strictly Ballroom, Luhrmann, Australia, 1992

Strike at Coaldale (The), Cullison, USA, 1914

Sunshine, Szabó, Hungary/Germany/Canada/Austria, 2000

Things to Come, Menzies, UK, 1936

Thunder Rock, Boulting, UK, 1942

Topper, McLeod, USA, 1937

Topper Returns, Del Ruth, USA, 1941

Topper Takes a Trip, McLeod, USA, 1939

Toy Story, Lasseter, USA, 1995

Toy Story 2, Lasseter, Unkrich and Brannon, USA, 1999

Tracking the Government, Warners Features, 1914

Traffic in Souls, George Loane Tucker, 1913

Trainspotting, Boyle, UK, 1996

Trial of Adolf Eichmann (The), USA, 1997

Trials of Oscar Wilde (The), (*The Man with the Green Carnation* in the USA) Hughes, UK, 1960

Vanity Fair, Nair, UK, 2004

Verdict for Tomorrow, Hurwitz, USA, 1961

Victim, Dearden, UK, 1961

Where are My Children?, Philips, Smalley and Weber, USA, 1916

Wild One (The), Benedek, USA, 1953

Wilde, Gilbert, UK, 1997

Wings of Desire, Wenders, Germany/France, 1987

Witnesses to the Holocaust, USA, 1987

Administration of Papua and New Guinea v Daera Guba (1973) 130 CLR 397

Amodu Tijani v Secretary, Southern Nigeria [1921] 2 AC 399

Advisory Opinion on Western Sahara (1975) ICJR, 12

Benjamin Bruce Andrew and Peter Clive Kane (1999) NSWSC 647, 2 July 1999 (unreported)

Block v City of Chicago (1909) 87 NE 1011, 239 Ill 251

Bramwell v Halcomb (1836) 2 My & Cr 737, 40 ER 1110

Buffalo Branch, Mutual Film Corporation v Breitinger (1915) 250 Pa 225

Burstyn v Wilson (1952) 343 US 459

Calder v Attorney General of British Columbia (1973) SCR at 416; (1973) 34 DLR (3d), 145

Campbell v Acuff-Rose Music Inc (1994) 114 S Ct 1164

Cary v Longman (1801) 1 East 358 102 ER 138

Case of Tanistry (1608) Davis 28; 80 ER 516

Claeryn/Klarein (1976) 7 IIC 420

Coe v Commonwealth (1979) 24 ALR 118

Commonwealth v Tasmania (1983) 158 CLR 1

Fejo v Northern Territory (1998) 156 ALR 721

Green v R, S172/1996 (10 December 1996)

Green v R (1997) 148 ALR 659 (High Court)

Johnson v McIntosh (1823) 8 Wheat 543

Leiber v Consumer Empowerment BV, (Hearing Transcript, 4 March 2002), www.eff.org/IP/ P2P/NMPA_v_MusicCity/20020304_leiber_hearing_transcript.html

Leiber v Consumer Empowerment BV, US District Court for the Central District of California, Western Div, CaseNo: CV-01-09923 GAF; see www.eff.org/IP/P2P/ NMPA_v_MusicCity/20011119_complaint.html

Mabo and Others v The State of Queensland (No 1) (1988) 166 CLR 186

Mabo and Others v The State of Queensland (No 2) (1992) 107 ALR 1

Message Photoplay Co v Bell (1917) 167 NYS 129

Metro-Goldwyn-Mayer Studios Inc v Grokster Ltd (Hearing Transcript, 4 March 2002), www.eff.org/IP/P2P/NMPA_v_MusicCity/20020304_mgm_hearing_transcript.html)

Metro-Goldwyn-Mayer Studios Inc v Grokster Ltd (Order of the United States Court of Appeal for the Ninth Circuit, 16 July 2003), www.eff.org/IP/P2P/ NMPA_v_MusicCity/20030716_court_order.pdf

Metro-Goldwyn-Mayer Studios Inc v Grokster Ltd (Order on Motions, 25 April 2003), www.eff.org/IP/P2P/NMPA_v_MusicCity/030425_order_on_motions.php

Metro-Goldwyn-Mayer Studios Inc v Grokster Ltd US District Court for the Central, District of California, Western Div, Case No: CV-01-08541 SVW; www.eff.org/IP/P2P/ NMPA_v_MusicCity/20011002_mgm_v_grokster_complaint.html

Milirrpum v Nabalco Pty Ltd (1970) 17 FLR 141

Mirage Studios v Counter-Feat Clothing [1991] FSR 145

Mutual Film Corp v Chicago (1915) 139 CCA 657, 224 Fed 201

Mutual Film Corp v Hodges (1915) 236 US 230

Mutual Film Corp v Industrial Commission of Ohio (1914) 215 Federal Reporter (September–October)

Mutual Film Corporation v Industrial Commission of Ohio (1915) 236 US 230

Pathé Exch v Cobb (1922) 202 App Div 450, 195 NY

R v Grmusa (1990) 50 A Crim R 358

R v Moffa (1977) 13 ALR 225 (High Court)

R v Preston (1992) 58 A Crim R 328

R v Pritchard (1990) A Crim R 67

R v Stiles (1990) 50 A Crim R 13

R v Tuncay (1998) 2 VR 19

R v Whittaker (1993) A Crim R 476

Rogers v Koons (1990) 751 F Supp 474 (SDNY 1990), aff'd, 960 F 2d 301 (2d Cir), cert denied, 113 S Ct 365 (1992)

Sabel v Puma [1998] RPC 199

Semayne's Case (1605) 5 Co Rep 91a

Sony Corp v Universal City Studios Inc (1984) 464 US 417

Time Warner Entertainments Company LP v Channel 4 Television Corporation plc (1994) EMLR 1

United States v Motion Picture Patents Co (1915) 225 F 800

United States v Motion Picture Patents Co (1918) 247 US 524

Universal City Studios, Inc v Corley (2001) US Court of Appeals for the Second Circuit, 28 November 2001, www.2600.com/news/112801-files/UniversalBrief_3.pdf

Universal City Studios, Inc v Shawn C Reimerdes (2000) 111 F Supp 2d 294

Wagamama Ltd v City Centre Restaurants [1995] FSR 713

Walt Disney Prods v Air Pirates (1978) 581 F 2d 751 9th Cir, cert denied 439 US 1132 (1979)

Warwick Film Productions Ltd v Eisenger and Others (1969) 1 Ch 508

West v Francis (1804) 5 B & Ald 737, 106 ER 1361

Western Australia v the Commonwealth (the Native Title Act Case) (1995) 183 CLR 373

Wik Peoples v The State of Queensland (1996) 141 CLR 129

Witrong and Blany (1674) 3 Keb 401